Praise for *Hon*

"Because [Liz Hauck] writes with such unvarnished clarity and pragmatism, sudden moments of tenderness burst open on the page. . . . It turns out that showing up to cook and eat with people once a week allows for startlingly deep moments of connection and community. That's all that happens. And it's extraordinary."

—KATE CHRISTENSEN, *The New York Times Book Review*

"*Home Made* is flawless. How someone, anyone, never mind a first-time author could write a page-turner about cooking one meal a week with teenage boys in state care who live in a group home is stunning. . . . *Home Made* reads like a movie and it's paced like a movie. But it isn't a movie. It's a true story about boys who got the short end of the stick through no fault of their own, inequality the most destructive and most indestructible monster of them all."

—BEVERLY BECKHAM, *The Boston Globe*

"When the author created a weekly cooking-and-dining program at a residential home for adolescent boys in state care, she transformed lives—including her own."

—*People*

"An affecting, thoughtful look at the lives of boys in transitional moments and a personal reflection on a father's legacy."

—*Booklist* (starred review)

"A moving memoir about how 'systems fail but food is revolutionary.' Hauck creates indelible portraits. . . . A captivating debut."

—*Kirkus Reviews* (starred review)

"The memoir is an honest account of community service, the kind, as Hauck puts it, where you show up on time, perform your small task to the best of your ability, improvise as needed, and leave. . . . Hauck's book chronicles a cooking program, but the food is beside the point: It's really about finding nourishment and community."
—*Boston College Magazine*

"Hauck writes with deep compassion, not only for the boys but for her grieving, idealistic younger self. . . . She captures the humor and pathos of interactions with young men already wary of well-meaning adults, and shares glimpses of the ordinary conversations that took place around the table. *Home Made* is not a prescription for sweeping social change or a story of a white woman saving young men of color (or even herself). Rather, it is a tender, insightful, often funny account of what happens when people show up—and keep showing up—to cook and eat together."
—KATIE NOAH GIBSON, *Shelf Awareness*

"A genuine page-turner, *Home Made* is a spellbinding tribute to Liz Hauck's great empathy and compassion, her commitment to the ideal of service, her generosity of spirit, and her irrepressible wit. Written as an act of love, it also manages to be an education, taking us into a world that few outside the system of child protective services have experienced firsthand."
—CHRISTINA THOMPSON, author of *Sea People: The Puzzle of Polynesia*

"In this wise and bighearted memoir, Liz Hauck shows us how grief can lead to generosity and how community can grow through sharing meals around a table, and she offers us an introduction to the complex world of the child welfare system. Written with style and grace with a flair for language and detail, the story of her three years of cooking and sharing meals with teenage boys living in a group home resonates long after the final page is read. I loved this book."
—BARBARA ABERCROMBIE, author of *The Language of Loss*

"*Home Made* is a tender story about the connections that form when people cook and eat. That this cooking and eating occurs in a group home, and that these people are children caught in the court system and striving to unknot the choices they've made from the choices that have been inflicted on them, means the fellowship Ms. Hauck writes about so elegantly is not just the difference between a decent meal and a lousy one. Here, the simple act of sharing a meal can stand as the difference between life and death. I for one am grateful to Ms. Hauck and the residents of 'the House' for sharing such meals with us; they have changed me, too."

—JEFF HOBBS, author of *The Short and Tragic Life of Robert Peace* and *Show Them You're Good*

"I could not wait to get home each night so I could get back to reading *Home Made*. I cared so much about everybody in it. Hauck's writing embodies what she knows about successful volunteering: show up on time when you said you would, do what you said you would do, and leave. I loved this book so much. I stayed up way later than I should have to just get one more chapter in before sleeping."

—GABRIELLE HAMILTON, *New York Times* bestselling author of *Blood, Bones & Butter*

"At every turn in *Home Made,* Liz Hauck suggests that we all ought to build a longer table, instead of a higher wall. With grace and tenderness, this memoir utterly affirms that it is the relationship that heals. Food brings us to the table, but cherishing leads us to joy and bravery. This is an important book because it reminds us not to venture to the margins to make a difference, but to allow the folks there to make us different. Your heart will be altered by this book."

—GREGORY BOYLE, S.J., *New York Times* bestselling author of *Tattoos on the Heart* and founder of Homeboy Industries

"Wise and empathetic, Liz Hauck describes the process of coming together through cooking and eating. *Home Made* is a meditation on hunger of all forms, of the limits and meaning of volunteerism, and the ways in which we continue the work of our deceased loved ones. Never cynical and always self-aware, Hauck knows that we may not rescue one another—but we can create a shared space where one is not alone."

—MICHELLE KUO, author of *Reading with Patrick*

"Liz Hauck reveals fascinating, sobering, and urgent truths about boyhood, inequality, and the power and promise of community."
—PIPER KERMAN, *New York Times* bestselling author of *Orange Is the New Black*

HOME MADE

HOME MADE

*A Story of Grief, Groceries,
Showing Up—and What We Make
When We Make Dinner*

LIZ HAUCK

THE DIAL PRESS
NEW YORK

Home Made is a work of nonfiction. Some names and identifying details have been changed.

2022 Dial Press Trade Paperback Edition

Published in the United States by The Dial Press, an imprint of Random House, a division of Penguin Random House LLC, New York.

THE DIAL PRESS is a registered trademark and the colophon is a trademark of Penguin Random House LLC.
RANDOM HOUSE BOOK CLUB and colophon are trademarks of Penguin Random House LLC.

Originally published in hardcover in the United States by The Dial Press, an imprint of Random House, a division of Penguin Random House LLC, in 2021.

LIBRARY OF CONGRESS CATALOGING-IN-PUBLICATION DATA
Names: Hauck, Liz, author.
Title: Home Made: a story of grief, groceries, showing up—and what we make when we make dinner / Liz Hauck.
Description: New York: The Dial Press, [2021]
Identifiers: LCCN 2020049180 (print) | LCCN 2020049181 (ebook) | ISBN 9780525512455 (paperback) | ISBN 9780525512448 (ebook)
Subjects: LCSH: Juvenile delinquents—Services for. | Juvenile delinquents—Rehabilitation. | Group homes—Food service.
Classification: LCC HV9275 .H385 2021 (print) | LCC HV9275 (ebook) | DDC 362.7483—dc23
LC record available at https://lccn.loc.gov/2020049180
LC ebook record available at https://lccn.loc.gov/2020049181

Printed in the United States of America on acid-free paper

randomhousebooks.com
randomhousebookclub.com

ScoutAutomatedPrintCode

Book design by Diane Hobbing

For my dad, Charlie Hauck,
who taught me that systems
fail but food is revolutionary

CONTENTS

PART 3: SOMETHING HAPPENED HERE

PROLOGUE

The Tester

On Sundays we went to church, but on Saturdays my father made pancakes. It was our job to assemble the ingredients in a line along the counter. We'd match the pictures on the back of the yellow box of mix: one egg, chubby plastic bottle of vegetable oil, cup of water, drum of grease, plus measuring spoons and the square skillet with olive-green sides that had a three-pronged scratch across its surface from the time someone used a fork instead of a spatula.

The first thing my dad would do was turn on the news. The world streamed into our kitchen in a steady pour as he hiked up his plaid pajama pants, tightened the soft belt of his robe, and shuffled toward the sink in his enormous size 16 slippers.

Hands washed and dried, he'd shake the mix then tip the oil into numbered metal cups and empty them into the bowl. Never one to estimate, he measured everything, his eyes small behind the thick lenses of his glasses. He'd crack the egg with two hands, shake out the gooey white, and set the shells aside; then he'd turn on the front burner, smear a slab of grease onto the griddle, and return to the mixture, breaking up the clumps, mixing its stickiness thinner, stirring breakfast into life. It made a round metallic sound, metal spoon against stainless steel, slow and then faster, fastest.

He'd drop a glob of batter onto the middle of the griddle to test its slick surface. We listened for the sizzle, watched the batter bubble then puff into a spongy thing. That first one was never bigger than a quarter. He called it "the tester." My sisters and I would fight for it; my brother would ignore us or swoop in for a sneak attack, his fork a predator claw out of nowhere. The tester was the best one. That first bite when you're hungry is electric: taste explodes against your tongue like heaven. We'd rush to set the table. Six plates, six forks and knives, six napkins, a glass at every place. Somebody would grab the syrup from the fridge, the butter dish, the OJ. Then we'd all sit down.

Before we ate, we prayed. We'd serve ourselves then lift up our hands in muscle memory, reaching for each other. We weren't hugging people, never *I love you* people; this was when we touched. No matter whose turn it was to say the prayer, my mother would add, "And let's remember the people who don't have what we have— especially the many children who don't have what the four of you have." She'd pause and we'd know she was thinking about the kids she had worked with, the ones my father still worked with. We heard stories about them, the kids who got in trouble and waited for parents who never came. My father would agree, a single nod. "We know," we'd say, hungry for the food on our plates. "We're lucky," we'd say, almost convinced. We'd let go of each other's hands. We'd bless ourselves. We'd eat.

It seemed like it would be like that forever.

The Back Burner Project

Some people are the kind of people who believe there's one right thing they're supposed to do with their life, a perfect person they're meant to share it with, and one place they're destined to live, forever. My father wasn't one of those people. When I told him I needed to find another job because the best part of my day was lunch, he said that the best part of everyone's day is lunch. My dad didn't believe in dream jobs. He was a better-safe-than-sorry guy. He parked in the first, farthest parking spot, just in case. He saved words like *perfect* and *love* for sacraments like food and baseball. And he didn't know that he was sick yet, though the cancer was already in his body, flowering like a noxious weed.

When I suggested to my dad that we start a cooking program in a residential home for adolescent boys who were living in state care, I was mostly joking. We were making dinner and splitting a beer, his half in the bottle by the meat he was tenderizing and mine in a foamy, half-full glass beside a cutting board as I diced vegetables. We had a cooking show on mute in the foreground, "Hey Julie" by Fountains of Wayne in the background, and a decent dinner on the horizon. We traded stories of our days and didn't cry because of the onions or anything else; we were tough like that. I was twenty-five, back in Boston, broke, and recalculating after having spent two years teaching in Chicago as an AmeriCorps volunteer after graduating from college. Thomas Wolfe wrote that you can't go home again, but he must not have had student loans. There I was, sleeping in my old bedroom and working the hospital job I had worked during summers home from college, living a life significantly less bold than the one I had imagined waiting for me on the other side of a diploma. One of my little sisters had just graduated and was also living at home, working all the time; the other was away at school. My older brother lived with his girlfriend outside the city, but he worked in a different department at the same hospital where I worked, so we'd coordinate lunches and coffee breaks like we had during our college summers, impersonating adult conversations over cheeseburger subs and soda, or iced coffees loaded with cream and sugar. My grandmother was stuck in the liminal haze of dementia, living in a convalescent home not far from our house, and my mom would go there after work to sit with her for dinner, to remind her who she was and make sure she ate. This is how my dad and I started making dinner together sometimes; growing up, it had rarely been just the two of us, except in the car, in between spaces. Now, home several months, I felt unsettled in my administrative job, unsure about who I wanted to be when I grew up, and convinced the One True Thing might reveal itself like a scream.

My dad had worked for the same nonprofit for over thirty years. He wasn't thinking about changing jobs but said he wanted to try something different. "I've been thinking about a way to get to know the kids at the House better," he said.

My father called the young people he worked with "the kids," and he called the building where his office was "the House." He was a social worker and chief financial officer of a nonprofit agency in Boston that provided residential services for youth in state care and adults with intellectual disabilities. The agency ran a fluctuating number of group homes; at that time there were eight. They were organized to meet the unique needs of the residents, who were supported by teams of caseworkers, social workers, counselors, doctors, and tutors. As a director, my dad's job was the paper-and-numbers part of social service: doing intake and transfer paperwork, writing grants and balancing budgets, attending meetings upon meetings, and showing up in court when called. He wasn't involved in the removals or the process that led to kids being removed from their guardians' care; he worked in one of the places that handled what happened after that. Most of his exchanges with the teenagers the agency served were formal. That night, while we were making dinner, he said that he missed the rapport he'd had with the kids he'd worked with in his early days as a direct-care provider.

My father's career in social work began as conscription. While he was finishing his senior year at Boston College, organizing peaceful protests of the Vietnam War, and filling out applications to the University of Chicago School of Divinity, he was drafted. So he applied for status as a conscientious objector, attended a hearing in front of a board who interrogated his pacifism and ultimately granted him CO status, and then postponed graduate school in order to complete his national service in an alternative civilian placement. In the summer of 1969, he shaved his beard and reported for duty in a group home for at-risk teens, wearing a tweed sport jacket with suede elbow patches and plaid polyester pants, carrying one suitcase of clothes and books. When his compulsory service was finished a few years later, he decided that there was still work to be done, so he deferred whatever he thought his life was going to be, and he stayed, and kept doing that work. For thirty-four years. His supervisor eventually became his business partner, and together they founded an agency that provided direct-care services for youth in state custody; their agency's radical mission was to keep vulnerable youth out of institutions and living in the community, surrounded by community care. The words for the population the agency served changed over time: delinquent, troubled, at-risk, needy, disadvantaged, under-resourced, displaced, poor. Poverty, or scarcity, was the common denominator. My dad always called his young clients "the kids." My whole life, he worked in the same un-air-conditioned corner office on the first floor of a redbrick building with a bright-green door. He rarely talked about the work he did at the House or why he did it; that it needed to be done was reason enough.

When my dad said he wanted to find a structured way to facilitate more casual interactions with his kids at the House, I had an idea. "What about a cooking class?" I suggested. "It could be like your own cooking show!" My dad loved cooking shows. He watched them from credits to credits, from the laying out of ingredients and prepping calisthenics to the first bite of a finished product and satisfied nod of approval. "All you'd have to do is go upstairs!" One of the residences the agency ran was located on the second floor of the House. I didn't know much about the kids he worked with, except for the stories I overheard him telling my mother, the ones he couldn't leave in the folders on his desk. A boy who spread lye on his stepmother's toilet seat; a girl who was twelve and pregnant with a relative's child; a kid who got locked in a closet. "Don't you think it could be great?" The joke of it was that I doubted he'd agree to a messy cooking class without a curriculum; he was shy and hated improvisation. "I would even help," I promised.

Over other dinners those first months after my move back home, I had recounted to my dad many beyond-the-classroom stories about the kids I had worked with in Chicago. I told him about the weekly tutoring program I'd run and retreats I'd helped facilitate, about funny conversations I'd had during hours on lunch duty and as a bus monitor. I liked the sense of community and back-and-forth that happened between kids and adults in those extracurricular spaces—the joking, the questions, the confiding, the growing; they reminded me of my own after-school experiences and the clubs and programs where I looked for amusement and found worlds that made sense to me and welcomed me in. When I was in high school, I was grateful for the teachers who taught art classes at the museum, led the gospel choir, ran the theater program, chaperoned the trip to Costa Rica, and moderated student council and public declamation. Other than one fleeting season with the sailing team, I never found my footing on sports teams like my siblings did, but I attended enough of their games to know that coaches also did that extra work. Still, I never appreciated that to facilitate my extracurricular experiences, those adults had mostly donated their time at the end of tiring days after working their real jobs—until I was the one hesitantly agreeing to oversee the break dancing club and chaperone the sophomore camping trip. Maybe part of my discontent with my office job was missing the messy goodness of working with kids. With all of that in mind, I raised my half-empty glass of

Sam Adams to toast my dad and me, and our cooking class, fairly certain that it would never actually happen.

My dad paused the way he paused while he was pondering an idea: deep breath, eyes closed, head askew. "Intriguing. We could be a team, like Roslindale's own Jacques and Claudine Pépin," he said, referencing our Boston neighborhood and the famous father-daughter cooking duo. He smiled, tickled by his own wit, fang tooth peeking out from beneath his upper lip.

I laughed and nodded and drank.

He took a sip of his Sam and said he was interested. "That would be neat."

How could I retract then, and admit that I hadn't been entirely serious?

We clinked glass to bottle to seal the deal. I had him at food. He had me at team.

Then he got sick and the plan for our cooking class went where plans go when somebody gets a capital-D diagnosis: onto the back burner, the bottom quadrant of my dad's to-do list. Other matters needed tending to. He went to medical appointments with yellow legal pads and black felt-tipped pens to take notes, and came home with naked pages as the weeks wore on. His doctor told him not to go online to search *mesothelioma*, and to walk as much as he could tolerate to increase his lung capacity. There was no cure. The best-case scenario was to slow the cancer, control the pain, and maintain some quality of life. The months that followed were swollen with experimental treatments, surgeries, a caravan of casseroles from friends, and so much walking.

Every day, he walked. At night, I walked with him. He assigned my siblings and me different jobs during the sick months; mine was walking. We had two routes, depending on his energy: a long route when he was feeling okay, or not okay but angry and ambitious, and a short route when he was feeling tired and sick, or very tired and even sicker.

On the walks, we didn't talk about the forever things people always mean to say or hope to hear. We talked mostly about food and baseball. I talked more about food and listened more about baseball.

My appreciation for sports has always been more holistic than statistical. Each night that fall of 2004, he gave me the breakdown of the chances the Red Sox would advance to their first World Series since 1918. Fans wore shirts that read "Believe" and "Why not us?" The Sox kept advancing, into October. Then they started losing. When they went into game four down three, I asked, "But don't you think it's effectively over?" My dad closed his eyes and shook his head. "It's unlikely, but possible," he assured me. He went on to explain three scenarios in which the chance of winning could play out. When the Sox came back to win four games straight and make fever-rising history, it was hard not to believe in miracles.

He died two months later, three months after his fifty-seventh birthday, six months after his diagnosis, eleven months after we made our Pépin plan. At four o'clock one Tuesday morning in December, as night shift staff bought croissants and coffee from the café in the hospital lobby, I walked with my mother through the huge revolving exit into a world without my dad. With the spin of an automatic door, the world as I knew it shifted into the past tense.

GRIEF IS THE ultimate marinade. You become more of whatever you were already: the lonely, lonelier; the angry, angrier; the restless, more restless. Sometimes the faithful manage to emerge more faithful. It's hard to describe the infinite loop of loss. The closest sensation might be hunger, if eyes and ears and fingertips could be hungry.

I missed my dad's voice. I replayed our last conversations in my mind like a favorite album on repeat. I kept papers with his writing on them as bookmarks. Months after his death, my dad didn't feel gone, yet. But I felt him disappearing. I asked a friend who'd lost his father how long it would take for the fog to lift. I thought it must disintegrate eventually; I wanted a time line. The friend hesitated then said the fog never really lifts, but I'd learn to see through it.

During the first year without my dad, I felt like I was sinking. As a child, I had a fear of quicksand. I imagined murky traps hidden beneath swampy grass and mud, and was astounded to learn how little quicksand there actually is in Massachusetts. But during the deep grief months, it felt real; small things like songs my dad used to sing along to on the radio were sinkholes in otherwise okay days. I needed to unstick myself. So I moved out of my childhood home, settled into a job teaching Spanish language and literature at my high school alongside two of my former teachers who became my mentors, and began graduate coursework in secondary education, taking classes in Spanish and Latin American literature and second language acquisition, and completing certification in teaching English language learners. Becoming a teacher felt like a step in the right direction of becoming a real grown-up with a job she believed in, if also one with chokingly short lunch breaks. "Education is architecture, not alchemy," I wrote in my personal statement. I had briefly considered moving away and trying to start over in a new place; I had lived in Spain for a year during college and liked losing myself in traveling, tasting flavors I'd never had before, and meeting people who knew me only as who I said I was. I wondered if my dad-less life would easier to process in translation. But instead I decided to stay close, not too far from my mom and siblings, and try to build something upon the foundations I knew, which largely consisted of words and food. I also decided to try the cooking idea, as a sort of back burner project.

Cooking at the House would be a way to finish one item on my father's largely unfinished to-do list, and running a weekly program at the House and funding it myself would be a small-scale community service project, like ones I'd participated in since I was ten. For all I didn't know about the world or what role I was supposed to play in it, I knew how to be a volunteer. I also knew how to cook; I wasn't a fancy cook, but I liked cooking. I enjoyed the process and presentation, the feeding and feeling fed. Cooking seemed more practical than grieving; at the time I believed they were distinct processes. The prospect of spending time in the place my father had spent so much of his time when he wasn't with us, and getting to know some of the other kids in his life, was intriguing. I didn't know whether the boys who lived in the residence upstairs from my dad's office already knew how to cook, or if they would want to cook with me. But I figured food is always good. And this project had been our idea. I would never make another meal with my dad, but cooking at the House with his other kids like we'd talked about would be a kind of final nod to him, an offering. One dinner at the House and I could check the box and move on to something else. "Just do the best you can," I could almost hear my dad say. "What do you have to lose?"

At a restaurant across the street from the House, I proposed the cooking idea to Gerry Wright, my father's business partner. Gerry had been working in human services for over sixty years and looked the part of a disheveled visionary, like Federico García Lorca's drawing of Walt Whitman with butterflies in his beard, but more dimensional and less romantic—white hair, white beard, white face, and with antifreeze-blue eyes. He had invited me to dinner to touch base and break bread. I don't like small talk and I wasn't ready for big talk; I was exhausted from trying to be fine all the time. I waited until the chicken arrived to start my service project pitch.

I told Gerry that I wanted to try cooking with the boys at the House, as a volunteer. I said it was a plan I'd made with my dad before he got sick, and I wanted to attempt it, in his memory. I described how my dad had been a little giddy at the prospect of trying this new thing with the residents at the House and how we imagined it as a joint venture; I swallowed hard, remembering the fleeting feeling of planning for a future. The format would be an approximately two-hour session once a week—we'd cook for an hour, then eat for an hour. The residents would pick the menus, I would bring the groceries. It wouldn't cost the agency anything; I'd pay for the food. I reminded Gerry that I was a licensed public high school teacher, so I had experience working with teenagers and the city had my criminal background check on file.

Gerry listened carefully, then rested his fork and knife against his plate and thanked but no thanked me. He said that the idea was interesting, but it didn't make sense at that time.

I saw doubt shade his eyes. I tried to convince him that I could handle the difference between a kitchen in a residential group home setting and my classroom in the rigorous exam school where I taught. I described other volunteer work I'd done as evidence that I was qualified to steer this community service project. "I tutored a teen in a homeless shelter who would pretend she was sleeping when she saw me coming," I said. "I led a prayer group in the women's unit of a prison by myself. I ran a tutoring program in a library in Chicago twice a week for two years. I dug an outhouse on a mountain. I've worked with people outside of classrooms." I was surprised by the urgency in my voice. "I won't disappoint the kids at the House."

"That is not what I am worried about. Let us leave it at this," he said, folding his hands. "I will let you know if anything changes."

A few months later, Gerry left me a voicemail. In an effort to defrost a hamburger with a steak knife, one of the residents had angrily stabbed himself in the hand, requiring a number of stitches. "So," Gerry said, "it appears that some sort of cooking program may be in order at this time. If you are still interested in giving this a go, come to the House next week and introduce your plan to the young people upstairs. And I suppose"—he paused, sounding wise and tired—"we'll just see what happens."

THIS IS THE story of what happened. It starts with a joke, or a meal, or a knife, depending on what you consider the beginning. And it ends with state budget cuts, or the death of a young man, or it hasn't ended yet, depending on what you accept as an ending. The kids picked the menus, I brought the groceries, and we cooked and ate together for two hours a week for nearly three years.

It sounds like a description for one of those "great white hope" stories involving kids facing difficult circumstances and a white twentysomething bleeding heart with crazy hair and good intentions, the kind that ends with upbeat music and rehabilitation. I look the part of the bleeding heart. But this is not one of those stories. I wasn't trying to save anyone. This is a story about food and conversations and extracurricular spaces, and how flavors and cooking remind you of other kitchens you've been in, and what happens when you sit down to eat with neighbors. This is one volunteer's story about a little community service project and a lot of cheese. Salvation was never on the table.

PART 1

MOVEABLE FEASTS

We've got to be as clear-headed about human beings as possible, because we are still each other's only hope.

—*James Baldwin*

La mejor salsa del mundo es el hambre.
Hunger is the best sauce in the world.

—*Miguel de Cervantes*

Cut away from yourself.

—*Charlie Hauck,*
on making food and not hurting yourself

Getting Started

The House is a two-story redbrick building, like the one the Big Bad Wolf couldn't blow down. It sits on a busy city corner, across from a funeral home on one side and an animal shelter on the other. One half mile to the left of it live some of the poorest people in the city of Boston; one half mile to the right live some of the richest. Gerry calls this the world's longest socioeconomic mile, and he says that there are strategy and symbolism in his having chosen this location for the headquarters of his agency. The doors, porch, and shutters that frame each window are painted a bright, flat Crayola green. There's usually graffiti to the left or right of the back door, which was rarely locked during daylight hours. The stairs leading up from the street make an aching sound when you walk on them; covered in carpeting the same gray as the sidewalk outside, they connect the building's two floors. The agency offices were located on the first, and one of the residences the agency ran for youth in state care was on the second, before everything changed. The residence upstairs from my dad's office was one of the boys' programs. At a given time, it housed up to eight of the agency's adolescent clients age fourteen to nineteen who were designated wards of the state, referred through other human service agencies, often after removal from their homes, failed placements with foster families, or short stays in juvenile detention facilities. For them, the House was a temporary group home placement, or at least somewhere to sleep and eat. It used to seem to me that upstairs and downstairs were two clearly divided worlds. Whenever I was at the House as a kid, it was to wait for my father, for a ride home. I'd sit in the waiting room on the couch, which was beige, the way that things that could be anybody's things are beige. Sometimes I would hear raised voices, or the thud of a basketball being dribbled hard against the other side of the ceiling. But for the first twenty-six years of my life, I never went upstairs.

I WENT TO the House to speak to Gerry a few days after receiving his voicemail. Ostensibly, I wanted to discuss the meeting he had scheduled for me with the residents. But really, this visit was a kind of dry run; I didn't want my first time back in the House after my father's death to be the night I met the kids. I didn't know how it would feel to be there without my father, and I didn't want to be messy; I knew I was already fighting other stereotypes. What would the boys think of me, or think I was trying to be? I took a deep breath before going in, noticing the veins in the late-September leaves on the tree between the House and the street, gilded in a final jolt of beauty before their inevitable fall. I pressed my hand against the familiar green door and it was open, so I went inside.

I walked up to the first-floor landing and turned the worn brass knob on the door that led to the office, like I had so many afternoons before. Inside, it looked and smelled the same: the walls, the floor, the stale coffee from that morning still in the coffeepot, the stack of magazines by the entryway. Gerry hadn't changed anything in the building since my father's last day, except for the ceiling, which he reluctantly allowed to be patched when someone warned him that if he didn't, it would fall in.

I made my way to the administrative coordinator's desk and told her I was there to talk to Gerry. My heart pounded. I stared at the typewriter as it sat in the front office. I remembered my dad at that exact typewriter: the mechanical *clink* as he filled in forms and typed up budgets, the *tink-tink* of each letter being hit, the *clack* and *whoosh* at the end of a line. His exasperated "Shit!" and slow *plack-plack* of backspacing. I could almost see his solid frame hunched over the outdated machine, glasses perched on his nose, bushy eyebrows furrowed in thought, hands moving slowly over the keys, silk tie thrown over his shoulder to save it from getting sucked in.

"I know, you'd think since we have computers, we could just get rid of that thing," the administrative coordinator said. "But Gerry won't let me. It's kind of ridiculous. You must be Liz."

I averted my eyes from the doorway to what had been my father's office, across the hall. I didn't want to see the pastel drawing of the House that he had commissioned by a local artist, or his chair or books or phone. Especially his phone. That phone looked ugly, plastic, and nondescript. But his for years, it had the patina of the diminishing supply of things he had touched.

I asked the administrative coordinator if she thought a cooking program might work upstairs.

"I don't really know," she said, smiling politely.

As we were talking, one of the boys walked in. He was Black, had caramel-brown eyes, stubble grabbing at his chin, and his head and shoulders tilted to one side. I had no idea how old he was, except that he was old enough to grow a beard but young enough to not live on his own. "You know when we're going to get our fall clothing allowance checks?" he asked. "'Cause I found some sneakers I like and I'm not sure how long they'll have my size."

"I think soon," the administrative coordinator replied, and then introduced us. "Leon, this's Liz. She might be starting a cooking program upstairs. And Liz, this's Leon."

"That's good," Leon said. "'Cause tell you the truth, I'm kind of hungry right now."

"Hey, Leon," I said, reaching out to shake his hand. He looked familiar.

"Nice to meet you," Leon said, placing his left hand over his stomach as he shook my hand, looking at me more out of his left eye than his right. "You're pretty tall, actually." The old floorboards creaked beneath us as he shifted from one foot to another.

"Nice to meet you, too," I said. I noticed that he was a few inches shorter than me, but I didn't say. I was used to people commenting on my height; I stand almost six feet tall and little kids, male students, and elderly folks tend to mention it. "I am pretty tall, and I think, maybe, we've met before. At Gerry's party." In February of that year, Gerry's wife had thrown him a seventieth birthday gathering. I'd stopped by with one of my sisters on our way to a basketball game with season tickets still printed in our dad's name. The event was a blur, except that I was sure I'd met Leon, briefly. I didn't remember his name, but I recognized his face. Meeting him and the other kid he was with at the party was part of what inspired me to resuscitate the cooking project idea.

He looked at me again. "Oh yeah, I was there. I think I remember you."

"You might not," I said. "There were a lot of people there."

"Yeah, I mean, I *think* I remember. But I met a *lot* of people that night," he said.

The administrative coordinator laughed. "You're very popular, Leon."

"It's true, I am," he told me seriously.

"Do you think the guys upstairs would be interested in cooking?" I asked.

"Yup. People like to eat," Leon said. "You cook and we eat?"

"I was thinking more of a *we all* cook, then *we all* eat kind of thing," I said.

"Oh," he said. "*People* don't really *cook*." He scrunched his nose.

"Well, that's kind of the idea," I said. "People would, like, *learn to cook*."

He thought about this for a second. "Tell you the truth," he said, "I think people would be more interested in *my* idea: *you cook,* and *we eat*."

"You're probably right," I agreed. "But would you help if we tried *everybody* cooking and *everybody* eating?"

Leon looked at me. "Yeah, I mean I'll probably help. 'Cause *I'm* like that," he said, his eyes widening. "But I'm not sure about anybody else."

"Maybe if you do, other people will, too," I suggested.

"Maybe." He shrugged. "But you don't know these people." His tone was somber, as if he were prepping me for a business meeting with foreign clients.

As Leon shook my hand goodbye, I decided that if he agreed to help, cooking could work. I headed toward Gerry's office and noticed the same old beige couch in the waiting room at the other end of the hall.

Gerry heard me coming and leaned into the hallway. "I've got to take an unexpected call," he said. "But you've met Leon. You'll come on Tuesday and meet the others. Are we still on?"

I said yes, and Gerry asked if there was anything else.

There was plenty else. How many boys lived upstairs? What should I know about them? What *could* I know about them? Did anyone have allergies? How equipped was the kitchen?

But there was no time for orientation. Our logistics meeting was over before it began. I figured there must be a stove and refrigerator upstairs, and hoped Leon would show up like he said he would so there'd be at least one participant. Everything else was negotiable.

THE FOLLOWING TUESDAY was my introductory meeting with the kids upstairs. I met Gerry in his office so we could go up together. There was a man with a camera standing beside him, a photographer for a local paper who was working on a story about Gerry's work in the community. It was a weird coincidence, and I felt uncomfortable with the camera and how the boys would understand me near it. Whose photo op was this? But who was I to question?

Gerry greeted me with outstretched arms. "Well, well, well," he said in the booming voice of a radio announcer. "Elizabeth! Are you ready?"

"As ready as I'm going to be, I think," I said, ignoring the photographer.

Gerry pointed to the tray of brownies I was carrying and raised his eyebrows. He'd told me not to bring anything.

"I'm not above bribery," I said. "You should know that from the beginning."

He laughed, I smiled, and the photographer snapped the first picture.

The trip upstairs was much shorter than I had always imagined it would be. The noise of our weight against the old wood announced our arrival. Before Gerry could knock on the second-floor door, it opened. Leon stepped out from behind it.

"Hello," Leon said. "I heard you all coming." I noticed his shoulders again, the left higher than the right. He shook my hand and the photographer's and nodded respectfully to Gerry. "Everybody's in the other room," he said as he led us through the kitchen toward the table in the dining room. "Except for James," he continued. "James isn't here. We're all *supposed* to be here but *James* isn't here." He looked at Gerry to make sure that Gerry had heard then he looked back at me. Already, Leon, with the handshake and angled posture and unshaved chin, was the spokesman, the elder, and the one who made the place feel less like a halfway house and more like a home.

The layout of the second floor of the House was nearly identical to the first. The rooms that were offices on the first floor were bedrooms on the second; what was the waiting room downstairs was a TV room upstairs. Leon led us through the kitchen and the pantry into the dining room. Four boys were sitting around a big wooden table that looked like a dock. A man with a clipboard leaned against the outside wall; he introduced himself as Greg, the houseparent on duty. I moved toward one of two unoccupied seats and set my tray of brownies on the table. I sat down, pushed up the sleeves of my salmon-colored sweater, and pressed the nails of my index fingers into the tips of my thumbs, the way I do when I'm nervous. The photographer was clicking away from the doorway, and while I appreciated that Gerry was being recognized for his service to the community, I felt increasingly conspicuous in the flickering flash.

As I surveyed the room, I wondered what the photographer was seeing, what he was trying to capture in this particular frame: four teenage boys, three Black, one Latino; Gerry, an elderly white man; the houseparent, a middle-aged Black man; me, a woman in my late twenties, white. At what angle did the story of us together at this table make sense?

Gerry greeted the boys and introduced me. He told them that my father had worked there for years, that I was a teacher, and that I wanted to cook with them.

The boys looked at Gerry, then at me, then back at him with uninterested-teenager-told-to-be-there faces.

Gerry reassured them that we would "take it one week at a time" and "just see how it goes," which we all knew were other ways of saying "this won't last long." He turned the table over to me.

I repeated my name and asked each of the boys to tell me his so that I could learn them: Frank, Carlos, Wesley, Leon. Leon was the only one who said more than just his name. He said, "Well, I think you know this already, but I'm Leon."

I tried not to seem like I was trying too hard. I didn't talk too fast or too much or too cheerfully. I repeated that I was a teacher; I taught Spanish at a high school not far from the House. I said I lived in the neighborhood, too, and that my father had worked downstairs. I could tell by the way they looked down at the table when I mentioned my dad that the houseparent must have told them that he had died. I didn't say that my father's death was part of why I was there, and why I wanted to start this cooking program, but I could see in their faces that they already knew. I wondered whether any of them had been at the House long enough to have known my dad. But I didn't ask.

I outlined my plan in four parts. One: We would cook for an hour, and then eat for an hour, together at the table, family style. Two: What we cooked would be up to them; they would pick the menus. If they wanted to cook meals they'd never tried before, we could do that. If they wanted to cook food they already knew they liked and wanted to learn how to make for themselves, we could do that, too. If they already knew how to make what they liked and wanted to teach the group, even better; I would bring the ingredients for that. I explained that the idea was that we would cook together so that they could learn to cook for themselves, or practice cooking for each other if they already knew how to cook. If I didn't know how to make something they wanted to make, I'd find the recipes; there'd be no homework involved for them, just showing up. Three: The dinner closest to someone's birthday would be his birthday dinner. The birthday person would choose the meal for that week and a kind of cake for dessert. Four: If anyone wanted to invite someone to dinner, he would be welcome to do that.

Carlos broke the silence on the other side of the table with a laugh. He was stocky, with a full face, close-cut hair, and coffee-colored eyes; he was the only one in the room who wasn't Black or white. His laugh was more of a snort.

The other boys looked at him.

"People aren't going to invite people here." Carlos shifted in his chair, moved his hands from his lap to the table, and enunciated clearly, pausing after every word for emphasis, like a political candidate reiterating his party's platform.

I looked around the table for other responses. Nobody agreed, but nobody disagreed.

"Okay," I said. "We can see about that." I handed out some surveys I had printed out, to gather information about what meals people would want to eat and who would want to cook them. There was a line for names at the top followed by five questions: What's your favorite food? Do you know how to make it? Are there any foods you're interested in learning how to cook? Are you willing to help make dinners? Are you available on Tuesdays? Beneath that, I had compiled a list of foods and asked them to circle the ones they liked and might want to make, and then write in other suggestions in the space below.

I hadn't anticipated that the surveys would look like quizzes to the boys, or how in handing them out I would solidify my identity as teacher, for better and for worse. For better because it put me in an identifiable category of person in their lives, for worse because teacher was a category of person they didn't necessarily care for.

"We can't do this. We don't have pens," Wesley said, pushing the page toward me. He had the slightest build of all the boys in the group, and the fiercest eyes.

"Yeah," Carlos agreed.

I pulled a handful of pens from my bag and passed them around.

Wesley sighed an exasperated sigh, dragged the paper back toward himself with his middle finger, and started writing.

As Wesley and Carlos and Leon wrote, Frank sat penless while Greg, the houseparent, took a seat beside him and read the questions and options aloud. Frank spoke his answers and Greg wrote them down. Frank was the tallest of the boys, and I would learn later that he was also the youngest and had been at the House the longest. When Greg finished recording Frank's answers, he passed the pen and paper over to Frank and told him to write his own name.

Wesley finished his sheet quickly and slid it across the table to me. He wrote "Cheesecake" for his favorite food and "N/A" for everything else, including his last name: Wesley Not Applicable.

Carlos handed me his paper and pointed to the tray of brownies. "Are those for us?"

"They are," I said, and reached to initiate distribution.

"I'll get a knife," Leon said, already on his way to get one.

"Look, she brought us brownies," Carlos told the other boys in a singsong way. "She put little candies in them and everything." To me, he said, "That's so cute."

I paused and nodded, noticing the dimples in his cheek as he smiled. I stopped myself before saying that I didn't appreciate his tone, like I would have if we were in my classroom.

Leon returned with a plastic knife and passed it to me. I sliced into the soft chocolate and asked who wanted a piece.

"I do, definitely," Leon said. He unfolded a napkin across his hand and held it toward me.

One by one, each boy reached out a hand.

While everyone was eating, I moved to my next agenda item. If people were available, we'd start the following week. "What should we make?" I took a chance with *we*.

"I like stir-fry chicken and it's been a real long time since I had it," Leon said.

I checked other faces for signs of agreement.

"And I've been trying to eat healthy, which isn't easy around here," Leon continued.

The other boys looked at him. Eyes rolled but no one said anything.

Leon looked at me. "So we could make stir-fry chicken?"

"Does everyone like stir-fry chicken?" I asked.

Frank shrugged. Wesley said nothing. Carlos stared at me.

"So, stir-fry chicken and veggies and rice," I said. "I was thinking I'd get some soda, too. Does anybody like soda? Or should I get juice or iced tea?" I'd seen massive canisters of tea mix in the pantry we walked through to get from the kitchen to the dining room and there was fruit punch on the table. But I thought soda might be a treat, like it had been in my house growing up, and like it was in meetings I attended at school.

"People like soda." "Yeah." "Uh-huh." "Everybody likes soda."

I should have led with soda. "What kind should I get?" I asked.

"Pepsi." "Mountain Dew Code Red." "Sprite." "No, Pepsi—" They fought for a consensus.

"Pepsi, Mountain Dew, Sprite. I can get one of each," I said. "There'll be a bunch of us, right? I'm sure we'll drink it or can leave leftovers in the fridge." I went all in with *us* and *we*.

"Mountain Dew *Code Red*," Frank corrected.

"Oh, is that different?" I asked.

"Yeah," Frank sighed. "It's red."

"Okay, I got it." I underlined *red* in my notes.

"What about dessert? Do you guys like dessert?" I asked.

"People like dessert," Leon said, gesturing to the brownie tray.

"How about strawberry shortcake?" I asked, noticing that somebody had circled it on one of the surveys.

"What does it have?" someone asked.

"Strawberries, whipped cream, and cake or biscuits," I listed.

"Yeah we could have that," someone else said.

"With cake," somebody added.

"Okay, so stir-fry chicken with rice and vegetables, and strawberry shortcake," I repeated, writing it down.

"Yeah, but could we have pie instead?" someone asked. "'Cause you wrote *pie* on the paper."

"Sure, we can make pie," I said, crossing out shortcake. "What kind?" I looked around.

There was shrugging.

"Apple pie is the healthiest," Leon said.

Someone sighed a slow, oozing sigh.

"So apple pie, then?" I asked. "Stir-fry chicken and vegetables with rice, and soda, with apple pie for dessert. What time should we say? Five o'clock to start cooking, and then six o'clock for eating? Does that sound okay?"

There was more shrugging and one nod.

The back door opened and then shut, and a figure appeared in the doorway.

"That's James," Leon stage-whispered to me. His bulging eyes suggested the rest of the introduction: James who was supposed to have been here since the beginning but wasn't.

I stood up. "James, it's good to meet you." I reached over to shake his hand.

"I had something," he said apologetically. James was nearly as tall as me, not as tall as Frank, but taller than Leon and Wesley, and also Black. As he reached his right hand toward mine, I saw a bandage wrapped across his left palm. I remembered him from Gerry's voicemail: James was the one who'd tried to defrost a hamburger with a knife, setting all of this in motion.

"Do you want a brownie?" I asked him.

He shrugged his broad shoulders. I was already cutting. I could see by the looks of disdain being exchanged around the table that the other boys didn't think it was fair to give James a brownie since he hadn't come to the meeting. As a middle sibling, I recognized the look. I knew this was a tricky precedent, but it felt like the right one.

"So I think that's it," I concluded, sensing that the boys had been told to stay until I dismissed them. "I'll see you all next week." I tried to say it as if it weren't a question.

The boys stood and moved away as if the doorways were magnetic.

"You leaving those brownies?" Leon asked.

"Well, I was going to," I told him. "If people might eat them, I'll leave them."

"People'll eat them," Leon said.

"Yeah," someone else agreed.

"Okay," I said. "I'm leaving the brownies." I smiled and reached out to shake hands goodbye.

No one except Leon met my smile with a smile, but one by one, each boy shook my hand on his way out. I said each of their names when I thanked them for coming to help me remember them: Wesley, the shortest and thinnest, who held his chin up highest; Frank, the tallest, with a space between his front teeth; Carlos, with a shaved head and crater dimples; James, with the soft eyes and bandaged hand; and Leon, with the uneven shoulders, the stubble, and the smile.

When I reached to shake the houseparent's hand, he leaned in toward me, so I leaned toward him. "I just want you to know," he said quietly, "that's not how we do things around here, with a table and everything."

I don't know what I expected him to say, but it wasn't that.

Before I could respond, he continued, "That's just not how it works around here. I don't even know if they're going to do any of this. I told them they had to be here tonight, because of Gerry. But after this, I don't know. I can't make them show up every time."

I nodded that I understood, and we shook on that. "We'll just try it next week." I shrugged.

I followed Gerry and the photographer down the stairs. On the landing, Gerry said, "Well, Elizabeth, you have your work cut out for you. You will take it from here. And—"

"I know," I interrupted. "We'll just see what happens."

Placement

If you're a kid who lives at the House, the state is your parent. For now, maybe for longer. You're a boy; if you're nonbinary, gender nonconforming, transgender, or a girl, you're probably placed somewhere else. You're fourteen, or fifteen, or sixteen, or seventeen—too young to be left alone. You might be eighteen, if you got a bonus year, or nineteen or twenty if you have some kind of disability that means the state is responsible for you for longer. On the outside, these years are called *adolescence*, a time for growing and learning and becoming a person in the world. On the inside, this is "transitional age," which means you'll be on your own soon. Something happened to land you here. Or a series of somethings. Maybe you have people who are fighting to get you back; maybe not. Maybe you think this is their fault, or maybe you think it's your fault, or maybe it's the fault of whoever got you taken away, or maybe it's too hard to untangle all the faults enough to understand how you got here, with all your stuff in a trash bag and the phone number of a caseworker in your pocket. You'll be here until you return to your parent or grandparent or aunt, or get placed somewhere else, or get kicked out, or run away. Or maybe you'll be adopted. Maybe you have some idea what will come next; maybe you're counting down to eighteen, when you can decide for yourself. For now, it's only sort of up to you. Maybe you're relieved to not still be wherever you were before. Maybe you're terrified of what comes next.

Your caseworker drove you here on the day you moved in. She's probably not your first caseworker. In the car, she told you everything is going to be okay. Maybe she believes that. She's probably young and white, and you probably think that she doesn't really know what she's talking about. She parked on the street outside of this building that looks like a dentist's office. You took your own stuff out of the trunk of her car. You didn't want her help.

You followed her through a bright green door and up noisy stairs. Another lady led you into a waiting room. Your caseworker told you to sit on the couch while she went over your paperwork with the staff here. You sat and stared at a poster with a peace sign and a scribbled rainbow and bird on the wall while they talked. You thought, *I won't be here long.* Then they brought you around to meet people in the other offices. People shook your hand and maybe told you, "Welcome." Maybe you said, "Thanks." Maybe you didn't.

When it was time to go upstairs, your caseworker asked if you wanted her to go up with you. You told her no, she could leave. You're fine on your own. She told you she'd call you tomorrow to see how it was going. You nodded okay. She asked if you had any questions. And maybe you had questions, but you probably told her you didn't. When your caseworker left, the lady who opened the door took you upstairs. All you felt was the weight of stuff in your bag pulling against your fingers.

A man opened the door to the second floor. He nodded at the lady who brought you up, then at you, and told you he's a houseparent. There's always staff on duty here. Afternoon staff orients the new kids; it's their job to give you a tour. The tour was short.

The House is probably not your first placement. It's a group home: a place to sleep when you have no place else to be. There are rules here, but you have a little more freedom than you would in a more restrictive residential placement, and a lot more freedom than you'd have in a juvenile detention facility. This isn't the worst place. If you've lived other places, you already know how this goes. If you haven't, you do now.

You get assigned a bed, a dresser with four drawers, and a closet barely as wide as your shoulders. Depending how many boys are here, you probably have a roommate. His bed is the one that's made; the side it's on is his side. You'll stay on your side, unless the door's on his side and you have to cross it to get in and out. Sometimes, clothes pile up along the invisible line that splits the room. Even if you get along, you never touch his stuff. There's probably a small TV in the middle of the room, with a remote. Whoever's been here longer has control of the remote when you're both in the room. Sometimes, the staff changes rooms around—like if someone steals from someone, or someone's snoring bothers someone, or someone hits someone. Whoever's been here the shorter amount of time gets moved. Four rooms are set up like this, each with two beds. If all eight beds are full and there's a problem in one room, everyone gets moved.

Down the hall in one direction are two bathrooms, side by side, each with a big ceramic bathtub. There's soap by the sink, but you carry everything else back and forth from your room in a little bucket or a plastic bag: toothbrush, toothpaste, shaving cream and razor, shampoo, brush or comb, deodorant. Nobody shares those things. Two people can't take showers with hot water at the same time; you have to go one at a time. You could take a shower at night to have hot water and avoid the rush in the morning. Nobody takes baths.

Down the hall in the other direction is the TV room. There're a couple of game systems and two controllers, unless someone got angry and broke one. People play videogames all the time. If there's a game on that people want to see, someone brings the TV from his room and hooks it up so people can play videogames on one and watch sports on the other at the same time. If you want to play, you wait and play the winner. The loser moves to the end of the line.

Off the TV room is a fifth room, the staff office. There's a bed, but it doesn't have sheets, because even the overnight staff doesn't sleep. There's a desk against the back wall; most of its drawers are locked. They lock up dangerous things and things people might want to steal, like scissors, knives, and money. They also lock up the medicine.

Not everybody takes medicine, but whatever people take is locked in that desk. If you have a prescription, your caseworker gave it to the staff when they checked you in; you can't keep drugs in your room. The bottom drawer of the staff desk is full of mood stabilizers, beta-blockers, antidepressants, Adderall, inhalers, and EpiPens. The pills are sorted into single doses and kept in little envelopes, licked shut and labeled with a name, day, and time the resident is supposed to take it. Serious painkillers, like if someone got shot or had surgery, are delivered one dose at a time so they can't be shared, sold, or taken all together. Hanging over the desk are two giant whiteboards with big grids of weeks with tilting lines. One is labeled MEDICINE, and has everybody's names. The staff on duty marks an erasable check to show who got his medicine. There's a code so people can't see what other people are taking, but after a while, everybody pretty much knows.

The other whiteboard is labeled CHORES. The chore chart is a huge grid with the days of the week in one direction and the list of chores in the other. The names of who's supposed to do which chore when are written in the boxes. There're eight chores: Kitchen A, Kitchen B, sweeping the front stairs, sweeping the back stairs, taking the garbage out, cleaning the TV room, and cleaning both bathrooms. Kitchen A means cleaning the sink and everything in it and sweeping the floor around the stove. Kitchen B means cleaning the dining room, sweeping it, and taking out the kitchen trash. The worst are the bathrooms, but everyone takes turns.

You get assigned chores one week at a time; they rotate, to make it fair. How many chores you get depends on how many people are living here. If the House is full, everyone gets one chore. Each chore pays two dollars per night. The staff on duty checks off who did what each night on the board, then counts the initials up to see who earned what. How much you get paid depends on how much you did. You get paid at the end of the week, at least fourteen dollars if you had one chore and did it every night.

Sometimes people make deals. You can trade chores, or share them. You can also let someone do your chore and split the money, so he gets a dollar for doing the chore and you keep a dollar since the chore was yours to start with; it works out for both of you. If you didn't come with money of your own and don't have an outside job, you do chores. Most people don't have jobs; pretty much every-one does chores to make some extra cash. People use the money for what they want, like Red Bull, subs, weed, and T-shirts.

You don't have to use chore money for haircuts, toothpaste, or stuff like that. They give you hygiene money twice a month for shaving cream and razors, deodorant, and shampoo. The staff takes you to a barber and pays for haircuts. Twice a year, if you're still here, you get a wardrobe allowance check to buy new clothes. How much you get depends on how much money there is. You can spend it how you want. Like if you want to spend most of it on sneakers and not get a coat because your coat from last year still fits, you get to decide that.

You have to clean your own clothes; nobody will do that for you. There's no washer at the House, so you need to go to one of the laundromats in the neighborhood. Most people bring their clothes in a pillowcase or a backpack. If you bring your own detergent, it's cheaper than buying the little boxes they sell there, but then you have to carry it back and forth. Sometimes people go do laundry together. People smoke then, too. On the way there, the way back, outside while you're waiting. You use hygiene money for laundry, not chore money.

You don't have to use chore money for buses or trains either. The staff gives you a bus pass to get around the city. People go to the Y to play basketball, lift weights, and hang out with friends; some peo-ple go back to their old neighborhoods. You can pretty much go wherever you want during the day. You're supposed to go to school, but no one follows you when you leave in the morning; staff won't know for a while where you're going, but they usually find out. Whatever you do, be back by curfew.

Curfew is 8 P.M. You have to be in the House, upstairs, before the staff locks the doors. If you get back late, you forfeit your chores, and chore money, because chores start right at eight. Plus you get in trouble. If you're going to be late, you'll get in less trouble if you call before curfew to tell the staff that you won't be there. There're a couple of exceptions. Like if you have an outside job. Or if you have a scheduled home visit, you might get permission to get back later. The first time you're late, you get a warning, unless you're drunk or high or bleeding. Every time you get in trouble, the staff writes it in the book. The staff writes everything in the book.

The book is a big black binder. The staff calls it "the log." It's full of reports from every shift. The staff writes down everything that happened. Normal stuff goes on white papers, like who took medicine at what time, if people went for haircuts, things like that. The colored paper sheets are for behavior stuff, like fights, fits, stealing, people acting out, people smoking up. If staff writes you up on a behavioral form, a copy gets put into your folder, too.

Everybody has a folder. They're all kept in one of the downstairs offices; they're supposed to be locked up, so nobody except the staff can read your business. Your folder has official papers in it: birth certificate, social security card, school transcripts, disciplinary records, court stuff, addresses—any paper thing they have for you is in there.

Everyone here will call you "FNG" in the beginning. It stands for Fuckin' New Guy. They'll call you that until someone else moves in. When someone leaves or gets kicked out or runs away and someone new moves in, you stop being the new guy. And people will call you your first name or your nickname or whatever you tell them to call you. Then you'll call the new guy FNG, too.

If you want to call someone on the outside, you use the landline in the dining room. If someone's on it when you need it, you have to wait your turn, but nobody ever talks too long.

Nobody really talks about how anybody got here. It's easier if you don't say too much, and if you stay out of trouble. Don't take other people's things. Don't fight. If you see something, don't say anything; if you talk, everyone will call you a snitch or a rat. Keep track of your own stuff; people will take it if you leave it around. You can eat what you can find here. Cereal for breakfast. You'll get free lunch at school. There are snacks in the pantry, and sometimes you can request the kind you can find. Sometimes the staff on duty cooks dinner. If they don't, you're on your own. There's food in the pantry and the refrigerator; you can help yourself to whatever you want. If you're hungry, you have to learn to feed yourself.

I DIDN'T KNOW most of this when I started the cooking nights at the House. I didn't know much about the kids who lived there. I didn't know how Leon and Frank and Wesley and Carlos and James had landed in state care, or where they had lived before the House, and I didn't know who would leave when or under what circumstances, or who would take their places then. I knew that, statistically, most of the boys had histories involving violence, but I didn't know the contours of their stories or the kinds of violence. I didn't know who took what medication or had which diagnosis; it took a while to learn why Leon walked the way he walked, and to understand the jokes other boys made about Frank's mother, and why nobody ever checked Carlos's room to see if he was around. Most of what I learned about the boys were stories they told me themselves, and most of what they told me, they told me near food because something we made or ate reminded them of other kitchens they had been in, and hands that had fed them there.

I never got a tour of the House. I would walk up the creaky back stairs into the kitchen, around the corner, through the TV room, and into the staff office to check in. Then I'd walk back to the kitchen to cook. When the food was ready, I'd walk through the pantry off the kitchen into the dining room for dinner. And when we were finished, I'd check out with the staff and leave, usually through the kitchen, back down the creaky stairs. I never went into any of the bedrooms; I never used the bathroom. My range of motion was small. I was only there for about two hours per week, so it took a while to learn the gist of how things went, beyond the kitchen choreography I was sort of making up as we went along. I was there to run a cooking program, so I focused on the food and what I could bring to get people to the table. I learned some things through observation and some because the boys told me, and there was plenty I never got to know. Some of it was obvious; some of it still doesn't make sense to me. Gerry would say later that his plan for me was total immersion.

What I knew about the agency's work and how the residences were run I knew in the context of the keywords: social work, group home, and community care. When I was younger, I understood that something bad had happened to the kids my dad worked with, and that was why they didn't get to live with their real families. (I also didn't appreciate that there are different kinds of real families.) At some point in middle school, I overheard a conversation and then asked my dad, "Is an adolescent the same as a juvenile delinquent?" He paused, bit his lip, and answered, "Not always." For the most part, he kept my siblings and me separate from his work kids. I used to think it was to protect us from their world, where fathers get arrested, mothers leave, and older kids get left home alone with younger siblings. I realized much later that my father wasn't trying to protect us from them; he wanted to protect them from us.

I understood when I started cooking at the House that there was a lot that I wouldn't get to know about the agency and all of the kids involved. I wasn't a social worker or a houseparent, or any kind of employee; I was a volunteer, there for two hours a week to do one small job. I didn't understand the galaxy of state care, or know the flowcharts and stipulations of the foster care system. I didn't know the operating budget of the agency, though I had the sense that there was never enough money; I knew the state allocated a certain amount of dollars per kid and that that allocation traveled with the kid to his placement, so the amount of money that the agency had depended on the number of kids placed in its care, and that Gerry sometimes received private donations for incidentals. I knew the agency had no religious affiliation, but I also knew my mom always said that atheists don't do that kind of work.

I had no idea what it must have been like to be a boy at the House, because I wasn't trained as staff or a social worker. I was a high school Spanish teacher who taught basic communication skills to second language learners and literary analysis to advanced students, with books and poems and lesson plans with rubrics and measurable outcomes. Because I was just a volunteer who showed up with food and helped cook it, and then left every week around the time it started to get really dark. Because when I was a kid sitting on that beige couch in the waiting room at the House, staring at the dove poster and counting the rungs on the rainbow, I was the girl who was only ever there for a few minutes, whose dad always came around the corner and brought her home.

Sometimes a Hole
(Or: How to Know Your Place
When It's Not Your Place)

Because I never had an official orientation to the House, I borrowed from my previous volunteer experiences, which always seemed to involve elements of picking up trash and keeping people company. I had completed trainings, reviewed and signed liability forms, and been told what was expected of me—in a veterans' hospital, in churches and camps, in a prison, in a homeless shelter, in a high school, and other service project placements. I liked to think I'd mastered the four guiding principles of volunteering: show up when you say you will show up; know your one small task and do it the best you can; be prepared to improvise, because you'll have to improvise, because inevitably something unforeseen will arise; and the easiest or hardest part—leave when you are supposed to leave, and then come back again.

In middle school, I volunteered for bingo lunches and special events at a soldiers' home. There, I was warned that sometimes the elderly residents would yell at me. I was assured that it wasn't my fault and told to not take it personally (which is always easier said than done). I wasn't told how a thirteen-year-old should mediate an argument between an octogenarian war hero and a cantankerous septuagenarian combat nurse, or what to do when he kicked her under the table with his one leg so hard that she cried out, or what to say next when I asked him to please stop and he replied, "For Christ's sake, I only have one leg."

When I taught Sunday school classes in high school, I was given lesson plans for my kindergarteners and told to schedule regular bathroom breaks. I knew there would be a lot of coloring and pee-ing, but I wasn't prepared for all of the lying, or how the child with the most elaborate lies would also make the most delicate drawings, or how one picture would nestle into my own theology. When I asked my kindergarteners to draw God on a day we finished early, a boy who had told me, among other things, that his grandmother was a frog drew God as an alien flower with a cluster of different-colored eyes in the center and arms with hands shooting out in every direction. When I asked him to explain the extraterrestrial bloom, he said, "If God can see everybody and hold everybody, He has to look like this. Right?"

Spring break of my first year at Boston College, I piled into a van with other volunteers to ride from Chestnut Hill, Massachusetts, to Buchanan County, Virginia, for an Appalachia Volunteers trip. I signed up to build an outhouse on the side of a mountain because I thought it sounded like something I might never do again—and also I had no sense of how hard it would be to dig a hole six feet down by six feet wide, and then build a wooden base to fit inside that space, and then a structure above it, complete with roof and door. We four women from cities didn't think we'd need the whole week to dig a hole and build a tiny house. I was offended when we intro-duced ourselves and tried to shake hands with the man who owned the property and he kept his hands in his pockets as he said, "I've been waiting two years for them to send people to do this, and now they sent me goddamned girls."

And I was annoyed when he invited his friend and nephew over to watch us four goddamned girls dig his outhouse. But when the man's friend jumped into the hole to teach us how to cut corners into the hard maroon dirt and he immediately started wheezing, a horrendous, harmonica-like rattle, I was stunned. And I was hum-bled when the man who owned the property toasted us four goddamned girls with a mason jar of moonshine when we put the last coat of paint on his outhouse, shrugged, and said, "We worked in the mines, so we got bad lungs. That's why we can't do this ourselves. I can't even do as much as he did, so we're grateful for y'all and what ya done here."

When I was a volunteer through chaplaincy at a prison the next year, the Jesuit who trained me asked me to organize a prayer group in Spanish on the women's unit as part of my four hours of weekly service. I told him I wasn't sure I was qualified to lead anyone in prayer, and he handed me a Bible and communion and told me I would figure it out. Then a different week, in the elevator we were swiped into after an hour with men on the protective custody unit, he asked if I would be willing to visit a woman in the hole, another name for an isolation cell. I agreed and asked what I should read or say, was there a particular text that made sense or should I just use the Saint Teresa of Ávila prayer of distress that I used with my women's group, mostly because it was short and I knew it by heart in two languages. He told me that the guard would walk me to the right place, and that once I was there I should just sit with the woman and listen to her, that the most important thing was the listening. But he didn't tell me how hard it would be to sit there, folding my tall body onto the floor in a way that I could hear the woman's voice through the small opening in the bottom of the door, only large enough to pass a plate through. "I don't really want to pray," she told me as we sat, our bodies awkwardly scrunched against opposite sides of the thin wall that separated our worlds, with our dignity and our chins nearly touching the floor. "I just wanted some company," she apologized, as if that was cheating.

Then, as an AmeriCorps volunteer after college graduation, I had to complete monthly time sheets with questions about impact and deliverables like, "How many people are in your school/community?" And then, "How many individuals in your school/community did your work impact during this reporting period?" My fellow volunteers and I would joke as we filled out these sheets, asking each other, "How many individuals did *you* impact this month?

Everyone? Just a handful? A cool hundred?" We mused about what would happen if we wrote "One." Is impacting one person enough? And what would happen if we answered honestly: "Maybe none"?

In AmeriCorps, I was placed in a school where I had some of the responsibilities of a teacher, so we had to learn protocols for safety and discipline. I learned to be aware of the closest exit in case of fire and practiced strategies for de-escalating conflict. I knew that when I was called to a bathroom to find a student crying on the floor, and she showed me thick bruises wrapped like purple ribbons around her thighs, I had to take her to the nurse's office. When the principal told me that I had to call child protective services because I was a mandated reporter, I remembered the form I had signed acknowledging that I understood my obligation. I also believed that I should tell the student I was making that call, because I felt obligated by the law and also by her trust, even if the order of operations troubled me.

But I wasn't prepared to have to keep calling her caseworker, because the girl kept asking me when they were going to come to her house, only for the state employee to tell me, "Ma'am, I can't say when I'll get to it. I have a lot of kids in my caseload and most of them are younger than fourteen. She's not on the top of my list, to be honest with you."

And I was less prepared for my father's reaction when I asked what he thought I should do. I called him during lunch to explain how worried I was about this student. I knew he would be home at 1 P.M. Eastern Standard Time to make a sandwich and watch my mother's soap opera. I complained about how dysfunctional The System was, as if it had actual gears and a clear mechanical advantage. I asked how it could take weeks to follow up on the case of a fourteen-year-old girl who had been assaulted by her parent. My dad listened. I asked what else I could do, and he told me that all I could do was wait. My voice shook as I told him that waiting didn't feel like enough. He remained quiet. I asked him what he was thinking and he said, "I'm thinking that whoever told you to make that call should be sitting with you right now and answering your questions. You had no business making that call, Elizabeth." I knew there was no sense in saying that it wasn't fair because I already knew what he'd say.

Life's not fair.

He was always telling my siblings and me that life wasn't fair. It was usually in regard to small things, like not getting stuff we wanted. Occasionally, it was about big things, like when my baby cousin died. Or the time he came home from jury duty and told us over dinner about a surprise encounter during his lunch break in town. At first he had avoided eye contact with a sex worker he saw near the courthouse, but when the woman called out to him, "Mr. Charlie?" he recognized her as a kid from the orphanage where he and my mother had worked years before. "That's what the kids called Daddy," my mother explained, recalling their past life.

My dad told us how he had bought the woman lunch, and how as they ate, the woman told stories about what she remembered from her early years at the orphanage—relay races, field trips, cafeteria meals. I imagined how it must have looked to anyone who saw them, my dad in his khakis and navy blazer, having lunch with a sex worker in a restaurant downtown. I thought about the woman, reaching out to him, her teacher. All I could think was that it wasn't fair, but I didn't say it.

Every time I think that something is unfair, I hear my father's voice: "Life's not fair."

So MUCH OF my understanding of right and wrong, and the discrepancy between what I think the world should be and what it actually is, was shaped by conversations with my father. The recurring theme in these dialogues was my wanting one right answer, and his frustration with my belief that there was one right answer or that I would use that belief as a guise to not think through the problem itself.

One of the nights when he was sick and we were walking, he asked me how my job was going. I was holding our giant, nearly blind German shepherd on her leash, steering her away from telephone poles and trees. I had been complaining about work for weeks on our walks. I was sure there was something I was supposed to be when I grew up; I wanted to know it already.

"I guess I'm just waiting for an epiphany," I said, as we passed a palatial church with stained glass windows that looked impressive even in the dark.

My dad didn't say anything.

"What?" I asked, wanting to hear what he wasn't saying.

"That's sentimentalist bullshit, Elizabeth," he said. He stopped walking. I knew he was serious when he called me Elizabeth, pronounced in four spitting syllables.

"Your life is happening all around you," he continued in a tone I wasn't expecting. "You have a job. You are surrounded by people who love you. If you think something needs to be changed, change it. That's up to you, not anyone else. Nobody is going to fix your life. It's your life. Do something. Or don't. But don't talk nonsense." He was angry, breathing fast. I was trying to be funny, but epiphanies aren't punch lines to dying men.

I COULDN'T IMAGINE a life without my father in it, but it happened anyway. When he died, I missed his voice and the moored feeling of standing near him. I would find myself wondering what he would have done or said in a particular situation. I tried to catalog our conversations so I could apply what he'd told me to similar quandaries—like multiple-choice options on a test. I could never remember everything; one of the stories I tell myself is that there is meaning in what I do remember. Certain things he used to say lend themselves better to the multiple-choice game than others. His "sentimentalist bullshit" critique makes sense in a lot of situations. And what he tended to say when pressed for advice is almost always applicable: "Just do the best you can." Translation: Make your own decision, and do it how you think it should be done. Simplified translation: Do something; don't be afraid.

It was the *do something* impulse that led me to the House in the months after my dad died, and what I had learned volunteering in the years before that had oriented me to the task of starting this small-scale service project as a way to be in community while also grieving my life-shaking loss. I copied some of the structural logic of the service-learning programs I had been a part of in college and facilitated in Chicago, designating a set day and fixed time window, identifying one small, accomplishable task, bringing most of the necessary materials with me, and expecting the unexpected, or trying to. You have to have a kind of discipline to be a volunteer, to show up for a small amount of time, work, and leave. This is true of teaching and other jobs, too, but when you are a volunteer, there's nothing keeping you in place except your word that you'd show up. Sometimes it's hard to leave. Sometimes it's harder to come back. Your range of motion is small. You have to stay on task. You'll probably be frustrated that you cannot do more. Sometimes it's hard not to take the little rejections personally. But if the frustration consumes you, you won't be effective. You have to learn the awkward, fluid posture of accompaniment; it's sitting, it's standing, it's reaching, it's digging, it's showing up, it's keeping company. Sometimes your only task is letting the other person know they are not alone; that affirmation of humanity is the smallest, biggest thing one person can do for another, and it's always graceful, and always reciprocal. Sometimes, you have to make the call. Sometimes the hole takes longer to dig than you thought; you have to decide whether you're going to stay and dig. Sometimes the hole is a metaphor, and sometimes it is actually a six-foot-by-six-foot hole that you know will eventually be filled up with shit, but you signed up to help dig it, so you do.

When I suggested cooking at the House, I had no idea how it would all turn out. But I believed that this little service project had the potential to take on a life of its own. Cooking with the boys wasn't random, because it had been my dad's and my idea; I wasn't random, because they understood me as his daughter and I understood my role as a volunteer. I knew that Leon was right when he said that people would definitely have preferred it if I just cooked and they just ate. And I understood that the houseparent's skepticism was legitimate; without a precedent for cooking and eating "with a table and everything," it wouldn't be easy. I was also familiar with the underlying tension: that in order for it to work, the boys would have to participate on their own terms, not under mandate—even though if cooking was voluntary, they might not participate. My plan was to try one dinner. I knew my dad would have told me to keep the food at the center of the thing, and try to not focus on what I didn't know, but on what I could find out: who liked what to eat, who wanted to learn how to cook, who liked to talk and what about, and what they hoped I might bring to the table—and whether I could. All of the surveys I collected at my first meeting with the boys had favorite foods circled and written in. Of the four, exactly one person answered *Yes* next to the question: *Are you willing to help?* One drew a question mark; one left it blank; one wrote *No*. I planned to show up for our first dinner with all of the food I said I would bring and a keen awareness that it might be the only dinner. But I thought there might be more, because that is the fundamental nature of cooking: that individual ingredients combined together add up to something more. It's a brand of science that sometimes feels more like faith.

Setting the Table

Leon was waiting when I arrived the first night. He stood with his back against the big green door, propping it open. He watched me through my windshield as I parked, got out of my car, and pulled grocery bags from the backseat.

I shouted hello and waited for him to offer to help.

"I was looking out the window," he said. "'Cause you said five and the stove clock says 5:06. I didn't know if that was you, but then I saw your hair, so I came down." He moved his hands around his head in a swirling motion to indicate my hair. "You're late. This's your whip?"

I apologized for my tardiness. "My what?" I asked, grabbing the last bag. "My whip?"

"You don't know what a whip is? You probably say *car*, but everybody says *whip*," he said.

"Oh. Then, yeah. This is my whip." I slammed the door with my hip.

He surveyed my car, widening his eyes at the dent in the door. "It looks kind of like a girl car, but that's all right. You could still take me driving in it." He said this as though we had already discussed my taking him driving. "When you think you'll take me?" he asked, stepping back against the green door to let me pass.

"Driving!" I wondered if it was the color that made my light-blue Toyota Matrix a girl car. "Should we see how cooking goes first?" I stopped in the doorway and turned to him. "Hey, can I give you one of these bags?"

Leon blinked, then offered two fingers to take a bag. "Okay, but

I'm *serious* about driving," he said. He looked at me, then reached over to take a second bag.

I said I was serious about cooking, echoing his emphasis on *serious*. I stepped into the House, to his right, and told him I would follow him up.

"Everybody!" he shouted as we walked up the creaky stairs. "She's here!"

The kitchen was empty when Leon let us in.

"Is anybody home?" I asked loudly enough for reluctant but curious ears to hear.

"Yeah, everybody's here," Leon said. "They're just not *here*," he said even louder.

As if on cue, Frank came around the corner. He looked like he might have been sleeping. His cheek had a seam in the side of it and his hair stood in a disheveled salute. He wore baggy jeans and a white T-shirt that could have been a sail for a small boat. One by one, he lifted every food item, scrutinizing each package like it was an artifact from an exotic land.

"Hey, Frank!" I tried to temper my excitement that he'd shown up.

"I thought you said we're having chicken," he said.

"We are!"

"Where's it?" he asked, searching the bags.

I fumbled through the food. "Oh, it's here!" I said, relieved, holding up the sleekly wrapped raw chicken strips.

He took the package from me and squinted at it. "That's not chicken."

"What do you mean?" I asked him to pass it to me so I could check the label and make sure I hadn't accidentally picked up pork or turkey. "It's chicken," I said. "See?" I pointed to the word *chicken*.

He took the package back from me and pushed against the soft flesh with a single finger. "It's got no bones in it," he said.

"Oh. No, it's boneless," I said.

He looked at it. "Chicken with no bones?" He was skeptical.

"I swear it's real chicken. It *had* bones for sure, but they were removed . . ." I stammered.

Frank left the kitchen, shouting to the houseparent in the TV room as he turned the corner: "Hey, Greg, you ever heard of chicken with no bones in it?"

"Yeah, Frank, you could buy it like that. Is that the kind she brought?" Greg asked. I recognized the voice as belonging to the houseparent who had told me the week before that this project probably wouldn't work.

"Yeah." Frank sounded unconvinced. He came back into the kitchen and picked up the second, identical package and studied both specimens.

"So, I usually get it like this so I don't have to deal with the bones," I explained. "I guess because I'm lazy and it's easier." I tried to catch his eye. "If you think people would like whole chicken pieces better, I can get those from now on." I unpacked the other food. I didn't have time to go back to the supermarket if the goal was to have dinner on the table in fifty minutes.

"Nobody eats it like this," Frank said, looking at the chicken and not at me. "How does it taste like?"

"I think it tastes like chicken." I shrugged, smiling. "How would you feel about cutting it up, Frank?"

"I'd cut it up but I can't 'cause of my eyes," Leon said from the sink, where he stood, washing vegetables.

I didn't know what Leon meant about his eyes, but I nodded as though I did. A thing I had learned working with teenagers is that sometimes it's better when they think you already know something to go along with it instead of asking for clarification, which sounds like faking it but feels more like a kind of empathy when you're doing it. And sometimes it's better to lean in to the teacher trope and ask questions that make space for the safe, small conversations that don't start themselves. Knowing when to do which depended on the situation and the level of severity of the thing you didn't know. At school, I did a lot of the latter and some of the former; at the House, I found myself doing a lot of the former, especially in the beginning.

"Yeah." Frank reluctantly agreed to cut the chicken. "I could."

I opened the narrow drawer by the side of the sink where I

thought knives might be kept. I saw a gray plastic organizer designed for knives, forks, and spoons, but it contained only one spoon. "You guys, where are the utensils?" I asked, looking up from the nearly empty drawer.

Leon and Frank looked at me. "The what?" Leon asked. Frank said nothing.

"Like, the knives," I said. "And forks and spoons. How are we going to cook and eat?"

"We got a lotta plastic ones in the closet that we eat with," Leon said. He dropped the peppers on the counter and disappeared into the pantry, returning with a cardboard trough of plastic utensils. "See? But you have to ask the staff for *real* knives."

I went around the corner to talk to Greg, who was in the staff office.

"Yeah, you could use 'em," Greg told me. He walked back toward the desk. "We keep the knives locked up. We have to." He jangled through the keys to find a tiny one that opened the desk. The first drawer he opened was full of pill bottles. The next was mostly paper. Behind a small envelope that said PETTY CASH was a big zippered plastic bag with two steak knives and a long chef's knife, the blades wrapped loosely in paper towels. He held them out to me and said, "They can't use the big one, but you could."

I told Greg that I'd take one of the steak knives to start. He handed it to me by the handle and locked the other knives away.

Back in the kitchen, Frank was leaning against the stove and Leon continued to wash vegetables. Frank looked at Leon then at me, with the knife. "Wash my hands first?" he asked.

"Yeah, that'd be great," I said. "Let's wash this knife, too."

And with that, Frank began a nearly three-year streak as the best sous-chef I could've wished for. And when Wesley would say later, too many times, that he wouldn't eat what Frank touched because Frank didn't ever wash his hands, I would tell him I knew for a fact that that wasn't true.

—

JAMES WAS THE next to show up. He stood in the doorway with his hands in his pockets. I said hello and he looked at the floor. I told him I was glad he came.

"*I'm* glad people *finally* got here," Leon said from the sink, over his shoulder.

"I had something last week," James explained. "Sorry again I wasn't here for the meeting," he said to the linoleum beneath my feet.

"No worries," I said. "I'm glad you made it for the last part, and that you're here tonight. Want to help? I'm thinking maybe nothing with knives this week."

"No knives would be good," he said. He held up his still-bandaged hand.

"Maybe the rice. How would you feel about making some rice?" I asked.

"Yeah, I could do the rice," he said, walking over to the pantry. "One box or two?"

"Well, I think we'll do white rice, not yellow, since we're having stir-fry with teriyaki sauce. We'll need two cups of water for every cup of rice for every two to three people, depending on how much each person eats." I held up the bag of white rice I had brought.

"I don't think we have white rice," he said from the pantry. "We just have yellow." He picked up two boxes and turned to face me and saw the bag of white rice I was holding.

"How much do you think people will eat?" I asked.

James shrugged and put the boxes of yellow rice back on the shelf. "Probably a lot."

From the sink, Leon said, "Well, *I* am trying to watch what I eat so I don't want a lot."

James rolled his eyes at Leon's diet plan and looked at me. "So how much?"

"So you, Leon, Frank, me. Do you think Carlos and Wesley will eat?"

"Damn, she knows everybody's names," Leon said, to no one in particular. "'Cause she's *a teacher.*"

James shrugged again.

"Some people'll probably think they could just come get food when it's ready," Leon called over his shoulder from the sink, "like last week when some people didn't come to the meeting but got a brownie." He held red peppers in each of his hands, swishing them back and forth under the rush of water, creating a kind of sprinkler effect.

James narrowed his eyes at Leon, and then looked at me.

I handed him the bag of rice. "Let's say ten cups of water and a little salt and some butter. Maybe use the biggest pot. If you use the cover it'll cook a lot faster," I added, not sure where we were with the physics of boiling.

"I don't know if I'm going to find the cover," James said.

"Well, maybe see if you can," I said. "One that's too big would be better than none."

"Okay," James said in a tone that indicated he would try but couldn't guarantee anything.

I went to check on Frank, who was cutting chicken on a small cutting board on the dining room table. When I agreed to stir-fry, I hadn't calculated the cutting index. There was more to cut than there were hands for cutting. Leon couldn't cut because of his eyes, James wouldn't cut because of his hand, and Wesley and Carlos didn't cut because they weren't around. This left Frank and me. Frank wasn't enthusiastic, but he was willing.

"This is how you want the blocks, miss?" he asked. He looked up from a soft pile of chicken, then looked back down.

"That's great, Frank," I said. "If you could get them a little smaller, that'd be perfect."

"Can't get 'em any smaller," he told me without looking up from the sticky stack.

"You know what?" I reconsidered. "I think they're actually perfect like that. If people want their chicken smaller, they can cut it smaller once it's cooked."

"How many I should cut?"

"I think all of them," I said. "That way, people can have as much as they want to eat."

He looked up quickly. "Cut all of 'em?"

"You don't think people'll be hungry?" I asked. I was worried about not having enough.

"No, I mean, they will. But it's a lot." He was worried about having too much to cut.

"Want me to make sure everyone's okay in the kitchen, then come back and help you with the chicken?" I proposed.

"Yup," he said.

IN THE KITCHEN, James had the rice under control and Leon had the peppers and carrots washed and ready to slice. To compensate for his inability to cut, Leon had washed and dried the vegetables multiple times.

"That dude keeps washing the peppers," James told me before I asked.

"*Some* people like to eat *clean* food," Leon said, to me but toward James, as he arranged the immaculate vegetables along the counter.

James shook his head at Leon and asked me, "What else?"

I asked him if he'd find a pan big enough to sauté the chicken, then wash it, put it on the stove, and turn the stove on. It was a gas stove, so I asked if anyone had a lighter. James laughed and said he was pretty sure everybody did. Then I asked Leon if he would help with the pie.

"Well, you know I can't *cut* the apples," he reminded me.

"I know. You can do the crust, then after I cut the apples, you can mix them with sugar and cinnamon and pour them into the crust. Want to do that?" I held the boxed crust out to him.

"I don't know how to *do* the crust," he said, hands by his sides, not taking the box.

"The crust is already made, rolled up in this box. You just carefully unroll it. It's really easy. Judging by how much attention you showed the carrots and peppers, I know you can do it."

James smiled to himself at the stove, shaking his head at both of us. I asked him to turn the burner down to medium, add some oil, and wait for a first batch of chicken from Frank.

"Frank, will you bring the chicken you already cut to James so he can cook it?" I called from the kitchen. "I'll be there to cut the rest in a minute. I didn't forget." I asked Leon to please carry the vegetables into the dining room. I grabbed the apples and crust, plus a stack of paper plates to use as a second cutting board, and followed Leon to the table.

Frank was still seated when I went in to see whether he was making a move to give James the chicken. He held his hands up in sticky surrender. "Could you give the plate to James? 'Cause my hands are nasty," he said, verifying that he'd heard me but had a different idea.

I placed all of my stuff on the table and brought the chicken in to James, who stood over the now-sizzling oil with a spatula in his able hand and his bandaged hand up in the air, ready to sauté, or joust.

I held the plate and tipped it into the pan as he tentatively scraped the chicken bits into the oil. The first two pieces fell in and crackled then spattered. James jumped back. I turned the heat down and added the rest of the meat. I asked him to salt and pepper it, then flip and repeat. He nodded and leaned back in, flicking the chicken with the spatula, bandaged hand still raised.

I reached over to preheat the oven, then went to see about dessert.

LEON SAT AT the table reading the instructions on the crust box as Frank worked on the chicken sitting across from him. The aesthetic of the dining room was something between rustic and indestructible. The table and chairs, heavy and shapeless, looked like they belonged in a woodsy cabin. There was an old desk tucked in the corner with only a phone on it. Nothing hung on the off-white walls. Worn white curtains covered three wide windows that looked down to the street below, two on one wall and one on another. A single, spiky plant in a white plastic planter dangled from a ceiling hook like proof of life.

"We don't have a round pan like this says and I don't think it's going to work in a square pan, so I guess we're not having pie," Leon told me. He put the box down, giving up on the pie.

"Did you check the other bag?" I asked.

He pulled the aluminum pie pan I'd just purchased out of the other bag. "We could probably use this," he said reluctantly.

"That's what I was thinking," I said.

I told him if he read the instructions and followed them, I'd cut the apples.

Leon picked the box back up and squinted as he read it aloud.

"Can't you just finish all of this?" Frank asked, placing the knife on top of the cutting board and sliding it over to me with the chicken.

I nodded and asked if he wanted to switch to cutting peppers.

Frank sighed. "One pepper?"

"Yes. I'll finish the chicken, you do one pepper, and I'll do the other peppers, plus carrots and onions." I listed what had yet to be cut, in case the litany inspired him to volunteer to do more. It didn't. I asked him to wash his hands between the chicken and the pepper and went to ask Greg to unlock a second knife for me.

"Who's going to help me with the crust?" Leon asked, still reading the directions.

"Leon, the crust is already made, you just have to open the box, unroll it, peel the plastic off, and then press it into the pan," I told him.

"I never *pressed* a crust," he said.

"You just have to peel it off the plastic, rest it in the pan, and push it down a little," I said.

"I could *break* it," he said.

"If you break it, we'll stick it back together. Dough is sticky."

"Then after I do this, can I make the biscuits?" he asked. "People *love* my biscuits."

Frank washed his hands and the knife and came back for a pepper. He brought a stack of paper plates instead of the cutting board so he wouldn't have to wash it again.

I finished the chicken and carried it to the kitchen, which felt warmer and smelled savory.

"How do you know if the chicken's done?" James asked.

I explained that the outside should be an almost-white color and that when you cut it, you shouldn't see pink inside. "If it's shiny or you can kind of see through it, it's not cooked."

He cut a piece open. "I think it's done."

"I think we should try it," I said. "You want to?"

"Like with my mouth?" he asked.

"Yeah, like to taste it," I said.

James nodded, then solemnly stuck a chunk with a plastic fork. He blew hard on it, then took a reluctant bite, eyes closed. "It's good," he said. His eyes snapped open in surprise.

"Okay, let's check the inside of the biggest piece," I said, cutting it in half. It was cooked.

"Can I finish this one?" he asked of the piece that remained of the one he had bitten. I said yes and asked if he'd repeat the same steps with the second batch of chicken: oil, drop, season, flip, repeat. He agreed, two quick nods while chewing.

I RETURNED TO the dining room to find Leon still reading the red crust box and Frank cutting one green pepper into jagged shards.

"This has mad seeds in it." Frank held up his hands, freckled with pepper innards.

"Oh, I should've cleaned that out for you." I cut a circle around the stem of the other pepper and pulled it out. Then I split it, trimmed the fibrous veins, and asked Frank to cut the halves into strips.

He took the two clean pieces and gave me the messy ones, flicking extra seeds from his hands onto my palm. He cut one slice and said, "This's mad easier."

I told Frank I should've done that with the other pepper from the start, and looked over at Leon, who was staring at the box. "Leon? Are you memorizing the directions?"

"I was just thinking that if I *rip* the crust, I'll *wreck* it," he said.

"You won't wreck it." I told him again if it ripped, we'd stick it back together.

"People like my *biscuits*." He put the box down, pouting. "People *love* my biscuits."

"I didn't buy biscuits," I said.

"We always have them. Arlette gets them because I always make them. She knows *everybody* likes when I make them," he told me. Arlette worked downstairs. In addition to other jobs she did, she was in charge of grocery shopping.

"Okay, then, sure. That sounds good. But will you still do the crust first?"

Leon was already on his way to the kitchen for the biscuits. The crust, still coiled in its red box, sat next to the empty pan, unopened.

"Okay, maybe Frank will want to do the pie anyway," I said in Frank's direction.

Frank looked up from the pepper. He met my eyes for the first time of the night and told me without saying a word that he didn't want to do the pie.

"I'm kidding," I said. "But do you want to do the onion?"

He looked at me again, the same look, and blinked.

"Or maybe," I suggested, "you want to take a break from cutting, watch a little TV, and come back when stuff is ready."

"Yup," he said, pushing away from the table with his elbows to go wash his hands.

I quickly finished cutting the vegetables and brought the medley in to James.

James and Leon were standing together in front of the stove, with parallel plastic forks of chicken, mid-bite when I walked in.

"James said I could have one." Leon threw James under the bus.

James shrugged, unfazed by blame.

"That's great," I said, appreciating that testers are the best tastes of the meal. "Is it ready? What do you guys think?"

James nodded.

"We could have the chicken?" Frank asked from the doorway, lured in by the smell.

"It tastes *good*," Leon said. "Second one's better than the first one."

"I'm taking two, too," Frank said, waiting for me to tell him no.

James and Leon exchanged glances. They looked at Frank and then at me.

"You have to test it, so you know it's done," I said.

Shoulder to shoulder they tasted and nodded in agreement.

I felt a tinge of confidence.

THREE MINUTES LATER, alone at the table with five pounds of apples to peel and cut and the hour of preparation time closing in fast, I was less sure. I debated giving up on the pie and borrowing one of the brownie mixes that I had noticed on the shelf in the pantry.

Leon came in with a cookie sheet, a tub of margarine larger than his head, and two blue tubes of biscuits. He explained again that he always made them on nights houseparents cooked.

"Do you think we need two packages?" I asked. "Sixteen biscuits for five people?"

He popped one tube open. "People *love* my biscuits," he said, emphasizing his statement by popping open the second one.

I tore a hole in the bag of apples, started peeling, and observed Leon's biscuit system.

He removed each biscuit from the tube and assigned it a place on the industrial cookie sheet. He patted each soft glob with his fingers, then used a plastic knife to spread a layer of margarine over them, once and then again, until they looked sweaty and yellow. When he dipped the knife for a third coat, I asked whether two extra layers of grease might be enough.

"People *love* my biscuits," Leon said again, and continued to lather the greasy mounds of dough. "The secret is that what *I* make, I make it from the *heart*."

"Are you sure the secret's not in the grease?" I asked.

"That's *hateful*, Liz," he said, not looking up from the knife. "It's *from the heart*."

"I can see that it's from the heart, Leon," I said more seriously.

When he was finished, he carried his biscuits into the kitchen to put them in the oven.

I could hear Frank and James negotiating who should hold the spatula, how much soy sauce was too much soy sauce, and how many testers they could each have before "she" would notice. I didn't weigh in when I went in to make sure nothing was burning; I let them decide.

WESLEY WAS THE next one to come into the kitchen. He wasn't so late as to miss all the cooking but was late enough to send the message that he wasn't afraid to not arrive on time. He stood in the doorway and watched the soy sauce debate. Frank offered him a tester and he took it. Leon walked through the pantry between the dining room and kitchen, counting plates and cups.

"Wes, you staying for dinner?" Leon asked, holding out a single paper plate.

Wesley answered with a noncommittal "Not sure yet."

I returned to the dining room table to finish the apples. When I had about six cups of slices piled into the dented stainless steel bowl, I folded in some cinnamon sugar. As I pressed the bottom crust into the aluminum pan, Wesley called from the doorway, "What're those for?"

"Oh, hey, Wesley." I looked up from the crust. "These apples? For the pie."

"Oh," he said, looking at the slices, slick and sandy in the sugar mixture.

"Do you not like apple pie?" I asked.

"No, I like it," he said. "But like, are there extra ones?"

"Apples? There are some whole ones left," I said. "Did you want one? You're welcome to have one—"

"I was thinking I could make applesauce if there's extra."

"Applesauce?" I wasn't expecting Wesley to offer to make applesauce. "Sure, there're enough for that. Do you know how, or would you like some help?"

"I think I could do it," he said.

"Okay. Did you want to use the whole apples? Or you want me to cut 'em up?" I asked.

"Yeah, that'd be good, actually," he said. "If you could cut 'em."

I asked what size he wanted them and he said that, actually, the ones I'd already cut were the size he had in mind. So I told him to take as many as he wanted, and he did. Then I followed him into the kitchen to rinse my hands and see how things were going.

"*People* finally showed up," Leon said to James or me or no one in particular.

I washed the smallest pot and handed it to Wesley.

"This dude's going to *cook*?" Leon asked me.

"Wesley's making applesauce," I said casually, washing the cutting board Frank had left in the sink.

Wesley put the pot on a burner and turned the dial on the stove all the way around, once and then again, studying the tiny words.

In case he didn't know what heat to set it to but didn't want to ask in front of everyone, I kept narrating, "You might start with medium heat. Then when it starts to bubble in a little while, because sugar heats quickly, you'll probably wanna turn the heat down, so the apples don't burn." I did the teacher thing, talking him through the steps; I figured if he already knew how to do it, he would shrug me off, and if he didn't, he could listen but act like he already knew.

Wesley took the wooden spoon I washed for him and stood over at the stove: baggy silhouette, hat tipped almost off his head, spoon in one hand, stirring, phone in the other, texting.

He asked me if he should add more sugar, and I told him to taste it, to see what he thought. I said he could make it as sweet as he wanted since it was his recipe, and suggested that he add a little salt to offset the flavor. "It sounds weird. But trust me, it'll taste better."

Wesley stirred and added more cinnamon sugar, and texted less. When almost nobody was looking, he shook some salt into the bubbling mixture. None of the other kids said anything to him as he stood at the stove, squinting into the pan.

"Hey, do you make applesauce a lot?" I asked from the doorway, about to finish the pie.

"Nope, I never did. But I saw my aunt make it before. It's not that hard." Wesley shrugged and kept stirring.

CARLOS WAS THE last to arrive. I was quickly peeling and cutting the rest of the apples at the dining room table, ever conscious of the promise of a six o'clock dinnertime. I cinnamon-sugared and then spooned the slices into the bottom crust.

"What kind of crust are you going to put on top?" he asked from the doorway as a hello.

I emptied the rest of the apples into the bottom crust with a plastic spoon. "I was just going to slice a hole into the middle of that one and put it on top of this one," I said, pointing to the second piecrust.

"You're not going to do one of those crisscross ones? Like they have in Stop and Shop and shit?"

I looked up at him, and I must have looked surprised.

"Sorry. Like the ones they have at Stop and Shop and stuff?" He edited himself.

It wasn't the swear that surprised me. "You want to do one of those? I can show you how, if you want."

He ducked out of the doorway.

As I lowered the plastic knife into the soft middle of the second crust, Carlos reemerged. He kicked a chair away from the table and sat down beside me.

"Okay, I washed my hands," he said.

I shifted gears, trying not to look too surprised by his interest. "Okay, so first, you want to cut the dough into about inch-wide strips . . ."

"Do I need a ruler or something?" he asked.

"No, just cut them a little wider than your thumb. They don't have to be exact."

"Like this?" He carefully cut two strips. The second was half the size of the first.

"That's great," I said. "Just do that with the rest of the crust."

He sliced through a month of moons in dough: sliver, crescent, quarter, until he reached the other side.

"Done," he announced. "Now what?"

"Okay, now you weave them together like when you were little, weaving paper in kindergarten," I said.

He looked up at me, his eyebrows crinkled. We didn't share that kindergarten memory.

I reframed. "Hold one and move it over another one, under the next, over the third, kind of like a braid. Start in one corner and then just keep doing the same thing. If they don't seem close enough, you can push them closer; the dough's flexible. Or undo them and start again."

"One strip over the other, like this, right?" he asked, lifting one inch of dough and tucking another underneath it, adding one strip at a time, lifting and putting down. His hands were small and smooth and his nails were perfectly filed, unlike mine.

"Yeah, exactly," I said.

Carlos tucked and untucked. I left to check on the kitchen crowd.

James was finishing the last of the chicken. I helped him combine it with the vegetables in the biggest pot and toss it all with teriyaki sauce. The rice and applesauce rested on back burners. The biscuits were almost done. With three minutes left in our prep hour, we were almost on track.

"Done!" Carlos called from the dining room.

I looked at the woven circle in front of him. "Awesome," I said.

"G, right?" he asked.

"Yeah, it looks pretty amazing, Carlos." I didn't think I could pull off calling the crust *gangster*. "You know, you'd make a great pastry chef, if you wanted."

He smiled. "Yeah, right? Like at Stop and Shop or something?"

"Sure," I said. "I think anywhere you want."

He nodded, still smiling. I noticed the dimples in his cheeks and chin.

"It looks really good," I said. "You want to put it on top of the pie now?"

"How am I supposed to do that?" He lifted his arms and moved away from the pie in a way that indicated that I was supposed to come over and show him without his actually having to ask me for help.

I sat down in the chair next to him and pulled it closer. I lifted his lattice crust and rested it on top of the apples and lower crust and showed him how to trim the edges with a plastic knife, then tuck and roll and pinch the perimeter so that the crusts wouldn't separate.

He carefully took the knife and finished the edge, trimming, tucking, and pinching. I remembered how, on my survey, Carlos had checked almost all of the foods listed under "What do you like to eat?" but had written "NO" next to "Will you help?"

"Want to put it into the oven now?" I asked. "I think it's ready."

He picked up the pie and looked at it from every angle, holding it away from his crisp white T-shirt. "Now, that looks like a pie," he said, not hiding his pride.

"It really does," I agreed, following him into the kitchen.

The rest of the boys had reconvened at the stove. Leon, Frank, James, and Wesley stood spearing teriyakied chicken from the pot with plastic forks, like ice fishermen plunging for sturgeon. Wesley kept stirring his applesauce with his other hand; he'd put his phone away.

I reached into their circle to open the oven, and they stepped aside to make way for Carlos and the pie.

There was only one oven rack inside, and Leon's biscuits were on it. "Where's the other oven rack?" I asked.

"Isn't one," someone said.

"There must be a second one," I said.

"There's not," someone said.

"Could be," Leon offered hopefully. He folded a dish towel, pulled his tray of biscuits from the oven, and rested them somewhat precariously across the sink to cool. "Could be somewhere. But it's not here. I don't think I've ever seen two."

Frank shook his head no and shut off the stove and stepped aside so Carlos could place the pie in the oven. Wesley scooped his apple-sauce into a Styrofoam bowl.

Then it was time. I held out the stack of paper plates and asked if people wanted to serve themselves in the kitchen buffet style, and eat in the TV room or at the table.

Leon reached over and grabbed the plates from me. "You said we're eating at the table together," he said. "Like a *family*. Not like a *buffet*. You didn't say it was going to be a buffet."

He was right. When we met the week before, I had said that the plan was to eat family style. But then Wesley said, "There's no family here." So I thought I should adjust the plan. The night was going pretty well so far; I didn't want to push too much too soon.

"You're right, Leon. I said that. I'd like to sit at the table and eat, too. So let's do that. And whoever wants to can. And whoever doesn't can eat in the TV room or wherever. Maybe we can put everything on the table and people can decide for themselves." I found a few tablespoons to use as serving spoons and hoped for the best.

Everyone carried a thing he'd had a hand in making to the table. Someone took the stir-fry, somebody else took the rice. Leon brought his biscuits. Someone asked about the soda, so I put down a stack of napkins and said I'd retrieve it from the kitchen. As I opened the fridge, I heard Wesley shout from the table, "I put the soda in the freezer so it could cool faster."

When I got back into the dining room, hugging a bundle of two-liter bottles to my chest, everyone was around the table. James was frisbeeing paper plates at the other boys, who were seated. They were catching them and setting them down in front of themselves, also grabbing plastic utensils and cups. All of the chairs at the table were full.

"Don't worry about me," I joked from the doorway. I was amazed that they had all sat down at the table and everything.

"There's a broken chair there at the desk where the phone is," Wesley said, nodding at it. "You could use that one."

Wesley sat at the head of the table by the window and Leon at the other, by the doorway to the pantry and kitchen. James and Frank sat with their backs to the windows on the long street-side wall. Carlos sat alone on the other side, facing them, closer to Leon than Wesley but not too close to anyone.

I handed cups of soda to outstretched hands and pulled the chair out from under the desk. As I dragged my seat toward the table by Carlos, he shifted his body away from me without actually moving his chair. Meanwhile, the arms of my chair pulled up out of their base so completely I thought the whole thing might collapse to the floor. "Oh shit!" I exclaimed.

"She said *shit*." Carlos laughed.

"Told you it was broken," Wesley said after a long sip of Pepsi.

"You did," I said, agreeing as I fit the arms back into the base and assessed whether the seat would hold my weight. "You think the whole thing is going to break if I sit in it?"

"Probably not." He shrugged.

As I debated whether probably not was good-enough odds to try sitting, the boys started serving themselves. Serving was a relatively quiet procedure with minimal eye contact. Everyone waited his turn to serve himself. No hands touched other hands. Distribution was followed by several minutes of eating then a round of calculated second servings. My attempts at conversation were mostly met with quick nos or yeahs or silence.

"So, gentlemen, how's school going?" I asked.

"Who're you calling gentlemen?" Wesley asked.

"What'd she say?" Carlos asked.

"She can hear you," I said. "I was calling you guys gentlemen. I was just asking about school."

"She's a *teacher*," Leon reminded them. "That's why she talks like that."

"School's school," Wesley said, as if this was a descriptive answer.

"Yup," Frank agreed.

Carlos and James didn't say anything.

"*People* don't really talk about *school*." Leon translated for me.

People ate. The table was a haze of hands and wood and food. Everyone, even James, was here and eating, elbows almost touching.

"Food's bomb," someone said, finally.

"Bomb," someone else agreed.

"And bomb's good, I hope?" I said.

"It's good," Wesley said. "That's what I said: it's *bomb*."

"This's what I'm talking about," Leon said, looking around the table. "See, I was right."

"You were right, Leon," I said.

"This is the truth," Leon said.

Everyone ate until his plate was empty, then ate a little more.

"I can't finish this, I'm too full," Wesley said. He pushed his plate of seconds away from his chest. "Is the pie ready?"

"How can you be thinking about pie if you're full?" I asked.

"Everybody's got room for dessert. No matter how much dinner you eat, there's a space left in your stomach, especially for dessert." Wesley stood up to make his point, holding his hands together, fingertips touching, making a small, almost circular shape. He lifted it over his stomach, to the left, just below his heart. "Right here. It stays empty for dessert. So there's always room for sweets. No matter what."

Everyone nodded and mmhmmed in agreement.

I went to get the pie from the oven and the applesauce from the stove.

The boys had pushed their dinner plates aside and Leon was handing out fresh ones for dessert. Between these and the ones that Frank and I had used as cutting boards, I estimated that we had used twenty-five paper plates for dinner. But we'd broach recycling a different night.

I offered Carlos the knife and asked if he wanted to cut his pie. He cut it, and he placed a slice on each plate I held out to him, saving the last, biggest piece for himself.

"Smells good in here!" Greg, the houseparent, came in from the other room.

"Food's bomb, Greg," Frank said.

"You should try it," Leon added.

"Please have some, there's plenty," I said. "Everybody pitched in."

"*Some* people did more than other people," Leon clarified.

"Carlos designed the top of the pie." I pointed to his crisscross crust.

"You did that?" Greg asked Carlos. "That's a serious pie, man."

Carlos nodded at his work. "G, right? She said I could get a job in a bakery."

"You could, man. If that's what you want to do," Greg agreed. "Y'all made applesauce, too?" Greg gestured to the dollops on people's plates.

"Wesley made it," I said, giving credit where credit was due.

He turned to Wesley and said, "Wes, *you* made this?"

Wesley nodded.

Greg tasted some and said, "This is good, man." He took another bite, scrunching his lips and nose. "It's real sweet." He laughed. "But it's good, man."

"I know, it's sweet, right?" Wesley smiled, heaping more onto his buckling plate. "That's how I like it." Then he held up the Pepsi. "Anybody want more? I'm about to do a facial."

"A facial?" I asked. I knew it couldn't mean what I thought it meant.

"You know, taking it to the face," he clarified.

I didn't know. "Taking the *bottle* to the face?"

"Yeah, dawg. A facial," Frank said.

Wesley drank from the two-liter bottle of Pepsi, holding it like a chalice, with both hands grasped around the base, eyes closed.

"That's a facial?" I asked. "Like because of the backwash?"

"What?" Wesley asked.

"You know, backwash: when germs from your mouth fall back into the drink when you take a sip of something," I said. "My brother used to do that, so we wouldn't drink his drinks."

"That's nasty, yo," Wesley said.

"Isn't that what you're talking about?"

"Nah, backwash? That's just nasty," he said, taking another swig of soda from the bottle. "This was a *facial*." He screwed the cap on and put it down in front of him.

When people finished eating, I asked what we should make the following week.

"Let's just do this again," Wesley said.

"Or we could pick something else," I suggested.

"Or we could pick this again," Wesley said, mimicking the pitch of my voice.

Everyone agreed with Wesley.

"Except for with the strawberry cake you said," someone said.

"Don't forget to get shrimp," Frank added. "So we could have shrimp, too."

I clarified that Frank meant shrimp in addition to chicken, as opposed to instead of chicken so he didn't have to cut it. He sighed and told me, "Yeah, dawg, I'll cut chicken, but could you get shrimp, too, because shrimp is good?" I said I would.

It had taken a while for all of the boys to come to the kitchen, hungry and each on his own terms, and they were slow to all sit down at the table, but when dinner was over, they disappeared quickly, all at once, in different directions.

On my way out, Greg shrugged and said, "I really didn't think it would go like this."

I shrugged, too, and said that I didn't either. I left down the achy stairs, empty-handed.

Despite myself, I looked up at my father's office on my way out to the car. The light was on. Gerry must have been doing work in there and hadn't shut it off when he left. My father's books, still perched on the radiator, looked like a tiny skyline against a halogen sun. My throat tightened. I heard a tap on the second-floor window. I looked farther up.

Leon was at the window, leaning against a broom. It was unclear whether he had tapped the pane accidentally or on purpose. He stood there, frozen behind the glass.

I knew he could see me. I waved.

He looked around the kitchen to see if anyone was watching him. After a few seconds, he waved back, two fingers lifted off the broomstick.

FOR MY DAD, life was a series of meals. Food was his favorite thing to talk about, and it never felt like small talk. Who did you go with? What did you eat? How was it served? Did you order dessert? Food was important to him, a frame for the world. When I lived in different cities and called home to touch base, we mostly talked about what we'd been eating. When I studied in Madrid during my junior year, and traveled through Western Europe over winter break, I sent him chocolate from every city I visited, and he kept notes about each kind on index cards to tell me later. Senior year, he'd meet me on campus at my college, which was also his college, to hear speakers like Daniel Berrigan and Jonathan Kozol and then grab dinner and talk about social justice activism and whatever we were eating, in almost equal measure. Then, when I was a volunteer in Chicago, living on three hundred dollars per month, he'd ask about school and what we were making to eat and how much it cost. I imagined what we would say, if we had the chance to talk about cooking at the House that first night. He would ask what we'd made, the way he always asked about food. I would tell him on a scale of one to ten; he was a numbers guy. I would say my night with the boys was a solid seven. The meal itself was okay, elevated by hand-cut blocks of chicken, unexpected applesauce, and a sculpted piecrust—artisanal, really. Far from gourmet, but we weren't going for gourmet, I would insist; we were function-not-form people. And participation was good, better than anticipated.

"You know how kids are," I would say, as if I knew, and he would nod, because he did. I'd have to admit that the conversation had been halting. "To be expected," he would have said. And then I would tell him about the biscuits. "But how can you even rate something made *with love*, when someone tells you *'This is from the heart'*?" I would ask. "Priceless," he might have replied. "And practically a bargain at $109.21!" I might have said, unfurling the receipt for the groceries. And he might have reviewed it carefully, assessing the cost of each ingredient and imagining how they all fit together into a meal, if only he could've been there to hold it.

As I pulled away from the House, I called the number named Home in my phone. It rang and rang. The answering machine picked up. There was a pause and then my father's voice, an apology: "I'm sorry," he said. "We are not here to take your call." Another pause. It had taken him three tries to record the message. He stammered like he did when he was nervous; the dog kept barking in the background. My mother couldn't bring herself to erase his voice yet. You could still hear him take a breath before he said, "Please leave a message." One more pause. Then he promised to call back.

If You Bring Soda,
They Will Come

The early weeks were instructive for all of us. That first night went more smoothly than any of us anticipated, but the next several dinners together were stickier.

The second week when I pulled up, I noticed that the bright-green door was ajar. When I squinted to get a better view, I saw Leon's face squished between the door and doorway, his fingers wrapped around the painted wood beneath his chin.

"It's 5:04!" he shouted.

I heard his voice through my open window.

"I know," I started, apologizing as I rolled up the window and pulled the keys out of the ignition. "Sorry I'm late." I had left school later than I should have, cursing as I tore through traffic to the store, and then up and down the aisles of the supermarket. I was trying to keep my costs as close to one hundred dollars per week as possible, and kept backtracking to compare prices. As I rushed to load groceries into the backseat, I questioned my motivation for the cooking program. What was I doing? Why did I think this was a good idea? Was cooking at the House helping me move forward or pulling me backward? Sitting in rush hour traffic, I questioned myself. Why was I always late? Why did I always think things would take less time than they took? By the time I was grabbing bags from the backseat, I was nearing an existential crisis. What did I really want to do with my life, and when was I going to do it?

"You said you were going to be here at five." Leon kept me grounded in the real. "And now you're late like last week."

"I know," I said. "I'm sorry." I was sorry. "I think we'll be okay if we work faster. Want to help me bring the bags up?"

"I helped last week," he reminded me from the doorway, his fingers drumming the door.

"I know, but there's more food this week, so what do you think?"

He thought about it.

"How about these two bags?" I asked. "Or will you lock my back door?"

"You still don't have one of those clickers?"

"Since last week?" I asked. "Nope."

"Everybody has them clickers."

"Well, maybe not everybody," I said, hooking the two last bags on my left wrist. "My car is a little low-tech," I admitted, locking the door with my right pinky.

"*Real* low-tech," Leon corrected. Then he thought for a moment, watching me walk from the street to the sidewalk toward the green door. "I'll still go driving in it, though," he said. "When'd you say you're taking me out?"

"To be determined," I said, shifting the twisting weight of six bags across my wrists.

"Something wrong with your hands?" Leon asked, watching me.

"Nope," I said. "How about yours?" I held out an arm of groceries to him, smiling.

"That was only a little funny." He looked at me, the way he did, out of one eye, head tilted. "I'll take a bag, but I took one last time. I'm not going to be doing everything around here."

"Noted," I said, following him up the creaky stairs. "Me either."

Leon stopped abruptly. He wanted to make a point but didn't want to lose his balance trying to look back while climbing. He turned his shoulders around and faced me. "I'm serious."

"Me too," I said, almost bumping into him. "I don't want to do everything either. Let's just let them do it."

Leon sighed like you sigh when someone suggests something

that is never going to happen, then he turned back around to finish the hike up the stairs.

In the kitchen, we unpacked the groceries and Leon found a snack I had brought to eat while cooking. "What's this?" he asked.

"Hummus. There are some pita chips in there, too. I thought people might be hungry while we're getting stuff ready."

"People aren't going to eat this," Leon said, shaking his head. "This here is college food; nobody eats this. You've got to bring us snacks we like if you want us to eat them." He put the hummus back in the bag and tied it shut like that was that, and then he opened the chips and chomped a few.

Frank came in and started to wash the knife he had already asked the staff to unlock. When I opened the freezer to deposit the soda for faster cooling, I saw a wholesale-size bag of frozen shrimp. I said, "Oh, there's already a lot of shrimp in the freezer."

"Yeah," Frank said nonchalantly.

"Frank, didn't you ask me last week to be sure to get shrimp, like it was an emergency?" I was so moved by his enthusiasm that I had bought shrimp even though it put me over budget.

"Yeah," he said. "Arlette always gets it for me." He paused. It made sense to me that Arlette kept track of who liked what. I had known her for years and hoped I'd get to see her one of these nights. Frank mused, "Man, I love shrimp so much, I could have it with everything." Frank only ever said *love* about shrimp and cheese.

"Like Bubba from *Forrest Gump*," I said, opening the cabinets to look for a colander.

Frank scrunched his lips into his nose and his nose into his cheeks. "Who?"

"Did you ever see *Forrest Gump*?" I asked. I reached into the short cabinet above the stove for the dented metal colander. "The movie with Tom Hanks?"

On one of our walks, I asked my dad who he thought could play him in a movie, and he said maybe Tom Hanks. He didn't usually indulge my hypothetical questions, but he answered this one. I asked why Tom Hanks and he said because he could see it. I had had a special affection for Tom Hanks since then—his kind face, wide forehead, crinkly eyes, thin fringe of wavy hair around his head, his dadness. I could see it, too.

"He's the retard. She's calling you a retard," Wesley told Frank, snapping me out of my memory. Like lightning before thunder, Wesley's words preceded him into the kitchen. He came in to pour himself a cup of milk. He looked at Frank, then at me. "Yeah, he *is* like him."

"Wesley! I didn't mean that. You know I didn't mean that. I meant Bubba, the friend in the army." To Frank, I clarified, "Because Bubba always talked about shrimp." I turned on the faucet and adjusted the water to a thin, cool stream. "Bubba is Forrest's best friend; he's the one who loves shrimp. I think Forrest is the one you are thinking about, Wesley." I opened the bag, dumped the shrimpcicles into the dented colander, and pushed it under the water. "Though I don't think we'd want to call him a *retard*. Or that we'd want to call anybody that."

"It's okay," Wesley said. "He *is* a retard." Then to Frank he said, "You *are* a retard."

"Wesley! Can you not keep saying that? You know that's not what I meant." I turned to Frank. "I meant because the character likes shrimp. The guys are friends and they're in the army together and when they're on the battlefield, one of them talks about how much he likes shrimp with everything. It's funny." I thought about Bubba's fate in the movie as I tossed the empty bag into the massive trash can. "He's like, 'shrimp cocktail, shrimp scampi, fried shrimp, buttered shrimp, shrimp with biscuits . . . ' The scenes keep changing and he's still talking about shrimp."

Frank nodded. "Yeah, that does sound like me."

Wesley nodded in agreement, gulped his last sip of milk, and said, "Because you're a *retard*." He looked at me. "That dude's retarded. He acts like he's on crack. Oh, wait, that's right." He looked at Frank. "You *is* on crack."

"Wesley." I said his name the way you say someone's name when you want to tell them that you know they know better than to say what they just said.

"My bad, Frank." Wesley corrected himself. "You *are* on crack."

Frank looked at him and said, "I know, right? My moms was sharing that shit with me since I was in her. I been high since then." He
pinched his lips together, squinted, and nodded.

Through jokes that weren't jokes was one of the ways I learned
some of the things I learned in the House. How Wesley learned
Frank was born substance dependent was never clear.

Wesley raised his eyebrows and finished his drink. He crunched
the cup into a ball and left the kitchen as quickly as he had come in,
dunking it into the trash can on his way out.

"Is he always so helpful?" I asked Frank.

"Yup," Frank said.

"So how do you like to make shrimp?" I asked. "Like, with what
kinds of spices?"

"Sazón," he said with an exaggerated accent, closing his eyes and
pursing his lips. He opened the cabinet near the stove to reveal the
spice shelf: a blue drum of salt, a pepper shaker, a jar of red pepper
flakes, another one of Adobo, and several boxes of yellow envelopes
of Sazón.

"What does it taste like?" I asked.

"Like Sazón." He squinted at me. "'Cause that's what it is." He
tore off two packets.

"Like, is it *spicy*?" I clarified. "Is it *hot*?"

"It's *good*," he said, and closed the spice cabinet for another day.

Then Frank cut the chicken into what we would come to refer to
as "blocks like last time" and sautéed it, and then he cooked the
shrimp the way he liked it. I cut the vegetables and he cooked those,
too. Leon insisted on making his biscuits again. James came back in
time to make the rice and test the chicken and shrimp with Frank
when they were ready. I assembled a strawberry shortcake with
angel food cake, whipped cream, and strawberries muddled in
sugar. And when everything was ready, people migrated to the
table, which Leon had set for four while his biscuits were baking. I
threw together a side salad with vegetables I'd brought, just in case.

Wesley and Carlos made their way to the table, late and with
paper plates tucked under their arms and plastic utensils in their

fists. There was some grumbling about whether they should be allowed to eat, but since there was plenty of food, nobody protested
too much.

I asked about school, the news, plans for the week. I pointed to
the salad that no one seemed to see.

The boys nodded, shrugged, and avoided eye contact as they kept
eating. It was hard to say whether they were less interested in my
questions or the salad.

"Well, just look at you all eating in here!" Arlette came up from
her office downstairs to check on us before she went home. She was
Black, with braids that almost reached her waist, and a British accent that made simple sentences sound like music. Her face had a
lighthouse quality to it, all strength and glow. She hadn't changed in
all the years I knew her. She stood in the doorway and greeted me
with her bright smile and open arms. "Hello, Liz!"

"Arlette!" I bent to hug her since she was much more petite than
I am.

"You two know each other?" Leon asked.

"We do," I said. "I've known Arlette since I was little, when I'd
come here after school."

"That's right," she said. "Good to see you here again. How's your
mum, Liz?"

"She's okay. She'll be happy to hear I saw you," I said. "Will you
stay for dinner?"

"Not tonight," Arlette said, like she might stay some night.
"How's the cooking going?"

"Okay," Frank answered.

"It's not just okay, it's bomb, Arlette," Leon said. "Frank's just
saying that."

She looked at me, eyebrows raised.

"We're mastering the art of stir-fry," I told her, since that was all
we'd made so far.

Arlette asked Frank if he liked it. "Not that much," he replied,
"'cause I'm vegetarian."

She laughed. "Is that right?" Frank's vegetarianism was news to

Arlette. Since she did the grocery shopping, she was the one who stocked the freezer with burgers, hot dogs, chicken thighs, and his special-request shrimp.

"Yup," Frank said. "I'm a vegetarian."

"Really now!" Arlette laughed, a big, deep laugh.

"You know that doesn't mean you hate vegetables, right, Frank? It means you *love* them." I said. "That's probably why Arlette's surprised to hear your news. Especially since she just got you that big bag of shrimp."

"Huh?" he asked.

"Vegetarians don't eat meat. Like, at all," I said. "No shrimp. Just vegetables. All the time. Tomatoes, mushrooms, peppers, carrots. Raw, cooked. They love them all."

Frank winced. "Yeah, I'm not vegetarian."

Arlette laughed her laugh again. "I think you're going to be just fine, Liz. Just fine."

Before the boys broke for chores, we picked the menu for the following Tuesday: shrimp and chicken quesadillas with strawberry shortcake for dessert; a little bit of what we'd made before, a little bit new. James asked if we could make caramel apples, since it was almost Halloween. I asked if they were his favorite fall dessert. He said he had one once, and that was enough for everyone to agree that we should definitely make caramel apples.

THE THIRD WEEK I arrived on time. As I pulled my keys out of the ignition, the green door opened like the magical gate in a fairy tale. Leon leaned out, squinting in the October sun, and recited what had happened during the week: who had gotten in trouble, who had done something wrong but didn't get in trouble, and what he thought about all of it.

"I'm surprised you're on time," Leon said between updates. "I almost didn't recognize you. But I saw your hair." He made the swirling motion around his ears. It was 5:58. The boys had voted to push our start time from five until six so they could have an extra

hour of free time before cooking instead of having it between finishing eating and starting chores and curfew.

Leon didn't reach for a bag, but took one wordlessly when I held
it out to him.

I followed him up the stairs, marveling a little at our routine. For
a solid fifteen seconds.

"Is the soda in your bags?" he shouted down to me. "'Cause it's
not in mine."

I cringed. We had a problem.

In the kitchen, I came clean.

"You didn't get soda?" Leon asked. He shook out each empty
plastic bag for emphasis.

I had gone to Trader Joe's to get the stuff for the quesadillas, and
because they didn't carry the big-brand sodas the boys requested, I
opted for organic lemonade and sweet tea. I thought they were acceptable alternatives, with complementary flavors for our chicken
and shrimp, but I thought wrong. I tried to convince Leon. I told him
the lemonade tasted homemade. I held up the bottle and pointed to
the arty sketch of lemons on the label. I pointed to the words *Not
from concentrate!* "It's delicious!" I said. "People *love* this lemonade."

"Not people like *us.*" Leon said. "She didn't get soda!" He shouted
a public service announcement into the TV room, which was quiet
but for the ping and sizzle of videogaming.

"Want to at least try it?" I asked. "I brought sweet tea, too."

"She didn't get soda?" Frank appeared in the doorway and scanned
the counter.

"She can hear you," I said.

"People thought you were getting soda. 'Cause you got it last
week," Leon told me. "And the week before. And when you asked if
people liked soda, people said *yes.* And then—" He finished his sentence with a sweeping hand gesture toward the sodaless counter.

"I've seen the canisters of iced tea mix. I know you guys drink
iced tea," I reasoned.

"People like that *okay,* but people really like *soda,*" Leon said.
"Who really likes soda?" he shouted past me into the TV room.

As Leon polled the others loudly about who would prefer soda, I rinsed the strawberries and stood at the counter next to the sink cutting them into slices with a knife the staff unlocked for me. My hands were sticky, red, and stuck with strawberry hulls. I asked if any of the boys wanted to go to the market around the corner to buy some soda.

"I could," Frank said, opting out of chicken cutting.

"Okay, great. In my vest pocket, there should be a five-dollar bill," I told him. "That should be enough for two bottles of soda. Want to grab it?"

"Could you get it for me?" Frank asked.

"It should be on the chair by the table," I said, walking over to make sure it was there.

Frank walked with me to the doorway and looked at the chair.

"Frank, that's it right there," I said. We stood almost shoulder to shoulder. I was taller than him, but barely. I pointed with strawberried fingers toward the chair. "That black vest. The only black vest there. The money's in the right pocket." I looked at my vest and then at him.

"Could you just get it for me?" he asked, arms by his sides, gaze fixed on my vest.

"Frank, it's right in the pocket. I'm sure it is. I just got change. My hands are sticky."

"We going or not?" Leon shouted from the back door. He had decided to go, too.

"Could you just give it to me, dawg?" Frank asked me, lowering his voice.

"My hands are gross, Frank," I said. "Would you please just grab it?" I didn't understand his resistance.

"Nah, I'm not doing it," he said, still staring at the chair.

I looked at him, wiped my hand on my jeans, and pulled the bill from my jacket pocket. Before I could say anything else, he said, "I don't go into anyone's pockets. I don't do that."

"Oh," I said. I felt embarrassed that I hadn't understood what was happening. "I'm sorry." I held out the money to him. "Frank, I wouldn't think that you'd take anything from me."

"I don't go into no one's pockets," he said in one quiet, declarative breath.

"I know," I said. "I'm sorry. I shouldn't have asked you to." I wanted to make a joke, to loosen the space between us, but there was no joke. "What kinds do you think you should get? Pepsi and Sierra Mist?" I asked.

He shrugged. "I like Mountain Dew Code Red," he said.

I traded the five for a ten. "Want to get all three, if you think people will drink it?"

"People will drink it," Leon shouted from the back door, listening all along. "And could we buy a snack for ourselves, too, since we're the ones who're going?"

While Frank and Leon were at the store, I defrosted the shrimp. Wesley's door was closed and there was no music spilling underneath so I figured he wasn't around. There was no sign of Carlos either. I finished the strawberries, washed my hands, and set to work at the dining room table, pulling the soft chicken tenders from their Styrofoam beds and trying to replicate Frank's blocks-like-last-time cut. I didn't hear James come in.

"Hey, Liz," he said shyly. "You cooking tonight?"

"I am," I said, cutting the chicken. "Are you?"

He smiled his gummy smile and said, "Yeah, I could. Lemme just wash my hands."

"Perfect," I said. "Want to get the pan ready and you can cook the chicken again?"

"Yeah, I could do that," he said. "I know how already."

I brought James the chicken and held the cutting board at an angle toward him. With a fork, he flicked the pieces into the heated pan. The first ones danced when they hit the hot oil.

We both stepped back.

"That's hotter than I thought," I said.

"I know, right?" he said. "Where's everybody?"

"We were here first," Leon shouted from the stairwell. "And we went to get soda for your ass." Leon handed me a fistful of change with the receipt crumpled into it.

James looked at me.

"That's true," I said. "Maybe except for the ass part." I looked at Leon. "Thank you both for going." I looked at Frank.

"I should cook the shrimp, right?" Frank asked.

"Sure, I thawed it." I lifted it out of the sink. "It's ready for your special seasoning."

Frank nodded, taking the colander. "It's 'bout to get spicy up in here," he said to the shrimp as he shook them, sending a drizzle of water droplets onto the linoleum floor.

"But not too spicy," Leon said. "'Cause not *every*body likes spicy."

"You're forcing it, LeBron," Frank said.

"Are you LeBron?" I asked Leon.

"Yeah, people call me that 'cause I look like him," he said, stroking his chin. "You know, LeBron James. But you're always calling people their government names, so."

"I see it!" I said. "You do kind of look like him."

"Do you even know who the basketball player LeBron James is?" Leon asked me.

"I do!" I said. "Do you even plan on eating shrimp quesadillas? Didn't you say you wanted chicken? Why do you care if Frank makes the shrimp spicy?"

"I mean, *I'll* probably have chicken," he said. "But I'm just saying. For *people*."

Ignoring Leon, Frank reached for a second envelope of Sazón, tore it open from the bottom, and sprinkled it onto the shrimp already simmering in a pool of grease in the pan.

As James and Frank worked at the stove, Leon helped me grease the tortillas. I taught him the buttering system I had picked up during my volunteer years in Chicago, when I lived in a neighborhood where the soft smell of fresh tortillas clung to the air and quesadillas were my go-to lunch. One of my roommates had developed a strategy to speed up the process of making dozens of quesadillas at a time, which we did whenever we cooked for our six-person household. "You over-butter a tortilla not quite to its edges. Then stick a second tortilla to the first one and twist, distributing the grease evenly on both sides." I demonstrated, pressing two tortillas together. "You need one sandwiched pair per quesadilla, and the tortillas will be slick when pulled apart so no additional grease is necessary. Then you put one butter-side down in the pan, fill it with shredded cheese and protein, then put the second tortilla on top, butter-side up. Then flip. And start again." Then I told Leon that given his biscuit-margarining technique, I knew he was the right man for the job. He reminded me that his biscuits were good, and that I was hateful.

We finished buttering and stacked the stuck pairs into a pile on a paper plate that Leon insisted on carrying into the kitchen to show the other two boys. I followed him into the kitchen as he balanced the teetering tower of tortillas, willing them not to tumble to the floor.

I washed my hands and dried them on the half apron I was wearing over my jeans.

Leon washed his hands and turned off the faucet, then he reached down, picked up the hem of my apron, and dried his hands on it, too. I watched as he patted his palms and individual fingers dry against my leg. "Are you drying your hands on me?" I asked.

"I thought that's what we're using," he said.

"Maybe next time we could use paper towels," I said.

"Maybe you could bring me one of those, too," he said, gesturing to my apron. "It's kind of rude to just bring one."

As I imagined Leon in his own wraparound floral apron, Frank and James came in from the TV room to start assembling their quesadillas. I started making the first round and told the boys they could make as many as they wanted after the first one, and that I'd help with flipping if they wanted since it was the hardest part.

"I'm here!" Wesley called from the TV room.

"Some people don't *deserve* to eat," Leon said to Frank.

"Some people are annoying as hell," Wesley said on his way into the kitchen.

"What kind of a thing is that to say?" I asked Leon. "Everyone deserves to eat." I thought it was important in the first weeks that we establish that everyone was welcome to the table, whether or not he cooked. The project was about cooking skills, but it was also about sitting down together and passing-other-people-food skills; it became pretty clear pretty quickly that the cooking was the easier part. "There're probably going to be nights when you have something you have to do, and Wesley will be the one cooking, and when you get back, he'll be like, 'Leon, I made this for you.'"

Leon looked at me in disbelief.

Wesley said, to no one in particular, "I don't know about that."

James shook his head and smiled.

Frank just listened, popping shredded cheese into his mouth.

There were a few quesadilla casualties: some blackened edges, some cheese spillage, some fall-away chicken and shrimp. Someone learned the hard way that you don't have time to take a phone call when it's your turn to use the burner. But ultimately, the boys were happy with the results. The sense of accomplishment in the kitchen was almost as palpable as the thick, buttery smoke we tried not to choke on.

I had brought an array of sides, some by request, some not: sour cream, salsa, hot sauce, guacamole. The guacamole was more of a posterity condiment; "nasty" was the House consensus. "And not the good kind of nasty," someone clarified, in case the scrunched noses, stuck-out tongues, and fast sips of soda that followed weren't clear enough context clues for me.

"No thank you," James said when I offered some to him. "I tried it before in a place I used to live." This was one of two references he made to a different house. "I don't like it."

"This right here," Leon said, scooping spoonfuls of salsa onto his plate, "is my favorite kind of *salad*."

"Mine too, dawg," Frank agreed.

"I'm not sure we can count salsa as salad," I said.

"What does salad have?" Leon asked, spooning a chunky red scoop out of the jar. "Vegetables." He answered his own question, studying the tomatoey heap on his spoon before dumping it onto his plate. "And what does salsa have?" he asked, this time in my direction.

"Vegetables." I nodded.

"You said it yourself," Leon said.

"Schooled the teacher," Wesley said.

"Yup," Frank agreed.

Between bites, the boys said that the quesadillas were bomb and that we should definitely make them again next week, as if there was definitely going to be a next week.

The caramel apples were significantly less successful. Nervous about burning hands on boiling caramel, I had bought a boxed kit that came with caramel sheets to wrap around apples and popsicle sticks to jab into them for handles. Frank held his with the stick in his fist and asked if we were supposed to eat them or play something with them. Wesley, who always had room for dessert, wasn't interested. James, who had requested them in the first place, took one bite and then politely wrapped the gluey glob in his napkin. When I looked at him expectantly, as if to say "You chose these!" he looked at me and said, "I just remembered I don't like these."

My attempt to facilitate a table-wide discussion dissolved into a sort of soliloquy on setting expectations for the rest of the school year plus random thoughts on weather and public transportation. As we cleared the table, I asked whether I should take the bottles of lemonade and sweet tea so they didn't go to waste. I lifted the bag of bottles off the telephone table.

"Nah, you could leave them," Wesley told me.

"What?" I asked. "I thought 'people like us don't drink lemonade.'"

"Nah, we drink it," Wesley said, finishing his Pepsi in one gulp. "But soda's better."

"Yeah, people'll drink it," Frank agreed between red sips.

Without saying anything, Leon walked over, took one bottle and then the other out of the plastic bag as I held it, and walked to the pantry to put them away. "You could keep that bag, though, if you want," he called over his shoulder. "'Cause now we got a lot of 'em."

BY THE FOURTH week, I thought we really had a routine. I was on time. I brought soda. I even brought an approved snack. The boys took turns setting the table, and everyone sat down to dinner. And we had the timing down: we had exactly one hour for cooking between my arrival and sitting down to eat, before hunger became grumpiness, and fifty-seven minutes to serve and eat dinner then dessert, pick the menu for the following week, and clear dishes by 7:58 so people could start chores right at eight. But while we were prepping dinner—pasta and meatballs and brownie sundaes for dessert—the boys staged an intervention in the dining room.

Leon brought in two Styrofoam bowls. "Could we just use these? Instead of that?"

I was holding the stainless steel mixing bowl and a tablespoon near the brownie mix.

Frank looked down at the ground beef he was rolling into meatballs of varying sizes.

"No, I don't think using two little bowls will work," I said, puzzled.

They sighed deeply, in stereo.

"Wait, why?" I asked. "Isn't it okay to use the stuff in the kitchen?"

"Yeah. But," Leon said. *But* on its own served as a kind of shorthand for an argument that didn't need to be made, or shouldn't have to be made.

"Is there a problem?" I asked.

Leon and Frank looked at each other.

"People like the food and everything. But," Leon said.

I looked at Leon and then at Frank. I needed the rest of the argument.

"No offense, but you use a mad lot of pots." Leon told it like it was.

Frank nodded in agreement.

"Oh." I laughed. This wasn't the first time I had heard this.

"Nobody wants Kitchen A when you come. It used to be like all the chores are pretty even. 'Cause they all pay the same and it doesn't matter which one you get," Leon explained.

Frank continued rolling, nodding.

"But the nights you come nobody wants Kitchen A. And it's not like people don't want you to come, 'cause the food's bomb. But." Leon looked down at the table as he shared the community concern that had apparently been simmering for some time.

"When you come, there's mad stuff in the sink," Frank cut to the chase, not looking up.

"I see." I nodded. "You know, I get that. One of my old room-mates told me that once, that there was a lot more to clean up on nights that I cooked."

"But you still do it?" Leon asked, as if it were easy to just change your behavior even when you have an idea that you should probably do things differently.

"Well, yeah," I said.

Frank and Leon exchanged glances.

"So, I still think we should use the bigger bowl," I continued. "But do you think that it would be better if I stayed to help with Kitchen A? To help whoever has it?"

"Like one week, or you thinking every week?" Leon asked.

"Well, maybe the weeks there are a lot of dishes?" I suggested.

"You use a lot every week," Leon said.

"Every week, dawg," Frank echoed.

"Okay, so let's say every week," I said.

"Starting tonight?" Leon asked.

"Yeah, I can start tonight," I said.

Leon looked at Frank.

Frank shrugged.

"At the same time," Leon continued, "you don't really have to start tonight 'cause Carlos has Kitchen A this week and that dude never helps anyone with anything."

"I don't mind starting tonight. I probably should've started sooner," I said. "With my pot problem and everything."

Frank looked at me. I smiled, but he didn't smile back. He blinked, looked at Leon, and resumed rolling the meatballs.

As part of a newly imagined food-is-not-born-in-plastic initiative, I had brought a cheese grater and a block of Parmesan instead of a bag of shredded cheese. When I left the kitchen to ask the house-parent a question, I came back to find Carlos holding the grater at a 93-degree angle to Wesley's face.

"I need ten minutes alone with you and this," Carlos said. "So I could scrape your face."

"Okay, Carlos, I'll take care of the cheese," I said, putting my hand out toward him.

He pressed the grater into my palm. I couldn't hear what he said on his way to his room but it was clear we had different ideas about what lessons the box grater held.

I had also brought ingredients for a tomato-basil salad. I insisted that Frank and Leon take in the smell of fresh basil, and they indulged me, nearly bumping heads when they leaned down to catch a whiff of the pungent leaves. "Wesley, you have to smell this, too!" I called to him too earnestly as he passed through the kitchen for a drink.

"Nope, I know that smell and I don't like it," he said.

"Wesley, when was the last time you smelled basil?" I asked him, too skeptically.

"One of the times I was locked up, I was in one of those farm programs and we had to pick a lot of that shit. So, yeah, I know that smell. And I know I don't like it." He patted the doorway for punctuation on his way out.

BY THE TIME we sat down to eat, everyone but James was at the table.

"I'm loving the meatballs and pasta," Leon told us.

The boys drifted into their usual seats, Wesley at one head of the table, Leon at the other, with Frank to his right, which enabled their occasional bickering. Carlos sat across from Frank, which was only technically near Wesley, since they didn't acknowledge each other. James wasn't around, but I left his chair empty in case he came back. I used the broken one, careful of its arms.

And everybody ate, dinner then dessert.

"This food is the truth," Leon said, after a minute.

Wesley agreed. Frank nodded. Carlos ate quietly.

I looked at Leon.

"When something's good," Leon explained, "we call it the truth." He took a bite of brownie. "Like," he said, taking another sweet bite and holding the rest of the square up to the light like a jewel, "this, right here, is the truth."

The boys nodded. By this definition, nothing bad could be the truth. This truth was not an abstraction. It was real. You could taste it.

After we finished, everyone got up to start chores, and I stayed to make good on my word. Still trying to fill all of the silences, I asked Frank what he was reading for school.

He looked at me like I had asked him for a kidney.

Pausing to lean on the broom he was sweeping with, Wesley piped into the conversation from the doorway. "Last book I read was about fairies and shit."

I thought for a second, then turned to him. "*Midsummer Night's Dream?*" I asked.

"I don't know. By some dude like Peter Gallagher or something," he said.

"She's asking about *school* books," Leon told him.

"I know, dawg. It is a *school book*," Wesley said.

"Like *you* read *books*," Leon said.

"Fine." Wesley resumed sweeping.

"Wes, I think I know the one you mean," I said. "There are couples in a forest and they drink something and start hooking up with each other, thinking they're each other's girlfriends and boyfriends. And there're fairies that talk to them and to the audience. Then when they wake up, one of the fairies tells the audience it was all a dream," I summarized.

"Yeah, I think so," he said. "By Peter Gallagher or something?"

"Yeah," I said. "William Shakespeare is the guy who wrote it, if it's the play I'm thinking of." I appreciated how names you're not used to saying can sound the same. "It's called *Midsummer Night's Dream.*"

"Yeah, that's it," Wesley said, smiling.

"How'd you even know what he was talking about?" Leon asked.

"I could tell by how he described it," I said. It was the first book that came to mind about fairies and shit that I thought might have been assigned in school. It was usually sophomore English curriculum, so I wondered if Wesley was a sophomore. The boys had written down their birthdays on that tiny lined piece of paper the first night, but I didn't remember who was how old, or know how their school years corresponded with their ages.

"Did you like it?" I asked Wesley.

"Well I didn't really *read* it," he said.

"I told you this dude doesn't read books," Leon said.

"Oh, did you act it out in class, since it's a play?" I asked.

"This dude doesn't know what a play *is*," Leon said, in an aside to his own audience.

"She knew what I meant, dawg," Wesley clarified. "Nah, I didn't act it out. Well, maybe they did. I wasn't really *there* all the days they did it."

"Oh," I said. I figured no one wanted to hear my monologue on truancy so I tried a different direction. "Hey, is there, like, a radio? Could we listen to music while we do chores?"

"We could listen to music, like loud?" Wesley asked.

"Sure," I said cheerfully.

"I'll get mine." He disappeared to his room, returned with a boom box, and pressed PLAY.

I wasn't expecting to hear so many expletives in such fast succession so loudly.

"You don't like this song?" Leon asked me, studying my face.

"Well, I was kind of thinking music with, like, a little less *motherfucker* in it," I said.

"Nobody here really has that kind of music," Wesley said, turning the volume down.

Frank shook his head.

"For real, though," Carlos said, brushing past me on his way to start Kitchen A.

I followed him to the sink. "So the guys were telling me that people think I use too many dishes and we thought it might be a good idea if I stayed to help with Kitchen A," I said.

"Yeah, there's mad dishes on Tuesdays now," Carlos agreed.

"I hear that," I said. "So would you mind if I stayed?"

"Like to help?"

I nodded.

"And we'd split the two dollars?" he asked.

"Oh no, you would keep the two dollars," I clarified. I wasn't asking for his chore money. "I'd just help with some of the washing. Or the drying, whichever you'd rather."

He thought for a second. "Oh. All right," he agreed, and shifted to make room for me at the sink. "You want to wash?" he asked, moving to the side of the sink.

"I do," I said, pushing my sleeves up.

He went to get a dish towel that was folded over the handle on the door of the stove. I turned on the water, squirted detergent onto a sponge, and started scrubbing the pots in the sink.

Carlos stood next to me. I turned to look at him. He looked at me for a second, then at my hands doing the dishes. It was easier if we didn't look directly at each other. Suds covered my hands, crept up my wrists. He was quiet.

Then he asked, "So you're a teacher or something?"

"I am, yeah," I said. "I teach Spanish at a high school in Boston, not too far from here." I rinsed, then handed him the dripping mixing bowl.

He took it by the rim, held it away from himself so it wouldn't drip on his sneakers. He wiped the outside, the inside, placed it by the sink. "You like school?" he asked.

"Most of the time," I said, not looking up. "You?" I washed and rinsed the serving spoons, held them out to him in a bouquet.

He reached for them. "Nah, not even sometimes."

Show Me How
You Make Your Chicken
and I'll Tell You Who You Are

Dinner was never just about food. When the boys said they wanted us to make fried chicken, I didn't want to tell them that I didn't know how. Most of the chicken I ate growing up had been shaken and baked, or roasted with indecently placed onions and slathered in vegetable oil and salt and pepper. I had eaten real, not-fast-food fried chicken exactly once, at the house of a friend whose mother was from Georgia. So when somebody said we should make fried chicken and everyone agreed, I said it sounded great. And I promptly called my friend's mom.

When I explained my cooking project and chicken predicament and asked for her help, my friend's mom dictated a list of ingredients and told me when to come over for a tutorial. I went with groceries and a notebook and left confident in her recipe, carrying the heaviest pan I have ever lifted: her mother's seasoned cast-iron frying pan that she insisted I borrow. Embracing the extra authenticity, I lugged the pan to my whip and left it on the backseat until the following Tuesday.

"I thought you said that we were making fried chicken," Leon said, as we unpacked the groceries. "People think we're making fried chicken."

"We are," I said, lifting the pan in his direction.

"What're the eggs for, then?" he asked me, pointing at the carton.

I casually said it was to dredge the chicken, as if dredging was something we did. "To, like, dip the chicken in eggs before rolling it in the flour mix," I said. "For the coating."

Frank joined in the questioning, "We're not having fried chicken?"

"We are," I told him, told them.

Someone put the soda in the freezer to cool.

"Looks like scrambled eggs," Frank said over my shoulder as I whisked the eggs with a plastic fork.

"It's for the coating!" I said. "To make it crispy."

"I didn't eat before 'cause I thought we were having fried chicken," Frank said.

"We are having fried chicken," I assured him.

"She probably doesn't know how to make it," Wesley told them, first from his room across the hall, then again in the kitchen.

She can hear you! I wanted to say. *And it's true, she doesn't really know how to make it. She's basically faking it, because she doesn't want to be disappointing, which I think we can all agree is something we all do sometimes.* Instead I said, "This is how I learned to make it."

"That's not how you make fried chicken." Wesley looked at my hands. "Nobody makes it like that."

Nobody ever agreed about anything, except when everyone agreed that I was wrong.

My confidence in the recipe wilted. *Does this look like the pan of someone who doesn't know how to make fried chicken?* I wanted to ask. I was stuck between a dozen eggs and an eight-pound pan, determined to not admit that I'd never actually made fried chicken on my own.

As the boys were all agreeing with each other, I quietly, stubbornly cracked three more eggs into the bowl.

Carlos, who had apparently also been listening from his room, came into the kitchen. He walked over to me and stood so close that his sleeve brushed my arm. He watched me whisk the eggs and said to the other boys, "Yeah, that's how white people make it."

"How would *you* know how *white* people make fried chicken?" Leon asked him.

"I had a white foster family once," Carlos said. He said "family" like he said "school," like an assigned institution. "That's how they made it."

Everyone got quiet.

I continued whisking, but slowed the strokes as I considered what to say. It hadn't occurred to me that my white friend's white mom's recipe might be different from what the kids had in mind, or that this meal would highlight my whiteness. Until the fried chicken, we hadn't really addressed race. It was obviously always present, but we never talked about the ways race inflected our food, our bodies, our everything. Until the fried chicken, we cooked around it.

"And they made chocolate cream pie, too," Carlos continued. "White people like chocolate cream pie and make fried chicken the way she does, with eggs," he told the boys. He turned to me. "You like chocolate cream pie, right?"

Everyone looked at me.

I had actually never made a chocolate cream pie either. I did have a different white friend who called them pudding pies and joked that her mother made them as apologies after family fights and would leave them in the fridge as offerings, but I didn't understand this as a white thing per se. We ate cake in my house: coffee cake, pound cake, birthday cake, ice cream cake—the full cake continuum. We rarely ate pie, except pumpkin and apple on Thanksgiving. Even though I couldn't remember the last time I'd eaten a slice of chocolate cream pie, it seemed more important in that moment to agree with Carlos than to prove him wrong. So I lied. "Yeah," I said. "Sometimes. Would you want to make chocolate cream pie? We can, if you want."

"Are we going to do one of those cookie crusts?" Carlos asked. The "we" surprised me.

Frank looked at Carlos and then at Leon. Wesley poured himself a cup of soda.

"We could do a graham cracker crust, or a pastry one like we did for the apple pie, or I think they have chocolate cookie ones," I said.

"The crunchy kind's better," Carlos said, washing his hands.

"Do white people have another way of cooking oil, too?" Wesley asked. "'Cause that's not even close to hot." With his chin, he gestured to the pot on the stove. "We're never eating."

Eyes moved from eggs to front burner to me.

The small pond of oil in the heavy pan was still. In my careful attention to avoid somebody getting burned, I had waited too long to turn on the stove. My underestimation of how long the oil would take to heat through, coupled with the fact that there was no cover to fit the pan, delayed dinner by forty-five minutes, which felt more like a year.

"Could I go do my laundry?" Wesley asked.

"Sure," I said. "I think it's going to be a while."

"So I could go?" he asked. "Now?"

"*You* weren't going to help *us* anyway, dawg, so why're you asking like you would?" Leon interjected, narrowing his eyes.

"I know, but I still want to eat. She said I could," Wesley replied, already in his room stuffing clothes into a backpack.

Carlos asked if he could go do his laundry, too. So I said sure, and asked if he and Wesley would go together. "There's two laundromats," Carlos clarified.

"Those two don't do anything together!" Leon called from the counter, where he was stirring salt and pepper into the flour with a plastic fork.

Carlos and Wesley left down different staircases, with dirty clothes in tow.

Frank had opened the chicken and was rinsing each piece and stacking wings, drumsticks, and thighs on clean paper plates.

"We don't have to use egg if you don't think we should," I conceded to Frank and Leon.

Frank shrugged.

"You think we should?" Leon asked me.

"I think it's pretty good." I shrugged. "But we could use milk or water if you think that's better. Up to you."

"We could just use the egg, dawg," Frank told me. "The oil's going to be hot already."

We made a line of bowls along the counter: egg, milk, and flour mixture. Frank and Leon dredged the drumsticks, dipping and flipping. The oil finally started to hum on the stove. I dropped in a gob of chicken skin to test the heat, and it bubbled and sizzled. With two real forks that someone had found somewhere since plastic ones would've puddled in the lava-like oil, I placed the chicken into the belly of the pot. Frank wordlessly took the forks from me and started moving pieces of chicken around.

"Please be careful," I said. "The oil's really hot. I don't want you to burn yourself."

"I know, dawg," he said. "But you have to tuck the wings in, so you could fit more in the pan that way." Carefully, with both forks, he turned the wings, tucking the tips underneath. Then he placed two more drumsticks into the pan. This was the only gesture toward a kitchen from his past that Frank ever made.

It was 7:40 when the first batch was done. We were way behind schedule. Wesley and Carlos were back, putting clean clothes away in their dressers. James was in the kitchen with Frank and Leon and me, having returned from wherever he'd been. We admired the inaugural lot of White People Fried Chicken as it sat steaming, oil seeping into the bed of newspapers beneath it. A second batch fried in the pan. The greasy smell swelled in the kitchen and seeped into our skin.

"I know this is taking way longer than expected," I said. "If you want one now, you can."

"We could have a piece right now?" Leon said.

"Yeah, as long as it's cool enough," I said.

"I'm having one," Wesley said from across the hall, making his way into the kitchen.

"Me too," Carlos said, on his way from his room.

"If they're having one, I'm having one," Leon said.

"Make sure it's cool enough," I said. "Please don't burn yourselves."

One by one, each of the boys pulled pieces off the newspapers, tapping the meat twice or three times against the paper to dab the grease.

"Chicken's good, dawg," Frank said first.

I asked again if it was cool enough to eat safely. I asked them to please be careful. I turned the second batch of chicken in the oil, tucking the wings under, like Frank taught me.

"White people know what's up with chicken," Leon said, surprised.

"Yeah, it's good, right?" Carlos said knowingly, as if he had predicted this.

"Bomb," Wesley said.

I stood near the stove and looked at them standing together, eating. "But is it still *white people* fried chicken if Leon and Frank made it with me?" I asked.

Heads nodded, someone mmmhmmed, and everyone kept eating.

"You're not even having one?" Leon asked me between bites.

I was going to say that I was waiting to eat until dinner started, when we sat down at the table. But dinner had started. I reached for a piece and felt its heat sear into my fingertips. Frank and Wesley stepped aside to let me into the semicircle. And we all stood, not really saying anything, looking mostly at the chicken and not at each other as we finished our first pieces in the crowded kitchen with the window open just wide enough to let some sky in. It was the truth.

THE NEXT TUESDAY, I brought ingredients for two chocolate cream pies, including a quart of heavy cream and a hand mixer to make fresh whipped cream for the top. Bolstered by the success of White People Fried Chicken, Carlos insisted the other boys also try the pies. Leon met me at the big green door and was already talking before I got out of the car. That weekend, they had gone on an outing to a massive amusement park with two of the houseparents. Because it was out of state, they had stayed overnight in a motel.

"Wait until you hear what happened with Wes," Leon said.

"What happened?"

"You're not going to believe it." He was excited, moving faster than usual up the stairs, carrying bags.

"Did you already tell her?" Frank called down into the stairwell as we walked up.

"I was just about to," Leon said.

"Could somebody just tell me?" I interjected, counting heads.

"Wes got locked up again," Leon reported.

"But it was mad funny," Frank jumped in.

"It doesn't sound funny," I said. I put the bags on the counter, the soda in the fridge.

James stood in the doorway, smiling but not saying anything, ready for the presentation.

"It was funny, dawg," Frank insisted.

"Locked up? Are you guys serious? How is this funny?" I unpacked the groceries and braced myself for the story. "What happened? Is he here? Is he okay?"

"We were about to tell you," Leon said.

"But you're asking mad questions," Frank said. "You don't listen."

"Can you just tell me if Wesley's okay?" I asked.

After they got back to the motel from the amusement park, they got bored with watching TV so they snuck out to go to McDonald's. It was unclear whose idea it was to leave their rooms. While they were walking along the side of the highway, some police stopped them.

"But why would you leave the motel? Hadn't you eaten dinner? How late was it? Were there cars on the highway? Did anyone get hurt?" I asked, kept asking.

"Just listen to the story, dawg," Frank said.

"But why did the police stop you?" I asked, not getting it.

"Because they did, dawg," Frank said. This wasn't a first time. "Just listen already."

"Do you think the police thought you needed help?" I asked, imagining the sight of them walking along the highway so late at night. "Did they think you were stranded?" I was trying to understand how Wesley had started the day on a roller coaster and ended it in a holding cell.

"Nah, dawg." Frank was bored by the privilege that shaped my assumption the police would be trying to help them. "Just listen."

"They picked us all up," Leon explained. "Us plus two of the guys from other residences that came with us. And they let us go, but since Wes had priors, they kept him there and the staff who took us had to come and bail him out. And they weren't happy about it."

"What's the funny part of this story?" I asked. "Where's Wesley now? Is he okay? I still don't get why the police got involved." I worried about Wesley. "Wes?" I called toward his door.

It opened. Wesley sauntered out of his room. "You telling her?" he asked them, smiling.

"We're trying but she's not listening," Frank said.

"I'm listening!" I said.

"When Wes was locked up, dude saw his cousin in there." Leon delivered what they all seemed to think was the punch line.

Wesley smiled and nodded. Everybody laughed.

I didn't know if they wanted me to laugh, too, or to be shocked. "Why did you walk to McDonald's? Hadn't you had dinner? Did you have permission to leave? What time was it? Wasn't it dangerous to walk along the shoulder of the road at night?" I asked the wrong questions. I was thinking it was dangerous because they could've been hit by cars not watching for pedestrians in the dark; I wasn't thinking it was dangerous because they would be picked up by police who weren't trying to help them. "Somebody could've gotten hurt."

"You're not even listening to the funny part, dawg," Frank said.

"Don't even tell her, yo. She's not listening," Carlos said.

"I *am* listening," I said. "I won't ask any more questions. I swear."

They were excited as they retold the story *Rashomon* style, each remembering different details of the night. Their smiles deepened as my eyes widened in disbelief.

"Dude's *cousin* was in there, too," Leon repeated the punch line. "You heard that part?"

"Your cousin? Wes, did you know that he was there?" How could I not ask?

"Nah, I mean I knew that, you know, he did stuff," Wesley said. "But I didn't know that he was going to be there. Like, then. It was funny, yo." He smiled. He stood, backlit by the fridge as he decided on a predinner drink, basking in being the center of the story.

"The important thing is, are you okay, Wes?" I asked.

"Yeah, I mean, I'm fine," he said.

"She said she wasn't going to keep asking questions," Frank said.

"How can I not ask questions, Frank?"

"That was a question, too, dawg," Frank said from the sink, washing his hands.

"Okay, but what were you thinking, Wes?" I asked him.

"Another question," Frank said.

Wesley shrugged. "What do you mean? Why'd I sneak out?" Wesley unscrewed the cap of the plastic gallon container and poured himself some milk. "We all did."

"Well, that too," I said. "But what did you think when you saw your cousin? Like, what did you think when you bumped into someone you knew—in jail—in a different state?"

He nodded and laughed and took a sip of his milk. The other boys laughed.

Wesley looked at me and asked, "Have you ever laughed so hard, whatever you were drinking came up out your nose?" He smiled just thinking of it. The more he thought about whatever it was that had been so funny, the more he giggled.

The other boys laughed at the thought of liquid flowing from places it shouldn't. Everyone said yes, and shared when it had happened to him, and what was so funny.

As everybody told their stories, giggling, I imagined them as little boys, before all of this. I laughed along with them, nodding along with the laughing.

"But seriously, Wes. Do you think this might be a good time to think about making some different choices?" I asked. It was easy for me to ask about choices; I had a lot of them.

"I mean, I wouldn't say it like that, exactly." Wesley smiled. "It was funny, yo."

"She's kind of right," Leon said to Wesley. "But at the same time"—he turned to me—"it *is* funny. Even *you* have to admit it."

"Okay, it *is* funny, because what are the chances you would see your cousin there?" Even I had to admit it. "But still." Here is where we might have talked about power, and police, and who gets the warning and who goes to jail, and who gets to make their own choices and whose choices are narrowed by the systems they live within—and by the people who make and remake those systems. But we didn't. That's not how we talked about the things we talked about.

"Whatever, yo," Wesley said. "It was funny. What're we having for dinner anyway?"

"Baked chicken Parmesan," I said. I had sold them on it the week before by describing it as similar to chicken parm subs with pasta instead of rolls. Wesley said he wasn't cooking but he would probably eat. Carlos said he would make the pudding for the pies. James said he would make the pasta and Leon said he would do his biscuits, of course. Frank asked if I wanted him to cut the chicken into blocks like last time, and I told him I'd cut it into cutlets, and asked if he'd help me with the sauce and cheese assembly. "Yup," he said, on his way to ask for a knife.

As Leon prepared his biscuits at one end of the dining room table, Frank and I set up at the other. He twisted the cover of the jar of sauce until it popped then dumped half the contents into the pan as I cut the chicken lengthwise, then salted and peppered the cutlets. Frank slid the pan across to me and I placed the chicken in the sauce. When I looked up, I saw him popping pinches of cheese into his mouth, head titled back to facilitate the landing.

Frank looked at me looking at him and said, "I love cheese."

"That dude's going to eat *all* our cheese," Leon said.

Frank tossed another pinch into his mouth and blinked in Leon's direction.

"There's going to be none left," Leon warned, rebuttering his biscuits.

"Sometimes a person just needs a little cheese, Leon," I said.

Frank held out the glossy envelope of cheese in my direction and lifted his eyebrows to communicate an offer. I took some and popped it into my mouth, replicating his technique. He nodded. Leon shook his head at both of us.

When dinner was in the oven, we started dessert. The mixer I brought to make fresh whipped cream was received with an enthusiasm I hadn't anticipated. Everyone wanted a chance with it. The boys passed it from hand to hand to hand. Even Wesley came out of his room to try it. They held it like a chain saw and then a machine gun, a microphone, a sword. My little mixer had never seen so much action.

That night, everyone sat down to the table without hesitation, the way people do when they are used to something. The chicken parm was cheesy enough. Nobody touched the salad I made, but everyone loved Leon's biscuits. And the chocolate cream pies with the crunchy kind of crust were as good as Carlos remembered them.

As we ate, I asked about school and the boys told me about other things, like Celtics scores and TV plotlines. We finally had a routine.

"She said that I could get a job in a bakery," Carlos reminded the table as we helped ourselves to second slices from the second pie.

I went to the pantry to grab more napkins.

As if he could not allow the moment to continue with everyone enjoying the pie he had made, Carlos said, "I would take any kind of job."

Nobody looked up at him.

"I'm serious, yo. I'd do anything for money." Carlos paused. "You know the difference between Black people and Hispanic people?" He looked around, then said, "Work."

"Carlos," I said sharply, surprised by the change in conversation.

"You people be lazy as shit," Carlos said to no one in particular.

"Carlos, stop," I pleaded. "Come on." I waited for the staff to come in from the other room to handle it. I could hear the shifting of papers in the office. I knew someone was there, listening. "Please. What're you even saying?"

"What? I'm not saying anything they don't know," Carlos said, inviting challengers.

The other boys kept eating. The room filled with the eerie quiet of calm before a storm.

"Carlos, you have to stop," I said. "We just had a great dinner, and you helped make two delicious pies. It was good. I don't get why you're trying to wreck it now, saying racist things and picking a fight. I'm not pretending that I work here or anything, but I'm asking you to be respectful." I wanted the table to be a neutral space. But this was sometimes impossible with everyone's fists so close together. "Please," I kept repeating.

"I'm about to leave anyway." Carlos picked up his plate and flung it into the barrel on his way out. And when his bike disappeared a few weeks later, there was little question as to whether it had been an inside job.

"So what're we having next week?" Leon asked the others. "'Cause personally, I been in the mood for stir-fry. 'Cause I've been *trying* to eat healthier around here. . . ."

Carlos came back to the table eventually, and we made fried chicken and chocolate cream pie other times. But the white foster family and the cousin from the holding cell were never mentioned again. Like sugar into cream under pressure, they just dissolved.

Moveable Feasts

Most of our dinners were pretty good, but the birthday dinners were the best. Each one was a tiny act of homemade grace on paper plates, with frosting. Leon was the only one who had demonstrated actual interest on the first night when I introduced the birthday prong of my plan. He went to the staff office for a pen and piece of paper and wrote his name, birthday, and preferred cake-and-frosting flavor combination on the top line. But when Leon handed me the sheet at the end of the night, I was surprised to see all of the boys' names and dates and cakes were there; sometime between the silences, each had made sure his birthday had been registered.

Wesley's sixteenth birthday was the first we celebrated. It was in November, the seventh dinner I made at the House. Wesley chose calzones, which we hadn't made before. I brought dough from a restaurant I liked in the interest of taste (it was already delicious) and time (we only had one hour to cook), a shortcut I'd take for pizza in the years ahead. It was becoming clearer and clearer that cooking at the House was more of an assembly operation than a scratch kitchen, and I had to adapt.

Frank poured each of the ingredients into a row of Styrofoam bowls: sautéed chicken in his signature cut, buffalo and barbecue sauces, pepperoni, meatballs, enough cheese to stuff a throw pillow, red sauce.

I cut the large disks of already-rolled-out dough into halves and gave each boy one soft half-moon to fill and fold. Everyone chose his combination carefully, snacking along the way. Cooking the cal-zones took over an hour because nobody knew where the second rack for the oven was and we could fit only three at a time on the one we had.

When we finally sat down to eat, Wesley gave a nod of approval. There was some groaning and exaggerated lip smacking. Survey said the calzones were "bomb" even though they took "mad long" to cook. Our bar for success was not tasting homemade, but restaurant-made; if a meal tasted like something they might buy in a restaurant, it passed. The calzones passed.

Wesley's birthday cake was a copy of the strawberry shortcake we made the second night, like he requested. It was a round angel food cake split through the middle, filled with sugary sliced straw-berries and whipped cream, with another layer of the soaked straw-berries on top, and frosted with more whipped cream. Instead of writing *Happy Birthday,* I arranged strawberry slices into a large *W* across the top and nestled the 1 and the 6 into eaves of the *W.*

"Do we have to sing?" somebody asked.

"Singing is lame," somebody added.

"I'm not singing," somebody said.

"Whoever wants to sing can sing," I said, carrying the cake in from the kitchen on a glass platter I had brought for the occasion.

Leon stood and switched off the lights and started the song in his loudest, most exaggerated falsetto, "Happy birthday to you . . ." Eyes closed and lips pursed for emphasis, he went for it: ". . . Happy birthday to you . . ."

By the time I reached Wesley and leaned down to place the cake in front of him, everyone had joined in, loud and off-key, almost shouting "Happy BIRTHDAY, DEAR WESLEY . . ."

Behind the chubby wax numbers, Wesley finger-conducted Keith Lockhart style, smiling all the while, his teeth bright in the light of the candles. He looked so young.

"Happy BIRTHDAY TO YOOOOOOOOOU," everybody sang shoutingly.

That sound—the boom of a roomful of teenage boys singing

"Happy Birthday to You," out of tune and at the top of their lungs, to a housemate who was something between stranger and brother to them—was as close to joy as we ever got.

When there was cake left over, Wesley asked if I was taking it with me. I said it was for him, so of course I was leaving it, right there in the fridge on my glass plate.

The next week I checked the sink and cabinets, then casually asked about the platter.

"That shit broke," Wesley said.

"Does anybody know how that shit broke?" I asked gently.

"Did you just swear?" Leon asked.

"Did somebody break my dish?" I asked.

"You don't usually swear," James said and Frank seconded.

"That shit doesn't usually just break," I said. "I just wondered about the plate."

The rest of the birthday cake sat unceremoniously on an aluminum foil–wrapped community cookie sheet.

LEON HAD THOUGHT through the details of his birthday dinner by the time Wesley's candles were lit, and possibly before that, though his birthday was not for another four months. In his careful and multiple mentions of his birthday, Leon reminded me of my dad, who had prized his birthday dinners. By the end of July, my dad would start drafting his birthday menu and list of possible gifts for his mid-September birthday. His gift wish list was always the same: new books, black socks, a dress shirt with extra-long sleeves. The menu was always the sacred trinity of meat, starch, and vegetable, but the flavors changed.

Leon told me the first version of his birthday dinner menu on the night of Wesley's, as we were washing dishes. Over the course of the next four months, he tweaked it week to week.

"I changed my mind about my birthday dinner . . ." he would begin again.

At some point, Leon changed his cake order to a request for ice cream sundaes. "Actually, I like sundaes better than cake, so I want to have those. Didn't you say that we could have whatever we want when it's our birthday?" he asked.

"Sundaes sound good," I told him.

"With candles, too. Just 'cause it's not a cake doesn't mean I can't have candles."

"I'll get candles," I promised.

"The number ones, like you got Wes—one and nine, 'cause I'm going to be nineteen." Leon was older than the other boys, and he was also the most specific about what he wanted, especially when it came to small things he thought he might actually get.

A week after Wesley's birthday, Frank and I were in the kitchen prepping food when he brought up the subject of his own birthday dinner, which would be in February.

"You're planning to get me candles like Wes's?" he asked.

"I did figure that we'd get candles. For all the birthdays. Unless somebody doesn't want them. Do you not want candles?" I asked.

"You think I'm going to cry or something?" he asked.

"What?" I laughed. I thought he was kidding.

"You think you're going to turn off the lights and people going to sing and I'm going to cry 'cause I never had a party like that or something?" Frank asked.

"Oh, Frank, no," I said as I realized he wasn't joking. "I wasn't thinking that at all."

He was looking away from me, looking down.

I shifted, tried to catch his eye. "Unless you mean cry because the singing is so bad . . ."

"I know, right? It's bad." I could see his cheek crack into a smile. Frank rarely smiled. When he did, he'd cover his mouth with a fist, as if he was holding an imaginary microphone in front of his lips to cover the gap between his two front teeth.

"No candles, Frank," I said, shifting my tone back to soft, to serious. "And we don't need to do a cake if you don't want a cake. We could do a pie or cookies. Or sundaes."

"I want a cake," he said quickly.

"Okay. What kind of cake are you thinking?"

"What kind is there?" he asked.

"Lots of kinds. A lot of people like vanilla or chocolate. And the vanilla can be white or yellow . . . some people like carrot."

"Carrots in their cake?" He scrunched his nose.

"Yeah, with walnuts in it, and usually you make it with cream cheese frosting. It's good. It's kind of spicy," I said. "I like it, actually."

"Sounds nasty," he said. "I don't want that."

"Okay, no carrot cake. There's also red velvet."

"Red cake?" he asked.

"Yeah, it tastes kind of like chocolate, but it's red. Like a really dark red, more than, like, Chicago Bulls red. And usually you put cream cheese frosting on that kind, too."

"Nobody says Chicago Bulls," he said. "People just say Bulls."

"Okay, it's not Bulls red," I said. "It's darker, like chocolate. Do you want red velvet?"

"No, red shit sounds nasty, too. No offense," he said.

"None taken," I said.

"Probably vanilla," he said after a pause.

"Cake or icing?" I asked.

"Both," he said.

"Okay. We can make it plain or there's also a kind of vanilla that's called Funfetti."

"Sounds gay," he said.

"Frank." I had started campaigning to curb the use of *gay* as an insult in the House.

"Sorry." He shrugged. "Just saying."

"Well, one of my friends really likes Funfetti cakes," I said. "It's vanilla cake with rainbow chips mixed in, so when you bake it, there are flecks of color in it."

"What's it taste like?" he asked.

"The cake is sweet and the flecks inside look like rainbow confetti and taste a little like candy." As I described it, I thought despite myself that it didn't sound particularly heterosexual.

"I want that," he said.

"You do?" I asked. "Funfetti cake?"

"Yeah," he said. "But those little cakes that everyone gets their own of, so nobody's touching mine."

I nodded. "Funfetti cupcakes. No candles. Sounds like a plan, Frank."

Then, just when I thought his apprehension about a birthday dinner was assuaged with talk of cake and Bulls and words like *shit* that we were used to hearing, he told me: "I don't want candles, 'cause I wished for lots of stuff and I didn't get none of it."

"No candles, Frank," I said again, because I didn't know what else to say.

Standby Dinner

One difference between food and love is that food is evenly divisible. We learn this division at home first, in some families sooner than others. Carlos was an expert in this kind of math. He wasn't often interested in helping cook, but he always knew exactly how much food was his before it hit the table. He'd swish into the kitchen and assess the groceries I'd brought, taking store of the total amount of what he was interested in and determining his allotted percentage by dividing the whole by the number of residents. He liked to take his portion up front: three quesadillas of fifteen, four pizza slices of twenty. He always asked me first if I was eating and whether he could take his share. He was always fair in his calculations, and never assumed that anyone else would be fair. He counted quickly on both hands with butterfly fingers.

When I brought two clearance bags of peanut butter cups three weeks after Halloween, Carlos asked if he could open the bags and count the candies. There were thirty pieces. "I'm going to take my six, okay?" he asked, holding them out as proof that he'd taken only six orange units. "Unless you want some." He waited for my nod before putting three pieces in one hoodie pocket and three in the other. He said thank you on his way out of the kitchen, and didn't return for dinner. This was how it went with Carlos, give or take a dinner and a thank-you.

Carlos wasn't wrong when he announced on the first night that none of the boys were interested in inviting people from the outside over for dinner. Nobody was more surprised than he was when his mother was our first guest.

—

FRANK AND JAMES and Wesley were clustered around the stove making quesadillas, which Leon started calling "quesa what-whats" and the other boys adopted into the House vernacular. Quesadillas had become our standby dinner, the way that all home cooks have standby dinners. They were the easy meal that everyone liked, the we-already-knew-it-was-good one that we defaulted to instead of trying something new, or made when no one suggested something better.

Carlos was ready and waiting in the TV room by the time I arrived with groceries. He was dressed up like a young man with plans: bright white T-shirt to his knees, ironed jeans, polished sneakers with artfully undone laces, slightly sideways hat with the sticker still stuck to the underpart of its unbent bill. I asked him if he had a date. "Nah," he said. "My moms is coming." I asked if he'd be back for dinner. He told me they were going out to eat; it was a scheduled home visit. She was supposed to take him for a haircut, too. Over the weekend when the houseparent had taken everyone to the barber, Carlos hadn't gone along; he said his mother was going to take him on the visit. I told him there was plenty of food and that, if he wanted, he was welcome to invite her for dinner. He was adamant that they had another plan.

When Carlos's mother arrived at the House, she walked in through the kitchen where Frank, Leon, Wesley, James, and I were working. I said hello and she said hello, picking up the bag of tortillas. "Real tortillas are easy to make," she told me. "You should try it sometime."

Carlos heard his mother's voice and came quickly. Hat on head, thumbs hooked through the string backpack on his shoulders, he was ready to go. "C'mon, Ma, it's six-ten."

She told Carlos to wait a minute, and he waited a minute as she laughed and called the other boys "baby" and told them how her man loved it when she cooked. Then he retreated to the TV room.

I reminded Carlos's mother that he was ready and she said they were leaving in a minute and took off her sweater. She flipped her ponytail and told the boys how much she liked to cook.

Over the next fifty minutes, Carlos came into the kitchen with time checks. "Ma, it's six-thirty and the place closes at seven." "We have a half hour to get there." "If we leave now, we'll be able to get there." "We could still get there if we leave already."

Each time Carlos came in, his mother said they would leave in a minute.

At five to seven, he asked, "Are we going to just go out and eat someplace?"

Leon, Frank, Wesley, and James took turns at the stove. Leon had buttered the tortillas, and everybody had filled his few the way he liked them. Now they were practicing the balancing act of flipping them.

"You think this one's ready to be flipped?" James asked Wesley. With the spatula, he lifted the toasted tortilla off the surface of the pan, carefully, to reveal the bottom.

Wesley leaned in to assess the situation. Their heads almost bumped.

Frank watched the exchange, tossing pinches of shredded cheddar into his mouth.

At the precise moment when I could almost hear the click of pieces falling into place as the boys helped each other, Carlos's mother wedged herself between them, playfully pried the spatula from James's hand, and said, "Nah, baby, I got that."

I watched as if in slow motion as James happily relinquished the spatula and Wesley said she could do his, too. I wanted to knock the spatula from her hand. "Nah, baby, I got that" was not the kitchen mission we were trying for.

The boys stood by, watching as Carlos's mom finished their quesadillas for them. They listened as she talked excitedly about how good she was at cooking for her family.

At 7:20, Carlos came in and told her in an almost-whisper, "If we don't go now, we won't get back by my curfew." She must have had some reason she didn't grab her purse and sweater and leave right then. When she told Carlos to just wait another minute, again, he went back to the TV room and stayed there.

Frank and James and Wesley carried their plates to the table and brought the soda and some napkins. Leon asked Carlos's mother if she was staying for dinner and she said baby, of course she was, that's why she came.

Before I sat down with the others, I went into the TV room and asked Carlos if he'd eat with us. He stared ahead at the screen. I asked if he wanted me to bring him a few quesadillas and he could eat them in there. He turned to look at me, then looked back at the TV.

"Don't worry about him, he has a bad attitude," Carlos's mother told me.

I wanted to tell Carlos's mother about the pies that he'd made, and how he often sat down to eat with us. And I wanted to tell her that I knew he'd been excited about going out with her that night, because he'd ironed his jeans and changed his shirt and put on his newest sneakers, and cologne. But I didn't think he'd want me to tell her any of that.

ON HER WAY out, Carlos's mother thanked me and told me that maybe we could get all the mothers to come cook. She said dinner was a really nice thing, that she'd definitely come back.

I thanked her and said maybe. It didn't seem like a moment to say anything else.

I went back into the TV room to see Carlos before I left. He was still sitting on the couch. He'd put his earbuds in. When I stepped in front of him, he looked up at me and took one earbud out, to listen.

I said I was sorry I'd wrecked his night. I figured someone owed him an apology.

He looked at me, then put the bud back in his ear and returned his gaze to the wall.

Whatever Normal Means

I wanted cooking the next week to be more normal, as if I could bring a right combination of ingredients to make some semblance of normalcy. Leon was at his post by the time I arrived at 5:54, standing with his back to the green door as I pulled the keys out of the ignition. When I said hello, he told me that he had a job interview. When I asked what he'd be doing, he said, "Making nine dollars an hour."

"It's Thursday, I think." He reached for a bag, and I handed him two. "'Cause tomorrow I got a doctor's appointment."

"A doctor's appointment?" I asked, locking the back door. "Is everything okay?" I didn't know what I should ask Leon about his medical situation. I thought he'd tell me what he wanted me to know, or Gerry would tell me if there was something I needed to know. I locked my door.

"Same old," he said, as if I knew what that meant. "You really need a clicker," he said on the way back into the House.

"They didn't tell you what you'll be doing for the job?"

"I'm going to be making nine dollars an hour, so that's all I need to know," he said over his shoulder. "When they said nine dollars an hour, I said I would go."

"That makes sense," I said, following him up the stairs.

"People who make nine dollars an hour have car clickers," he said, letting us into the kitchen.

Frank was waiting in the doorway by the stove, fingertips hooked into its wooden frame, his lanky body leaning forward. "Can't cook, dawg," he told me. "Got to drop and roll."

"You have to what?" I asked, emptying the bags.

"Drop and roll, dawg. You never seen those fire films?" he asked.

"I have," I laughed. "Have *you* seen those fire prevention ads, Frank? Aren't you too young for them? They were on TV when I was little."

"Yeah, dawg. I'm old as dirt," he said, lips pursed, looking off into the distance.

"Okay, well, when you're done dropping and rolling, will you cut the chicken?" I asked. "Into your blocks?" We were having stir-fry again, with brownies for dessert, more of the same.

Frank sighed and agreed. I went to ask the staff for knives.

When I came back into the kitchen, Frank was putting the soda in the freezer and Leon had picked up a piece of mini corn and was squeezing it between a thumb and an index finger. "You brought fake food?" he asked. "What's this, some kind of toy?"

"No," I said. "It's corn!" I'd brought it for the stir-fry. "Real corn!" I thought the boys would like it. I thought if I brought more interesting vegetables, they might eat them.

"It doesn't look like corn," Leon said. "I mean it kind of *does*, but like, little. And fake."

"It's not fake, and it *is* little, but it's real." I plucked one out of the bag and held it with two hands, nibbling a tiny side, like Tom Hanks in *Big*. I held a second out to him. "Want to try it?"

Leon and Frank watched me then exchanged glances, their eyes widening.

"I'm just kidding," I said. "You just eat it regular." I put the rest of the tiny cob in my mouth and crunched. I tried to give the second one to Leon.

"Nope," he said, holding both hands up.

"Frank?" I asked. I held the bag of little ears in his direction.

"Nah," Frank said. "I'm good." He had washed his hands and started cutting the chicken.

James came around the corner.

"James will try it!" I held a handful of mini corns out to James.

"Not even," James said, shaking his head no.

"Really?" I asked.

"Really," Leon said. "Nobody wants your fake food. We just like it regular."

"Yup," Frank agreed, flipping and seasoning chicken chunks in the sizzling grease.

"I also brought your favorite, Frank." I held up a can of water chestnuts.

Frank squinted at it. "Nobody wants that shit either, dawg." He sighed. "No offense."

"Okay, I know," I said. I'd brought water chestnuts the last time we had stir-fry. Frank had called them water crunchies and said, "They should be called *water nasties,* 'cause they are." I'd read that you have to try things a few times before you can like them, but nobody was interested in opening a can of water chestnuts a second time. "I thought we needed some texture," I said. "I really thought people would like the little corn and the pea pods."

"This is the pea pods?" Leon reached into the bag and pulled one out, grasping it by the tip of the pod as if it were a dirty tissue. "Who's going to get all the peas out of these?"

"Not me, dawg," Frank said over his shoulder from the stove.

"You eat the whole thing!" I said, taking the pea pod from Leon. I snapped its tip, peeled the fiber away from the side, popped the pod into my mouth, and crunched. "I love these!" I'd never been so enthusiastic about peas, or anything. "They get softer and a little sweeter when you cook them."

The boys looked at me like I'd eaten the dirty tissue. Then Frank returned to the chicken, and Leon broke open the brownie box to start dessert, and James made the rice. Wesley came in to pour himself a drink, like he did almost every time we cooked. He didn't really want to participate in the preparation, but his weekly 6:15 drinks suggested that he didn't want to be left out either.

"So, should we talk about our weeks?" I asked, eager to fill the silence between the sizzling, scraping, and sipping sounds.

"*Some* of us have interviews this week," Leon said, assembling brownie ingredients.

Wesley rolled his eyes, crushed his cup with one hand. "My girl's coming over. I'm out."

"Do we get to meet her?" I asked. "Is she coming to dinner? Does she know you make applesauce?" I had enough questions for all of us.

"Don't tell her about that," Wesley said. He looked at me. "I'm serious, yo. I don't want her to know I can do that shit."

"I think she'll be impressed," I said.

"I'm serious," he said. "Don't tell her that shit."

"Okay, I won't say anything," I said. "Does that mean I get to meet her?"

Wesley shrugged and threw the cup into the enormous trash barrel. Then he went to his room across the hall, closed the door, and turned up his music until it thumped against the wall.

Frank shut off the stove, moved the pan to a different burner, and asked if he could go play videogames until we sat down to dinner. I nodded and said I'd finish up.

"What do you think you'll wear for the interview?" I asked Leon.

"Probably a shirt," he said. "Could you do this for a second?" He handed me the spoon.

I continued mixing and realized he hadn't added any oil, so I poured some in and smoothed the clumps, inhaling the cloyingly sweet, chocolaty smell of batter.

Leon returned with two shirts. One was a yellow collared shirt that looked like he might have pulled it out from under a lounging hippopotamus. The other was a blue-and-lighter-blue-striped short-sleeve shirt.

"Either would work, but I'd maybe wear the yellow," I said. "Is there an iron? I could iron it for you after dinner."

"I was thinking the yellow. And I was already going to iron it. Could you just finish the brownies? 'Cause I'm busy. I've got to ask the staff about the iron," he said, disappearing into the hallway.

I spread the batter in the ungreased pan and placed the bowl and spoon in the sink. Then I placed the pan in the preheated oven and turned to the sink to start washing the dirty dishes to get a head start for whoever was on Kitchen A.

James came into the kitchen and said hello. "You think I could have this?" he asked as he pulled the batter-streaked bowl from the basin.

"Yeah," I said. "I was just going to wash it."

"I was just going to lick it." He smiled and leaned against the counter near me.

"I used to do that all the time when I was little." I nodded. With my mother, with my aunts, with my grandmother, I remembered.

"Yeah, me too," he said. As he cradled the bowl in the crook of his left elbow, I noticed his hand was bandage-less, finally healed.

I knew approximately four things about James: he was sixteen, turning seventeen in May, according to the birthday sheet; his favorite cake was chocolate with vanilla frosting, which was also my favorite; he special-requested caramel apples because he had one once at a Halloween party; and something had made him so angry that he'd stabbed his own hand nearly through, ostensibly while trying to defrost a hamburger.

"A crazy thing happened today," he said. He was almost as tall as I was and lean, with broad shoulders and dark brown eyes. He started scraping the bowl with the spatula.

"What happened?" I asked. I turned on the water and squeezed blue soap onto a yellow sponge. As I hunched at the sink, washing dishes from the week, and James leaned against the counter, polishing off the batter, we were on the same level.

"I was at Forest Hills, and this dude I don't know was all staring at me. So I stared back at him. And finally this dude comes up to me and goes, 'Are you from the Archdale projects? 'Cause you look just like this dude I know there. Who's your pops?'" As he spoke, James scraped the batter from the sides of the bowl one thin chocolate line at a time. "And he said this dude's name, and I said that I was from there but didn't know him, 'cause I left those projects in 1993." James would have been three in 1993, old enough to recognize faces but not describe them, to say a word for *father* but not know first or last names.

"Oh my goodness, James," I said. I stopped washing and let the water run. I turned to look at him and tried to read his face. "That's intense."

"I know, right?" He looked into the bowl and licked the spatula every three or four strokes. "Then this dude goes, 'I'm pretty sure that dude's your father.' He goes, 'No joke, you look just like him with a younger face, he's got to be your pops.' Then he was all, 'He still lives in there and you should go by and see him, 'cause you're probably his kid. I'm going to tell him I saw you.'" He didn't look up from the bowl. "That's crazy, right?" It wasn't a question.

"That's so crazy, James," I said. I looked over at him in profile. The water made a shushing sound. "You were just having a regular day, thinking about other things, waiting for the bus, and some stranger stares at you and then starts talking to you because you look so much like some guy he knows that he tells you he's pretty sure that guy is your father. And it kind of blows your day apart because you weren't expecting it, you were just, like, waiting for a bus."

"Yeah," he said obviously. He pulled the spatula to his lips. He didn't need the recap.

"So?" I asked. I thought of times I had been stopped by strangers who asked if I was my sisters' sister, or my father's daughter because our faces are so alike. It was a strange feeling to be recognized and stranger, I figured, if unfamiliar with the related face. I started washing again.

"So what?" he asked. He put the spatula in the bowl and stood for a second.

"What happened then? What did you say? What did he do?" I asked. I didn't know why James was telling me all this. I kept asking in case there was a question he wanted to answer.

He shrugged and licked his lips. "The bus came and I got on it."

"What do you do now?" I asked. I dried the cutting board, the knives. "What do you think about all of this?" I looked at him. The rich aroma of chocolate was rising in the room around us.

He shrugged again. "I got stuff I've got to do before dinner," he said.

I reached for the bowl and James gently placed it in my hands. He was done.

"Thanks," he said. I nodded. He left.

I went into the TV room to see if I could convince Frank to cut the rest of the vegetables. He agreed and I followed him into the kitchen. He washed his hands quickly and flicked the water off his fingers before picking up the knife.

"Do you know where the pot holders went?" I asked.

I had brought a set of pot holders because I was tired of using dish towels or quartered paper towels to retrieve hot pans from the oven. I understood how the bowls and spoons could disappear: bowls were carried out full of cereal or SpaghettiOs and abandoned to grow mold in the privacy of corners or under beds. But where could the pot holders be?

"Nope," Frank said. Nobody saw them. Nobody saw anything.

I folded a dish towel and opened the oven to check the brownies. I started to pull the pan out and burned my fingers. "Fuck!" I swore instinctively.

Frank stepped into my path, sort of bumping me out of the way. I assured him I was fine, but he said, "Nah, I got it, dawg," and pulled his sleeve over his hand, grabbed one side of the pan, and transferred it from oven to counter.

When I thanked Frank, he said it was nothing even though it felt like something. Then he shook his hands, as if the heat could be flung off them like water.

EVERYONE EXCEPT CARLOS sat down to dinner. By that point in November, there was a flow to our dinner conversations. I was a broken record, asking questions about school and people's weeks and telling random stories from the news that I thought they might find interesting. Leon usually kept the conversations moving, agreeing or sharing anecdotes. When Carlos was there, he sometimes said things to stop it. James rarely said much. Wesley would launch one-liners, but focused mostly on his plate and was the first to excuse himself.

Frank was the constant, and the wild card. I never knew what he was thinking, or what he'd say, or if he'd say anything. He was a man of few words but well-chosen ones. And he was always listening though he liked to say he didn't care. He usually lingered at the table while the others fled to chores. But that night he got up hastily while people were still eating dessert.

This incited suspicion amongst the masses. It wasn't eight, the phone hadn't rung, Frank never hurried, and he had no place else to be. Heads turned, but no one said anything.

"I'm about to take a dump," he announced.

The other boys' eyes got wide. They looked at Frank and then at me, to see my reaction.

I looked at them and then at Frank.

"A dashizzle," Frank continued. "I'm about to—" Now he was gesticulating. He pressed his hands to his thighs, bent his torso to mimic sitting, and shimmied his hips.

Giggling started like a slow boil.

"Okay, Frank, we don't need to know *exactly* where you're going," I said. I fought my own laugh, not wanting to lose the credibility I had been trying to establish as Neutral Grown-up Exuding Unconditional Positive Regard.

"It's about to be a big one, too," Frank said, still wiggling his hips. "I could feel it."

"Frank!" I exclaimed.

The room burst with laughter.

Frank turned quickly in the doorway. He looked at me and said, "Aren't you always telling us to tell the truth? And I'm just trying to tell the truth." He shook his finger in my direction. "But if you didn't really mean it, dawg, that's okay. I mean, I thought you wanted us to be real honest with you. But if you want us to lie, we could lie." He played to the room like a preacher to a packed church.

Everyone mmhmmed in stereo sound. Some of the uh-huhs sounded more like amens.

"Did I say that?" I asked. I didn't remember saying anything about the truth.

Everyone laughed harder, louder. Heads nodded.

"He. Told. You," Wesley said. "Schooled the teacher."

"Dude makes a point," Carlos said, his dimples deepening as he smiled.

"No offense but he's kind of *right*, Liz," Leon said.

James smiled widely.

I shrugged and they laughed. They knew I knew it was true.

By 7:58, I was wiping down the table and everyone dispersed for chores. Leon returned to the dining room with his yellow shirt and the iron.

"See, I was going to iron it right now," he said. "Even if you didn't tell me."

I dried half of the table with a clean paper towel and sat down in my broken chair to watch him iron and ask him practice questions. "Why do you want this job?"

"'Cause I could use the money," he said. "But I probably shouldn't say that."

"Maybe don't lead with that," I said. "You could say something about learning new skills and meeting people." I tried another angle. "What if they ask you why you are qualified for this job? Usually there is some kind of question about what your strengths are."

"Those are some good questions," he said. He ironed back and forth in even strides. He didn't look up. "I wish you could just go for me."

"If you don't think they'll be able to tell us apart," I said, "I'll go."

He looked up from the shirt to see if I was joking, shifting his shoulders so he could look at me, then looked back down at the shirt. He resumed ironing in long, fast strokes.

"When they ask about your strengths, talk about customer service. No matter what the job is, people skills are important. And you have a great way with people. You're polite. You're a good listener. You get people. You help. Mention all of these things when they ask."

"I wish you had a job you could give me," he said.

"Me too," I said. "I hope you get it."

"Me too. You think this's done?" He held the shirt up like a warm, pressed wish.

—

THE NEXT WEEK, Leon met me at the door and reached for the groceries without being asked. He updated me on what was happening in the House: who was going to school, who wasn't, who got in trouble, and for what. The big news, he told me, was that Greg, the houseparent, had started bringing a puppy to the House. Greg trained dogs as a side job and got permission to bring the puppy because none of the boys had allergies, and they could play with him if they wanted to. It was a blond Lab the size of a loaf of bread.

"It's mad little. And real cute," Leon told me. "I just hope it doesn't pee inside."

When we got upstairs, I casually asked him about the job as we unpacked the food.

"What job?" he asked.

"The one we talked about last week," I said. "With the interview shirt?"

"Oh, that," he said. He pulled the soda bottles out of bags. "I didn't get it."

I asked if they had given him any feedback on why he hadn't gotten the job.

"Could be 'cause I can't look them in the eye," he said, placing the bottles on the counter.

"It can't be that," I said. The puppy whimpered in the staff office.

"It's what they said," Leon said. He crumpled the plastic bags.

"It's what who said? Is that what your counselor told you?"

"Yeah, she said it could be they need people to look people in the eye, and I can't." He threw the bags away.

"She said that?" I asked.

Leon picked up the soda, a bottle in each hand, and shrugged. I didn't know exactly what Leon's medical condition was, but I knew it caused his head to tilt to one side, and that he couldn't hold steady eye contact.

"But didn't your counselor tell them it's not your fault? She knows you can't control it." The words got stuck in my throat.

"I don't know," he said. "I guess." He moved toward the freezer. "But if that's the problem"—he took a deep breath and continued, his back to me as he opened the freezer door—"I'll never get a job. I can't help it that I can't be looking people in the eye like other people. This is how I am." He wiggled the bottles until they fit among the frozen food. "I was born like this. There's nothing I can do about it," he said quietly, closing the freezer door. "They can't fix me." He walked to the sink. "They already tried."

My throat felt tight. "That interviewer's wrong, Leon," I said. "I'd hire you in a minute."

"But you know me," he said. "They don't know me and they don't want to." He turned on the faucet, started washing the vegetables.

"I'm sorry people are stupid," I said. "I think your counselor's wrong, too." How could she tell him something like that? I swallowed hard.

"Maybe my counselor's right," Leon said. "But if she is, I'll never get a job. Because this is just how I am." He paused, his hands underwater, and shrugged. "I'm always going to be like this. I can't help it." The water ran around the surface of a pepper, down into the drain.

"She's not right, Leon." I blinked quickly; my cheeks felt hot. "I think I forgot some of the soda in my car. I'm going to run down and grab it. Can you get the rice started?"

My heart was hummingbirding when I reached the sidewalk. I gulped the brisk November air and looked up. The light was off in my dad's office. His chair, his desk, his books were shadows. Everything he'd touched there was dark. What was I doing here? I couldn't do anything about Leon and his body, James and his father's face, Carlos and his mother, Wesley and his locking up, Frank and his being born addicted. I peered into the darkness of my father's place.

I walked to the 7-Eleven on the corner for soda. There was none in my trunk; it was an excuse to leave, to catch my breath. The clerk asked if I wanted a bag for the bottles and I said no, because Leon would catch my lie about already having the soda if I came back with a different bag. I rushed back to the House and climbed the stairs two at a time to the kitchen.

"You were gone mad long," Leon said when I opened the door. "Didn't you say the soda was in your car?"

"Yeah," I lied again.

"'Cause people tell me I'm slow," he continued. "But you're *slow*. No offense."

I laughed, grateful for laughter.

"What? It's true." Almost to himself, he added, "Least I got an excuse to be slow."

Goodwill toward Men

The first week of December, the TV room at the House blinked and glittered. Gold garland was draped in the doorways and multicolored lights were strung against the walls. A tree, decked in two economy packs of metallic globes, almost touched the ceiling. It was artificial, but all the effort felt like tropism. Five green Celtics jerseys flashed back and forth across the TV screen; one occasional red buzzer buzzing completed the scene. Three boys on the couch watched the game, wholly unimpressed by their surroundings.

"Wow!" I said when I came around the corner.

"James did it all," Greg, the houseparent on duty, told me.

"James, you did all this?" I asked him.

James shrugged from his spot on the couch.

"Did anybody help you?" I scanned the couch for a glimmer of recognition.

James shrugged again.

"I helped him put the nails in and stuff, but he pretty much did everything," Greg explained. "We don't usually put up everything that's in the boxes of decorations. We just do a couple, you know what I mean? But James said he wanted to do it all, so I let him."

"I think it looks great," I said.

"I think it looks gay," Wesley said.

"She doesn't like it when you say *gay*," Leon corrected him from a doorway.

I contemplated introducing a "Don we now our gay apparel: when it's okay to say *gay*" clause to my anti-hate-speech campaign, but didn't want to confuse my targeted "Let's make a concerted effort to avoid homophobic slurs for two hours a week" agenda that was finally starting to gain momentum.

"James, how long did this take?" I asked.

"Like an hour," he said with a shrug.

"At least that, I'm sure." I nodded. I thought about the constellation of little rituals that make the holidays the holidays. Decorations, lights, cards, cookies. I imagined the memories of star-spangled Christmases James must have stored in his body that moved him to unpack every ornament and each string of lights, to hang them, to plug them in so they would shine.

"Did you bring soda?" Leon cut to the chase.

"I did," I said, still thinking about my own muscle memory of Christmas, of decorating, of baking, of giving and taking.

"You didn't get the diet kind again, did you?" he asked.

"No," I assured him. "I told you that was an accident."

"Because people don't like that." Leon hammered his point home. "Which you knew but you got it anyway."

A different week, I'd bought diet Sprite instead of Sprite. I didn't realize the mistake until we sat down to dinner. I noted how similar the labels were and laughed. I told Leon that my dad had bought diet root beer instead of regular root beer on more than one occasion, and how disappointed my sisters and I would be because having soda was such a treat and the diet kind wasn't as good, especially the generic brand, which is what he mostly bought when he got it. And he would try to convince us that it was an easy mistake since the labels looked alike and that, besides, they tasted pretty much the same. And we would get so mad and argue that they weren't at all the same, and then we'd drink it just the same.

"And you did this anyway?" Leon asked gravely.

"I've never done it before!" I thought we both could see the humor in the situation.

"You just did it. You know it's bad, you did it anyway," he said. "And you're laughing."

"I won't bring diet soda again," I promised that night, as seriously as I could manage. After that, Leon carefully inspected the soda labels as we unpacked.

"I got plenty of soda," I assured him. "No diet. Plus stuff for the steak-and-cheese subs."

"Nobody likes diet soda," Leon reiterated on his way to the kitchen.

"Did you bring mushrooms?" Frank asked.

"I may have brought diet mushrooms," I said for Leon's benefit. He looked back at me from under the garland and shook his head.

Frank scrunched his nose.

"Just kidding, Frank," I said. "They're regular mushrooms. And peppers and onions. And cheese, plenty of cheese."

In the kitchen we did our usual, which was starting to feel like our usual.

I WANTED TO do something a little different for the boys for Christmas but didn't know what. Holidays are hard for a lot of people because of all the traffic and feelings, but at the House, they were even harder. Gerry had told me that after Mother's Day, Christmas is the day when the most kids act out. He explained that it wasn't that anyone had delusions about Santa Claus or presents, but even the older kids still believed that their families would come through for them on Christmas. The trauma of grief, buried like land mines, was triggered by other people's celebrations, which functioned as reminders of the kids' own losses: what they had had and lost, what they wanted and never had, who they had or didn't have to lose. When families didn't show up, things got ugly. Fights, drugs, drinking, property damage. I started thinking about what I could bring for them that was small but good.

For Thanksgiving, I had brought pies. When I learned that some of the boys had home visits and some didn't, and the houseparent on duty was going to make a chicken as a stand-in for a turkey, I said I would bring pie. When I made it clear that nobody needed to help, they ordered three. I suggested what I thought was the usual triumvirate: apple, cherry, and pumpkin.

"Nobody eats pumpkin pie. That sounds nasty." Leon was the voice of the people.

"People like sweet potato," Wesley told me.

Pumpkin pie is just like sweet potato, I would have argued. Except that I didn't really know; I'd never tasted a sweet potato pie, but the color was similar and texture looked the same. Instead of pushing pumpkin, I went home, searched for a sweet potato pie recipe, and delivered the three kinds they wanted.

I wanted to do something more than dessert for Christmas. At the same time, I didn't want to ask the boys what they wanted and then not be able to afford the things they asked for. Gerry had sent me a couple of checks that covered part of my costs for groceries, which I hadn't expected, but still—between student loans and grad school fees, rent, car, food, phone, life stuff, and things for my classroom—I didn't have a big enough operating budget to buy anything substantial even with my teacher's starting salary, which was more than I had made in my other jobs. I called Gerry to ask if he thought it would be appropriate to get gifts for each of the boys. He said he thought it would be fine and asked what I was thinking. I said I didn't know yet.

When I came for dinner the second week of December, Arlette came upstairs to say hello and to remind the boys about the deadline for their wish lists in order for her to be able to shop and wrap for Christmas Day. Each boy could submit a Christmas list for items totaling up to $150; the money came from a combination of state allowance and private donations. It was separate from the seasonal clothing budget they received twice a year, before school in the fall and again in the spring. There was an additional holiday fund from an anonymous donor who had come through the system. The wish lists consisted largely of electronics and sneakers; most of the TVs, radios, and game system controllers in the boys' rooms were gifts from Christmases past.

Every year, Arlette also made the boys with knotted ends fleece blankets for Christmas. Arlette's dedication to the kids in the different residences run by the agency stretched beyond her job description and paycheck, and they felt it. Most of the boys kept the blankets

Arlette had made for them on their beds. Frank and Leon had multiple blankets, layered, from multiple holidays.

"Arlette's cool 'cause she does the mom things, you know?" Leon would tell me.

I agreed. Arlette is one of those people who really sees people when she looks at them. When she looks at me, I can sometimes see her seeing my father in my face. That night, she asked about my mother, and our Christmas plans. I told her that this time of year was especially hard for my mom. Arlette nodded that she understood and said that she would pray for us.

"No offense, but I don't believe in that shit," Wesley said. In keeping with the theology of abandonment, he didn't believe in what he could not see.

"None taken," I said. I don't think that Arlette or I realized that Wesley had been listening to us. Leon had gone to find his list, and James and Carlos weren't around. Frank had been sitting at the table, too, but he left for chores. "You're entitled to your own beliefs, Wes."

"I don't have any," he said, sipping his drink.

"Everybody believes in something, Wesley," Arlette said. Her voice was even.

"I don't," he said.

"I know you do," she said. Arlette radiated faith.

"Fine," he said. "I believe people get what they deserve."

Arlette looked at me, her eyebrows raised. I looked at her, then at Wesley. I asked him what he meant by that.

"Everybody gets what they deserve," he said, and took another sip of Pepsi.

"Do you really believe that's true?" I asked him.

"Yeah," Wesley said, and sipped again.

Arlette was quiet. She folded and unfolded her hands.

"You can't believe that you deserve this, Wes, to be here." Arlette looked at me when I said it, so I knew I'd said it out loud. I felt like a traitor. And a stranger. But I also felt like it had to be said.

"I do," he said. "I did stuff. I got what I deserve."

"But you can't believe that you deserve to not have what you don't have," I said. I looked at Arlette. She shook her head at me, or him, or all of us, this world. Wesley didn't walk away. We had never talked like this. "You're just a kid, Wes. You have to know that this isn't all your fault," I said. I lowered my voice. A game was on in the other room. We heard the pounding sound of running, the buzzer screeching. "You can't believe that you deserve this." I talked to his forehead. He looked into his cup.

"Yeah, I do," he said, not looking up. "People get what they deserve."

I wanted to tell him that I've heard people say that the God of love and the God of fear are the same, but that even on my best day, I have trouble with that idea. I wanted to say again that this wasn't his fault. But I knew Wesley was accustomed to being both blamed and pitied and didn't like either. And given the choice, he would take blame any day.

"No offense," he said, as he'd said before, still sipping, still not looking at Arlette or me, "but I don't believe in that church shit."

Arlette's eyes were closed, her head was tilted downward. She might have been praying.

Wesley scraped the last of the strawberry shortcake off his plate in three slow swipes of a plastic spoon. "I don't believe in any of it," he said, before taking the last big bite.

"Well, what're you thinking about Christmas, present-wise?" I asked him, figuring that now that faith was off the table, we could return to the holiday's practical implications. "Do you guys get gifts from your caseworkers, too?"

"Yeah, but no," Wesley said. He was already on his way to the trash barrel.

Arlette laughed a big burst of a laugh. I asked Wesley what *Yeah, but no* meant.

"I mean, my caseworker's probably going to get me another blue size-medium sweater."

Arlette nodded, laughing, agreeing with Wesley.

"No," I said, thinking he was exaggerating. "Don't you wear like a double X?" His shoulders were narrow and he was lanky, but he chose clothes that fell away from his body.

"I'm serious, yo," he said. "Every year, she gets me a size-medium sweater, like blue or something."

"Not really," I said again, looking at Arlette for confirmation.

Arlette was still nodding yes, still laughing. "It's true," she said.

"What am I supposed to do with that shit?" Wesley asked rhetorically.

I said I didn't know. "Size medium won't fit me or Arlette, so we're not interested in that shit either," I joked. We all laughed. "But I really don't get why she'd get you that."

Wesley shrugged. He had tossed his plate in the barrel and returned to the table to pour himself a third cup of Pepsi. He stood by us, sipping.

"Like, does she know it's for you?" I asked. "Does she know you?"

Wesley wore black and white almost exclusively. Shirts, sweaters, sweatshirts, sneakers. Jackets. He had exactly one red short-sleeve shirt and a pair of black sneakers with a red Swoosh that he wore with it. A size medium might have fit his torso technically, but that wasn't the size he wore.

I looked at Arlette, who was laughing and nodding, and asked whether the caseworker would've picked that out for him or would it have been from donations or something.

"Yeah, she *knew* it was for me," Wesley said. "She's been my caseworker since the longest."

"I don't understand why she'd get you a blue size-medium sweater"—I looked over at Arlette to see if I was missing something— "since you never wear blue and don't wear medium."

Arlette shook her head no. She had stopped laughing.

"What did you do with it?" I asked.

Wesley shrugged and crushed the cup in one hand. He had already said more than he ever did. "Just left it somewhere."

WITH THOSE BLUE size-medium sweaters in mind, I decided that clothing was the something small but not random that I could bring to each of the boys. I couldn't begin to fill the holes left by people who weren't in their lives for now or forever, or address real material deficit, or answer big questions with any kind of certainty, but I could take advantage of post-holiday pricing and get some shirts and sweaters in the right colors and sizes. I knew that trying for surprises was not a good path, not least because I'm terrible at receiving gifts, and surprises in general—a combination of not really registering excitement on my face ever, and always preferring that things be a little different than they are. So I told the boys my idea ahead of time, explaining that this was separate from the list they generated for Arlette, and asked for suggestions.

I told them that if they told me what they wanted, I'd have a better chance at finding it, and that I was going to wait until after Christmas, so I could buy better things on sale with the same budget. I asked what colors and styles they liked, and what sizes they wore. I said that for whoever didn't tell me, I would have to get a size-medium blue sweater. They laughed and told me sizes and color preferences, some with more specificity than others. Carlos wasn't there the night I asked, and James just shrugged, so I knew their gifts would be a gamble. Wesley said something in XXL in black or white. Frank said anything in XXXL. Leon said a new shirt for interviews—white, then striped, and then he settled on blue.

After two and a half hours, three gift cards, and one awkward exchange with a guy in the men's section whom I misread, thinking he would be happier to render an opinion than he actually was, I left TJ Maxx feeling fairly confident about four of my five purchases. The next week, I had boxes for everyone: a shirt and tie for Leon; a sweater for Carlos by a designer I'd noticed he liked; a black slicker for Frank, who snuck out in short sleeves to smoke in the rain; an orange sweater for James, who wore more colors than the other boys; and a black zip-up sweater, size XXL, for Wesley.

I wrapped the boxes, hoped for the best, and braced myself for honest reactions.

LEON WAS ON the sidewalk in front of my usual spot as I parked between snowbanks. He said off the bat that he would carry the gifts upstairs. He checked the tags and took his and Frank's and Wesley's.

When he opened the door and announced "She brought the presents!" everyone poured into the TV room. The houseparent on duty lingered in the doorway to the staff office to watch the big reveal. "She even wrapped them!" he said. My stomach clenched like before a test.

As the boys opened their packages and compared items, each seemed to prefer his own, which I thought was a good sign.

"She got me a shirt and tie," Leon said, stroking the silk tie.

I told him it was for his next interview.

"I'm going to be all, *Excuse me, sir,*" he said. Leon unfolded the shirt and put it on his chest with the tie flung over his shoulder, holding the cuffs of the sleeves with his hands. He tucked his chin to hold the collar in place and made exaggerated gestures with his arms. "Yes, I'm here to make twelve dollars an hour . . . What's that you say? Fifteen? Okay, make it twenty!"

The other boys laughed and unfolded and refolded.

Wesley opened his box, closed it, and quickly brought it to his room.

"This is real nice," Carlos said softly. He lifted his sweater out of its box.

"Do you like it?" I asked him. "I remember you said that you liked that brand. I thought I could maybe see you wearing it." It was a gray zip-up with a small logo on the chest. "I guessed on the size. I can take it back to switch it for a bigger one if you want." I had gone back and forth between the L, XL, and XXL. I estimated that his true size was large, and that he wore his clothes big, but not as baggy as Wesley, so I went with XL.

He unzipped it, put it on, and zipped it up. He held out his arms to test the sleeves. "Nah, it's perfect," he said. "Thank you." Then he looked at Leon. "That's a real nice shirt and tie, LeBron."

Leon was putting on a show. He had expanded his bit to include a head bobble. "What's that?" He lifted a sleeve to his ear, smacked his lips. He was his own marionette. "I'm fancy? Yes, I'm fancy."

"Frank, do you like yours?" I asked him.

"Yeah," he said unconvincingly. "What is it?"

"What do you mean? Did you take it out of the box?" I looked at the closed box.

"Nah, but I saw it. It's shiny and black," he said. "What's it, a laundry bag?"

"Frank, it's a rain jacket!" I pulled it out of the box and held it up. "Since you're always going out to smoke in a T-shirt when it's raining," I explained. "It's plain black, XXXL, like you said. I thought it'd keep you dry on your secret smoke breaks and on the way to the laundromat."

He looked at me.

"Do you think you'll use it?" I asked.

"Nah," he said. "But it's cool."

"Oh, then give it back to me and I'll get you something else," I said. "Please."

"I might use it," he said. He took it from my hand, shoved it into the box, and tucked it under his arm.

"Really? Are you sure?" I asked. I was no longer convinced it was a good choice. I debated wrestling it away from him.

He looked at me, sighed, and brought it to his room.

I turned to James, who was sitting on the couch laughing at Leon, who was now doing a version of the robot, with the new shirt tucked over his shoulders and the tie tied Rambo style around his head. "What do you think of yours, James?" I'd picked something bright for him since he seemed to like Life Savers colors.

"I like it okay," he said.

"You don't really, do you?" I scrunched my nose.

"I mean, it's nice, but."

"I thought you might like a sweater," I said.

"It's nice, but I don't really have anywhere to wear something like that," he said apologetically. "I like the color, but it's kind of fancy."

"James, I can bring it back. No problem. I'd rather do that and get you something you'll actually wear," I said.

He got up and left without saying anything.

"Are we ever going to eat anything?" Frank asked. He was doing the thing he did in the doorway, hooking his fingers on the top of the wooden doorframe and sort of hanging forward.

I told him yes and followed him into the kitchen. We started quesadillas. While I was buttering the tortillas and Frank was cutting up chicken, James came in with three shirts folded over his arms.

"Like, these are the kind I like." They were rugby shirts in primary colors, with collars. "You could still get orange," he said.

"You don't have to say orange since I picked it," I said. "I can get a different color."

"No, I like the orange. I do." He paused. "I could just keep the sweater."

"No, I'm not letting you keep that terrible sweater," I said.

He smiled his gummy smile. "It's not terrible."

"Can I tell you something?" I asked James. He looked at me. I wanted to tell him that I am the worst gift getter, that I always return things that are given to me, and my poor mom and sisters are so patient about it. But how could I say this without sounding like I was flaunting that I have a mom and sisters who give me presents, and I'm so ungrateful I don't even appreciate the artifacts of their care? So I said, a little louder, "It's no problem to return it because I'm returning Frank's, too. I'll probably just sneak into his room and grab it from his desk since he won't give it to me."

James laughed and looked at Frank.

Frank looked at me and then at James. "She won't," he said.

"I might," I said. "I know which room is yours, Frank. You think I don't know things."

Frank sighed deeply. "I said I'm keeping it, dawg. I'm about to use it. Just finish the tortillas already 'cause this chicken's about to be done."

I was unsure whether Frank would ever wear the jacket, but I loved it when he called me dawg. Two weeks late, without lights or a manger in sight, it felt a lot like Christmas.

Help Is a Four-Letter Word

When Gerry invited me to dinner a couple of weeks later, I knew that in addition to discussing how cooking was going at the House, he'd also want to talk about the Christmas that made me hate Christmas. It was two Decembers ago already. I didn't want to talk about it.

The last time I spoke to my father, I was making my favorite Christmas cookies for my teacher friends at school. My godmother calls the cookies "snowballs" because they are round and white, embedded with walnuts, and dusted in powdered sugar. I had used her recipe, multiplying it by six and rolling the cookies smaller than usual, so there were hundreds of snowballs, a full storm of cookies on the stove. My hands had batter on them when my dad came home from dinner with my mom. I heard him come through the door and went over to meet him. I held out a sample for him to try and he said that he was having trouble breathing. He walked through the doorway and stopped to lean against a chair, to steady himself. I dropped the cookie onto the rug. I wiped my hands on my jeans, as if it mattered whether my hands were clean. I grabbed his shoulders. I guided his body down to the floor as he fell. In my memory, I see the intricate floral pattern of the rug surround my father's face, the flowers and their vines. This part repeats: him through the door, his face when he looks at me, into the living room, the chair, the stickiness of my hands, his eyes closed, how the rug swallows him. I cannot disentangle the memory from the taste of those cookies; powdered sugar makes me choke. Even when I re-dream the scene, I can never hold him up.

—

I MET GERRY at the restaurant across the street from the House, the same place we had dinner when I asked about starting the program. When I was in high school, the place had been a dive bar; now it was a trendy gastropub, with mood lighting, servers in dark glasses and high-waisted pants, and tap water that tasted like cucumber. I arrived late and told the hostess I was looking for an older man who could pass for an off-season Santa Claus, possibly in a plaid shirt. She nodded and led me straight to Gerry.

He stood to greet me with arms extended. "Well, well, well," he said.

We embraced, and I said, "Here we are, back where we began."

He said that was always the way. As I took off my coat, he told me that he had heard from one of the houseparents about the gifts.

I told him I had decided to go with shirts and sweaters. I thought I was three for five.

He said he heard that I was five for five.

I said the houseparent mustn't have seen the James negotiation or the Frank jacket fiasco.

"He said it was apparent from the choices you made that you know these young men, Elizabeth," Gerry said. He is one of the only people who call me Elizabeth. He paused. "The houseparent said, 'She knows them.' He said, 'You can tell she's Charlie's daughter, Gerry.'" His voice was wistful.

It physically hurt to listen to people talk about my dad, especially at that two-year mark when the freeze of grief was thawing, and everything felt like something, and it all stung.

"Do you think it's the giant forehead," I asked, referring to how similar my face is to my father's, "that gives me away as his daughter?" Multiple houseparents who'd known my father had commented to me that I looked like him. Once, Leon came to my defense and said it was "kind of messed up for someone to tell a girl she looks like a dude." I assured him that I had heard it before and didn't mind. Fighting the truth was a losing battle.

"I think it's much more than that," Gerry said. His eyes were glossy with tears.

I knew Gerry missed my father. For over thirty-three years they had worked together in the trenches of human services, in that same brick building. They had served hundreds of youth surviving the havoc of systematic inequalities and savagely unfair lives. For one battle over state funding and the institutionalization of young people, Gerry had literally chained himself to the gates of the state-house in protest. My dad was there, too, but not in chains. My dad was a do-the-duty-closest-to-you guy, not a dramatic, big-gesture person. He was the Sancho Panza to Gerry's Don Quixote, the pragmatic optimist to Gerry's visionary.

And I knew I reminded Gerry of my father, more than just the way my face echoed his, the way I stammer like he used to when I'm trying to say something I haven't said out loud before, and the way I'm also always late. More than once when I answered one of Gerry's questions, he had said, "Now see there, that is something your father would say."

What I didn't know that evening, sitting across the table from Gerry, was that the future of the House was uncertain. I knew that the agency's operating budget was contingent upon placements, that there were fluctuations in numbers of kids and how long they would stay, and that those placements were impossible to predict. I remembered the urgency and speculation from the decades that my father maneuvered the budgets, but I didn't know until much later how many years there had been without raises. I've never understood the way that salaries are so vastly incommensurate with work; it doesn't make sense that some people are paid so little to do so much.

I listened that night as Gerry told me that he sensed a shift coming in the infrastructure of managed care, and how this would likely have ramifications for the agency. I listened as he explained who the major players were and what discussions were on the table. I listened, and nodded as if I understood. But I didn't think it was possible that the agency wouldn't endure whatever changes were on the horizon. The world of human services was always in flux; there were always changes—more money, less money, new policies, different leadership. The agency had always survived the changes. It was inconceivable to think that the House could ever close.

We toasted.

I held up my gin and tonic. "To a new year and new beginnings!"

Gerry touched his glass to mine and sipped his ruby wine. Then he asked me about school and Christmas, and I answered in anecdotes and rhetorical questions. When the bread came, we broke it. He circled back to Tuesdays with the boys.

"I felt terribly about that night that Carlos's mother crashed our dinner," I said. "He was so angry, I thought something was going to happen between him and the other boys. I wanted to tell her to leave but didn't think it was my place. And the houseparent didn't say anything. And Carlos just sat there in the TV room, watching her from the doorway."

Gerry listened as I remembered the night.

"When she told James 'Nah, baby, I got that,' it made me so mad," I admitted. *"Nah, baby, I got that* is, like, the opposite of what I'm going for with this whole thing."

Gerry laughed his low laugh.

"I'm serious! And then on her way out, she told me that she thought all of the mothers should get involved. And I sort of nodded, but I don't think that's a good idea; it's not really what I had in mind. Plus it was so unhelpful for Carlos. Do you think it would be a good idea, to get the mothers involved?"

"What mothers?" Gerry answered my question with a question.

I started to say something and then sipped my drink instead.

He took a sip of his, then asked, "How do you feel it is going otherwise?"

"Well, it's mostly forced labor if you ask Frank," I said.

He laughed. "Frank Jones," Gerry said, using his whole name. "He is a unique individual."

"He is," I said. "You know, I told him that he's my best helper."

"Is that right?" Gerry asked.

"Hands down," I said. "And when I told him, you know what he said?"

Gerry looked at me, his eyebrows furrowed.

"That yeah, he knows already, and could I please keep it on the down low."

Gerry laughed a firecracker laugh.

"Apparently, Frank doesn't want to wreck his reputation at the House by people finding out he *helps*," I said. The lime and fizz of my drink tingled against my tongue. "Because *help* is a four-letter word."

Gerry nodded. " 'Help' is a four-letter word."

"*Help* is apparently on the very short list of four-letter words that are the unspeakable ones in the House. Like *love*. And *hope*," I said. Gerry nodded. I took a drink. "Except about food—also four letters. I can ask for help in the kitchen. Frank is open about his love for cheese. Leon hopes against hope that we have brownie sundaes and I remember the cherries." Dinner was a parallel world where there could be unabashed love, the give-and-take of help, the expression of hope for a possible future. At dinner, at least one kind of hunger could be satiated. There could be enough, for a few minutes. "And you know," I continued, "Leon Williams continues to be a super-star."

Gerry nodded that he knew.

"Could we find a stipend for him as project manager?" I asked, only sort of kidding. "He keeps everyone on track. Or tries to."

Gerry laughed.

"And I refuse to give up on Wesley Not Applicable," I said, a reference to his first-night survey.

"Wesley Not Applicable." Gerry shook his head. "That says it all, now, doesn't it?" He paused. "Does he come to the cooking sessions?"

"Most of the time!" I said. "He's not what we'd call a helper per se. But he's definitely an eater, and occasionally a conversationalist."

Gerry nodded appreciatively.

"I don't know very much about James," I said. "He seems withdrawn."

"Withdrawn," Gerry repeated, as if to taste the word again. I thought he might say more about James, but he didn't. "Indeed; he is withdrawn."

I kept talking. About food and memory, fried chicken and white-ness. About Leon's desire for me to get a clicker for my car; Frank's fear of birthday candles and the disappointment of unanswered wishes; James's encounter with the stranger who thought he knew his father; Carlos's perfect lattice piecrust; and Wesley's theory about getting what we deserve, and the space we all have in our stomachs for dessert.

Gerry sat, listening, finishing his salad. "They are all exquisitely unique individuals."

I agreed, even though there was so much that I didn't know.

The server brought our check tucked into a small notebook and explained that we should write on a page about our meal.

"What did she say, now?" Gerry asked when she stepped away.

"That we could write about our meal," I said.

"We could fill the whole thing with what we have talked about," he said. "And more." He put on his glasses to read the bill.

"Gerry," I asked, "how sick is Leon?"

He looked up at me. "What was that?"

I didn't know if it was that he hadn't heard me in the noisy restau-rant or that I shouldn't have asked. "Leon Williams," I said. "He's talked about doctor appointments and his eyes. And alludes to things he thinks I know. But I don't know. I get that he's sick, but how sick?"

Gerry held up the little book. "I would need three of these," he said. He slid his credit card into the cover and the server swooped it away. "Leon is a very sick young man," Gerry said. "But that is a story for another time."

I nodded, as if it was enough of an answer.

Gerry took his last sip of wine. "Now, are you thinking that you would like to continue this cooking program of yours? Into the new year?" He looked at me. "Has it been the experience you were look-ing for?"

I couldn't say what I thought cooking would be when I asked for permission to do it. I didn't know how long it would last, or how long I wanted it to last. But I knew that Frank was ready to help make steak bombs the following Tuesday. And Leon was hoping for brownie sundaes, with cherries. And I knew that I liked being there, making dinners with the boys and talking to Gerry about things that felt real, participating in a sliver of the life that had once belonged to my dad. I knew it was about cooking, but I was slowly discovering that the project was also about belonging. I answered Gerry's question with a question. "Does this mean I've passed my trial period?"

He laughed. "It seems that it does." And it seemed like it did, the way a thing can seem one way right up until it becomes another. It was the end of a beginning. And the beginning of another end.

PART 2

ENTERTAINING ANGELS

But don't forget to be friendly to outsiders; for in so doing, some people, without knowing it, have entertained angels.
—*Hebrews 13:2, The Complete Jewish Bible*

The ache for home lives in all of us, the safe place where we can go as we are and not be questioned.
—*Maya Angelou*

Why don't you see if you can stick it out.
—*Charlie Hauck, on taking sick days and quitting, never in the form of a question*

Test Kitchen

They say the more things change, the more they stay the same, but I have found that to be true only about kitchens, churches, and convenience stores, which look similar on the inside wherever they are. One late January morning when the air was crisp like paper, I found myself sick, sitting in my parked car in the tiny lot of the 7-Eleven near the House. It was the same store I had gone to for chips or candy and soda so many afternoons after art class in high school, waiting for my dad to finish work and drive us home.

Three school years into teaching, I was still not accustomed to the inundation of germs that infested my classroom in waves in the winter. My head was pounding, my nose was leaking. I could feel my pulse in my thumbs. I was talking to my sister on my cellphone. "Do you need me to bring you anything?" she asked.

My younger, not youngest, sister, Juli, has the amazing tendency to answer the phone almost every time I call her. "Where are you?" she'll say as she picks up, knowing I often call while lost on highways, asking for directions, describing vague indicators of where I am. Her sense of direction is as good as mine is bad; when we were younger, our differences were the sources of our fights but somehow over time they have become how we help to orient each other.

I told her I didn't need anything, that I was about to grab a few items and then go home to sleep. I asked her how things were going with her boyfriend.

"They're good," she said. They were serious; it was strange to think that she would marry a man who had never met our dad.

A shadow fell across my lap. I looked up to see a hooded figure looming over me. Then I recognized him: Frank was squinting at me through my driver's side window.

"Someone's at my car," I said. "I have to go."

"What?" she asked. "Are you okay?"

"Yeah, I'm fine," I said. "It's one of the kids. I'm going to go."

"One of your students?"

"No, one of the kids from Community Care," I explained, using the old name of the agency. I had told my mom and siblings about my cooking project in broad terms like "dad" and "comfort food." I preemptively addressed their skepticism with Gerry's we-can-stop-at-any-time time frame. I was five months into it, and nobody had asked any follow-up questions. Still lodged in the fog of grief, we were all busy at trying to be busy enough to at least feel busy.

"Okay, bye, call me later," she said. "Love you." At some point she decided this was a thing we should say out loud to each other, so she introduced it into the family lexicon.

"Love you, too," I said, pulling my wallet from my schoolbag.

Frank watched me put my phone away and unsnap my seatbelt and stepped away from the car just enough to let me squeeze by.

We faced each other on the pavement. There was no hello or a how-are-you. But what we lacked in pleasantries, we made up for in situational irony.

"Aren't you supposed to be in school?" he asked me first.

"Yeah," I said. "The nurse sent me home, because I'm sick." I sniffled to increase my credibility. "Aren't *you* supposed to be in school, too, Frank?"

He squinted into the sun. "Yeah, I left early," he said. "I was tired."

Greg, the houseparent, had told me that Frank had been cutting school. Except that instead of skipping the whole day, he was going for math class and leaving after that.

"I thought that was your whip," Frank said, nodding toward my car.

"Where's your winter coat, Frank? Aren't you cold?" I was surprised that he stopped.

"Nah, I'm not cold," he said. He blinked. He didn't walk away.

"I was just going to go into the store, to get some ginger ale and stuff," I said. "Do you want a drink or some food?"

He blinked. "Okay. A Red Bull?"

We walked into the store, almost shoulder to shoulder. Frank was shorter and broader than I was, but not by much; when we turned to talk to each other, we were nearly eye to eye.

The clerk watched us come in. He flashed me a look of concern.

"Good morning." I nodded, greeting him as we moved toward the drink aisle.

"You know him?" Frank asked me, loud enough for the clerk to hear.

"Not really," I said in a lowered voice, scanning the shelves for the items on my list: ginger ale, orange Gatorade, chicken noodle soup. The aisles felt narrower than I remembered them; I knew it was a trick of memory, the way that time shrinks and expands the familiar.

Frank kept looking over his shoulder at the clerk. "That dude's still looking at you."

I looked across the store to the counter. The clerk was staring at us. I could see in his eyes that the clerk thought I was in trouble. I read his concern for me as rooted in assumptions he seemed to be making about Frank rather than anything about my behavior that suggested that I was in trouble. Meanwhile, Frank was concerned for me because he could feel the clerk's gaze on me and couldn't make sense of it. "You think he thinks I'm about to steal this Gatorade?" I asked Frank, nodding toward the energy drink I'd tucked under my armpit so I could fit the cans of soup and liters of soda in my hands.

"Could be," Frank said, staring back at the clerk, who then looked away.

"Want to grab your drink?" I said as we stood in front of the case with energy drinks.

Frank lifted a slim silver can and turned it to see the price tag. He started to put it back.

"Isn't that the one you wanted?" I asked.

"It's 2.99," he said.

"That's okay. Do you want something to eat, too?" I asked.

"Nah, just this," he said.

We went to check out and I unloaded my armful of salt and plastic. Frank placed his can on the counter in front of himself, then slid it toward my pile with one finger, a quick, quiet slide.

The clerk kept checking us out as he scanned our things. The *ding* of the scan-gun sounded loud. He handed me the bag and I thanked him, eager to exit the store.

Out in the parking lot, Frank and I faced each other like before, but this time with stuff in our hands. The crystal bits in the pavement under our feet glittered in the sun.

"Are you sure you don't want anything to eat?" I asked him again.

"Nah, just this," he said, holding up the can. "So I could wake up."

"And go back to school?" I asked, scrunching my nose and smiling at him.

"Maybe," he said. He smiled back at me, his real smile, lifting the can to hide the gap between his front teeth. "Probably not." He snapped the can open and it gasped.

"Yeah, me neither," I said. I inhaled the morning air.

"Well," Frank said finally, as if it was enough of a salutation, like *Goodbye* or *See you later*. He extended a fist toward me, easily, as if this was something we had done before.

I shifted both bags into my left hand and pushed my right fist toward his.

"Okay," I said, touching our knuckles together for a second. "Be safe."

He nodded and then turned away.

"See you Tuesday, Frank," I said, as if it wasn't a question.

"Yup," he replied, his back to me, already slicing through the morning toward the House.

THE NEXT WEEK, Frank was in the kitchen when I reached the top step. He opened the door, washed his hands, and helped me unpack the ingredients for steak-and-cheese subs.

"So you're from Randolph?" I asked him as we stood at the stove with our backs to the snow falling outside the kitchen windows. January was almost over; so far, it was one of the least snowy winters in history. But it was too soon to know what February and March would bring, other than birthdays. Frank's birthday was in February, and Leon's and Carlos's were in March. The menus were already set. (Mine was in March, too, but it wasn't on the agenda.)

"I'm not from Randolph. Why you think that?" Frank asked me, laughing at the thought that he might be from the suburb.

"Oh, I thought you were from Randolph. Where are you from?" I tried to redirect. Leon wasn't around and Wesley had come for milk and left with laundry. It was the two of us in the kitchen, Frank pulling apart the shredded steak and dropping it into the frying pan a pile at a time, me at the counter perpendicular to him, slicing peppers and onions for steak bombs.

"But why you think I was from there? Randolph?" He was amused. He lifted the knife and turned to me as if we were in a cooking show and this was part of a bit.

"I don't know," I said. "Because you said something before, about playing outside, and about how there are mad trees in Randolph. A while ago, when everybody was talking. You told a story about being outside when you were really little, and the trees. So I thought that maybe that's where you're from."

"Nah, I'm not from there. I mean, I *lived* there. But I'm not *from* there." He turned back to the meat.

"Oh, I just thought maybe, when you said you were little and lived there . . ." I rinsed the Styrofoamy mushrooms and dropped them into a bowl.

"I lived so many places," Frank said, adjusting the dial for heat. "But I'm not *from* any of 'em."

How many places? I wanted to ask. *What do you remember about them? What did you eat and play when you were little? Who was there?* Instead, I put the second frying pan on the burner next to his and spun the heat to medium. I pointed to the dial that required pliers to move because someone broke it, which sat on top of the refrigerator like a tease, so close to where it was supposed to be. "You think anyone is ever going to fix that dial?" I asked.

"Probably not, dawg," Frank said. He lifted the steak with the spatula and shook it to let some of the grease fall through the slots before putting it onto a paper plate. He started the next batch of meat. "You remembered the cheese?" he asked me.

"I did," I said. "The sliced kind everybody likes. I brought extra, just in case." I left the onions and peppers to simmer in the pan and unwrapped the cube of cheese by the side of the sink. I peeled a piece off the top and offered it to him. "Want one?"

He took a slice of American between his thumb and index finger and ate it in three folded bites. The outside door opened then slammed, and the stairs creaked as somebody climbed them. Leon opened the door. Frank nodded at him, and Leon nodded back.

"I'm back from school," Leon announced. "It's mad cold outside. You're lucky you're inside." He and James were enrolled in a job-training program in a different part of the city, a train and two buses away from the House. "What're we making?"

"We, dawg?" Frank said, moving the third plate of steak to the top of the bookcase in the kitchen that we used as our ready station.

"Subs?" Leon asked. "I love it when we make subs. I'm about to put my jacket away and come make us brownies." He pinched a slice of cheese off the stack on his way to his room.

I pulled the brownie pan from the cabinet, washed it, and set it to the side of the sink. "I think he meant he loves it when you make subs," I told Frank.

Frank shook his head and finished the last batch of meat. He put the pan in the sink and it sizzled, then he squirted a blue blob of soap onto it and let the water run. "Want me to do the mushrooms?" he asked, watching the bubbles grow.

"Sure," I said. I transferred the onions and peppers onto a plate and set it next to the meat.

Leon returned, pushed up his sleeves, and started making the brownies on the short stretch of counter next to the sink. He did an impression of a student in his class, bopping his head back and forth. Frank laughed and I laughed, and Leon laughed at himself.

Carlos came into the kitchen with hard eyes and dirty hands. He stood at the sink washing them, talking to himself but loud enough for us to hear. "These fuckin' people don't know what they're talking about. They fucking think that—"

"Hey, Carlos, is everything okay?" I asked. Sometimes he cursed at the other boys in Spanish. Sometimes I would ask him in Spanish to watch what he was saying and he'd dare me in English, "Oh, I forget that you understand it. I don't care, tell them what I'm saying." More than once, I'd seen one or the other of his eyes black-and-blue. When I'd ask him what happened, he'd tell me to mind my own business.

It was unclear who *they* were or what they didn't know they were talking about, but with every *fucking,* Carlos's voice got louder.

Frank and Leon looked at each other, then at me.

"Hey, Carlos, we're kind of trying to keep it clean in here," I said, which mostly meant trying not to swear or call each other gay as an insult.

"I don't need to listen to another fucking white bitch telling me what to fucking do," Carlos announced to the drain, and to all of us.

Leon widened his eyes and looked at me. Frank looked down.

"Want to maybe take a break then come back for dinner, Carlos?" I suggested. I knew it was his place and not mine, but I felt like I had to say something. "We're having steak-and-cheese subs. There's one for you, if you want it."

"I'm already leaving anyway," he said. Then he left.

Leon, Frank, and I stood for a minute before we resumed cooking.

"He shouldn't've said that to you," Leon said to me apologetically.

"Nobody likes that dude," Frank added, drying the frying pan.

"I don't think it's really about me," I said. I didn't want the boys to see me as just another white female teacher, social worker, probation officer, counselor, lawyer, or judge trying to save or punish them. But I knew that I fit into that kind of familiar, transient anonymity and cumulative stress. With Carlos especially, I sometimes felt like a face with a voice and hands, filling a role. It wasn't easy to not take it personally because they were my face, my voice, my hands. But working with teenagers had taught me that particular kind of target practice.

"At the same time," Leon said, looking at Frank, then at me, "it was definitely about you. No offense." He wanted to make sure that I understood the exchange. "Carlos shouldn't've said it, but he did. The first part was about the staff. The second part was *definitely* about *you*."

Frank nodded quietly in agreement as he jabbed at the shards of steak in the hot pan as they sizzled from pink into brown.

I appreciated that Frank and Leon were looking out for me and thanked them for it. But I didn't want Carlos to hear us from the hallway and think we were against him. I had the sense he already felt that way. We got back to cooking and talking about normal things, like how many maraschino cherries a person can eat before throwing up. Leon thought two jars, and he was willing to try.

Carlos didn't come back for dinner that night, and he stayed away the next week. The week after that, he came into the kitchen to look in the fridge while I was cutting vegetables and Leon was making brownies. I told Carlos he was welcome to soda if he wanted some and asked if he'd be around for dinner. He said he didn't know. I told him that there was plenty of food and hoped he knew that he was welcome whenever he wanted. I said I knew that he knew how to talk to people, and that everybody has bad nights. He walked away.

But then he came back to the table. Even though people had seen him in the kitchen and could hear him rumbling in his room, nobody set a place for him. He came in and sat down quietly, with a flag of surrender in the form of a white paper plate and plastic utensils.

WEATHER AND OTHER conditions shifted the week before Frank's birthday in February. A Valentine's Day blizzard left snow on the ground, piled high on sidewalks, with dirty, icy snowcaps, and Frank changed his mind about candles. There was no more talk of wishes, but he established that he did want the number kind for his Funfetti cupcakes.

"I do want candles," Frank told me while cutting the chicken into his signature blocks.

"Okay," I told him.

"What numbers you going to get anyway?" It sounded like a trick question.

"Well, how old are you going to be?" I couldn't remember what he had written on the little birthday sheet from the first night.

"Fifteen," he said.

"So, I'll get a one and a five, then?" I said, still feeling like there was a catch.

"Yeah," he said. "Get those."

"Dude is going to be *four*teen not *fif*teen," Wesley interjected, coming around the corner, appearing out of nowhere.

"Wait, what?" I was confused. "Frank, how old are you now?"

"Fourteen," Frank said, emphasizing the *four*.

"Dude's *thir*teen. Dude's lying about his age," Wesley said to me, not Frank. Wesley was always more willing to provide information about other people than about himself.

"I'm not lying, dawg," Frank told me. It was always serious when he called me dawg. "I'm not lying, Wes," he snapped. Then he turned to me, softened his tone, repeating, "I'm not."

"Okay, Frank. I was just asking because I don't know how old you are," I said.

"So what candles you getting?" he narrowed his eyes and asked.

"One and five," I said, not as a question this time.

"Yeah," he said.

Later, I went downstairs to the offices to ask Arlette. "They're both right." She laughed. "We don't know for sure when Frank's birthday is. He says he's fourteen, he's been consistent about that. We think he's thirteen by some of the school records. But we don't know for sure."

"What about his birth certificate?" I asked, too quickly.

She nodded and then shrugged. "That would be helpful. If we had one."

"How can there be no birth certificate? Here, or at any of the schools? On file somewhere?" I asked, kept asking.

Arlette tilted her head and looked at me, one eyebrow raised. The discussion was over.

"Okay." I nodded as if I understood. "So, I'm thinking get a one and a five?"

Arlette laughed her big, deep laugh. "You do that."

On Frank's birthday, I lit the 1 and the 5 and arranged the cupcakes into an *F*. And when Leon asked Frank if we should sing, Frank said yes.

"But leave the lights on, dawg," Frank said, as if lights could keep wishes at bay.

THE NEXT WEEK my grades were due in school, so on cooking night I brought meatballs from one of the restaurants my sister managed to make subs, to save time; she donated them to the cause. Dinner went quick; Leon and Frank ate and left to do laundry and probably smoke. By the time Wesley came back to the House, the others were gone and I was wrapping things up at the table.

"Do you want a sub?" I asked him.

"Nah, I'm not even hungry," he said quickly.

"If you want one, I'll make it," I said.

Wesley assessed the ingredients on the table.

"Meatball. Want one?" I asked again.

"If you make it, yeah," he said. "Thanks."

When Wesley sat to eat it, I sat across from him. I asked questions about school and he answered in mmhmms and uh-huhs. We heard Carlos come up the front stairs and check in with the staff.

"Want to make Carlos a sub?" I asked hopefully.

"I'm not making him anything. 'Cause I'm not gay," he added, as if his logic followed.

"What?" I asked.

"You heard me," he told me. He wiped his mouth with a napkin.

I had heard him. "Well, I must be really gay, because I just made four sandwiches!"

"It's not the same, yo." Wesley laughed.

"If making one sandwich would make you gay, then making four sandwiches must make me *really* gay," I said.

He shook his head. "You know what I mean."

"Right," I said, opening another soft sub roll with my thumbs.

"It's different for girls," he clarified.

"Because girls are supposed to serve people," I finished the thought.

"You know what I mean," Wesley said, laughing.

"So is that really a no on a sub for Carlos?" I asked.

"Uh, yeah. It's really a no." He shook his head. "Besides, people like Carlos is one of my hot spots. So I can't anyway."

"What's a hot spot?" I asked.

"My counselor said things that I know make me angry are my hot spots, and I've got to stay away from them so I don't get in trouble," he explained. "So I stay away from that dude."

I couldn't argue with that but wouldn't let it go. "Maybe next time," I said.

"Maybe not." Wesley laughed. He crumpled his plate and stood up. Before he left, he said, "But thanks, though. For the sandwich."

I heard Carlos rooting around in the refrigerator and met him in the kitchen.

"Hey, Carlos, I can make you a meatball sub if you're hungry," I offered. "It's what we had tonight. The plan was for people to make their own, or make them for each other, but I pretty much made all of them."

He looked at me, for the catch.

"Want one?" I asked. "I think there's a whole soda left, too."

He shrugged.

"Do you want cheese?" I asked, already on my way to the tray of meatballs.

As I made the sandwich, he disappeared into the pantry and returned with two paper towels. When I finished lining the roll with a fourth triangle of cheese, Carlos held out his hands with the paper towels instead of a plate and I placed the sub gently between them.

"Thanks, Liz," he said, as if he had known my name all along.

THAT NIGHT, I met a houseparent named Leonard whom the boys called Prof because he taught history for his day job. Tall, thin, and Black, with salt-and-pepper hair and wire-rimmed glasses, he looked the part of a professor. When I was running late, or Prof was running early, we crossed paths.

"You Charlie's girl?" Prof asked me.

"I am," I said. "Did you know my dad?" I followed him into the TV room. He sat on the couch and gestured for me to sit, too.

He nodded. "People tell you ya look like him?"

I nodded.

"You look just like him." Prof folded his hands. "He was a good man, your pops."

My throat tightened. I nodded. "He was a good man."

"Hey, Prof, how much you think I could get for this?" James came in with a suit hung on a hanger hooked over his hand. James hadn't been around for the past few dinners.

"Hey, James," I said. "Want a sub? The boys are done, but I'd make you one if you want."

"No, thanks. I already ate," he said to me. "How much you think, Prof?"

"That's a nice suit," Prof said. "Maybe fifty dollars?"

"It is nice," I agreed. "Shouldn't you keep it in case you need it for something?"

James shook his head at me and asked Prof, "That's it? You don't think I could get more? I only wore it once or something."

Prof shrugged. James left. I just sat there.

FOR LEON'S BIRTHDAY in March, we had stir-fry chicken with rice and vegetables and ice cream sundaes. Leon insisted that he shouldn't have to help because he was the one being celebrated. Frank said that this wasn't fair since he had cut chicken for his own birthday dinner. Leon told us we were lucky that he was planning to make biscuits anyway, and that he had to be the one to make the rice so it came out the way he liked it.

When the time came for dessert, Leon shut the lights off himself and sang along as everybody sang to him. "Happy birrrrrrrthday dear LeBro-on! Happy birthday to meeeeeeeeeeeee!" He sang the loudest.

Carlos was on Kitchen A, so he had to wash the dishes that night. I stayed to help, as I said I would, even though Leon reminded me that I shouldn't help him "after the whole bitch thing." I reminded Leon that people deserve second chances, and he told me that nobody was ever trying to give him chances.

I washed and Carlos dried, careful not to let water drip on his sneakers.

"Now that right there is a good pan," he said of the coated frying pan I'd bought after a disastrous attempt at omelets. "You don't have to scrub it real hard or nothing."

"You really like it? It's Teflon." Good was a four-letter word I hadn't heard Carlos say.

"The rest of the pans here are mad cheap," he declared.

"Well." I didn't disagree. I rinsed.

"Everything here is cheap," he continued.

I handed him the pan, watched the water beads roll. "You know, Teflon kills some birds."

"What?" he asked, taking it from me.

"Seriously. I'm pretty sure that Teflon kills canaries when it's heated to a certain temperature. I think I read that. They die from the fumes; it's like their kryptonite."

"That's messed up." He laughed, looking at the pan. "Are you taking it with you?"

"No, I was going to leave it," I said. "You weren't here when we made breakfast for dinner, but it was a mess. The eggs all stuck to that big frying pan. Frank was really nice about it, but it wasn't great. I thought if I got this one, people could use it instead."

Carlos nodded that he approved, putting the pan down and then drying his hands on a paper towel. "You probably drink when you leave here, huh," he said, turning to leave.

I laughed. I thought he was kidding.

"Do you?" he asked me seriously.

When I asked him questions, Carlos usually answered in monosyllables or shrugs like the other boys, but sometimes he offered a little bit more: he had other siblings; he used the money he earned to buy sneakers; he spoke Spanish but didn't like the school kind, no offense. And, yeah, he did kind of like baking. The only time he asked me questions was at the sink, when I was washing and he was drying. It was a kitchen mercy, the ease of that space by the sink.

"Not usually." I shrugged. "I like coming to hang out with you guys and cook."

"That's a lie," he said. Carlos never seemed to trust my answers, but he listened for them.

"Hey, your birthday's coming up," I said. "Do you still want what you wrote on the paper the first night?" I remembered it was his birthday because it was close to my birthday. I was going to be twenty-nine. When I was younger, I had flagged twenty-eight as the starting year for being a real grown-up—someone with a house, a husband, a meaningful job. I imagined that life must galvanize by then, that you become who you're supposed to be, and you know it.

"What'd I write?" Carlos asked. He bit his thumbnail as he listened for his answer.

"Ice cream cake, I think," I said. "And I think you specified with chocolate cookie crumbles." Now I knew I was wrong about my grown-up fantasy. I was twenty-eight and decidedly not galvanized. I lived in an apartment, had no husband, and wasn't convinced I was doing what I was supposed to be doing with my life. And all I could think on my birthday that year was that by the time my father was my age, he had lived half his life already, and he had no idea.

"Yeah, that's my favorite," Carlos said. "I mean, I don't have it that much, but I like it."

"Sounds good," I said, shutting the faucet off. "See you next week?"

"Probably," he said, tossing the paper towel into the trash can and flicking his hand up into a wave. "See ya."

I MADE AN ice cream cake in my own kitchen and brought it to the House for Carlos's birthday dinner; I didn't think it would have time to set otherwise. I pressed a gallon of Oreo ice cream into a pan, spread a layer of hot fudge and smashed Oreo crumbles in the middle, added a gallon of vanilla, and then frosted it with whipped cream. I wrote *Carlos* in cookie pieces. He said it was just what he wanted. He smiled big as he blew out the 1 and 6 candles.

I was shocked when I learned Carlos was gone a few weeks later. "He's not-here gone, or like gone-gone?" I asked finally, when we had all sat down to dinner and Carlos never came.

"Gone-gone," Frank clarified.

"When did he leave?" I asked. "Where did he go?"

"He's dead," somebody said.

"He died?" I gasped.

Somebody laughed.

"Oh, I get it, not really," I said. "But really, then where did he go?"

"Nobody knows," Leon said.

"Nobody cares," Wesley said. "People talked to him when you were around, but that doesn't mean that people talked to him."

Open Wounds

James was next to leave. He left and then came back and then left again for good; he was the only one with two last dinners. It was late March; you could feel the sun on your cheeks, not just see it, and things were finally growing.

The last time I saw James was in the kitchen, in between times he ran away. People say "run away" and it conjures the image of a person running. A body in motion: there's speed and drama in it. Maybe it's like that sometimes. But sometimes, it's just one hand over the other putting things in a bag, methodically, like adding ingredients to a mixing bowl, and then one foot in front of the other until you're out the door, down the street, and eventually someplace else.

That's how it was with James. James, who didn't say much and spoke in a voice just louder than a whisper. James, who kept his hair cut close to his head and wore candy-colored shirts with turned-down collars. James, whose smile was a subtle, gummy glimmer. James, who sliced his hand open while thawing a frozen hamburger with a knife, starting everything.

When I asked where James was, the other boys said what they'd said about Carlos: dead.

"Come on, you guys," I pleaded. "Where is he?"

"*Come on, you guys,*" Wesley mimicked.

"Dude's dead," Frank said.

"No, seriously."

"*No, seriously,*" Wesley said, "he's across the street," referring to the funeral home that faced the House.

I asked if he had packed a bag, or if he told anyone where he was going. Everyone was quiet. There were six days between cooking nights, plenty of time for plenty to happen. I asked Leon, since he and James took the bus together to their job-training program. I thought if anyone would know, Leon would, and if anyone might tell me, Leon might.

"One day he just didn't come back here," Leon said. "He started staying with these people who were doing stuff," he began, reluctantly relating a longer story, elaborating on the stuff. "And I told him, man, that shit's going to get you in trouble."

Two weeks later, as Leon mixed brownies and I cut vegetables, James walked into the kitchen. I was so relieved when I saw his face that I opened my arms and exclaimed, "James! Welcome back!" Before I could drop my arms to my sides and regain my usual posture and safe distance, James walked into my hug. His fingertips touched my back.

"Thanks," he said quietly, before we both let go.

Leon, mixing and watching, said, "What? Now, why does this dude get a hug? I been here the whole time and nobody's trying to give me loving. You're a hater, Liz. I see how it is. That's not right." He walked out of the kitchen in protest, only half joking.

I started to wash the dishes for whoever was on Kitchen A. James picked up the bowl with the remnants of brownie batter, licked the spatula, and then asked if he could have it. He leaned against the counter, next to me at the sink, like he had the time before. When he bent to move his mouth toward the spatula, I saw a gash on the back of his neck below his hairline. It looked like a gob of fresh pink bubble gum smeared across pavement.

"James, that looks terrible. How did it happen?" I'd heard a version of the story.

"I was sleeping on the couch where I was staying," he said. "And this dude was smoking, and I guess he wanted to see if I would wake up if he put it on my neck."

"Put what on your neck?" I asked. When Leon met me on the sidewalk to bring the groceries up, he had told me that James was back because he had gotten burned with a crack pipe. He hadn't said the burn was on James's neck or that he had been sleeping.

"A cigarette or something," James said.

I didn't say I'd heard otherwise. I asked, "Did you wake up?"

"Yeah, I woke up. 'Cause it hurt like hell," he said, licking the spatula between words.

"You woke up to being burned? Where were you? Did you know the guy?" I asked.

"Yeah, I knew him," he said, not looking at me.

"Why would he do this? What did your friend say?" I kept looking at his neck.

He shrugged, moving the spoon to his mouth in one fell swoop. He was done talking about it.

"Does it still hurt?" I asked.

He shrugged.

"Are you supposed to have it covered? It could get dirty. You wouldn't want it to get infected . . ." I continued my monologue. "You know what might help? Cocoa butter."

"What?" he asked, apparently listening.

"Cocoa butter. It'll soothe the sting a little and prevent a scar from forming."

"You think I should put butter on it?" he asked, finishing the batter.

"Well, not butter, cocoa butter," I said. "Seriously, it works. It'll smooth the wound and help your skin to heal. There won't be a scar. Or there'll be less of one."

He shrugged his shrug. "Okay, if it works. I could try it." He kept swiping the bowl.

"Yeah, I know it works," I started. I debated whether I should share my cocoa butter story; I offered it as proof. "I had a burn on my cheek once." I told him an abbreviated version of the story. "I was walking with my dad to one of my brother's baseball games. I was fourteen and talking, and my dad was listening and smoking a cigar. I asked him a question, and when he turned to answer it, the cigar he was clenching in his teeth burned my cheek. The skin sizzled. I heard it. It left this perfect crispy circle on the side of my face." I traced a circle on my cheek.

"That's messed up," James interjected.

"My grandmother told him to get me cocoa butter, so he did. It smelled like chocolate, felt like margarine, and in like two weeks, smoothed the burn to nothing. It was basically erased." I pointed to my scarless cheek. I thought I had sold the product with *erase*. I didn't usually tell my own stories in the kitchen, but that night felt different. James was hurt and listening. I kept talking so he wouldn't walk away.

"That's real messed up," he said again. He shook his head and licked the spoon. "Your father burned you like that."

My face flushed. I wanted to backtrack. My father hadn't burned me on purpose. I knew he hadn't meant to hurt me and that he felt terrible about it. But given the situation of James's injury and his larger circumstances, how could I try to make him understand my father's remorse or emphasize how deeply I knew that my dad would never intentionally have harmed me? I shrugged. "I'm pretty sure it was an accident," I downplayed. "His apology was implied in his tone of voice when he shouted, 'Oh shit!' when it happened."

James laughed and shook his head when I imitated my dad swearing. He took one more lick, then he put the spatula into the bowl and the bowl into the sink. Now he was really done.

The next day, I bought a small tub of cocoa butter and gave it to Gerry to give to James.

And I remembered the part of my cocoa butter memory that I hadn't shared at the sink. After the cancer surgery that was supposed to buy my dad more time, he had a scar that stretched from the middle of his back along his waist above his beltline to the front, then up the side of his torso, and then hooked under his armpit, to the back. His body looked like he'd been sawed in half, because he'd been sawed in half. I suggested cocoa butter for the scars and reminded him about the burn incident, and how he'd finished smoking the cigar as my skin was peeling off. "Because"—I quoted his own words back to him—"the harm was already done. No point in wasting a good cigar."

He stood behind his logic and joked that for his surgery scars, he'd need a barrel of cocoa butter. "The industrial bucket size they use in ice cream shops! I'd need a scoop!" He chuckled. And why did he need to fix his scars anyway, he asked, dismissing vanity he had no use for. In the event that someone called from a Frankenstein-of-the-month calendar, he assured me, he'd send me out for some. And we laughed, and he winced from the pain of the wounds.

BY THE NEXT dinner, James was gone again. The police had brought him back the night he was burned, which is why I saw him when I did. But he ran again. Or he walked. That time, he was really gone. Gone-gone.

I asked Arlette what happened to James. She shrugged and said he was on the run, as if *on the run* was a place a person could be.

I asked the staff and the other boys. They all told me different stories.

The first was that James was dead. This was their favorite, the running joke about whoever left, I would learn. Where's Carlos? Has anyone heard from James? When I asked where a gone boy was, the others would tell me he died. Gerry has suggested that from a psychoanalytical perspective, this response is rooted in the transience of their relationships with each other and the ill-fated nature of the direction they know life to follow.

"Seriously, does anyone know where James is living now?" I asked the others. I was horrified when they said he could be dead.

"*Seriously*, he's across the street." Wesley echoed the tone of my voice and pointed to the funeral home we could see from the kitchen window.

The second story was that James was in jail, or had been in jail. More than one kid said that he got locked up for stealing cars, that he was the fall guy in a string of car thefts. The other people involved were the people from the place he ran to.

When he ran away the second time, he ran back to the place where he had been burned. By some accounts, it was an apartment with a lot of people crashing there; by other accounts, it was a drug house. The person who invited him there, the one James referred to loosely as his friend, was a kid he met in the job-training program he was in with Leon. A friend of that friend gouged a cigarette or pipe into the back of his neck. The boys said that the incident involved James being scourged with the pipe, then stripped of his clothes and beaten, naked, on the sidewalk outside the apartment. All this was videoed and put online; some of the boys said they had seen it and asked if I wanted to see. Somebody called the police, who called his caseworker and brought him back to the House. He didn't come back because he wanted to. Days later, he had a conversation with the staff that made it seem like things were better. But then he ran again.

The story went that after that, he got caught in a stolen car and he was taken in. When he was questioned, he did not give the names of the other people involved.

"Obviously," Wesley had said.

But I didn't know which part was obvious, that James had stolen a car, that he got caught, that he didn't name the others involved, or that he had ended up in jail. Or all of it.

The third story was that James was crashing at some other kid's place, a different friend from the one in the second story. They are *more than just friends*, Wesley insinuated.

"The friend lives in another residential program. James hides under the kid's bed until bed check. He sleeps there 'cause he doesn't have another place to go. He's legit on the run," Leon said, as if sleeping under another kid's bed in another group home made it more legit.

"He's so gay," Wesley said.

"What did we say about gay?" I asked.

"No, really," Wesley told me. "That dude really is gay. I seen it. One time I was in the office and his folder was on top and no one was around and so I read it. He. Is. Gay. It says it right in his folder. If you don't believe me, you could ask Arlette."

It was never clear when or if Wesley gained access to James's folder, or how he might have seen some documentation of abuse James had suffered in one of his placements, or why he would translate an assault into calling James gay. I wondered whether Wesley had said something to James about it during an argument or through a joke that wasn't a joke. The boys were accustomed to having bits of their own stories thrown at them like lit matches, like Leon's physical limitations or Frank's having been born substance dependent. I wondered if somebody had said something, if that was why James had run.

I hated the idea of James sleeping under another kid's bed with no place else to go. I hated the idea of him on the run, with a bag of stuff and no money, with two families that didn't work out and friends who were never friends.

"I would love to see James," I said. "If you talk to him, will you invite him for dinner?"

"Yeah, I will," Frank would tell me when I asked, the way he said he would about cutting up the chicken, which he always did. But also the way he said he would about going to school for the whole day, which he almost never did.

THE FOURTH STORY was my favorite. In that version, James is a manager at a Best Buy. It wasn't Frank or Wesley who told me. It was Michael Peters, a boy who lived in one of the other residences who started coming to our dinners sometime after James left.

"Really?" I asked. This story was so different from the dead, jail, and on-the-run ones.

"Yeah, somebody seen him there. With the manager name tag and everything," Michael Peters said, forming his fingers into a small rectangle on the right side of his chest, where a name tag might be pinned.

I fill in my own details in this version of the story: James shares an apartment in the city with a roommate who also works at the big box store. He has his own room. He meets a person, eventually, who comforts him, and listens when he talks about his past with specific words. The only running he does is through a park near his apartment, to clear his mind. The scars on his hand and the back of his neck are gone.

Adaptations, Replacements, and Substitutions

When Carlos left and then James left, new boys were assigned to their rooms. There were never formal introductions when new kids arrived, just a mutual acceptance of vague backstories.

"So, what's the new kid's name?" I would ask.

"FNG," Wesley would answer.

"But what's his *name*?" I'd ask again.

"That's his *name*," Wesley would say, imitating my intonation.

"I think it's Mikey or something like that," Frank would say. He added the "or something like that" as a disclaimer, to indicate he wasn't really listening or didn't really care. But the new kid's name was always Mikey, or whatever Frank said before "or something like that."

"It's Mikey," Leon would say. Leon always knew the new kid's name.

For the beginning of a new kid's stay, the others called him the letters instead of his name. When I asked what *FNG* stood for, Wesley said, "Fuckin' New Guy," as if it were obvious.

When the FNG had a real name, and he always had a real name, it was only a first name, or sometimes a nickname that started in the House or was brought in from outside. Like Leon, who another kid started calling "LeBron" because Leon looked sort of like LeBron James, and LeBron sounded sort of like *Leon*, and Leon liked it, so it stuck.

Last names, for some of the boys, were lingering connections to the families they came from. Like the words *youth* and *adolescent,* last names were words mainly used on paper. I only knew the last names of the boys who were there on the first night, who filled out my surveys; on the line that said Name, everyone except Wesley wrote his first and last names. Occasionally, I called Leon and Frank by their first and last names. When I did, Leon would say, "Man, Liz. There you go again, using people's government names. I guess you're used to that, though, since you're a teacher, using people's government names all the time." (*All the time* was four or five times.) I asked if there was something wrong with using last names, and Leon said, "No, but people just don't." Government names were aliases, used only in the government parts of their lives, like school and court and hospitals.

An FNG at the House wasn't usually new to the system. By the time he was here, he'd been somewhere else, or a string of some-where elses: a foster family that didn't work out, a juvie facility, an interim placement, a medical institution. Sometimes the FNG was already known to another of the residents from someplace before: a previous program, a lockup, a neighborhood or school. In that case, the resident acquaintance would serve as a buffer for the FNG. Otherwise, the FNG had nothing between him and the other boys, until a new guy arrived and became the FNG, and then the resident formerly known as FNG became Mikey, or something like that.

Mikey was the second FNG I met; he had colorful tattoos and brought our dessert game to another level. The first FNG was a quiet kid named David with intricate braids and terrible acne who showed up in the kitchen after James left and said somebody told him he should come.

But there were weeks between when Carlos and then James left, and when we sat down to eat again, with FNGs in their seats at the table.

FRANK AND LEON and Wesley stopped coming to dinner for a while. Even though they sort of knew me and I sort of knew them and we sort of had a dinner routine with a table and everything, there were weeks that spring after Carlos and James left when nobody was interested in cooking. I would arrive on time, inevitably having left school late and rushed through the supermarket to park and lug groceries up the noisy stairs, only to find myself alone in the kitchen. Fingers stinging from the weight of stuff, gentle April breeze blowing through open windows onto my cheeks, I was sure that if I touched the TV, it would still be warm. I finally felt the opposition that Gerry and the houseparent had predicted in the beginning.

"How's your cooking club?" one of my friends asked during one of those weeks.

"I don't know if we can call it a *club*," I told him. "And I'm not sure it's anything anymore." I told myself I understood why the no-showing kept happening. Leon had gotten a new job through a work program with the help of his caseworker. Wesley had better things to do and was never interested in the first place. Frank didn't want to be the only one who wanted to cook. Besides, the boys expected me to stop coming anyway; it would be less disappointing to end on their own terms. Maybe it was a fluke that the program had lasted so long.

A part of me was relieved to go home to my apartment and make myself dinner, walk around the park in the neighborhood, get work done, rest. I was teaching classes, taking classes, and trying to figure out how to figure out what to do with my one allegedly wild and precious life. Somehow, I felt both restless and tired. I threw some dinner parties for friends and made my favorite tapas, ones that my host mom in Spain during my year abroad had taught me to make and ones I tried to replicate from little bars in Madrid and Sevilla, the ones I hadn't been able to convince the boys that they might like to try. (I was sure people would love *croquetas de jamón* and *patatas bravas* with different dipping sauces, and Leon was sure it would be better if we just made something normal like French fries or quesadillas.)

I started planning my summer; I enjoyed the students and the literature facets of my teaching job, but I loved the summers. A perk of the teaching schedule is two full months to recalculate, and I intended to travel somewhere but didn't know where. Another aspect of the school calendar I appreciated was how time was chunked into familiar blocks like last time: the year was clearly grouped in days and weeks and terms, with three vacations and two new year's days (one in September, one in January) to start again. If something doesn't work, you reevaluate and make changes or replace the unit altogether; revision is part of the process—of teaching, of writing, of everything. I had hoped for one dinner at the House; we had already exceeded expectations. If the cooking project had a one-semester lifespan, I would accept that—or try to. I had a bad habit of not knowing when enough was enough, or just being grateful for enough. Still, I wouldn't be the one to quit. I needed to be told it was over.

The first two ghost dinners, I assured the houseparent on duty that it was not a big deal ("No problem!"). I left my phone number with a request to please call me the next week ("Just text!"), to let me know if I should come. (No one ever contacted me.) I asked Greg one of the empty nights when he was in the office but nobody was around if he thought cooking was over; he said I should ask somebody else.

I started calling the House before I left school, before I went to the supermarket. (Three consecutive weeks, I bought ingredients for the last meal that Leon had suggested and everyone had agreed to: chicken stir-fry.) I'd ask whoever answered if anyone would be around for dinner and said I wanted to verify the menu. When Greg was on duty, he'd say, "Well, Frank'll be here 'cause he's got no-where else to go."

That Frank had no place else to go didn't mean he wanted to cook with me. One night, he turned his radio up in his room when he heard me on the stairs. I heard the music get louder as I got closer to the kitchen. When I knocked on his door, Frank opened it wide enough to speak to me through the crack. "I'm not cooking today," he said. I nodded and asked whether he wanted any of the food I'd brought. He nodded. "Just the soda. You could just leave it in the fridge."

Another one of those April nights, Frank opened his door all the way and said nobody else was around but he guessed he'd cook, since I brought shrimp and he was hungry.

Greg had told me that Frank's attendance at school continued to be an issue. As a volunteer, I would check in with staff when I arrived at the House and then check out before I left. Greg often worked the day shifts on the Tuesdays I went to cook, so it was usually him I talked to, and our weekly exchanges had grown more familiar. I would tell him funny things that happened in the kitchen, or sometimes I might flag a thing that came up in conversation with the boys, just in case, which he said he appreciated. My default setting in adult mode was *teacher*, even though I knew I wasn't a teacher at the House; in the kitchen with the kids, I still felt compelled by some of the obligations to protocol and manners of care that I felt and practiced in my real job at school. As a volunteer, I navigated an in-between space at the House: I was there to serve the residents, and to report to the staff. I felt accountable both to the adults running the show and the young people living it; in that sense, it was a lot like school. As a white female adult, I looked more like the administrative assistant downstairs than I looked like anyone else in the House. I was older than she was by a few years, but I was significantly less cool, as Leon had told me once. When I asked for tips on how to be cooler, he shook his head like you do when someone asks you to explain a thing they couldn't possibly understand and said, "Well you're a teacher, so." So even if I tried, I couldn't shake my teacher mentality.

I was distressed to learn from Greg that Frank was having truancy issues. When we had bumped into each other that morning in the convenience store parking lot, I had seen a glimpse into Frank's school day: he woke up, got dressed, took the bus to school, went to class. It wasn't that he wasn't *going* to school, it was that he wasn't *staying* at school. Something was happening that compelled him to leave early. I suspected it had to do with reading because I had noticed that for all Frank helped in the kitchen, none of the tasks he took on required reading directions, like on the bags of rice and frozen vegetables or the boxes of cake mix. And I remembered that the first night when I had passed out surveys, the other kids filled out their own, but Greg had read Frank the questions and recorded his answers; Frank had written only his name.

So while Frank was fixing the shrimp and I was cutting vegetables, I decided to try to learn more about what was happening at school. I always asked the boys about school when we talked (or when I talked); it was a question that adults in my life had always asked me when I was a kid, and in theory, it was something the boys and I had in common, since we all spent part of our days in school. Over the course of our dinners, they had come to expect me to ask "How's school?" and I had come to expect the quick answers they provided in the form of shrugs, okays, and Wesley's favorite: "School is school." This time, I thought that since it was only Frank and me in the kitchen, I might try for a longer answer, though I didn't necessarily know what I would do, or could do, with the longer answer if I got one. After we speculated about where everyone else was and whether they would be back for chores, and how much shrimp one person could safely eat, Frank started cooking them, I started the rice, and I asked him how school was going.

"I been going," he answered, as if I had asked whether he was showing up and not what was happening once he had arrived.

"Oh good," I said. "Every day?"

"Yup," he said.

"So no more cutting classes, like what Greg was telling me?"

"Well. There's still problems," he said.

"What kind of problems, if you're going every day?" I asked.

"I leave sometimes, after math class," he said. "But they know I leave."

"Oh, like the morning we met in the parking lot," I said. "So what do the people at school do about that?"

"Nothing," he said. "I mean, nothing really."

"But is there, like, a punishment for that?" I figured there must be some kind of plan, and that some kind of punishment was probably part of the plan.

"I'm supposed to write some kind of paper or something," Frank explained.

"Every time?" I looked up from the cutting board as I finished the peppers. "Do you write them?"

"Nope," he said. He flipped the shrimp.

"So then what's the punishment for that, for not doing the punishment?" I knew how punishments compound.

"Gotta write more of 'em," he said.

"Well, that seems like a stupid idea, huh?" I summed up Frank's school life as I understood it, filling in some gaps and counting on Frank to correct me where I was wrong: "So, you go to school for math because you like math, but you leave before the other classes because you get frustrated, maybe because of the books in the other classes. But your punishment for leaving early is writing an essay, which you don't do because I bet you hate writing—because when reading is hard, writing's harder. So then you don't write them. So then you get in more trouble. Which is probably frustrating because you'd write them if it was easier, and maybe you'd stay the whole day anyway if you didn't hate reading. But none of it's getting any better. So it just feels like a lot of punishment, and too many words. Except for math, which you like, which is why you go."

"Yup." Frank didn't look up from the stove. "See, you get it." He turned down the heat when the shrimp started to vibrate in the hot oil.

I watched him flip the shrimp again. I imagined him getting up every day, getting dressed, taking the bus to school, going to math class, leaving. I wondered about his teachers. I turned the rice off and fluffed it with a plastic fork.

"You think we could eat dinner and watch the game in the TV room instead of at the table, since we already talked a lot and nobody else's coming?" he asked.

"Sure," I said. "I didn't even know basketball's still on. I thought it was baseball season."

"We could?" he asked, already packing up a plate for the TV room. On the way to the couch he told me over his shoulder, "Yeah, it's still on. It's the playoffs."

"I heard you guys went to a game," I said. When I called to ask

Gerry whether we should reconsider the cooking project or switch nights since people weren't showing up, he apologized for the confusion and said that one of the nights a friend of the agency had donated some Celtics tickets and one of the houseparents had taken whoever wanted to go to a game.

"Yeah, this guy got us tickets," Frank said. "It was cool."

After two quarters of watching the game with plates in our laps, I asked Frank if during the next commercial we could mute the TV and would he read something to me out loud. It was an uncool teacher ask. I had some literacy training and was certified in teaching English language learners, in addition to the courses in second language teaching methodology I had completed for my degree and practiced daily in my position as a Spanish teacher. Teaching literature was my favorite part of the day, but teaching and assessing students' reading comprehension, listening comprehension, speaking, and writing were a big part of my job. Outside of school, I tutored a student with dyslexia and worked with her in English on her reading and writing skills. I'm not sure what I was thinking Frank and I might accomplish with this little reading exercise except that I thought this was a way to expand our exploratory conversation about Frank's reading and his experience in school, if he wanted to expand it, during this unusually quiet window with none of the other guys around.

Greg was seated in the staff office, which was just off the TV room where Frank and I were sitting, so I knew he could hear us. When Greg had told me initially about Frank's attendance issues, I asked if he thought something more was going on, and he shrugged and told me to ask Frank myself. The truth is that when I asked Frank that night if he would read something to me out loud, so I could get a sense of how he put letters together, I didn't really think he would agree to do it. But he did.

"Yeah, I could," he said between bites.

"Okay, do you have any books or magazines in your room?" I had nothing with words on it; I never brought my schoolbag into the House, just my wallet and keys zipped into my coat pocket and the groceries.

"Nah, but I'm about to get one tomorrow," he said, muting the controller.

"Is there a book we could use?"

"Yeah, I think under the cabinet," he said.

I rooted around and found one. "Did you mean this yellow book?" I held it up so he could see it. "Frank, this is a *phone* book." I almost laughed.

"You said a book, and it's a book, dawg." He sighed.

After more fumbling, I found a coverless copy of a poetry anthology that had been published in the 1970s and possibly deposited in that cabinet soon thereafter. It smelled musty but its spine was perfect. It would have to do. I skimmed the table of contents for a poem that looked familiar to me; I wouldn't ask Frank to read something I didn't know. Poetry wasn't ideal for this exercise because though poems look easier than prose since they often are made with fewer words, the language tends to make them more complicated. But poetry was all we had, and Frank had already agreed. I opened to a poem by Emily Dickinson, which I picked for its short lines and small words. Eight lines total, the longest line had eight words—it was the first line, and like most of hers, also the title: "Tell all the truth but tell it slant." Longest word, four syllables: *explanation*. Most difficult word, in my prediction: *Circuit*, because of *c*'s with two different sounds, plus the dissolved second *i*, and the capital *C* to begin—hard, harder, and hardest to explain if Frank asked. I dog-eared the page, took another bite of my spicy shrimp, and waited for the next commercial.

When the players flashed off and the advertisement started, Frank sighed, hit mute, and traded me remote control for book.

I prefaced the poem with a brief biography of America's most poetic agoraphobic xenophobe, trying to pique Frank's interest. "She was from Massachusetts . . . She wrote her poems on scraps of paper . . . She was kind of weird and stayed inside most of her life . . . And her work wasn't published until after she died, because she didn't want anyone to read it . . . Some people believe her poems changed American poetry."

Frank sighed. I thought he might have changed his mind. But

then, he quietly began to read. He interchanged sight words that began with the same letter like *the* and *too* and *as* and *and,* and stumbled over words he didn't recognize, which were many. By the last two lines, "The Truth must dazzle gradually / Or every man be blind—," he was exhausted. After *blind,* he said, "See, that's why I don't like reading," as if that were the real last line of the poem, except that he pronounced it more fluently than any of the rest. He sighed again, traded me back, book for remote, and pressed the mute button to release the rushing and stomping of the game back into the space between us. At the next commercial, he muted the remote a third time and said, without prompting, "I know. I have one of them three levels."

I took that to mean someone must have told Frank that he read at a third-grade reading level. I was hoping we could find a way to work on his reading; I didn't think his school situation could change without addressing it, and I was afraid that nobody at school was really addressing it. I had no idea what Frank's teachers were trying, but I knew that Frank kept leaving. Still, I wasn't sure this had been a helpful exercise for him. I thought I might be able to help, though I didn't know what that would look like. "Does anyone ever help you with reading?" I asked. "Would you maybe want some extra help?" During the early months of the cooking program, I had asked if anyone would be interested in me coming an additional night to run a drop-in homework group, complete with snacks; the idea was vetoed unanimously. Even free snacks could not redeem homework. I thought if Frank was interested now, we could make a different arrangement.

"You ask too much questions," he said. "No offense."

"None taken." I smiled. "You aren't the first person to tell me that."

"'Cause you do, dawg." He took two more bites of food. "Shrimp's good though."

"Yeah. You did a good job with it," I said. "You always do."

He looked at me. "And you have mad small eyes."

"What?"

"You're real tall, but you have real small eyes." He had an ad hoc assessment of his own. "Can you even see out of them?"

I laughed. I do have small eyes, and I was wearing my glasses instead of contact lenses, which made my eyes appear even smaller behind the thick lenses of my strong prescription.

"I'm serious, dawg. No offense," he said seriously, leaning in close to my face. Our noses almost touched as the Truth dazzled gradually. "I can barely see them. That's messed up."

"Yes, I can see out of my small eyes," I assured him, opening my eyes as wide as I could.

He leaned back and finished his food.

"Hey, is there a book you'd want to read if I brought it to you?" I asked. "Since I don't think anybody's going to be reading that poetry book again for a while."

"*Harry Potter*, I guess," he said.

"Which one? There's a bunch, I think." I hadn't read them.

"The one with the magic stuff in it," he said.

WHEN I CALLED to tell Gerry about our poetry experience the day after it happened and to ask if there was anything I could do to support Frank's school goals, he asked if that was something Frank seemed interested in; I said I thought he might be. But the next week, Frank asserted his position on the matter. I brought him a copy of the first book of the *Harry Potter* series as I said I would, and he reached through his barely opened door to accept it and tell me he wasn't cooking. Or reading. "Just don't want to," he told me.

But then the week after that, he was in the kitchen when I arrived. "Still don't want to cook, but . . ." He dragged out the *but* as if he hadn't decided whether to finish the thought.

"But what?" I didn't start unpacking the groceries.

"But do you have, like, three dollars?" He looked down.

"For what?"

"Batteries," he said. "For my remote. It needs batteries but they don't work no more."

"Oh, sure," I said. "We can get batteries. I can walk with you to CVS now." There was one not far from the House.

"What?" he asked.

"Do you have time to go now? We could get them right now." I was happy to buy the batteries but I knew handing Frank cash outright would set a tricky precedent.

"Like right now, right now?" he asked. "Yeah, I'll get my coat." He came back with a sweatshirt, which he pulled over his head as he took the stairs two at a time, ahead of me.

On the sidewalk, Frank sighed deeply in the early May breeze before we started our journey. Door to door, the store was about four hundred steps from the House. As we crossed the street, I asked Frank about school and he asked me if he could just have the money. I said I needed to get something, too, because I didn't want to tell him that I didn't think I was supposed to just give him the money. We bought the batteries and some drinks and I tried to keep the questions to a minimum, but on the way back, I had to ask about the book.

"Have you started *Harry Potter*?"

"Yup," he said. "I did, dawg. I'm not lying."

"What page are you on?"

"Two," he said.

"Really?"

"Yeah," he told me. "I read one page. I'm not lying, dawg."

"Is it good? I haven't read it. Do you think you'll keep reading it?"

"Maybe, dawg," he said in an open-ended way, shrugging. "I read one page a year. And now I read it already."

"Fair enough," I said, hearing myself say something my dad used to say.

We crossed the street in front of the House. I stopped on the sidewalk. Frank stood in the doorway, his hand on the green door. "So you probably wish we could just keep talking all night, but I think I'm going to head out," I said. "You think people will want to cook next week?"

"Probably will," he said.

"Even though we haven't for a while, you think next week'll be different?"

"Probably will," he said again. "People just weren't hungry, dawg."

I asked him what I should bring and he said, "Probably steak bombs. With a lot of cheese," he added, like I might've forgotten the cheese.

"Okay," I said. "See you next week? With extra cheese?"

"Yup." Frank turned in toward the House. "Thanks," he said, mostly to the green door as he pushed it open with his left hand and lifted the bag almost like a wave with his right.

My eyes traveled up to the windows of my dad's office. The light was on. The line of books on the radiator looked faded and dusty in the daylight. I squinted, as if I could see what mattered about that place. If I stood there long enough, maybe I would know what of him I could save. My dad never moved out of his office in those last months; he had planned to go back. I could pack his books in boxes, unhang his pictures, unplug his phone. I could take it all with me. I could own what was his and surround myself with piles of his stuff. I could sift through it all to make sense of what he did here at this place, where he was when he wasn't with us. What was his work, the impact? It was too late to ask him questions about who he was or how I was supposed to know who I was supposed to be. His voice on my mother's answering machine had started to sound tinny, his books in the basement smelled stale. What was left of him? I squinted into the windows, as if I might see what was left of a lifetime of work when the body was gone.

"You're leaving already?" a voice asked from behind me. It was Prof, the houseparent I had met a few weeks earlier, who worked evenings—the other teacher.

"I am, yeah," I said. "The boys don't want to cook tonight, so I'm going. Before I get charged with loitering, you know."

He laughed. "Sometimes they don't know what's good for them. Lot of times, probably."

I nodded like I understood. "I keep thinking James might come back," I said.

Prof shook his head no. He told me that he would give each resident two handshakes: one when he meets them and one when they graduate high school. "I don't usually get the opportunity for that second handshake," he said.

"All I could think when I heard James ran again was of him asking you about that suit, and how much you thought he could sell it for." I searched Prof's face. "I mean, he must've known, right? That he was going? That must be why he asked you about money?"

Prof shrugged. "It's like I said before."

"And Carlos," I said. "Have you heard anything about either of them?"

Prof shook his head no again.

"I think we might be done with the cooking. It's been a few weeks now that no one has wanted to do it, so I should take the hint, right?" I asked the sidewalk.

Prof shrugged. "Well, you have a good night, now. See you next week," he added, already inside.

I nodded goodbye and looked up into the window of my father's office one more time. I wanted the light to flicker or something. I didn't believe in signs, but I wanted one. The stupid bulb shone steadily.

The Other Oregano

Everybody made it to the table the next week, less for the company and more for the steak-and-cheese subs. Frank helped, like he said he would. Leon came back from his job in time to make brownies. There was no talk of the pause and there were two new faces. One was David, who was Black with long braids, an easy smile, bad acne, and a blue bike that he parked on the landing behind the trash barrels. He asked me if it was true people could just eat and not cook. I said it was, and he said maybe he would help anyway.

When everyone had eaten enough and we were figuring out the menu for the following week, someone suggested lasagna. We were easing out of our hiatus, and lasagna didn't feel like a May food, so I suggested American chop suey instead, since it contains nearly the same ingredients but requires significantly less work. I thought it was a perfect alternative: easy, meaty, filling, good. I also thought it could be a great go-to recipe for the boys in their someday kitchens, when they were on their own to cook for themselves.

"Nah, I don't want that." Wesley was the first to say no.

"Me neither," Frank agreed.

"Are you sure?" I didn't understand why I was being vetoed. "Do you know the meal I mean? It's hamburger, pasta, tomato sauce, sometimes with cheese. It tastes like lasagna, but doesn't take as long to make . . . and the next day you can reheat the leftovers and add some ketchup. . . . It'd be something you could make on your own, too . . . on not Tuesdays here . . . and when you have your own places. . . . You guys like all of the ingredients . . ." I had a tendency to keep talking until somebody agreed with me or interrupted.

American chop suey was the ultimate comfort food, in my opinion. It had been a favorite in my house when I was little. A pot of it on the stove was as ubiquitous in winter as snow, wool, and catching colds. My memories of scooping the saucy pasta into a ceramic bowl and adding ketchup for extra tang are not marked with specific dates or times; my hands are all different sizes, but the pot is always the same. My grandmother's version of the dish was blander than my mother's and she never made as much of it. When she served it, she always served my grandfather last. She gave him his portion in the pan she had cooked it in; he'd insist she not dirty another dish and she'd oblige him, knowing that this was a show for us. We sat captivated by the sight of him: hunched over the table with a dish towel tucked into the collar of his shirt and a fistful of bread from the loaf, eating straight from the pan, like the illustrated giant in our copy of *Jack and the Beanstalk*.

"No. I mean, yeah, I know what you're talking about," Wesley said, "but I don't want it. No offense, but for me that's an institutional food. They serve it all the time at places I've been before."

"True. They serve it like every week at—" Before Frank could name whichever place he was going to name from his résumé, someone cut him off.

"More than that, right?" the FNG jumped in. His name was Miguel but he went by Mikey because it was easier, he said. He was heavier-set than the other kids, Latino, with freckles, perfect eyebrows and a giggle of a laugh. When Mikey talked, he waved his hands around, rendering the tattoos on his arms into a swirling blur of color against the clear canvas of his white T-shirt. "Like every other night. The cooks cook that shit up like we forgot we just had it the night before."

Everybody laughed.

"Yeah, it's good and everything, but I had enough of it. And it reminds me of being in those places." Wesley made his closing argument. "It's institutional food."

"Yeah, right?" Mikey agreed. He nodded at the plate of brownies across the table.

"Yup," Frank said, pushing the plate toward Mikey.

Leon looked at me and shrugged.

My comfort food was the boys' discomfort food. The same flavors that made me think about snow days and wooden spoons in cozy kitchens triggered memories in them of juvenile detention facilities, stainless steel trays, and uniforms. *Institutional* was the only five-syllable word I ever heard around that table, and everybody could use it in a sentence. The boys nodded and laughed and listened to each other talk about faceless cooks in white aprons with metal troughs of oily pasta and boiled baby carrots.

At some point, Mikey, the FNG who didn't seem to have any allegiances to other boys yet, left the table. He returned in an off-white jumpsuit. It looked like something a mechanic might wear, but it was the color of mashed potatoes, with snaps instead of zippers. He appeared in the doorway, swung his hips in an exaggerated way toward his chair, and did a little spin.

Everybody laughed.

Someone said, "No, he didn't just do that."

Someone else confirmed that "Yeah, dawg, he just did."

"Yeah, dawg," Mikey said to me. "I got a bunch of these." He put his hands on his hips and posed purposefully, like a model, looking off in the distance.

"Aren't you supposed to give those back before you leave?" I couldn't resist asking.

"I mean, you could," he shrugged. "But you could take them."

This sounded unlikely, but I knew he knew better than me.

David, the other new guy, left the table and returned in a denim version of the same outfit several sizes smaller, to fit his body. He didn't spin; he just walked to his chair, smiling.

Not to be upstaged, Mikey left again and came back in a two-piece outfit that looked like hospital scrubs, in a shade of brown somewhere between safari and UPS. He had two other folded uniforms hung over his arm the way a butler might carry towels.

He really did have a bunch of those.

Mikey rested the pile of clothes on the back of his chair, then shook out the outfits one by one for his audience: a two-piece in the electric clementine of traffic cones, a one-piece snap-up in dark denim, and a third set that looked like scrubs, similar to the one he was wearing, but in a dull, desert-camouflage tan. As he held each up, he said the name of the facility it came from, as if it were a fashion center like Paris, Milan, or Barcelona. The crowd laughed and cheered and shared who else had worn what, where, and when.

"Are you sure you're *allowed* to take them?" I was hung up on logistics.

"Well, I did and nobody stopped me," Mikey said.

"But are you *supposed* to take them?" I kept asking teacher questions.

"They check your bags on the way out and nobody took them away from me."

"Okay, but why would you *want* to take them? Did you think you'd wear them again?"

"Well, I'm wearing them now, aren't I?" Mikey asked, beaming.

The crowd burst into mmhmms and a gurgle of giggles because Mikey was right. "Schooled the teacher!" Wesley said. He raised his cup of Pepsi in triumph.

I couldn't argue with that. I opened my palms in a concession of defeat.

When the show was over, Wesley wiped tears from his eyes from laughing so hard. "I was *not* expecting that," he said to no one in particular, and to all of us.

"I know, dawg," Frank said seriously. "That was some funny shit."

"So, lasagna." I conceded. "Does everyone even like lasagna?"

"Yeah," Wesley said, answering for everyone. "We said lasagna in the first place, yo."

"Here's the thing, though," I said. "Lasagna takes a while to make. So we'll be eating later . . . there're a bunch of steps . . . people need to help . . . okay?"

"Okay!" someone said.

"I'm serious. I'm not interested in making it by myself. I don't even like lasagna."

"Oookaay," someone else reiterated.

"We get it." Wesley poured himself the last sips of Pepsi. "You're forcing it already, yo."

WHEN I ARRIVED at the House the next week, no one was waiting at the green door. I had fought the urge to buy a tray of lasagna from my sister's restaurant, but I figured we should try for the real thing. In search of the most practical variation, I chose no-boil noodles and dutifully collected the other ingredients listed on the back of the package. As I grabbed the bags from my backseat, I wondered what the chances were that anyone was in the kitchen. I looked up at the window and thought I saw a curtain flutter.

Frank greeted me in the doorway at the top of the stairs, his fingers hooked to the top of the frame as he leaned forward. "Nobody's here, dawg."

"Is Leon at work?" I asked.

"No, dawg," Frank said. "LeBron's sick, in the hospital or something."

"In the hospital?" I asked. "Is he okay?"

"Yeah," Frank said. "I mean no, but yeah." He stepped aside to let me in. "He's how he is."

"What do you mean, Frank?" *In the hospital* sounded serious to me.

"Don't know, dawg. LeBron's in the hospital. You've got to ask someone."

"I'm asking someone." I pointed at him.

"I'm not someone, dawg." He sighed heavily. "You know what I mean."

"So do you think we shouldn't make the lasagna, if it's just the two of us?"

He shrugged. "Yeah, I mean we still could do it."

I looked at him and squinted a little.

"What, dawg? How do you even see out of those little eyes?" He squinted back. "I'm here. Let's just make it already."

As the meat was browning, I asked Frank to grab the other spice from the staff office. I'd received a spice rack as a gift and donated it to our cause, but someone had decided it should be locked up in the staff desk with the other contraband.

Frank left and returned with the tower of small jars. "What's this one say?" he asked, holding one with a label that started with *O*.

"Oregano," I said.

"Really? This's oregano? Oh, I'm taking this shit," he said, tucking it into his armpit. "I'm about to smoke this right now."

"What?" I asked.

"You're so stupid, dawg," Wesley said, appearing in the doorway like he did, with an insult heralding his arrival. "It's not real oregano." He reached into the fridge for milk.

I must have looked confused, because Wesley clarified for me, "I mean it *is* really oregano." Then he looked at Frank. "But it's real *oregano*. Not like you think."

"What, dawg?" Frank asked.

"Oh, like, it's not *marijuana*, Frank," I said. "It's really just a spice called *oregano*."

Wesley and Frank looked at each other and then at me.

"I'm guessing that's what you guys are talking about," I said. "Am I wrong?" I sometimes smelled the piney, skunky smell of pot in the staircase or on the boys' sweatshirts; I usually just cooked around it.

Wesley smiled. "Or you could know from experience," he said into his cup.

"Why'd they call it that then?" Frank asked.

"Oregano, the spice? Probably from the Latin, *oreganum* or something. Or you mean why do they call marijuana oregano?" I asked. "Do people really call it oregano?"

"Yup," Frank said. Wesley nodded.

"Maybe because it looks like the same little dried leaves, so it's like a nickname, like weed or grass."

"Nobody calls marijuana grass," Wesley said.

I moved on. "I think the only spice in that set that you could actually smoke is cloves."

Frank squinted at me and spun the rack to find it. "Which one is it? This one?" He held out something else that started with *C*.

"That's cinnamon," I said. "You'll recognize the smell of that one, but you can't smoke it." I unscrewed the jar and we inhaled and he nodded. Wesley wasn't interested. "This one is cloves." I shook the bottle so Frank could hear the cloves click against the tin top. I poured some into my hand so he could see their shape, like tiny wooden screws without the winding sides.

"This?" Frank pinched one between his thumb and index finger and squinted at it. "This looks nasty. I wouldn't smoke this."

"Well, I really wasn't thinking we'd be smoking any of this to-night," I said.

"Told you you smoked," Wesley said, smiling, on his way out.

"You also told me you were going to help with the lasagna," I called over to him.

"That dude was never going to help," Frank said, shaking his head.

"Which is why I'm lucky I have you, Frank."

He shook his head again. "Wash my hands?"

"Yeah," I said. "I've got to wash mine, too." I followed Frank to the sink and we washed our hands, shoulder to shoulder.

I made cookies and Frank cooked and seasoned the meat, then turned the burner off and moved the pan off the stove. He carried it into the dining room as I laid the other ingredients out in a line on the table next to the pan: sauce, noodles, meat, and three kinds of cheese.

"You think anybody else is coming to help?" I asked Frank.

"Nope," he said, popping a handful of mozzarella from the glossy envelope into his mouth.

AFTER FIFTY-FIVE MINUTES of preparation and forty-five minutes of baking, Frank put on the new pot holders and took his steaming cheesy opus out of the oven. Some combination of noise and smell and hunger drew everyone to the table, which someone set with paper plates and plastic forks. Frank carried in his lasagna. The boys watched as he placed it on the table, bubbling and oozing. I buttered slices of white bread and everyone reached out for some. Nobody touched the salad I made.

For several quiet minutes, everyone ate.

The phone rang.

"Liz, it's for you," Greg, the houseparent on duty, called from the other room.

"How's it going to be for her if she doesn't live here?" Frank asked what I was thinking.

I went into the staff office and took the phone from Greg. I thought it might be Gerry.

"Hello?" I answered.

"Liz, I'm sorry I can't cook tonight." It was Leon. "What're we having?"

"Hey Leon," I said, softening my voice as I said his name. "Lasagna."

"Sounds so good," Leon said. "Nobody helped you, right?"

"Frank did a great job," I said, loud enough for Frank to hear.

"You're saying that 'cause he can hear you, huh?"

"How are you, Leon? Frank said you're in the hospital?"

"Yeah. It kind of sucks," he said. "Sorry to use bad language, but it does."

"Are you okay?" I asked. "When do you get out? Will you be back next week?"

"Should be," Leon said. "Long as these doctors can figure my shit out."

I was quiet. I did not know what I should ask, or what I was allowed to know.

"Sorry about saying shit, too," Leon said.

"Leon. I'm really sorry you're sick."

"It's all right. It's the same old," he said. "You've probably got to go now, right? 'Cause everybody's at the table."

"I probably should," I said. "But can you have visitors?

"I mean I can, but I'm supposed to get out tomorrow. You can come next time."

"Leon says hello," I told the others when I returned to the table.

"That's so gay," Wesley said.

I looked at him. He looked away.

"She don't like you to say *gay*, dawg," Frank said quietly.

I asked who wanted more bread and started buttering. "So, what do people think of the lasagna?"

"Mad good," Mikey said, nodding approvingly.

"Real good," David said, also back for dinner.

"Bomb," Wesley added, biting, sipping, swallowing.

"It's good," Frank said, his voice full of hesitation. "But this shit takes mad long."

I kept buttering bread until hands stopped reaching for it, three quarters of a loaf. This was my favorite part of my nights at the House, the giving and taking that made generic white bread taste a little like manna.

"Shit's bomb," Wesley said again.

"You didn't help, dawg," Frank said, lifting a loaded plastic forkful into his mouth. "None of y'all helped," he added, gesturing around the table with his empty plastic fork.

"So what do you think?" I looked at Frank. "Is it worth all the time it took?"

"Don't know, dawg," he said, scraping the last piece onto his plate. Everyone took seconds, and Frank had thirds; the other boys left him the last square. "But it's good, though."

How to Make a Difference

In May, Gerry called to tell me that my work was really taking root. "Progress!" he said. Six months and so much chicken later, he said he could literally smell the boys' increasing confidence in the kitchen. He reported that on at least two occasions, on afternoons I wasn't there, the scent of sweet chocolate had wafted downstairs as proof. "Incredible!" he said. I accepted the win, but thought there must be more to the story. I knew who to ask.

Leon met me at the green door that week. He was out of the hospital. His head was shaved, but he didn't want to talk about it. He took one bag and I took the rest. On the stairs, I asked about the brownies. He stopped on the step ahead of me and turned around.

"How'd you know about the brownies?" he asked in a whisper.

"Gerry told me," I said.

"Gerry knows about the brownies?" Leon asked, in a faster whisper.

"Yeah, he smelled them," I said. "Leon, what's there to know about the brownies?"

"You've got to ask Mikey," Leon said. "You know, the FNG."

I didn't know very much about Mikey besides the uniforms and other things I could see, like his tattoos and his distinctive eyebrows, which were ink-black and meticulously plucked into perfect parentheses that curved over his deep brown eyes. One night at dinner, he explained that he had them done at school. He'd recently transferred to a high school with a vocational technical curriculum, and the program he chose was esthetics; instead of electricity, culinary, technology, or mechanics, he picked beauty.

"Some people say it's gay," he said. "But it's the opposite of gay. You're surrounded by females all day and they touch you and put shit on you and wipe it off you. I'm the only dude in the program. It's just me and mad females who want to practice on me and my face. So anyone can call me gay, but I know I'm not, so I don't care."

"She doesn't like it when people say *gay,* dawg," Wesley warned him.

Mikey waved his hands around when he told stories and when he did, his arms told stories of their own. He had a tattoo of a praying woman on his right arm and a jagged scar that roped across the forearm of the other. He said the Mary tattoo was Our Lady of Something, but he couldn't remember what exactly. He said he had her put there so she would always watch out for him. I asked him whether he ever prayed to her, and he said that he didn't have to, because he already had her right there. When he said "right here," he pointed to the cartoonish Virgin with closed eyes resting between his left wrist and elbow. She was draped in an Oreo-wrapper-blue head scarf and she had a banana-yellow halo. Her face and praying hands were the color of cappuccino, the color of the inside of his arm, not inked. The scar on his other arm was white and pink and looked like fusilli under his skin. It was twisted and raised with tissue built up around it, the way some scars puff and harden instead of fully healing.

"I was getting onto a bus in *my* country," he said, to distinguish his country from this one. "I was holding money, and somebody cut my arm and ripped me off." He traced the lumpy line of the scar with an immaculately manicured index finger. "It's real poor there. The worst part was that the driver wouldn't even let me on the bus 'cause of all the blood, so I had to walk a long way to the hospital."

That didn't seem like the worst part.

Mikey was never specific about how he got from his country to this one, except that there was a relative who was supposed to take him, before something had happened.

When Mikey helped in the kitchen, he helped with dessert. He made sugar cookies methodically. He preheated, measured and mixed and stirred with solemn precision. He read the recipe twice.

Before he reached for a whisk or poured milk into a measuring cup, he wiggled his fingers as if he had to wake them up to work. For M&M cookies, he'd divide the total number of candies by the number of cookies and place them carefully apart in evenly spaced mounds of pale batter. For a perfect second while he was holding a fistful of M&M's in his hand above the cookie sheet, the colored chocolate pieces matched Mary's flowers, head scarf, and halo so well it was as if the candy in his hand and the lady on his arm were where they were supposed to be.

So I can't say I was surprised when I asked him about the brownies and he said that yeah, he'd made them. But he seemed surprised when I asked whether that meant he'd make them for us from now on; he smiled widely as he answered that yes, he definitely would. He said he had to go to his room to get his special ingredient. Then I understood.

"The only special ingredient we use here is love," I said, quickly realizing that the smell of independence that had so moved Gerry was the smell of oregano brownies, but not, like, real oregano. I debated whether I should tell Gerry about the marijuana brownies, or leave the boys' independent snacking to his imagination.

"That's mad cheesy." Mikey laughed.

"That's *hateful*, Liz," Leon said. "Everybody loves my brownies."

"I know," I said.

"Not as much as they love mine, dawg." Mikey laughed.

WHILE MIKEY WAS at the counter making cookies and I was buttering tortillas for quesadillas, we started talking. I asked him about school and he asked which one, because he had a couple. The one he'd just transferred from was a school where a friend of mine had worked; we had taught together in a summer program for English language learners. My friend had since moved out of the country, and Mikey had transferred to a new school, but I thought they might've crossed paths while they were both in the same building.

"Hey, I think you might know a friend of mine," I said, making small talk as I greased the tortillas. "Did you ever have José Anaya?

Mr. Anaya? We worked together a couple of summers ago in an ESL program for students who'd recently arrived in the U.S., to help build English language skills before the school year started."

"Yeah, I know people who did that class. I think I know who you mean. Kind of a small dude? With dark hair? Colombian or something?"

"Dominican." I nodded. "He taught English."

"Yeah, I never had him, but I know who he is. He's your friend? He's straight." When Mikey said straight, it meant cool. José was easygoing, funny, and handsome. I'd witnessed how he interacted with students. It made sense he'd have a reputation for being cool. Mikey paused. "Can I ask you something?"

I thought he might be thinking of his own experience as an English language learner. Mikey sometimes used an expression in Spanish when it made more sense in context, or asked me how to say a particular word in English. "Is Mr. Anaya gay?" he asked as if he was asking for a quick translation or how long to cream the butter and sugar.

I hesitated to out my friend. José wasn't a teacher at the school anymore; he'd moved to France the year before. Mikey wasn't a student there anymore. If I said no, it would be a lie. If I avoided the question or asked why it mattered, Mikey would assume yes and I'd be confirming that being gay should be secret.

"Yeah, he's gay," I said, as if it was a quick translation or how long it takes to cream butter and sugar together. I briefly considered the difference between privacy and secrecy.

"I fucking knew it!" Mikey clapped his hands and spit out a tangle of slurs about my friend.

"Mikey," I winced at his words, at my mistake.

"No, I mean if a dude's not into pussy, that's cool. I don't get it, but that's cool," he said.

I looked at him. "C'mon, Mikey," I pleaded.

"What's going down in here?" Leon came in, floorboards creaking under his uneven walk.

I looked at Leon. Leon looked at Mikey.

"I'm just saying, what'd you say, dawg?" Leon said to Mikey.

"'Cause when Liz gives you the Liz eyes, looking at you all hard, it means you must've said something. And I wasn't here, so I just want to know what it was." Leon turned his body to look from Mikey to me, then back to Mikey. "So I don't say it and she doesn't look at me like that."

"The Liz eyes?" I asked, looking at him.

"Those," Leon said. "Don't give 'em to me. I'm trying to help." He shielded his eyes from me with a hand and turned to Mikey.

"What? I don't know. Ask her. 'Cause I don't know." Mikey looked down at the dough.

"Mikey," I said his name again, as if it were a reset button.

Leon looked at me and then at Mikey.

"Seriously, dawg. I don't know. What'd I say?" Mikey looked at me then repeated what he'd said for Leon to hear.

Leon looked at Mikey then at me.

"Mikey, there are, like, five words in the English language that I'm genuinely offended by. Of all possible words, like, five that I think are so ugly that I'd rather they not be used in the kitchen, at least when I'm here. Five. And you just managed to use four of them one after the other in like thirty seconds."

Leon looked back at Mikey.

"Sorry," Mikey said. "But, I mean, that seems like a lot."

"Five words out of the entire dictionary are a lot?" I asked.

"Yeah. Kind of is," Mikey said.

"Okay, for the record that's not an apology. When you say *sorry* to preface a reason you don't think you're wrong, it's not really an apology."

"Well, sorry, but, okay, I mean not sorry, but maybe I'm offended by your words, too." Mikey saw my request for an apology and raised me one of his own.

"What? Which of my words? How did I offend you?"

"Like, what you just said. *Preface.* I think I know what that means, but it sounds like it could be something nasty. You could be saying something nasty to me right now. And I don't know what it means. So that's worse. Least you know what I'm saying."

"Yeah, it does, dawg," Leon agreed with Mikey. He tried it out for effect: "I want to *preface* you right here . . ." He scrunched his nose when he said *preface* and spit it out. "Yup, it sounds nasty. I've got to be with Mikey on this one."

"It does *not* mean something nasty," I said. "Preface refers to something that comes *before*—what you say or write *before* something else. Like the preface to a book, or prefacing one idea with another."

"But how do we know that? You could just be telling us that," Mikey said. "Insulting us."

"Yup," Leon agreed.

"Well, a dictionary, for example, would settle it," I said. "Or you could search it online."

"Told you she don't like it when you say *gay*." Wesley appeared in the doorway. He'd been in his bedroom, not helping, but apparently listening. "She don't like it when you say *gay*," Wesley said over my shoulder. "She always be reacting like that. Don't know why. 'Cause if you're gay, you're gay."

"Right," someone agreed.

"Mmmhmm." Everyone was in agreement.

"Besides," Mikey said in my direction, "you even said he was gay."

"Yeah, I did say he was gay. He is gay. It's not wrong to say *gay* when someone's gay. But when you guys say *gay*, you don't mean it as a fact. You mean it as an insult. That's what I don't like. It's the hate speech part that's offensive." I debated pulling the step stool out of the pantry and going full Speakers' Corner in front of the refrigerator. "Like when you say 'He's so gay,' you mean it like it's the worst thing you could say about another guy. Or like if someone is gay, there's something wrong with them, something weak, something not masculine, whatever that means. Something bad. You know what I mean." I thought of all the times in the House, and at school, that I heard teenage boys call each other *gay* or *fag* or *fairy* or *pussy* or some other derivative, as if it was the worst thing they could say about the other person's personhood. I had never made this speech before because I knew that the boys knew why it was bad to call each other *gay* as an insult; that's precisely why they did it. "You know the difference."

"People like that are different," Mikey said seriously. Then, he turned to Leon and repeated what he'd said in the first place.

"Please don't be hateful," I said. "And what does it even matter to you who people love . . ." My voice drifted. I didn't know what else to say. What did it mean to attempt this argument here, on the basis of unconditional love or unconditional respect?

Leon counted on the fingers of one hand. "Fag, fucking, pus—"

"Okay, thank you, Leon." I cut him off. "We don't need a full recap."

He mouthed the third and fourth words, touching his middle and ring fingers. "What's the fifth word?" he asked me, tapping his pinky.

"Leon!" I said.

"Ass?" Leon guessed, shielding his eyes.

Mikey laughed.

"What?" Leon asked. "I mean, I want to know. So if I'm going to say it, I stop myself so that you don't look at me all hard like that." He scrunched his nose at me and waved an open hand in the direction of my face. "Don't give me the Liz eyes."

I looked at him, biting my lip to keep from smiling.

"Those are the Liz eyes!" He covered his eyes with both hands and kept guessing. "Bitch?"

"Do you have a backpack I could borrow?" Mikey asked.

"No." I answered Leon's question.

"You know, I think *preface* might be one of my five," Leon said in my direction.

"You don't have a backpack?" Mikey asked.

"*Preface* can't be one of your offensive words! It just means *goes before*," I said.

"I don't even know if it really means that, so it *is* offensive," Leon said, cringing.

"Do *I* have a backpack?" I turned to Mikey, surprised he was asking me for this, now.

"Yeah," he repeated. "Do you have a backpack?"

"I do, yeah," I told Mikey, confused.

"Is it girly?" he asked.

"What?" Was this a test?

"'Cause I was going to ask, could I borrow it. Not have it or anything. But I'm going on this camping trip with school . . ." He kept talking. "We're going on this overnight and we have to take clothes, you know, for the next day, but I don't have a backpack that could fit clothes. I have a bag, but it's real big, it'd look dumb to bring it. . . . But I could just use some of these plastic supermarket bags. I just thought, everyone else is going to probably have backpacks . . . and maybe you have one and could let me use it. . . ."

"Oh," I said, slow to process what he was asking. "Yeah, I have one. You can use it."

"Cool," he said. "Is it?"

"Is it what?" I asked, probably curtly.

"Girly? Is it, you know, like, girly colors?"

My mind was racing. "No. It's red. Red and black; it's unisex."

"It's sexy?" Mikey asked, confused.

"No, sorry. Unisex, like for both men and women," I said. "It's not girly, you'll see."

By the time dinner was over, I felt exasperated. The boys said the food was the truth, and people agreed that Mikey's cookies had just the right M&M–to–cookie dough ratio. He counted them out like that, he said; he knew they were good. I stayed to help with Kitchen A. I washed the dishes quickly. I was ready to call it a night.

Mikey pushed the broom into the room and stood behind me at the sink until I turned around. "So you're going to come right back?" he asked.

"Tonight?" I asked.

"You know." He paused. "With the backpack?"

I hadn't realized he needed it for the next day. "Did you need it today?"

"Yeah, 'cause we're going tomorrow. That's okay if you can't. I could just use plastic bags or something," he said. "I could use those ones you brought tonight. The grocery ones. That's fine."

I imagined Mikey on this field trip with classmates, with his clothes and toiletries in plastic bags, making a joke about himself before anybody else could.

"No, no, I just— I didn't realize you needed it today. Yeah, I can come back. In, like, ten minutes. I just need to run to my place and pick it up."

As I rode home, parked, then jogged up the four flights of stairs to my apartment, tore through my closet to find the backpack, then ran back down the stairs to my car, the night replayed in my mind. I remembered Mikey's disdain when he said he knew José was gay, and his smirk when he said the word *pussy*. I didn't feel like driving back to give him my backpack. I was tired and annoyed and wished I had better hobbies. Why was I doing this? I thought of Mikey and his meticulous eyebrows, and his counting nine M&M's for every cookie, and his collection of uniforms from juvie lockups. I imagined him packing and unpacking his one big bag at every new placement. I thought of the scar on his arm, and how he had walked to the hospital bleeding.

WHEN I PULLED up to the House, Mikey was standing outside smoking. He nodded a hello and looked at the backpack as I pulled it out of the passenger seat. He smashed the tip of his cigarette against a brick and tossed it down to the sidewalk.

I held my red backpack out to him. "Not too girly, right?" I shrugged.

He took it. "No, it's nice." He zippered and unzippered the zippers. "Real nice. I like it."

"You really don't have a schoolbag?" I asked. "How do you carry your books to school?"

"Nah," he said. "I mean, I have one of those string ones, but it's real small. I don't know about books." He laughed. He tried to slide his arm through a backpack strap, but it was tight. "I could just carry it." He looped two fingers through the handle.

"Oh, the straps are adjustable," I said. "You can move them." I put my hand out and he passed the bag back to me. I lengthened one strap and then the other.

"You don't have to go do all that," he said. "I could just carry the handle."

"It's no trouble," I said. "It's meant to be worn." I held the loosened straps out to him like a coat to be put on sleeve by sleeve. "Try it now."

He hunched his big shoulders and slid one arm and then the other into the straps.

"This's good," he said. He hooked his thumbs through the loops, exposing his forearms. Mary on his arm held a rose the same red as the fabric. "Actually, it's perfect."

I agreed, then asked, "Hey, have you ever been camping?"

"Nah." He laughed.

"I put some bug spray in the front pocket," I said. "Just in case."

"Thanks. I appreciate it," he said. "The bag, I mean. The spray, too. Both."

I nodded.

We stood for a moment, him on the stoop, me on the sidewalk. A siren screeched in the distance. The moon was a bright scratch on the big black wall of night.

"Be safe, okay?" I said.

"I will," he said. "I'll make sure nothing happens to the backpack. I'll take real good care of it." His meticulous eyebrows rose as he spoke. He pressed a manicured hand against the green door and turned back to smile a goodbye.

"I'm not so worried about the backpack," I said.

"Oh, I gotcha," Mikey said, nodding knowingly. He lifted his hand off the door to wave, then turned toward me. "But you do have to admit. *Preface* does sound kind of nasty, if you don't know what it means." He smiled and winked, and I waved good night. He turned to the door. The indelible prayer on his arm was a shadow in the streetlight as he disappeared into the House.

Shortcut to Heaven

"Nobody told you?" Leon shouted from the doorway one June evening, his hands behind his back, leaning against the big green door. School was almost out. Someone had planted flowers between the sidewalk and the House and the buds were open and bright.

"Told me what?" I asked, pulling bags from my backseat. The answer to any question about whether anybody told me anything was usually no.

"I don't think we're cooking anymore," he said.

"Why?" I asked.

"A lot of stuff happened," he said.

"Like what?" I asked, balancing the bags. "Are we really not cooking?"

"People haven't *exactly* been washing the dishes so some of the staff's frustrated," Leon said. "I'm not saying *me*. But *people*." He looked at Frank.

Frank, who had met us inside on the landing, looked away but reached over for groceries.

"And there's some FNGs you haven't met," Leon added as we climbed the stairs. "And one of them's *white*." He whispered *white* like he'd whispered about the pot brownies, as if we had to be careful about what we talked about. "Actually, I think both of them might be, but one of them *definitely* is."

I tried to imagine Leon's rubric for definitely white versus possibly white. To date, the only whiteness in the kitchen had been my own, and we had talked about it only in the context of fried chicken, chocolate cream pies, and school. "You think they'll help?" I asked. "Cooking?"

Frank shrugged. He kicked the kitchen door open since his hands were full of groceries.

"One's not here right now, and I doubt the other dude will. But thing is," Leon said, "there's no knives."

Not washing dishes wasn't a new phenomenon. The House's pay-by-chore system was efficient, but adherence to the practice of cleaning up after oneself, which didn't pay anything, was at best sporadic, which was why the pantry was loaded with disposable products.

We needed the knives to cook, and I figured they must be some-where. I went to ask Judy, the houseparent on duty; I was sure if I asked her, she'd give them to me. But she shrugged and demon-strated how her key opened an empty drawer, and that she didn't have any other keys.

Frank agreed to cut the chicken with a plastic knife. Leon started the brownies with a plastic spoon. I went down the hallway to intro-duce myself to the FNG, and to ask if he wanted to help cook. He said his name was Tom and no to cooking, then asked, "But what time're we eating?"

"This is mad hard, fam," Frank told me as I came back into the kitchen and washed my hands and he sawed through a chicken breast with a plastic knife.

"I know, I'm sorry." I started trying to cut an onion with a plastic knife on a stack of paper plates. The knife got lodged in a middle layer. I laughed at the absurdity of it.

"I'm serious, though," Frank said, sighing. "This shit's dumb."

I wiped onion tears from my eyes with the back of my hand. I lived close enough to run home and get my own knives, but neither Gerry nor Arlette was downstairs to ask if that would be okay. Bringing sharp objects into a group home for minors with behav-ioral and emotional disorders without permission didn't seem like a great idea. So we continued hacking, Frank at the chicken and I at the onion. What should've taken ten minutes took us twenty-five. "This shit *is* dumb," I said.

"Oh, people're just swearing tonight?" Leon said, on his way in with a pan of brownies.

"I'm not doing the rice now," Frank said. "I'm taking a break."

"That's fair," I said. "I'll do the rice."

"You ask the FNG?" Leon asked. "You see what I mean about him?" he whispered.

The FNG was tall and thin with irritated skin, but what Leon meant for me to see was that the new guy was white. During our brief exchange, the FNG told me "Tom" and "no" in ways that implied he knew I already knew his name and thought I should already know he wasn't interested in helping. "Maybe next week he'll help," I said.

"Doubt that," Frank said on his way out of the kitchen.

"*I'll* do the rice, even though I *already* did the brownies," Leon said, closing the oven.

I cut the rest of the vegetables for the stir-fry. Leon made the rice while his brownies baked. Frank returned to mix and season the chicken and vegetables. Wesley came in for milk and said he'd be back to eat. Leon set the table for five, the four of us plus the FNG.

After everything was on the table, Frank and Leon and I sat down to eat. Then Tom, the FNG, came around the corner with a paper plate tucked under his arm and a cup in one hand and a fistful of utensils and napkin in the other. He pushed aside the ones Leon had set for him and used the ones he got for himself. He served himself quietly and started eating.

Over dinner, I asked when Mikey and David had left and if they were part of the lot of stuff that happened. Nobody knew about David. Leon said that Mikey had left in a rush, and that he left some new T-shirts behind when he went, which the remaining boys divided among themselves.

Then they told me about the other FNG, who'd moved in before Tom but wasn't there now. His name was Joseph. "He's a real big dude," Leon said. "*Real* big," Frank reiterated. Right after he moved in, Joseph had some sort of medical episode and punched Greg, the houseparent, in the face. Greg called the police, and two cars came. The boys described the sirens and swirling lights and how the officers parked with their tires up on the sidewalk. They said that while the paramedics carried him out, Joseph kicked the window out of one of the doors, shattering the glass. Frank imitated the popping sound of the pane as they told me. Leon said they took Joseph away in an ambulance followed by the two police cars. He imitated the shrieking sound of the sirens as they took off.

"That dude's big. *And* he's bipolar or some shit like that," Wesley said. "He's crazy." He sipped his Pepsi. "But legit crazy."

"Bipolar," said Tom, who hadn't said a word until then, without looking up from his plate. "I got that shit, too." Then he stood up, crumpled up his napkin onto his plate, flung his trash into the barrel, and left the way he came in.

"So, that dude's crazy, too," Wesley said, finishing his Pepsi.

"Let's try not to talk about people," I suggested.

"Told you she was going to like him better 'cause he's white," Leon told Frank.

"I'm not saying that because he's white," I said.

"She's saying it 'cause he's crazy," Wesley said, smiling.

"So is he the one who's definitely white or probably white?" I asked.

"He's the one who's crazy." Wesley laughed. "They both are."

Maybe I should have anticipated how the next week would play out. I didn't.

THE NEXT WEEK, everything was gone: the pots and pans and spices, along with the knives and spoons. Judy was on duty again. She checked the desk and closet; we did the key dance again.

Why didn't anyone call me? I wanted to ask. "I guess we should just go out to eat," I suggested to Leon instead.

Everyone mobilized in the kitchen in what felt like seconds. The two who were playing a videogame in the TV room and the ones who had been in their bedrooms all somehow heard me. Even Tom was standing, waiting. Walls that had seemed soundproof the weeks that I loudly unpacked the supermarket bags and called for help were suddenly porous.

"Should we go to the Cuban place around the corner?" I asked. "I love that place!" I thought my high recommendation coupled with the fact that I was paying made it a shoo-in.

"Nah," Leon vetoed. "People like Heaven so we could just go there." Gina's Pizza Heaven was a pizza and sub place two blocks away. I'd seen it walking around the neighborhood.

I told Judy our plan. I knew that the boys could be out until curfew, so technically we didn't need permission; we'd just be going to Heaven, together. Still, I felt I should tell her.

"That's cute," she said.

I didn't think it was cute. I was annoyed about the pots and pans and spending money on subs in addition to groceries that might not last until the following week. I could make do with the lack of information, but I couldn't make anything without pots and knives. But the boys seemed more excited for our field trip than they did about cooking, even I had to admit that.

Judy told me that Joseph was supposed to take a pill with dinner and asked if I would give it to him. She handed me a tiny envelope with a tinier bulge in it.

"Do you think it's okay for Joseph to come with us?" I asked. I looked over at him. He had been discharged from wherever he had been and was now standing apart from the other boys in the kitchen. I thought about what they told me, about him punching Greg in the face, the police, the ambulance. Greg was bigger than me, and Joseph was bigger than Greg. "Real big," like Frank and Leon said.

"Oh yeah," Judy said. "He's real sweet, most of the time." I turned to go and she added, "It should be okay. Besides, you could just call the police if something happens."

I nodded as if this sounded reasonable even though the police didn't seem like the best remedy if Joseph's mental illness interrupted our dinner plan. I zipped the pill into my wallet. And we were off.

THE BOYS FELL into formation on our way to Gina's Pizza Heaven. They walked in twos, not touching, spanning the width of the sidewalk. Frank and Wesley in front, Leon a bit behind them, Tom to his right, and Joseph behind them. I walked near Joseph, who said nothing, even when I asked him questions.

People walked around us. Some held their bags tighter to their bodies, or physically contracted their shoulders and arms to pass by, or crossed the street; some avoided eye contact. Some looked at me, at my clothes and into my face, as if trying to discern my relationship to the boys, as if their relationship to each other was more obvious. Who were we to each other?

Nine silent minutes later, we arrived at the restaurant. The place was small, had more chairs than people, and smelled like bread and grease and comfort. Leon explained to me that the boys liked it because it wasn't too far from the House, they could buy a large sub and a drink for eight dollars, four days of chore money, and it was good.

While I wrestled with questions about breakdowns in communication and why was I trying so hard to make this program work, the boys were happily deciding whether they wanted extra cheese or *extra* extra cheese on their usuals. Large steak bombs with everything for Frank and Wesley, and a large chicken parm for Leon. Joseph ordered himself a cheese pizza. Tom asked if he could really get anything and would I pay for it. As I said "Yeah," I searched the menu for the most expensive item and wondered what the chances were that he'd order himself a fried seafood platter for two.

"Steak bomb," Tom told the guy behind the counter. "American cheese, no onions."

"What size?" the guy asked.

Tom looked at me.

"Large?" I asked.

"Large," he told the guy.

I told him that he should also get a drink. I had to tell all of the boys to order drinks and encourage them to get chips. Their conscious hesitation about asking for too much made me want to offer them more.

We sat at two tables because we didn't fit at one, and after the period of silence during which each boy devoured his meal, there was even some conversation. As if he could sense my ambivalence, Leon played the role of me at the table, asking everyone about school. Except unlike when I asked, everybody answered him, salt-and-peppering, in between bites.

On the walk home, Frank paused on the sidewalk ahead of us, outside another pizza place. He was squinting, looking in the window. We caught up with him.

"Are you checking out the menu?" I asked. "Should we try there next time?" It felt like there would be a next time.

"Nah," Frank said, still squinting. "I think that lady cop in there arrested me one time."

I looked in the window. Two uniformed officers were at the counter, a Black male with a pizza box and a white female with red hair holding a Styrofoam container.

"Yup, that's her," Frank said, his gaze fixed on the female officer as she turned around. I wondered what he saw watching the officer order dinner, waiting for it to be ready, as if she was a normal person.

"We can wait for you if you want to go in and say hi," I joked, a stupid joke.

Tom looked into the window, then at me, and asked Frank, "Is she serious?"

"Nah," Frank said to Tom, then looked at me and rolled his eyes. "I'm good."

We kept walking.

When we got back to the House, Judy asked Frank for the other half of his sub. He looked at the wrapped package in his hand, and I could see him thinking about whether he should give it to her, and that he didn't want to.

I couldn't believe she was asking for the rest of his sandwich. Who asks a kid for some of his food? Then I thought about how anytime I invited her to eat after the boys had, she would take a heaping plate and be grateful. I didn't often think about how little the houseparents made, how most held multiple jobs; I should have asked her before we left if we could bring her something back.

"You know, I think Frank was saving that for lunch tomorrow," I said.

"You are?" she asked him.

"Yeah," he said, relieved.

"Oh, I was just kidding about asking you for it anyway." Judy laughed. "You gave Joseph his pill, right?"

"Shit! No!" I said. "I totally forgot." I pulled the envelope out of my wallet.

"That's okay," she said. "I'll give it to him now. It'll probably be okay."

I hoped it would all be okay.

With Cherries on Top

We decided to take the summer off from cooking. By *we decided*, I mean that I asked the boys if they wanted to keep doing our cooking nights through the summer, and Leon explained that I could come if I wanted, but nobody else was going to show up. They had other plans.

I spent July and August reading and traveling, my two favorite parallel universes. I met a friend in London for a week. I liked the escape of getting away; I liked being a stranger someplace else. I liked paying extra attention to the height of buildings and the way things tasted. My terrible sense of direction was less noticeable in places I wasn't supposed to know my way around. London was the first place I'd ever gone abroad, with my sister Juli and my dad; it was his first time on another continent, too. He slept with our passports under his pillow, found a local breakfast place that served sausage because he didn't consider the jam and bread the hotel served acceptable, and insisted we visit the Inns of Court rather than the Jack the Ripper tour my sister and I begged to do. It was strange to be back there, in a city I had only ever been to with him. It was another in the litany of empty firsts without him, when things weighed differently even though their shapes were the same. I found myself looking for him there as if I might find him around some corner, misplaced. It had started happening less frequently in Boston, that I would think I saw him at a distance in the hunch of somebody else's shoulders as he walked on a sidewalk, in another father's face waiting in a crowd at the airport. Part of missing is that looking and mistaking in the fog. Part of grief is that grasping, all of those almosts.

I RETURNED TO the House a few weeks after school started, at the end of September. In addition to groceries, I brought my own knives. I swore to Gerry I would keep track of them and he gave me permission to bring them and his word that the staff would unlock the pots and spices. There were five boys living in the House when we left off in June: Frank, Leon, Wesley, Joseph, and an FNG named Mark who liked eating mangoes, asking questions, and not going to school. Tom was already gone. When I asked what happened to him, the boys told me there'd been a fight. Wesley said he'd told me Tom was crazy and that he was right, and Leon said, "He called us fucked-up stuff," and Frank nodded that all of it was true. It was hard to predict what new boys and stories the summer might bring.

I should've known that something was up when Frank was in the kitchen, already washing his hands, when I arrived. The windows were open; there was no breeze. His hair was disheveled, his eyes were bloodshot, and he was barefoot. He didn't look at me.

"Hey, Frank!" I said, unpacking groceries. "How was the summer?"

"Fine," he said. He ripped a paper towel from the roll and dried his hands in three pats. Front of the hands, back of the hands, front of the hands.

"How's school so far?" I asked.

"How you want me to cut the chicken?" he asked. "Like before, in blocks?"

"Sure, your usual is great," I said. "Is Leon around?"

Frank shrugged and opened the cabinets to look for the cutting board.

"Leon?" I called down the hall. "Will you help me with the groceries?" I talked to his closed door. "There're still bags in the car."

Leon pulled a white T-shirt over a white undershirt on his way into the kitchen. His hair was big and his eyes were heavy with sleep. The red numbers on the clock on the back of the stove read 5:55. "Yeah, Liz, I'll help you," he said.

"Hey, I'm early and you didn't even notice," I said.

He dropped one sneaker and wiggled his bare foot into it.

"Leon?" I asked. "Were you sleeping?"

"I smell a rat," Frank said from the sink, rinsing the cutting board.

"I was taking a nap," Leon told me. He looked at Frank, narrowed his eyes, and looked away. He wiggled into his second shoe. "This place makes me tired."

As the peeling green door shut behind us, Leon started to speak quickly. "Things've been crazy since a few weeks ago."

"What happened?" I asked.

"Everybody's got court dates and Arlette said I have to tell the truth, so Frank's calling me a rat," he said.

"But what happened? Why do people have court dates?" I asked.

"I was walking with Frank and another guy and they were tipsy and wanted more alcohol so they gave a homeless guy two dollars." Leon reached for a bag, didn't look at me.

"Wait, this is about two dollars?" I asked. "Who was the other guy? Wesley?"

"I know," he said. "That's what I was telling them. . . . But Frank tipped the guy and stomped him. The homeless guy was tipsy so he wasn't right, and Frank wasn't taking his medicine, so he was how he gets."

I wanted to ask for clarification about how much alcohol "more alcohol" was, and what "tipping and stomping" was. I wanted to talk about judgment, and ask how often Frank had been getting "how he gets," and what that even meant. But I wasn't anybody's caseworker. I wasn't really sure what the volunteer who ran a cooking program was supposed to do in this situation. I reached into my car for a bag, processing what Leon had told me. "Was the other kid Wesley?"

"Nah, an FNG. You don't know him." Leon reached for another bag.

"They robbed and beat a homeless man for two dollars?" I couldn't look at Leon.

"Well, it was Frank's money, so it wasn't really robbing him," Leon reasoned.

"Leon—" I started, not interested in technicalities.

"What? *I* didn't do it," he said. "But Frank gave the dude two dollars to get one of those little bottles of alcohol that you can get at the checkout." He made a claw with his thumb and index finger to indicate the size of the container.

"And then what?" I asked. "What happened then?"

Leon shrugged. "The dude took off with the money. So Frank got real mad and followed him." He reached for another bag. "Then he tipped him and stomped him. I told you already."

"And you were with them?" I asked, searching his face.

"I mean I *was*, but *I* didn't touch the guy," he said. "Did you get whipped cream?" He looked in the bags he was holding, then peeked into mine.

I pulled the soda from the backseat. "So what now?" I asked.

"I guess we have to have sundaes without whipped cream since you didn't get any."

"Leon, I mean what now with the court dates," I clarified.

"I *told you* already. We all got court dates," Leon said. "Separate ones. But Arlette said it's different for me 'cause I'm old now. I'm nineteen so I go to real court, not juvie. They get to go to juvie, so it doesn't matter so much for them. I've got to look out for myself, 'cause I don't have that many chances anymore." He paused. "So Frank's calling me a rat."

"Yeah, you've got to listen to Arlette," I said. I locked the door and slammed it.

"You really need one of those clickers," Leon said.

Back in the kitchen with Frank, I cut vegetables as he cut the chicken. Wesley came in and stood in the spotlight of the open refrigerator. With a plastic cup in his teeth, he twisted the cap open to pour himself a predinner drink.

"Liz!" Leon called from the dining room where he'd gone to mix the brownies. "Liz! Could you come here for a minute?"

"*Liz! Could you come here for a minute?*" Wesley mimicked. "You sound like you're special needs, LeBron!"

"Wesley!" I whispered.

"I'm just saying," Wesley said, shrugging. "Someone had to say it so I'm saying it."

"Liz?" Leon called again.

"Nobody had to say that," I said to Wesley on my way into the dining room.

"But I said it anyway." Wesley smiled a big smile. "You're welcome."

Leon was sitting at the table with his hands in his lap.

"What's up, Leon? I thought you were making the brownies. Are you making them?"

The red box of brownie mix, a one-fourth measuring cup of canola oil, water, and egg were sitting in a row in front of him, in the order of assembly. "They're not my specialty anymore, they're Mikey's specialty," he said, pouting.

"Is Mikey back?" I asked.

"No," Leon said. "But everybody still likes his better."

"C'mon, Leon, you know how to make brownies. And everyone likes how you make them. With love," I added, reminding him.

"I forget how to make them," he said, squinting at the box out of the corner of his eye, his head shaking the way it shook when he fixed his focus on something. He sighed and tore the box open, pulling out the plastic bag of brown powder and biting it open with his teeth. He emptied the mix into the bowl and added the oil and water. "One, two, three, four, five, six, seven," he counted as he mixed. Then he cracked the egg; the shell broke but no liquid spilled out.

"What's this?" Leon scrunched his nose.

"Oh my goodness!" I'd never seen frozen eggs.

"Someone turned the refrigerator too cold," he said. "How am I supposed to mix them?"

"Oh, you can't use those. Mix it some, and I'll go to the store for fresh eggs," I said.

"How many times?" Leon asked, squinting at the box. "It says to mix it fifty times total."

"Just beat it until it's blended," I said. "You can finish when I bring back better eggs."

"Can you get whipped cream?" he asked. "Since you forgot it."

"Yes." I reached for a ten-dollar bill in my wallet.

"And cherries?" he asked.

"Cherries?" I asked. Everyone had court dates, and who knows what had happened to the homeless man. And we were talking about cherries.

"Well, you said brownie *sundaes*. Ice cream and whipped cream is good and everything, but *sundaes* have *cherries*," he said.

"And cherries. I'll get eggs, whipped cream, and cherries." I grabbed my wallet.

Mark, who had moved in before we broke for summer, said he'd come with me to the store and poured himself a cup of soda for the walk. I asked him if he'd heard about the incident in question and he said, "Yeah, but I didn't go out with them, 'cause I quit smoking for a while, 'cause I've got to take a pee test for a job application." Of course, there was more to the story.

When we got to the parking lot, he put his empty cup on a light post instead of in the trash.

"Are we the kind of people who litter?" I asked, picking up the cup.

"Maybe you're not." He laughed.

I threw it away near the entrance. At the door, he stepped aside to let me walk through first. When we got inside the store, a small woman followed us to the dairy aisle and then asked me in Spanish if I would get something for her from a top shelf on the other side of the store. After we walked with her and I retrieved the jar and she walked away, Mark looked at me and started laughing.

"What? Don't people ever ask you to get stuff? You're tall, too," I said. "Taller than me."

"Nobody ever asks me for anything," he said, still laughing.

WHEN WE RETURNED to the House with the groceries, a pan of chicken and vegetables was resting on one back burner and a pot of rice on the other. The bowl of partially blended brownie batter lay abandoned on the dining room table. The only sign of boys around was the ping and whir of videogame gunfire dinging in the near distance. But with the promise of chips as an interim snack, Frank and Leon returned to their stations.

When Leon finished the brownies, I put them in the oven. Mark took it upon himself to set the table. He dumped a pile of plastic silverware into the middle of the table and threw paper plates like Frisbees toward each spot at the table. He overthrew one, and it fell to the floor. He walked over, picked the plate up, then placed it where Frank usually sat. I looked at him.

He narrowed his eyes at me and shrugged. "Frank won't notice anyway," he said. He tossed another plate to a different spot, across the table. It landed. Mark looked at me to be sure I had seen it and smiled his widest smile.

Dinner was faster and quieter than usual. Frank, Leon, Wesley, Mark, and Tony, the FNG who had been arrested with Leon and Frank, all came to dinner. Joseph, who spent all of the prep time in his room, made his way out of his room when Leon knocked and told him it was time.

Leon brought three different bottles of hot sauce to the table and pushed them into the middle. The boys reached for the bottles, but no one would look at him, let alone thank him.

By the time I was rinsing my two knives and putting them in my purse, the clock on the stove read 7:44 P.M. The boys scattered for sixteen minutes of freedom before chores, so I decided to leave. I went to find Frank, who I thought might be smoking outside. I walked around to the front of the House. From the sidewalk, I saw him standing with his back to me on the porch. When I called his name, he crushed his cigarette against the House and tossed the butt into the mulch. He turned to me, hands shoved into the front pockets of his jeans.

"Hey Frank," I said, turning my car keys in my hand.

"Who told you?" he asked.

"It doesn't matter, Frank. It's big news, and I'm worried," I said.

"I'm worried about rats," he said.

"You know Leon's in a different situation, Frank," I said. "You and the new guy will go through the juvie system. But Leon has to go to adult court now. He said he's afraid he could catch real assault charges for this." The boys said "catch charges" like sometimes they hit you and sometimes they didn't. "You wouldn't want him to get in trouble if it wasn't his fault, would you?" I looked at him. He looked at his feet. "Frank?"

"What?" Frank asked. He paused. "Yeah, I get it."

"Are you okay?" I asked.

"If I do something, I do it. I take the consequences," he said.

"I know," I said. "You know what this reminds me of?"

"Hmmm?" He looked over my shoulder at the street.

"It reminds me of the PlayStation controllers. How you work to earn money, to buy yourself a controller. Then when you get angry, you break it. Then buy another one when you have enough to. But you only break your own, only the ones you bought with your own money."

He looked at the porch floorboards.

"Arlette told me about that. And I think it must make sense to you, because it's your money; you're only hurting yourself." I looked at him. "But you're hurting yourself, Frank."

He studied the bricks on the side of the House.

"And that man, whoever he was—" I started.

"You don't have to worry," he said.

"It's not about me, Frank. It's about you. You know, I can't even imagine you hurting someone like that," I said. "I only know you to be good. To be helping."

"You don't really know me," he said.

"I know," I said. I looked down at the sidewalk, turning my keys in my hand.

"I didn't mean it like that," he said. "It's just how I get sometimes."

"What happens now, Frank?" I asked.

"Don't know. I'll see at my court date," he said. "It's the last time."

"Will you tell me what happens?" I asked. He had told me the last time he had gotten in trouble with police was the last time. "I do worry about you, Frank," I said again. I wanted him to hear that I cared about him, for whatever that was worth.

"Yeah," he said to my shoulder. "I've got to go already. I've got to go to the bathroom."

"Okay, I'm leaving," I said.

"Never mind, I could hold it," he said quickly.

"No, go to the bathroom." I laughed. "Thanks for helping tonight. And I'll see you next week?"

"Yup," he said, already pushing the door open. "Don't worry about me."

WHEN I GOT back to my apartment, I went to my room, fell across my bed, and stared at the print on my wall of a Klimt woman with wild hair, open eyes, tangled in a constellation of golden flowers; I loved how Klimt embellished the real. Eventually I called my mother, because I couldn't call my father. I talked quickly, breathlessly. About Frank and the PlayStation controllers, about the homeless man and the two dollars, about how my role in all of this felt insignificant. And by *all of this* I meant life in general, the way I do when I feel angry, sad, and tired.

"He could've jumped anybody else in the neighborhood for more money than that. He just wanted his own money back." In his mind, he was justified. "I'm not defending him. But who does he have to defend him, Mom?"

"That's how it is with those kids, Liz," she said. "It won't do you any good to get so worked up." Her voice was tender. "Daddy would say you can do more from a step away." Her voice was the same as when we were little and she'd tell my siblings and me stories about the kids at the orphanage where she and my dad worked when they met each other, kids who set things on fire and waited for parents who never came.

"Two dollars," I said, as if it were about two dollars. I knew if I kept talking, she'd tell me I should stop going. I said goodbye and called my sister Juli.

My sister listened as I talked in circles, the terrible parts, the funny parts, the silences between them. Then she asked me, "Why do you go?" I could hear her voice waver on the other end of the line; she had no interest in going to the House without our dad. It was a terrible story inside of a terrible story. She said, "I just don't understand why you keep going."

The going wasn't the hard part. It had been nearly a year of starting and stopping and starting over. The rhythm at the House was tumultuous; it was fast and changing and there was no stopping for the kids. As a volunteer, I just had to show up for a while, and leave, and then come back again. And I knew my mother was right, that I shouldn't keep going if I couldn't accept the limitations of what I was able to do and then exit the space two hours later and be in my own life. My father had told me this once, when I called him from Chicago, crying about a student who had been expelled. "You've got to take a step back," he said. "And if you can't do that, you have no business being there."

"That doesn't make sense," I had said, thinking of the short term.

"That's the only thing that makes sense," he had said, thinking of the long term.

The taking the step back was the hard part, the keeping a distance, the leaving, the knowing when enough was enough. Going to the House was a way into what had been the other part of my father's life. Cooking was a way to practice something with a beginning, a middle, an end, every time complete. Every time, we made something good and practical, however small. That was my tiny job there: helping make dinner once a week. I knew what my dad would say: Just do what you can do; do the best you can. And if you can't take a step back, you have no business being there.

I couldn't fall asleep. My heart was pounding. I closed my eyes. I imagined the long walk my dad and I would do those nights after the diagnosis. It's what I did when I couldn't fall asleep; I remembered it into a dream. I walked out the door of my parents' house and down the stairs. I turned right at the end of the driveway. I walked up the street, past the telephone poles to the corner, and turned right at the end of the sidewalk. I fell asleep then. I could feel my father walking next to me. My breathing slowed. He didn't say anything. I felt him shift to adjust his hat, the dark-green scally cap he wore with a navy fleece when it was cool outside, the one I packed up with my things when I moved out of my parents' house. I kept leaning closer to his face, to breathe him in. I strained to see the pores on his nose, a lost eyelash on his cheek. I tried to see his eyes. I wanted him to say words I'd never heard him say before. I wanted him to be real.

Shit Bag

Several weeks later, as Frank was cutting chicken into blocks like last time and I was preparing the vegetables, the phone rang at the House. It was Mark. Mark, who had told me he was quitting smoking and was going to get a job. Mark, who called me "Liz" while most of the boys called me "Miss," "Um, Excuse Me?" or nothing at all. Mark, who had stepped out of the way to let me into the supermarket ahead of him. Mark was in the hospital. He'd been shot and was recovering from surgery. He asked to talk to me because nobody else would talk to him.

Mark had moved into the House just before summer and had been a regular at the table in the fall. When he helped on cooking nights, he liked to ask questions. "Why do you always get Mexican mangoes? Look at me," he told me once, showing me his arm. "I'm Haitian. I like Haitian mangoes." A different night, he asked, "Can't we ask for stuff we want you to make? You think you could make a pineapple cake sometime? With, like, cherries in it?"

I asked if pineapple upside-down cake was his favorite.

He shrugged. "My aunt made one of those once. It was good. I was just thinking about it." But don't wait for his birthday, he told me. Because his birthday was before he moved in, and he'd probably be gone before his next one.

Mark asked me questions that spanned beyond the usual "Could you pass me that?" and "Is this ready?" and "What time you think we're eating?"

"Do you have any kids, Liz?" he asked me once, leaning into the kitchen from a doorway.

"What? Nooo," I said. I was pulling something out of the oven with my sweater sleeves pulled over my hands because I couldn't find pot holders, trying not to get burned. "No kids."

"You don't want them, right?" he said. "Because kids wreck your life. I don't blame you."

I looked up from the pan, into his face. He looked at me, smiling his wide white smile.

"No, I didn't mean it like that," I backtracked. "I just mean, not now. I need to get my life in order before I bring other people into it, you know?" I shrugged. It felt like the wrong answer.

"Whatever you say," he said, still smiling. "But you're right," he said, nodding at me. "It's true kids wreck your life. What're you making for dinner anyway?"

ON THE PHONE, Mark's voice was low and scratchy. "Heyyy, Liz. What're you making for dinner?"

"Just stir-fry again," I said. "How're you feeling?"

"You know," he said.

I didn't know what it felt like to be shot then sewn back together. "Tired and in lots of pain?" I guessed.

"What's in the stir-fry? Chicken?" he asked.

"Yeah, chicken and vegetables."

He started to groan. "It hurts so bad, Liz. It hurts so bad."

"Did you ask for more medicine?" I assumed because he was on the phone with me, he was alone in his hospital room. I didn't know if he knew how to advocate for himself. "They can adjust the dosage of your medicine if you ask them. To help with the pain. If you tell them how much it hurts, they'll be able to give you a little more," I said. "Have you had visitors?"

"No," he said. "Just Arlette."

"Has your mom been by?" I asked. I knew his mother was local, that he had home visits.

"No, my moms doesn't want to see me." He started groaning again. "It hurts so bad, Liz."

I didn't know what to say. I held the phone for a minute and listened. "Mark, tell the nurse you want some medicine, so you can sleep. You won't fall asleep without it because I think you're in too much pain. The nurse will give it to you when you ask, and it'll help you fall asleep." I didn't know his situation, but I knew this routine.

"Okay, hold on," he said. I could hear the machines beeping in the background, a woman's voice. "Hey, could I get some medicine?" he asked the voice. "I could?" Then to me he said, "Okay, yeah, Liz. I'm going to go. They're going to give me medicine, and I'm going to sleep." He said something to the nurse. "Thank you," he said to me. "Bye."

I listened for his end to click before I hung up.

When I walked back into the kitchen, I asked why no one wanted to say hello to Mark. Wesley shook his head. Leon looked away. Frank said, "Just didn't."

"He could use some support," I said. "When he comes home, it won't be easy for him."

"This isn't anybody's home," Wesley said, before leaving the kitchen.

Frank and Leon didn't say anything.

Later that night, Arlette came upstairs to talk to one of the staff, and I asked about Mark.

"He's just had surgery," she said. "When I heard, I thought that he was going to be sent back to us in a chair, too." By *too*, I knew she was referring to Ronald, a resident who'd been paralyzed in a gang shooting during my dad's last summer.

Ronald had lived in one of the agency's residences before he was paralyzed. My dad told me about him on our walks. I learned his story in installments: in the hospital, not knowing whether he'd ever walk again; finding out he couldn't; figuring out how to accommodate a kid with a wheelchair whose family was out of the picture; finding a place he could live and go to school; determining who would pay for all of it. My dad was sick by then, but we didn't know how sick yet. Talking about Ronald became a way to talk about other things.

But Ronald was living someplace else now, and Arlette was telling me about Mark. "And I thought to myself," Arlette continued, "Lord, I can't go through this again. I can't do this with another one." She closed her eyes and shook her head slowly. "But he's going to be all right. He's got a colostomy bag for now. But he's going to be all right."

I THINK IT was Leon who told me how Mark ended up in the hospital. Mark had gone home to visit his mother in the projects. There was a back-and-forth between some people looking for drugs and people selling them and the runners who facilitated the transactions. Mark and his friend had an idea. The friend would tell a guy who came looking that they knew where the drugs were, and if he gave them the money, they'd run for them and then come back with the drugs and keep some of the money. They did this a couple of times. One afternoon, they decided to try it a different way: the guy would come, and instead of taking his money and running back with the drugs, they would just take all of the money and run. It worked the first time, and a couple of other times. Mark had bragged to the boys at the House about the money he was making, the times they got away with it. But this time, a disgruntled return customer came back with a gun. This time, it was the customer who ran away. Mark and his friend were carried off on stretchers in a mess of blood and a bath of blaring sirens and swirling lights.

Mark was in the hospital for almost a month. His stomach was blown apart. No charges were filed. General consensus in the House was that Mark got what he deserved.

"I'm not saying that Mark should've been shot, or that God would want that to happen to anyone, but *in a way* he got what he deserved." Leon's tone was apologetic when he told me. He looked at me, head tilted, out of the bottom corner of his eye, to see if I was shocked or saddened by what he said.

"That dude's just stupid." Wesley was less diplomatic. "He did what he did and got himself shot for it. He was bragging about how much money he's got, and how he doesn't need to be doing chores here. Now he can't even shit by himself. He's got to wear a shit bag, which is just nasty."

I was struck by Wesley's knowledge of colostomy bags. I asked him if he knew other people who had had them, and he said, "Yup," as if it were obvious. He listed names, how he knew them, and where they'd gotten shot. He counted on one hand as he ticked them off, and moved to a second before he was done.

THE NIGHT MARK was discharged from the hospital to the House was a cooking night. He arrived all slur and frizz and stagger and stink. When he limped in, holding his side, his hair stretched up in a wild halo, not tied back into his usual wide, tight braids, he said, "It's good to be back." He lowered himself slowly into a chair at the table. He was wearing a hospital gown over his jeans, with an un-zipped navy-blue hoodie over the gown; Arlette had brought a new set of clothes for him to wear out, since the ones he had worn in were cut off him in the emergency room. The plastic colostomy bag protruded through the gown's thin fabric, slightly. Its sharp rectangular shape wasn't as obvious as the smell.

Mark sat hunched in a chair at the table, determined to not go back to bed because, he said, he'd been in bed for a month. Each time he shifted, he winced and groaned. Each time he made a noise, the other boys looked at him and then looked away. Nobody said much to him. He said that he wanted to eat what we were eating and asked if he could. He was on a special diet because of the colos-tomy bag. The houseparent looked for the green paper that had his diet printed on it. He couldn't eat anything with seeds, nuts, or cas-ings. Our pasta and chicken with broccoli and Alfredo sauce was fine.

I also made him a pineapple upside-down cake, like the one he'd asked for weeks before. Mark smiled and nodded when he saw it. "That's the one I wanted," he said.

———

He left not long after that. But before his departure, Mark asked me a question in the kitchen that burrowed deep into my brain. The boys had gone out to smoke before dinner. They came in giggling, with bloodshot eyes.

"I don't understand why you do this," I said to them, about getting high on school nights.

"Man, Liz," Mark said in his smooth, sweet voice, opening his arms wide like he was about to take off. "You be trying to change us, like that's ever going to happen." Then he paused and asked, "Why can't you just accept us how we are?"

Seventeen Candles

"You forgot Wesley's birthday," Leon told me, shaking his head, as soon as I opened the door to the kitchen that November. The windows were closed. It was more than chilly outside; it was cold.

"What? Isn't it next week?" I had a sinking feeling.

"Nope. Last week. You forgot it," Leon said.

"Yeah, you did," Frank said seriously.

"What? Last week? How come nobody told me?" I asked. I was there the week before, and the week before that; we had cooked and the boys decided menus, and we cooked again. "We were here! We cooked! Why didn't anybody tell me?"

"You should've known," Leon said, still shaking his head.

"Wes?" I called into his room. "Did we forget your birthday?"

Wesley opened the door. "Yeah, you did," he said, taking everyone else out of it. "It's all right. It doesn't matter."

We made calzones per Wesley's request the following week, with a strawberry shortcake, his favorite. I made the W with strawberries on top, like I'd made the year before, and brought 1 and 7 numbered candles. But Wesley said not to light them, because it wasn't his birthday anymore.

Transfer

Meanwhile, Joseph spent most of his time in his room, watching movies on his laptop and listening to music. His first months, he would come to dinner sometimes, when he wasn't at appointments or on home visits, but he wasn't interested in making anything. Then he started showing up in the kitchen while we were working, to watch. He'd stand, eyeing me as I unloaded the groceries and I'd tell him what we were cooking that night. Whatever it was, his response was the same: "Ookaay, that's a good idea." Except when we were having pizza, then he would add, giddily, "I like pizza so much it's funny."

Joseph didn't interact much with the other boys; they tended to move around him as if he were a piece of furniture. And he would contort his body to not touch them, without saying anything, to pass them in the hallway on the way to his room. But at the table, facing each other, they couldn't deny their mutual existence. Sometimes people talked.

"Joseph's killing the food," Frank said one night, watching as Joseph served himself seconds while the others were still eating firsts. "Joe, you should be a sumo," he told him.

"Frank, he's not big enough for that," I said. I didn't know how Joseph would react to that, or how he thought about his size, or what his triggers were, except that I knew he had them. And I didn't think anybody called him Joe, but I figured one thing at a time.

"Just wait," Frank said, shaking his head. "He's about to be."

Joseph laughed, kept eating. And we all kept eating.

I learned later that Joseph's placement at the House was a kind of experiment that he and his brother agreed to. Before he lived in the House, Joseph had lived in an institution for individuals with profound physical, emotional, and intellectual disabilities. The experiment was to see how he would do in a less-restrictive group home setting. The agency's mission was to provide care to young people in a community setting rather than an institutional setting for as long as possible. Gerry had been a pioneer in this work in the 1960s; some continued to think his ideas were radical. All the boys at the House had complicated emotional and physical histories that intersected homes and schools and jails and hospitals, but Joseph stood out. In my conversations with Joseph, I could tell he was different from the other boys, but I didn't understand that for him, it was unlikely that he would ever live on his own in the world.

JOSEPH HEARD VOICES; sometimes he did what they said. He called his psychotic breaks "episodes," and he talked about them the way other boys talked about home visits and skipping school. He said he wasn't himself during his episodes, as if there were a clear division of his selves, like a white and a yolk, with an obvious distinction after a crack.

"I tried to hang myself once," Joseph said during one dinner, looking down at his plate.

We were all sitting around the table, finishing dessert, talking about a gruesome triple-homicide-suicide story in the news. A teenager killed his sisters and then himself, and the three siblings were being waked and buried together out of a nearby church. My youngest sister, Laura, who was also a teacher, had taught one of the sisters and attended the wake. Laura inherited our father's math brain and she can put anything together, with or without instructions. She wept as she described the scene; nothing about the story held a natural order of things.

"That's messed up," Leon had said, "that they buried the brother next to sisters he killed."

I didn't disagree, but repeated what my sister had heard, that the mother said they were all her children and wanted to bury them together.

Joseph had said he knew something that was messed up, and then shared about one of the times he attempted suicide, when he tried to hang himself. "From an overpass," he explained. He described the location, not far from where we were sitting. He talked not to the other boys, but near them. "I was working at a supermarket, and you know those ropes they use for the carts?"

The other boys got quiet. They looked at me.

"I think so," I said. I'd never really looked at the rope, but I'd seen people wrangle carts.

"I used one of those," Joseph said. "I took it from work. I got the idea when I was bringing carts in."

"Who saved you?" I asked the obvious question.

"A cop. He got me down from there," Joseph said. "And brought me to a hospital."

"It's good he found you," I said.

"Yeah. He saw me when I was getting ready to do it, so he was right there," he said. In Joseph's stories, police officers always seemed to be there to save him, which wasn't the case in the other boys' stories.

The table remained quiet. Joseph kept talking. "Then there was the time I jumped into a frozen pond." He laughed a little. "But that time it was just because I was so excited about life."

Other boys pushed away from the table, relieved to be free before chores.

"Who saved you that time?" I asked.

"I saved myself," he said. "I only jumped half in. Then I got out." He shrugged.

"Have you had feelings like that recently?" I thought I should ask.

"Yeah, I have. Like when I cut my hand and I didn't want to kill myself, I just wanted to hurt myself. Did I tell you that? I had a knife. It was just an episode," he explained between bites. "I wasn't myself."

"No, you didn't tell me that," I said. I wondered if he remembered his episodes like dreams. I wanted to ask him who he thought he was when he was himself. And I wondered where he'd gotten the knife.

I counted my knives twice before putting them in my purse that night, and examined their serrated blades. Before I left, I told the houseparent on duty what Joseph had said so he could put it in a log entry for the shift, because it seemed like something that should be recorded somewhere. I wasn't in the practice of telling on the boys or reporting our conversations unless they felt dangerous. I called the next day to tell Gerry, too, and I talked to Arlette. "Oh, yes, Joseph has attempted," she said in shorthand: "attempted," leaving *suicide* silent.

JOSEPH WAS ALSO a poet. He wrote his poems in bubbly lowercase letters, lightly, in pencil, on loose-leaf paper. At arm's length, the pages looked like they might be covered with spiderwebs. Joseph kept hundreds of them stacked in piles, stuffed in manila folders on his desk. When he told me he was a poet, I asked him if I might read one of his poems, because I liked poetry, too, and he started bringing the folders to the table after dinner, on his good nights.

After we cleared the table and the others started chores, Joseph disappeared to his room and returned with the pale folders. He'd sit across from me and push some pages over in my direction, and watch me read. I asked questions about his word pairings and line breaks and commented on imagery. Each time I looked up, Joseph's eyes were already on me. Leon called these ten minutes of poetry "Joe-and-Liz time at the table." Everyone was invited to stay. Almost nobody ever did.

"Sometimes I write words 'cause I like what they mean," Joseph told me. "Sometimes it's just words for words." When he spoke, his voice was usually flat unless he was talking about pizza, but his poems were spiked with question marks and exclamation points. Some had questions that I never heard him ask out loud, like, "If I'm so normal, then why / can't I just kiss a girl?"

—

A THING THAT repeated in Joseph's days like a refrain in one of his poems was that he kept getting lost. He knew where he was supposed to be and got where he was going without incident, but on the way back he often got lost—after short trips, like to appointments in the city, and longer ones, like visits to family out of state. When it happened the Sunday after Thanksgiving, after spending the weekend at his brother's, he almost got arrested.

One night at the table Joseph told us that what he wanted was to live with his brother all the time, but his brother told him he couldn't, because he had his own family. Sometimes Joseph seemed to understand what his brother meant by this; sometimes he didn't. "But I *am* his own family," he would say, shrugging. "And he's my own family."

One time, right after his brother moved out of state, Joseph lost his transfer ticket on the bus ride back from a visit and he wasn't sure what to do, so he walked in circles around the bus station for hours before a police officer picked him up and directed him. The next time, he got off the bus at the wrong stop and thought he'd try to walk; he walked a long time before being picked up by another police officer in a different town, who took him back to the bus station to start again. Another time, he just kept walking and made it back on his own; it took seven hours and his feet were bleeding when he took his socks off. He decided not to get lost the time after that, Thanksgiving weekend.

But it was Sunday and it was getting dark, so when he missed the second bus and there wasn't another one coming anytime soon, he decided to take a taxi. He read the address of the House off a paper he kept in his wallet, but when the cab pulled up to the brick building, he got out and told the driver he was sorry but he didn't have any money. The driver yelled that he was going to call the police. The driver rang the doorbell to try to get somebody to pay the fare. Judy, the houseparent on duty, came downstairs and said she didn't have any money either.

"But," Joseph said when he told me the story of that night, "Judy explained how I am and he didn't call the cops. The guy was mad, but he left."

I knew what he meant when he referred to how he was because he'd told me before. "That's my disorder," Joseph would say, when he talked about that part of his life. "I have two: schizo disorder and bipolar." He counted them among his possessions, like his laptop, his DVD collection, and his tie-dye T-shirts; he talked about his two disorders the way you talk about things you inherited but never asked for, and only know a little bit about.

When I asked Judy what happened over Thanksgiving, she said she felt terrible about the driver, because people deserve to get paid for their work, but there wasn't enough money in the petty cash envelope to pay him and she didn't have cash to pay him herself. "But I explained that Joseph isn't right, and asked him not to call the cops, and he didn't. He was still yelling and swearing, saying somebody up there must have money. I told him nobody did, and he finally drove away, speeding down the street," she said. "Some people are just like that, you know?"

I nodded, but I wasn't sure if she meant the driver or Joseph.

JOSEPH WAS GOING to turn nineteen on Christmas Eve. Like Leon, he was older than the other boys and allowed to stay longer because his disabilities meant there were different parameters for his care. I asked if he wanted to celebrate his birthday before winter break or after. He said before. When I asked him what he thought we should make for dinner, he looked puzzled.

"I think you already know." He smiled and his cheeks pushed his glasses up higher.

"Pizza?" I asked. On three occasions, I had seen him eat entire pies, one slice at a time.

"Yeah. You know it." He smiled again.

When I asked what cake he wanted, his answer was also simple: "I like everything."

I said we could make enough pizzas on Joseph's birthday for everyone to have his own.

"I like pizza so much it's funny," Joseph said. "And I like Elvis." He paused and looked down at the fluorescent Elvis shirt he was wearing, as if he was noticing it for the first time. "My mother got me this shirt," he said. "There's a name for it. It's called tie-dye. I went to visit her where she lived, and I saw it at a store and said I liked it. She remembered."

"That's cool," I said. "I like it." He had brought his mother up in conversation once before. One of the boys asked Joseph what he was, and he said he was pretty much white, because his mother was white. His father was from El Salvador, he said, but he didn't know him because he was in jail for a long time, and he didn't speak Spanish either, so when people asked, he said he was pretty much white. The boys exchanged glances but didn't say anything. I realized this was what Leon had meant when he told me Joseph was "sort of white," as opposed to definitely white.

"I like Elvis, and T-shirts like this," he said, smoothing his chest.

"That's a pretty perfect shirt for people who like Elvis and tie-dye," I said.

"My mom remembered I liked it," Joseph repeated. "In the beginning, she was a good cook. She could make anything. Without a recipe even. She just knew." The way he said beginning implied there was an end.

I asked if he ever got to see her, because his brother was all he talked about as family.

"Something happened a long time ago and I can't go home. Something happened and I flipped out," he said, still sitting at the table, looking at his greasy, empty paper plate and half-full cup of Sprite. I learned later that part of the something that had happened was that Joseph's mother took his social security checks and his medicine. "Should I get my poems now?"

I said sure, and he left to collect his spiderwebbed pages.

Giving Trees

By the third Tuesday of the second December, the tree was up in the TV room, wrapped in a coil of blinking lights. Glittery ropes of garland were nailed to the doorways; a cardboard Santa with his jolly white face was taped to the wall. It was nothing like the year before, when James had emptied all of the boxes and hung up every sparkling thing. This was an abbreviated version, two days of Christmas versus all twelve.

"Nobody wanted to help Greg with the ornaments?" I asked Wesley, who was sitting in his usual spot on the couch, watching TV as the houseparent explained the decoration situation.

"Nope," Wesley said. "That shit's gay anyway."

"You know she doesn't like it when you say *gay*," Leon said, coming around the corner. "Are we cooking this week or what?"

"We are," I told Leon, even though he knew because I had just left him in the kitchen to empty the bags while I came into the TV room to wrangle more help.

"Has anyone heard from James?" I asked. The display made me wonder where he was.

"Nope," Wesley said again. "He's gay, too," he added, smiling.

"C'mon, Wes," I said.

He shook his head and stared ahead at the TV.

"Anyway, we're making empanadas tonight. As always you're welcome to join us in the kitchen for an hour of fun before we eat," I said. It was another borrowed recipe. One of my students had brought in empanadas for a class project and I'd asked him how to make them because I thought the boys would like them, since they were a perfect combination of dough, grease, and spicy beef.

"Empanatas, empanantas, empananatas!" Leon liked to say *empanadas* as much as he liked to eat them. He'd scrunch his nose and trill his tongue and snap the word in the air like an elastic band against a desk, moving his arms and dancing as if shaking imaginary maracas.

I followed him into the kitchen. Frank agreed to help sauté and spice the beef and onions, fill and fold the dough disks, and pinch the edges together to fry them into pockets of goodness.

"You're not even going to ask me about school?" Leon asked.

"How's school?" I didn't know he had been going.

"School's school," he said. "Except there's a bunch of people like me there, so it's cool."

"What do you mean people like you?" I asked.

"Well, not exactly like me. But like people with the same kind of problems, so they get how it is sometimes," he said. "You know."

I didn't really; I waited for him to say more, but he didn't. He said he was going to make brownies. I asked if he would make the rice.

"Joseph's making the rice," he said, nodding at Joseph, who'd just lumbered into the kitchen.

"I don't know how," Joseph said. "I never made it before."

"Read the box, dawg," Leon told him.

I gave Leon Liz eyes.

"Or let's make it to-ge-ther," he singsonged to Joseph. "First, you boil the water. You don't know how to boil the water?" He pulled the biggest pot from the lower cabinet and carried it to the sink. "Okay, you put the water in"—he stepped aside and gestured to Joseph to take over—"then you turn the stove on, then when you see little bubbles jump at the top, it's ready."

"To add the rice," I added.

"See, you could just help him," he told me. "Even though people like Mikey's brownies better, I'm just going to make them my way. You know."

I nodded. "Old school, from the heart."

"Exactly," he said. "Brrrrrrrownies!" he sort of sang, trilling the *r*, carrying the pan through the pantry into the dining room.

I helped Joseph with rice and Frank made the beef then filled the dough disks, and we sealed them together. At some point in the process, Arlette came upstairs to check on us. She watched from the doorway as Frank flipped empanadas in the pan.

"Arlette, how come we never get a tree?" Frank asked her.

"What do you mean, Frank? We *have* a tree. It's up in the living room right now. You've seen it."

"Yeah," he said. "But I mean a real tree."

"We have a real tree. It's right there, in the living room," Arlette said.

"But like a *real* tree," Frank said. "You know what I mean."

I knew what he meant.

"And who's going to water a real tree, Frank?" Arlette asked.

"People would," he said.

She looked at him. "Nobody's going to water that tree, Frank. And it's going to dry out, and one day when someone puts the lights on, or forgets a cigarette, it's going to catch fire and burn the whole place down."

"Yeah, but," Frank said.

"But what, Frank?" She looked at him.

"Nothing," he said quietly. "Yeah, you right. We'd probably burn this shit down."

I asked Arlette before she left what had happened with the court dates, since when I asked the boys, they'd told me, "Nothing, really." She shrugged and said the homeless man didn't show up to court, and the judge told the boys they were lucky.

WHEN I CAME the next week, I told Frank I had something small for him. While grocery shopping, I had seen a display of pint-size pine trees at the checkout and decided this was a stand-in real tree for Frank—small, but real. At CVS, I found a tiny string of battery-operated lights with bulbs the size of sunflower seeds, and acrylic

SpongeBob ornaments the size of grapes I'd chosen over Mickey Mouse, the only other option. I held the bag out to him.

"It's food?" Frank asked, reaching for the bag.

"Well, no," I said.

"Oh." His voice dropped. "I'll put it in my room."

I followed him to his room and stood in the doorway as he rolled the top of the bag closed and put it on the floor under his desk. I wasn't sure what he imagined the bag contained. I feared he might not open it until the tiny tree was a scoop of mulch, so I asked him to open it.

He did. "You got me a plant?"

"No!" I said. "Pull it out!"

He held it up, his thumb and index finger around the base of the pot. He looked at it. "It's not a plant?"

"It's a little tree," I said. "Like, a real tree!"

He squinted at it. *Tree* was pushing it; it was more of a sapling. In fact, it was a plant. Frank dropped it back into the bag.

"Okay, Frank, it *is* a plant. But there're lights in the bag, too. And ornaments," I said. "So you can put them all together, like a little, real Christmas tree."

He opened the bag and peered into it, tilting his torso forward to have a better look.

"Want to decorate it?" I asked from the doorway. I thought we might share a moment.

"I might later," he said. He put the plant back in the bag, dropped the lights and ornaments on top of it, rolled the top of the bag closed, and put it all under his desk. "What're we making again?" he asked, pushing past me through the doorway, to the kitchen.

"Pizza," I said, accepting the mulch trajectory as a definite possibility. "For Joseph's birthday."

FOR CHRISTMAS PRESENTS, I figured I'd get the boys more shirts and sweaters. I asked them again to tell me what colors and what sizes so I could get something they wanted and would wear. There were only four boys living at the House. Wesley said he wanted something like last year. Leon said he didn't, because he only needed one interview shirt and he already had a job anyway, so he wanted a sweater like I'd gotten Carlos, with a zipper. Frank wasn't taking any chances; he told me he wanted a black hoodie and two white T-shirts, same size, and where specifically to go to find them. In the store, the sleeves looked short to me, so I tried the sweatshirt on over my cardigan, which must have seemed strange to the clerk, who just stared at me instead of asking if I needed any help. There wasn't the surprise effect of the year before, but the sharing of a tiny tradition held its own kind of magic. I knew Frank was pleased with it when he put it on immediately upon receipt. Wesley tried his on and sang *"Thank you"* on his way to put it away in his room. The real Christmas miracle was finding an XXXL tie-dye T-shirt for Joseph at the first store on my list in January, on the clearance rack. Like Frank, he felt inspired to change, out of one psychedelic T-shirt and into another, before dinner. Leon closed his box and said he was saving his. I asked for what, and he said he wasn't sure yet.

I HAD DINNER with Gerry in the new year at the restaurant he had started calling our usual place. There were wine and chicken, and there were questions about the turnover, which was higher than usual. So many FNGs had come and gone over the course of the year; it felt overwhelming.

"What now?" he asked.

"New kids," I said. "There are so many. By the time I learn their names, they're gone."

Gerry nodded. He didn't offer much information about the new guys, or why there seemed to be so many more arriving—and so few who stayed. He listened as I talked through my questions.

"Any word on the boys who left?" I asked about the ones who were gone: Carlos, James, David, Mikey, Tom, Mark. "I ask the others and they tell me everyone is dead."

Gerry sipped his wine.

"And what about the marijuana?" I asked hesitantly, moving down my list. I had never asked because I didn't know if I should ask, but

I'd been noticing it more and more. In my school life, I knew my role. I knew what constituted right and wrong, and how I was expected to document the space between them.

"What about it?" Gerry asked.

"Are the boys supposed to smoke?" I asked. They smoked; we sometimes talked about smoking. "And those brownies, do you know those brownies you smelled wafting downstairs when I wasn't there were pot brownies? I feel weirdly responsible for them."

Gerry laughed. "Elizabeth, what is *supposed to* in this context?"

"So you know," I said. I wasn't looking for a rhetorical question.

"Some of the young people smoke." Gerry shrugged. "It's part of how they navigate the situations they must learn to navigate on their own. . . . It is not ideal, but we are not dealing in the ideal."

"So you're saying it's self-medication?" I asked.

"Now, you've just said it's self-medication," he said, sipping his wine.

"And what about Frank's reading?" I asked, moving down my list.

"What about Frank's reading?" Gerry asked.

"He can barely read. He's in high school. Greg told me about his truancy issues. And I think if he could read better, school would be easier for him," I said, risking overstepping my place.

"Of course it would," Gerry agreed.

"So do you think I can help?" I asked.

"You are helping," he said.

"I mean with the reading," I said.

"Does Frank want you to help him?" Gerry asked, squinting at me.

I laughed. "No, no, I'm pretty sure he doesn't. He said I ask too many questions."

Gerry laughed. "Well then, you have your answer. Frank gave it to you himself."

"What about Leon's driving?" I asked. If I was going to limit how I tried to help to requests for help I had actually received, not projected, I figured I should ask about driving.

"Now, what's this about Leon driving?" Gerry asked, as if he hadn't heard me correctly.

"Well, sometimes Leon asks me about taking him for driving lessons. Should I try to take him for a driving lesson?"

"Oh, no," Gerry said gravely. "Leon cannot drive."

"Like, cannot or should not?"

"I don't think Leon Williams will ever drive; I don't think he physically can," Gerry said.

"Does he know that?" I asked. "Does he think I know that?"

Gerry laughed and nodded. "I believe he must," he said. He returned to his drink and left me to come to my own conclusion, which was that I had to find a kind of peace with the unfinishedness of all of it. He talked about changes on the horizon, but they still sounded like distant possibilities to me.

When dinner was over and we left the restaurant and crossed the street, him to the House and me to my car, we passed a teenager in a hooded sweatshirt and hat and baggy jeans who was standing on the corner, waiting.

"Well, well, well," Gerry said in his booming, knowing voice. "Who do we have here?"

"Hey, Gerry," the boy nodded at him.

Gerry extended his hand; the boy shook it.

"Do you remember who this is?" Gerry asked him, gesturing in my direction.

"Yeah, I remember her." The boy looked at me, lifted his eyes to meet mine. He nodded.

"Carlos!" I hadn't recognized him until that second. He was taller, looked thinner. It had only been months but somehow he looked different, older.

"Hey," he said.

I wanted to ask where he was sleeping, how things were going. Instead I said, kept saying, "Good to see you. Really good to see you, Carlos."

He nodded again.

I reached out my hand for his. He looked at it, then up at my face, then shook my hand, looked down at the ground. His hand was cold.

"Well, then," Gerry said to him. "Arlette said that you came around?"

"Yeah." Carlos nodded.

"She said that you're coming back on Thursday. Is that right?" Gerry asked.

"Yeah." Carlos nodded.

"Well, then I will see you on Thursday," Gerry said.

"Okay." Carlos nodded.

"Good night, then," Gerry said.

"Good night, Gerry," he said to Gerry. "Bye, Liz," he said to me.

We walked away from him, across the snowbanks on the sidewalk, icy and dirty at the edges. I turned my keys in my hand. "I didn't recognize him," I said. "Do you know where Carlos lives now, where he's been? Did he move home?" I recalled his mother in the kitchen.

Gerry shook his head no. He said that he didn't know many more details, but that Carlos had come back for some of his paperwork. In addition to his folder, Arlette had presented him with a letter that his mother had written to him. Carlos took the envelope from Arlette and, without reading it, dropped it into the trash. Arlette had said something to him like, "Whoever she is, she's your mother." Arlette took the letter out of the trash and tried to hand it to Carlos, but he wouldn't open his fists. He said, "That woman does nothing for me." Gerry took a deep breath as he recounted the story. "She was never who he needed her to be," he said, in the past tense, as if it was over for Carlos and his mother.

"That night she came to the House, all he wanted was for her to take him to dinner." I remembered it so clearly. "I wanted to push her toward him."

Gerry laughed. "Well, I'm glad you didn't push her."

"Frank and Leon held me back," I joked. I looked up at the stars, barely visible behind the streetlights, then over toward the corner where Carlos had been standing; he was gone. I looked over Gerry's shoulder at the House, at my father's office window. The light was on.

"Is Leon in recovery, Gerry?" I asked him outright. Leon had been saying things that made me think that he thought I already knew about that, too—about drinking, coping, smoking, and people like him. I had the sense he wasn't referring to the neurological issue that prevented him from walking straight and, apparently, from driving.

"Yes," Gerry said, staring into my face. "But aren't we all in recovery?"

I nodded. We are all in recovery. I looked up at the partial moon.

"Well," Gerry continued, "next week, you will start again. Is that right?"

"How do we even know what is right?" I asked, a question for a question, one of many that populated our conversations, about food and security and violence and trust and mothers. These questions loomed all over the House, above the stove like the smell of burning, in the sink like mold, around the table like ghosts.

Entertaining Angels

Extending the table to visitors was the part of the cooking project that took the longest to enact. The boys were hesitant to invite people from the outside in to eat with us. It wasn't about having new bodies at the table; the census was up, which meant most of the beds were full, and turnover after the first few months was high, so there were often new faces one week to the next. People who slept there didn't count; inviting company in was hard. Asking for anything is hard when the potential for rejection is everywhere.

I grew up in the kind of house where there were always extra chairs and there was enough food for whoever might occupy them, and serving size was just a suggestion. At the same time every night, we sat down to eat together, the five of us, and after my baby sister was born, the six of us. Dinner was part of the sacramentality of our everyday; those rolls that pop out of blue aluminum tubes were another brand of communion. Even as a child, I appreciated the holiness of sitting down together, passing food from hands to hands, and talking the way that people talk around a table, elbows almost touching. I have always had questions about religion and the logic of faith-based institutions, but I believe in sharing food and conversations over bread. I thought that letting the boys invite people was a way to give them ownership of the space, to have something that was theirs. Sharing means having less of what you have, but also knowing what is yours to give; there's a multiplication in the division.

Carlos had laughed on the first night when he asserted that nobody would ever invite people over for dinner. "People. Are. Not.

Going to *invite* people. Here," he had said. Then his mother was our first guest, though technically she was never invited.

Destiny was our second guest; our first few guests were female. Destiny was a teenager who lived in one of the girls' programs and came to cook a couple of times. She was petite and Black and talked quickly and smiled a lot. I didn't know who had asked her to stay, but she was friendly with most of the boys, and me, and eager to help in the kitchen. Whenever I asked for help, if Destiny was around, the boys would say, "Destiny'll do it." And she'd agree, "I could do that for them." Unlike the boys, Destiny chatted constantly; she was as animated talking about sitcom reruns as she was talking about the time she was in a towel coming out of the bathroom in her group home and a staff member said something inappropriate to her, but when she reported it, they said she was lying. "Some people are funny but some people are so nasty," she said.

Deirdre was our third guest. She was a sophomore from a local college who came to the House as part of a social justice internship. She competed with the boys' stories at the table, saying how she knew people who did crazier things than that, cooler, better things. Some of the older boys mistook her way of talking for flirting. "I definitely wanted to work someplace like this when I graduate," she said, "except I kind of need to find a job that pays more."

Exactly once, Wesley brought a lady friend to the House. When I arrived, he was on the couch with a girl who waved enthusiastically as I approached the TV room. I waved and said I remembered her, too. A few Saturdays before, when I was on my way to brunch in our neighborhood, I had bumped into Wesley with a girl on the street. He noticed me first. He said hey and I said hey and we kept walking. He never introduced me to the girl, and I wondered how or if he explained me to her later.

But the girl on the couch looked confused and said she didn't think we had met before. Wesley widened his eyes and slid his free hand across his neck behind her, in the universal sign for *Cut it out, stop talking, this is why I never tell you anything.* So I retracted, apologizing, saying that I was confusing her with Frank's friend. (Frank gave me a puzzled look, but generously did not correct me.) "I don't really know what I'm talking about," I assured her, admitting it out loud for once. I extended my hand and she shook it. I didn't say anything else; I knew that Wesley knew that if he wanted to invite her for dinner, he could. She was gone before the table was set.

SOMETIME IN THAT second year, the boys started inviting other guys to dinner. The leap from being at the House to staying for dinner was, like all things, a combination of faith, hunger, and coincidence.

Two Michaels who lived at other residences were among the first to come. The Michaels were the only boys who used their last names. Since there were two of them, their second names distinguished one from the other. Michael Peters had a stutter, acne, and an immaculate Chicago White Sox hat with an unbent brim that he wore for the colors, not for the team, he told me. He also had some issues with anger management and a medical condition he referred to only as "my diagnosis" in a tone that curbed follow-up questions. He was also white. I never discovered exactly why he was in state care, but this wasn't unusual. The one thing I knew about most of the boys was that I didn't really know their stories.

"Did Frank invite you to dinner?" I asked Michael Peters on the sidewalk one afternoon. I was unloading groceries; he and Frank were on their way out of the House, headed somewhere.

"Nah," Michael Peters said.

Frank, a full head and shoulders taller, just stood there.

"Frank, I told you to invite Michael for dinner," I said. I had seen Michael Peters before, noticed how he would leave as soon as Frank started washing his hands to cook.

"I'm not gay," Frank said.

"I'm not suggesting that dinner might be followed by a movie and snuggling, I'm just saying since he's here, and since we have enough food, ask him if he wants to stay."

Michael Peters laughed the gravelly laugh of a smoker twice his age.

Frank blinked. "You could," he told me.

Michael Peters looked at me, blinkingly.

"You're very welcome to stay to eat, Michael," I said. "But I can't promise you romance." I looked at Frank.

Frank narrowed his eyes at me.

Michael Peters laughed his rumbly laugh again, and he stayed for dinner. When he sat down to the table, the last to sit after the other boys took their usual seats, he took his hat off, rested it on his knee, and bowed his head to pause in a way that looked like prayer.

Michael Peters came back for dinner with some regularity after that. One of the nights he stayed, we had fried plantains, yellow rice, and beef empanadas that Frank had seasoned to the uppermost spicy threshold. Michael Peters served himself thirds of the sweet plantains, which were largely neglected by the other boys.

"These taste like my auntie's," he told me.

"Thank you," I said. "I'm going to take that as a compliment."

"You should," he said between bites.

"I think they taste nasty," Frank interjected. "They taste like banana-y potatoes," he said, which wasn't entirely inaccurate.

When there was food left over, Michael asked, "What're you doing with the extra?"

"What'd you have in mind?" I asked. We didn't usually have leftovers, but that night we did.

"Tell you the truth," he told me, "my roommate would appreciate the extra."

"Who's your roommate?" I asked.

"His name's Ronald," he said. "He's the one in a wheelchair," he said as if there were only one. "He likes yellow rice and food like this."

I told Michael that I knew who Ronald was and that I knew that we had aluminum foil and he was welcome to take what was left for his roommate. I hadn't realized that Ronald was still living in one of the agency's residences. I felt relieved to know he was close by, and alive; I felt like I knew him because of the conversations I'd had with my dad about his journey. I suddenly wanted to tell my dad; I hadn't felt that urgency to call him in a while. Michael Peters quietly packed up what was left of the plantains, yellow rice, and empanadas, and placed it all carefully into two plastic grocery bags that I held open for him one at a time. He washed his hands and dried them carefully on a paper towel before putting on the hat he'd taken off for the duration of dinner. Then, he nodded, said, "Thank you, miss," and took the makeshift takeout to the bus stop.

MICHAEL SMITH WAS the other Michael, also a resident in one of the agency's other group homes. He had a distinctive look: he wore a plaid flannel bathrobe, corduroy slippers, and thick dark glasses that Truman Capote might have chosen; he carried his PlayStation controller in the pocket of his robe. The first time I met him, I asked if he was the FNG, because he looked like he was ready for bed. But the other boys told me that he was just visiting and that was just what he wore. Michael Smith made himself at home everywhere, or made everywhere a home for himself, so he always looked either out of place in his pajamas or like he belonged, depending on how you looked at it. The first time he ate with us, he came for videogames but stayed for dinner. He asked the boys about me as if I didn't speak the same language they were speaking.

"How often does she come?" "What does she do?" "How long does she stay?" He Anderson Coopered whomever he was electronically shooting and whoever else was watching and waiting his turn.

I heard him asking and went into the TV room to answer his questions directly. I thought I would come to him. I thought I was so approachable. He talked around me. Each time he came, it was the same routine.

"You know, you can just ask me, Michael," I tried. I thought using his first name made me sound more familiar, but Leon told me I sounded like such a teacher, because nobody talked to each other like that.

"Why does she come?" "Do they pay her?" His questions continued at the table. When he sat down to dinner, in his perpetual robe and glasses, he held his plastic cup of soda like a brandy snifter in one hand and twirled a plastic fork in the other. "She wasn't always here, was she?"

"I'm white, not deaf," I said to him, as I'd said to all of them at different times, only half joking. It had become a kind of refrain.

"Is she being funny?" he asked anyone else in the room.

Sometimes I went ahead and answered his questions in the third person. "She comes to cook. She's a volunteer; they don't pay her, but Gerry sometimes gives her grocery money. She's a teacher, but she doesn't know whether she wants to do that forever. Yes, she has seen *Rob and Big,* but she didn't really like it until the episode when Big takes Rob home."

Frank's brother, P, came to the House once on a cooking night. He was so tall, he ducked to pass through the doorways, and his walk was more of a lunge. P had lived at the House before moving to wherever he was visiting from. "Something like five years ago," he said. I calculated that P would've been there when my father was there. I wanted to ask if he'd known my dad, because I thought he must have, but I was afraid he might just say *Yeah* or *I don't remember,* and I'd embarrass myself by wishing for more.

"We didn't have programs like this when I was here," P said authoritatively.

"It's not really a program, dawg," Frank told him. Frank didn't give P any indication that he washed and cut and cooked and seasoned more than any of the other boys when I came. He didn't want his brother to know that he helped make this whatever it was.

"It's not a program? It *look* like a program, dawg." Frank's brother knew about programs.

"It's not, dawg," Frank told him. "She just comes."

Like some kind of vagabond, I just came. I asked P if he'd stay to eat with us, but he said no, he had someplace else to be.

When I remarked to Frank later about how tall P was, Frank told me that he and P had different fathers, and he had another brother in a different place like this, and an older sister who was locked up. Having siblings in other facilities in the system throughout the city was a common story, true for a number of boys at the House. I didn't know why the siblings weren't placed together. When I'd ask Frank about P periodically after that, Frank would ask who wanted to know or narrow his eyes and say that he was fine in a defensive way as if he thought I had heard different. The last time I asked about P, Frank said he was on the run in Atlanta. He said it like Arlette had said that James was on the run, as if On The Run were a particular city.

EVERY NOW AND again there were other friends, from school or old neighborhoods. Some asked for soda or ice cream and left before dinner was served. Some were quick to say they'd stay, and then slow to sit down.

We had a routine by then. Someone would set the table. People would carry the stuff over from the stove. On nights Leon didn't make his biscuits, I buttered slices of bread since somebody said it was easier if I just did it, since it didn't rip when I did it; I kept buttering until hands stopped reaching out.

"You eat like this every day? Sitting down and everything, like Thanksgiving and shit?" a friend of Wesley's asked once, balancing a buttered slice of bread across the flat palm of his left hand, and taking a bite of food off the plastic fork in his right.

"No, not every day, dawg. Just Tuesdays." Leon was matter-of-fact.

"Bomb, right?" Frank interjected.

"Man, I would kill for my family to sit down like this, just once in my life," the boy said. He carefully set his slice of bread on the corner of his plate and placed his fork on his napkin and filled a plastic cup with Sprite.

"I know, right? Me too." Leon was matter-of-fact.

"It's not always like this, dawg," Frank interjected.

"Just when she's here." Wesley took the smooth green bottle of Sprite from the guest and poured some into his cup, to the rim as he usually did. Then he pulled the drink to his lips and pushed his lips toward the cup in slow motion, barely moving it so it wouldn't spill.

—

THERE'S A BIBLE passage in Hebrews about radical hospitality that talks about welcoming people into your home. It implores that you do this, suggests that in so doing, you may be entertaining not just strangers, but angels. The message is graceful, yet noncommittal: you might be entertaining angels, which implies that you might not. When outsiders and FNGs asked questions about who I was and why I came, I listened for the answers the other boys gave them. I relied on these explanations to understand how they understood who I was to them, and how the boys explained who we were to each other.

"Is that chick still here?" one FNG asked.

"She's not a chick, dawg," I heard Wesley correct him.

"Who?" Frank's voice changed as he asked about the presence of a female in the House.

"Liz," Wesley told Frank.

"Oh," Frank responded flatly. "Yeah, nah. She's not a chick, dawg."

"What is she, then?" the new voice asked.

There was a pause.

I strained from the kitchen to hear what I was.

"She's like"—Wesley started—"a"—he paused again—"teacher." I could hear his shrug.

"What? Why's there a teacher here?" the FNG asked.

"That's what she is, dawg. Don't force it." Wesley preempted further questions.

"Seriously, dawg, she's not a *chick*," Frank reiterated, for emphasis.

I appreciated that "teacher" was the easiest way to approximate who I was to them.

Sometimes someone would say, "Her father worked here or something." Sometimes the someone would add, "He died or something."

I would wait for what came after "or something" but it always stopped there. As if that was enough. As if mystical things like food and death and fathers were explanation enough.

When You Can't Go Home

I kept thinking that eventually we would start cooking real food. Part of the issue with this was that the boys and I had different ideas about what *real* meant. What is real food? Who are your real friends? When does your real life start? What is real?

"This tastes like *real* pizza!" Frank exclaimed the first time we made pizza.

"It *is* real pizza," I said.

"You know what I mean." Frank rolled his eyes at me.

I knew what he meant. He meant that it tasted like food from a restaurant, probably because I bought the dough, in softball-size portions, from a restaurant. I kept thinking that eventually we would start making homemade crust so the boys could learn the patience of letting dough rise and feeling the sticky softness of kneading it and stretching it out. I kept thinking they would taste the difference of knowing that they made it from scratch, from flour to pie. I kept suggesting we try homemade, and they kept asking if we could just make it the same as last time. I pushed for new!, different!, better! things before I appreciated that the boys craved familiar, and that for them, familiar was exotic. It took longer for me to realize that familiar was what I was craving, too.

ONE NIGHT MY second January in the House, we made pizza as usual, except that Leon wasn't around because he was in the hospital, which I had learned by then was its own kind of usual. With Leon gone, there were three: Frank, Wesley, and Joseph. I didn't know why there weren't more boys assigned to the House that winter. I did know that my best chance for assistance in the kitchen was Frank.

"Hey, who's ready for cooking?" I called into the TV room from the empty kitchen.

Nobody responded, but I could hear the click of fingers on a keyboard. I rounded the corner hoping to find Frank. He was in the throes of social networking. He sat at the desk in the TV room, casually, with his right hand on the mouse, looking at the screen sideways. He wore the serious expression of a person doing research. I had never seen him at the computer; I had never seen any of the boys at the computer. I leaned down to see what he was reading. It was an online friend forum. In bold was a name like *Sugar123*. Frank squinted toward the upper-left-hand side, where her photo was posted. Sugar123 was looking up at the camera; you could see down her abbreviated shirt. The selfie was captured in a way that you could see her face, chest, and thighs in the shot, lots of skin in a little frame. Her mouth was open slightly, suggestively.

"Who's she?" I asked breezily. I leaned closer and closer to the screen over Frank's shoulder, to see how long it would take him to turn around and look at me.

"My friend," he said definitively, not turning around.

"What's your friend's name?" Her lips didn't suggest *friend*.

"I forget." He clicked the corner icon to shrink the page.

"What do you know about her?" I asked.

"Huh?"

"I mean, like, what do you guys talk about?"

"She's nice," he said, clicking again to close the page.

"Really?" I asked.

"Yeah," he said, to the screen.

"She looks like she'd be a really good friend," I said.

He almost smiled.

"What's her name, again? I should friend her, too. We could have a friend in common. I love nice people."

Without meeting my eyes, he logged out of the site then the browser in two quick clicks.

"What're we having anyway?" he asked, laughing, already walking toward the kitchen.

THE SHRILL RING of the phone jolted our calm kitchen routine. One pizza was already in the oven, another was on the counter, made and waiting. Frank, who appeared to be setting the table in slow motion, didn't move to answer it.

"Liz, the phone's for you," Greg called from the staff office.

"Who keeps calling her? She don't even live here," Frank said loudly to no one in particular.

It was Leon calling from the hospital, again. Until recently, I hadn't understood what his medical condition was. I finally asked Gerry outright for clarification of what "a very sick young man" meant. He told me that Leon had been born with a neurological disorder, which impacted his vision and his balance. When he was a baby, his doctors had placed a drain in the back of his head; it had been monitored constantly and replaced regularly his whole life. He was used to the hospitalizations by now. The only part he complained about was his hair. He hated how they shaved it for surgery, and how slowly it grew back in. This time, he went in for a routine appointment, and his doctor had found a bigger issue and was keeping him for observation and possibly another surgery.

"What're we making?" Leon asked.

"Just pizza," I told him.

He asked questions about making pizza that he knew the answers to: what kind, how much sauce, what color cheese. He didn't want to get off the phone. "That pizza is the truth," he said wistfully. "Is it ready yet?" I could hear in his voice how he wished he were at the House. He was waiting for me to say I had to go. I was in the TV room with the extension cord stretched all the way from the desk in the staff office through the doorway. The cord didn't reach far so I stood awkwardly, leaning against the wall. I asked him how he was feeling; I didn't know what else to say. I could smell the pizza starting to burn.

Frank had moved from setting the table to sitting on the couch, playing videogames, swearing, an arm's length away from me.

"You're not really missing anything new here, Leon," I said. "Frank still has the same potty mouth, in case you were wondering." I spoke in Frank's direction.

"Tell him he's running up the bill," Frank replied in my direction.

"Frank says he misses you," I translated.

"Nuh-uh. I didn't say that. I don't miss no one," Frank said loudly.

Wesley came in and asked me if the pizza was ready. Wesley didn't acknowledge that I was on the phone, or ask who was on the other line.

I sort of held the phone out to him, to show him that I was on it, and told him I was talking to Leon; I asked him if he'd please go check the pizza.

Wesley seemed to go into the kitchen, but then circled back to the TV room and said he didn't know, but he was going to get his laundry together.

I called to Frank, who had gone into the kitchen for soda, to please check the pizza.

He appeared in the doorway, his fingers hooked into the doorframe, leaning forward. "How'm I supposed to know if the pizza's done or not?" he asked.

"The crust should be toasty brown, and the cheese should be melty," I said.

He scrunched his nose. "How you mean toasty?" He left, only to return seconds later, and tell me, "Can't do it, dawg. You got to."

We had a silent exchange: I held the phone out to him. Frank shook his head no while keeping his arms stiff by his sides to indicate that he wasn't going to take it. I looked toward the kitchen then back at the phone and shrugged, as if to ask him what he thought we should do.

Meanwhile, Leon breathed loudly on the other end of the line. "Hello? What's going on?"

Frank sighed deeply for my benefit and took the phone. "Hey, LeBron, what's boppin'?" he said. He made small talk about sports and food as I pulled the pizza from the upper rack out of the oven, then put the second one in. Frank called to Wesley, who was in the hallway, with his laundry bag up on his shoulder, about to go out. "Wes, your man's on the phone."

Wesley put his bag down, took the phone from Frank, and asked Leon, "What's happening, LeBron?" As he listened, his tone changed. "Why didn't they figure that shit out before, so they didn't have to cut open your shit?" he asked.

It was the million-dollar question.

I pulled the second pizza out of the oven and rested it on the counter to cool.

Wesley talked for a few minutes, then called to me, "Liz, your husband's on the phone."

I shot Wesley the look that Leon called Liz eyes. He smiled widely and handed me the phone.

"People here are worried about you, LeBron." I didn't usually use his nickname.

"Nah, they know like I know. They're used to this, it's just same old. It's how it is with me. Some of the nurses here are ones who known me since I was little. One's a bodybuilder, too, so he has mad muscles, you know, and he's always telling people I was a baby with a bald-ass head."

"That's a long time, Leon."

"I know, and that's messed up 'cause he got bald in the time I known him. So when he says that, I'm like, 'Yeah, but now who's bald?' And he laughs. We're cool like that."

I imagined this man, and all these nurses and doctors, who had cared for Leon since he was a baby. "I'm sorry, Leon," I said.

"You can't be sorry, Liz," Leon said. "This is how it is with me."

What could I say to that? As I stood in the door to the staff office, with the phone cord pulled as far as it would go, I overheard Frank tell Greg, who was on duty that night, that the pizza we made was bomb so he should try it when it was ready. Then I heard Greg say to him, "Man, you're so much calmer when she's here." And Frank said something like, "Nah, dawg, it's just that I'm hungry."

"You could come visit me, if you want," Leon said after a pause.

I had told him the last time that I would come the next time. I was thinking I didn't have the clearance to visit. "How do I get permission to come?" I asked.

"Anybody could come," he said. "All kinds of people come here. You could come any day if I'm still here. You could call first. But I'll probably still be here."

"I'll come," I said. "What can I bring you? Want some books or magazines?"

"You don't have to bring anything," he told me. "But you could bring Cherry Garcia if you *really* wanted to bring something."

"Ben and Jerry's, you mean? The ice cream?"

"Yeah," he said.

"I can definitely bring Cherry Garcia," I promised. "Can you eat it? Is ice cream okay?"

"Yeah, I could eat it, if people bring it to me. The problem is that nobody brings it to me, that's why I haven't been eating it," he said. "Did you make three pizzas? So everyone could have a lot? You did, didn't you? Man, I just wish I was there."

"You'll be back soon," I said, as if I knew.

We said goodbye, and I listened for Leon to hang up before I did.

I heard him breathing. "Why didn't you hang up already?" he asked.

I laughed. "I was waiting for you to hang up first."

"All right," he said. The phone fumbled and then clicked.

WHEN I GOT off the phone, Frank and Wesley carried the pizzas to the table. I knocked on Joseph's door to tell him dinner was ready. They poured soda and I started serving.

"Can you get me that one? The one with all the cheese?" Frank asked.

I gestured to a middle piece and he said, "Yeah, that's the one I want." I looked at him and raised my eyebrows.

"What, dawg? I already said please too much times today," he told me. "Cut it, keep cutting, I want a perfect block."

As I contemplated the idea of Frank reaching his *please* quota for the day, I burned my hand on the pan when I turned the knife. I swore under my breath and shook off the sting of heat.

"Oh, you burned your hand?" Frank said. "Too bad. Just make sure none of the cheese comes off, 'cause I want all of it."

"Thanks, Frank, that's nice," I said, thinking that his change in tone was so Greg could overhear that he didn't lose his toughness around me. "I'd really love to know where you used all of your pleases today."

Joseph sat quietly, keeping to himself, eating. When he finished a last bite he paused, then reached for more pieces, looking to me mid-reach for a nod to proceed.

I'd give him the nod, and he'd repeat the process wordlessly, taking three slices at a time. "I like pizza so much it's funny," he said, smiling.

"It's pretty good, right?" I asked.

"It's half bomb, half crap." Frank downgraded his initial assessment.

"I already heard you tell Greg it was bomb," I said.

"You're lucky I said half," he told me.

"I feel lucky," I said.

Wesley ate his slices, drank some soda, and said he had to get his laundry before chores.

Frank said he was about to leave, too. He stood up, took a last gulp of Mountain Dew Code Red, and looked over at Joseph, who was still eating. He put his empty cup on his plate and walked away, leaving me with the mostly wordless Joseph.

"I like pizza so much it's funny," Joseph repeated, reaching for another slice.

I told him that I liked pizza, too, and explained that Leon was in the hospital. I couldn't tell whether he felt left out by the call earlier, how Frank and Wesley had talked, but nobody called Joseph to the phone.

Joseph gave no indication that he was listening. No nod, no eye contact. When he finished his last slice, he wiped red sauce from his mouth with a napkin. He looked at me over the rim of his glasses and said, "Where I was before was kind of like a hospital, but more like a jail."

When the clock struck 7:58, Frank and Wesley reemerged for chores. "You doing chores, Joe?" Wesley asked Joseph. When Joseph responded, "Not tonight," staring straight ahead, Wesley and Frank happily divided the eight chores by two and went to work.

Joseph remained at the table. "I'm a little antisocial," he told me. The way he talked about himself felt like he was repeating things he'd heard other people say about him. Some of his phrases sounded like mash-ups of common proverbs and popular songs. Like when he said, "I don't really talk to people. Talking to them is like blowing in the wind, you know?"

I didn't exactly understand what he meant, but I said I did. I stood to leave and he stood, too, and followed me to the door. When I got to my car, I looked up and saw that he was back in his room, on his laptop, searching for something, light inside of light.

I CALLED GERRY the next day to ask whether he thought it would be appropriate for me to visit Leon in the hospital. He said he didn't see why not. So I asked what unit Leon was on, where I should park, and if he knew where I could buy a pint of ice cream nearby.

When I checked in at the nurses' station, they asked me twice what my relationship to Leon was. For lack of a better word, I said "friend," which was apparently so unconvincing they asked me to repeat it. A nurse led me to his room and announced my arrival from the doorway. "Do you know this person?" she asked him, smiling.

"Yup," he said. "She brought me ice cream." Always one to get to the heart of a matter, in lieu of hello, Leon greeted me, "Did you bring the Cherry Garcia?"

"I did," I said, procuring the carton from my purse. "And I even stopped at the cafeteria for a plastic spoon."

"Good," he said, reaching for the stuff. "How else was I going to eat it?" Leon looked like a young old man in bed. Unshaved, his cheeks and chin were scraggly and he was tucked in, with one of the blankets Arlette made covering him up.

When the nurse left, he leaned over to tell me something, so I leaned in closer to his face to hear him. His voice was hoarse. "I think that nurse has a thing for me," he whispered.

"Is she one of your usual ones?" I asked him.

"No," he said, his eyes following her into the hallway. "She just started today."

"Then how do you know?" I reviewed the limited interactions with the nurse I had witnessed, trying hard to read the subtext. Apparently, when I understood "Do you know this person?" to mean "Your friend is here," what he heard was, "I like you." When I heard, "Do you need anything for the moment?" what he heard was, "I have a thing for you." And when I heard, "Would you like some ice chips?" he heard, "I think we need to be together."

"What do you think I should do about it?" he asked me.

I confessed that I'm not very good at those kinds of things, so I was probably the wrong person to ask. I have a hard time reading between the ice chips.

When the nurse came back a half hour later to say that she was going on a break, Leon smiled at her and said, "Okay." When she left, he said, "Yeah, you saw it, right? You saw how she was looking at me?"

"I think it's her job to look at you," I suggested.

"That was hateful, Liz," he said.

I asked Leon how he'd been spending his days, and he said he was mostly watching TV and calling people on the phone. "The phone's right here, and I can make as many calls as I want," he said. "The other day I called where I used to live."

"Oh, wow," I said. "Who did you talk to?" I had never heard him mention that place.

"Sometimes I just call to see who answers," he said.

"What do you say?" I didn't understand why he called.

"Nothing," he said. "I just hang up."

"You remember the number?" I didn't know how long it had been since he lived there.

"'Course I remember it. That was my number. How am I supposed to forget that number?" As he talked to me, his gaze was focused on the nurses in the hallway.

"Do you call a lot?" I asked.

"I call sometimes," he answered.

From the time he was two until the time he was thirteen, Leon
had lived with a family who had adopted him. But when he was
thirteen, during one of his hospitalizations, they returned him to
state care, as if he were an appliance still under warranty. His
sickness was too much for them, they said. I knew this because
when I asked Gerry about Leon's hospital situation, he also told me
this family situation. For all Leon talked, he never talked about
them.

"When was the last time you did that," I asked, "the last time you
called that house?"

"The other day," he answered. "Thursday, I think. Yeah, it was
Thursday."

"Last week?" I was surprised that he had called so recently. It had
been years since he lived with them. "Who answered?"

"The grandfather," he said. "He usually answers. He's always
there. He doesn't really go anywhere."

"But you didn't say anything to him?" I asked.

"Nope," he said.

"What did you do?" I asked.

"Hung up," he said.

I thought about him, calling that house so many years later, listening for the hello on the other end of the line to see if he recognized the voice. I thought of him calling, standing at the phone in
the dining room at the House; he probably didn't even sit down,
because he knew it wouldn't take too long. I thought of him calling
from this hospital room, alone.

"Do you ever say anything?" I asked, not wanting to be the one to
change the subject.

"Nope," he answered. "What am I going to say?" He looked at
me for the first time.

He wanted them to recognize him, to call him back, to want him back. Leon kept giving them opportunities to redeem themselves, but they never tried.

I sat there across from Leon in his room a while longer. I hated the smell of hospitals, the blend of ammonia and flowers and sickness and hopeless hope. I wondered how the world could be so breathtakingly unfair, and watched Leon mine the pint for cherries.

PART 3

SOMETHING HAPPENED HERE

Sometimes at that moment a wave of light breaks into our darkness, and it is as though a voice were saying: "You are accepted. You are accepted, accepted by that which is greater than you, and the name of which you do not know. Do not ask for the name now; perhaps you will find it later."

—*Paul Tillich*

We are each other's harvest; we are each other's business; we are each other's magnitude and bond.

—*Gwendolyn Brooks*

Give it a try. Just do the best you can.

—*Charlie Hauck, when pressed for advice on just about anything*

Grown-Up

When I was younger, I used to love the dinner party question: If you could invite five people, living or dead, to dinner, who would they be? I used to configure and reconfigure what I thought was the perfect party, based on what I was reading or whom I was thinking about.

One of the high school evenings when my father was driving me home, I asked him who he would, "like, invite to his, like, hypothetical dinner party." He pulled the car over, put it in park, and leaned in to my face, his pupils wide behind the thick lenses of his glasses. I could feel his breath on my cheek. He told me to stop saying *like* so much. It was getting out of hand, he said. My thoughts were getting lost between the likes, he said. And I was getting too old for it. He had told me this before.

I said, "Okay, *fine,*" and asked the question again: Who were his five people?

He sighed and said his mother, he supposed. She had died the year before. I asked about the other four, and he shrugged as we pulled back into traffic.

Didn't he think that was boring? I asked. Just Grandma? He had had so many dinners with her already, wouldn't he rather choose famous people? Interesting people?

He shook his head no. If he could have a meal with anyone, he would choose one more with her.

Then he took a deep breath and I knew he was going to ask me about my future. He asked the same dreaded questions every time we were alone in the car together between freshman year and senior year of high school: What colleges do you think you will apply to? What would you like to study? Have you thought about what you'd like to do for work?

I would become exasperated and say that I didn't know exactly. How could I already know what I wanted to be when I grew up? How could I figure out something so big? Then he would become exasperated and say that I had the wrong attitude, and the wrong idea about knowing. "You make a decision," he'd say, as if it were that easy. "Top three for each, if you had to decide today," he'd ask, not counting art school, because it wasn't a practical option. He wouldn't let me out of the green minivan until I had a working list of possibilities, three per category. He didn't say it was for my own good, but that was implied in the way he counted off my reluctant answers on one hand before pulling the keys from the ignition and releasing the locks on the doors.

It's hard to say what was stranger about being at the House with the boys, the feeling that I was there and my father wasn't, or the realization that the boys there now were the same ages I had been all of the times I was there when I was growing up, when I was waiting downstairs for my father to take me home. I still didn't know what I wanted to be when I grew up, but now I wasn't so convinced of one true anything.

WHEN I ASKED Frank about his little tree in February, just before his fifteenth or sixteenth birthday, he told me he was just about to water it. He went to his room and I followed him. Sitting on his windowsill, the plant was now a twig stuck in a pot of dirt, strangled by tiny unlit lights. The pine needles had fallen and formed a ring around its base. A single sneeze would have sent the whole thing flying.

"I think it might be dead, Frank," I said from his doorway.

He picked up the plant. "I watered it sometimes," he said, looking at it.

"I know," I said. "You took care of it. It lasted a while."

He picked up a pen and started flicking dry dirt out of the pot, into his trash can.

"It's like you're chipping my heart out, Frank," I joked.

He sighed. "I watered it sometimes, dawg," he said again as he dropped the pot into the trash and walked past me through his doorway. "C'mon, let's go make the food already."

Leon joined us in the kitchen. He had been discharged from the hospital after another surgery and was already back to work. He was about to turn twenty and move out of the House and into another residence with less supervision. As part of a transition to more independent living, he got a job at a big box store, two buses and a train away. "I have to wear these pants," he told us, about his uniform. "They're called khakis. They're actually pretty comfortable." He wiggled a little to demonstrate, reminding himself to get a belt as they slipped down his hips. He liked stocking shelves, he said. "Some people have to work," he told Frank. "Someday, you'll understand."

Leon was also going to school on what seemed like a regular basis. His school "with people like me" was an evening program for young adults who struggle with substance dependency and seek to complete their GEDs in a therapeutic environment. But Leon didn't use words like *substance* or *dependent;* he talked about being "how I was" and other people at school who "had the same kinds of problems." One night at the table, he told us about school.

"I'm a badass there," Leon asserted.

Frank and Wesley shook their heads and continued to eat. Joseph just sat, eating and listening, the way he usually did.

"I know what you're thinking," Leon said, looking in Wesley's direction. "'Cause here, I'm just so-so badass." He tilted his hand back and forth when he said *so-so.*

"Not even," Wesley said between sips.

"Okay, here I'm not as badass as other people." He narrowed his eyes at Wesley. Wesley looked down at his plate. "But *there*"—he emphasized the otherness of the mostly suburban population the school served—"there, everybody has names like *Amber* and *JP.* They don't know that many Black people, so I'm the G-est person they know." He puffed out his chest, expanding his gangster-ness by making his body bigger as he explained, "Some of 'em are even afraid of me." He nodded, agreeing with himself. "It's cool."

Wesley rolled his eyes. The others ate and listened. Nobody knew exactly what anybody else looked like in his life outside the House.

FOR HIS BIRTHDAY dinner in March, Leon ordered his usual: chicken stir-fry and ice cream sundaes for dessert, with number candles— a 2 and a 0. Just because he wanted sundaes instead of cake, he reminded me, didn't mean he didn't want candles. Wesley told me he wasn't going to be around for dinner.

"Do you want me to leave you a plate in the microwave?" I asked him.

He paused and said, "If you want."

"Will you eat it?" I asked. "I'll leave it if you'll eat it."

"I mean, yeah, I'll eat it," he said.

"Okay, so it'll be in the microwave when you get back," I said. I had to catch myself before saying *when you get home*, because every time I said that, he'd say, "This is not my home."

In college, I volunteered at a homeless shelter. The staff member who trained me was an old hippie in recovery who taught me about what he called the ministry of presence. At the shelter, this meant sitting near people. Not next to someone, necessarily, and not speaking, unless spoken to. "Your only job is to let them know they're not alone," the guy had said. I was never great at silent ministries. But in the House, my loose interpretation of accompaniment was making a plate for somebody and leaving it in the microwave for when he was ready to eat. The somebody was usually Wesley.

"All right," he agreed. And before he left, he came through the kitchen to say "Thanks, Liz."

Leon thought this was messed up. In general, but especially for his birthday dinner.

"Wes doesn't help and he gets to eat anyway. It's no fair," he said.

"Leon, you're the oldest one here and I'm going to tell you a secret that's not really a secret: you're the kindest one, too." I looked at him, and he looked at me. "Wes isn't used to kindness. Everything for him comes with strings; this is something that we can give him without strings attached. He doesn't expect us to offer him dinner. But if we do, I think it'll help him to be kinder, or think about being kinder."

Leon relished these talks, when it was just the two of us and I confirmed for him what he already knew, that I thought he was special, and not just because of his sickness. Of course, all of them were special, but Leon was most unabashed in his longing to hear it. And maybe I shouldn't have told him that I thought he was the kindest, but I did.

"That's tricky right there, Liz. I see what you're saying." Leon nodded. "But that dude should still help."

"I don't disagree with you. But I think it's the right thing to do, and I think you think so too."

"Because *we* are good people," he said. Then he added under his breath, but loudly, "And Wesley is *not*."

"Leon Williams." I focused my green eyes on his brown ones.

He looked away from my Liz eyes. "Don't *Leon Williams* me, Liz. You know it's true."

I ENLISTED JOSEPH to help make the brownies for the sundaes. Joseph had started helping, but his task had to be a small thing that didn't involve knives or heat or too much water or too much texture, like making rice. I thought brownies would also fit within the parameters of his interest and ability. While Frank was cubing the chicken, I asked Joseph to crack the eggs, and showed him how to do it.

I put a bowl down into the sink in front of him, separate from the other bowl, in case we needed to fish out shells before adding the eggs to the mix; I'd bought a dozen, and knew that we had a decent margin for error. I held an egg with both hands, using three fingers each in a sandwich formation, and mimed knocking it against the corner of the counter then opening it up. I asked Joseph if he had any questions. When he said no, I gave him the egg and moved to cut the vegetables.

Leon came back into the kitchen to supervise. If Wesley could eat and not cook, he wasn't going to cook either, he said. Especially for his own birthday dinner.

"Where should I put this?" Joseph asked me, holding the egg.

"You can just put it there." I pointed to the bowl in the sink.

"Are you sure?" Joseph asked, looking at the sink.

"Yeah. There's good," I said, turning to the vegetables.

"Ookaay," Joseph said, cracking the egg against the counter.

I looked over just as the liberated white and yolk were sliding across the sink in a slow race toward the drain, inches away from the empty bowl.

"Did it," he said, smiling proudly as the drain swallowed the egg.

"Good job," I said. There were no bits of shell in the basin; what I had thought would be the hardest part wasn't. "How about for the next two eggs, you crack them into the bowl in the sink, and then we'll pour them from that bowl into the bigger bowl with the oil and mix." I touched each bowl as I said *bowl* so it was clear that the next eggs should land in bowls.

"Ookaay," Joseph said. "Iiiiiiin the boooooowl."

"And you're really letting that dude make my special birthday-brownie-sundae brownies?" Leon continued his running critique of me, shaking his head in disbelief.

EVEN AFTER LEON moved out of the House, he would come back for dinner. The first night he came back, I had what I thought was a funny story. As we sat down to eat, I told the boys how my uncle had recently said that his cousin was having renovations done to her house in New York, and her contractor, who was supposedly psychic, had told her that somebody with a name that started with C was trying to make contact from the other side. "So she told my uncle to tell us that my dad has a message for us from the other side! Isn't that crazy?" I asked. "Isn't it so funny?"

Frank widened his eyes and he looked down at his plate. Wesley shook his head, sipped his soda; though I wanted to think the disdain was aimed at my second cousin, I was pretty sure it was at me, and my ghosts. Joseph ate without pause.

"How's that supposed to be funny?" Leon asked.

"Well, I just think the idea of my dad trying to send a message to us through a psychic who does construction and also happens to be working on his cousin's house in New York is funny," I said. It had been three years and two months since my dad died. It wasn't that I wasn't interested in a message from him. In fact, I constantly thought about what he might say about family entanglements, political developments, decisions I had to make. The longer he was gone, the longer the list of things I wished to know. But if he wanted to reach through from the other side, it seemed unlikely that he would use his cousin's contractor as a medium.

"Maybe if you took it seriously, he would talk to you instead," Leon said. "Kind of seems like you have a bad attitude."

I laughed and told him that was funny because that was something my father would tell me when I was younger, that I needed to adjust my attitude.

"See?" Leon said, agreeing. "Dude sounds smart."

After dinner, I offered to drive Leon home. His new place was another residence the agency ran, a few blocks away; it was where Michael Peters and Ronald lived. I told him if he wanted, I'd give him a ride so he didn't have to take another bus in the dark.

"I knew I was going to get to ride in your whip," he said. "I told you since the beginning."

Leon's disappointment that I didn't have automatic locks had not waned. "Chict-chict." He sort of spit out a clicking sound as I unlocked the passenger door. "Your whip's antique," he said.

"It's only five years old," I told him. "It's practically new."

"Not even," he said, making the clicking sound, like locking and unlocking, on and off the whole ride home.

When I pulled into the driveway of his apartment, the first floor of a three-family house, Leon didn't reach for the door.

"Isn't this where you live now?" I recognized the house because it was the only one with a wheelchair ramp that wrapped around the first floor; it had been built for Ronald.

"Aren't we going to talk for a couple of minutes?" he asked. He rolled down the window. It creaked a little as he cranked it. "Figures you have old-fashioned windows, too."

I was exhausted. "What did you want to talk about?" I asked.

"And why are you opening the window? It's like forty degrees outside."

"So," he started. He hooked his elbow out the window, as if it were a midsummer day. "You're not a car person, huh?"

I said I was more of a cake person, and Leon said he could see that. Then he picked up the small picture I keep in the change tray near my cup holder. "This is your pops?"

I nodded. I forgot the picture was there.

"He looks gangster," Leon said.

"You think?" I asked. The picture was of my father sitting on his bed, his elbows folded behind his head. I liked it because just before I took it, I had said, "Hey, Dad?" and he looked over at me. So the look on his face is his expectant one, like when he picked me up at the airport, or listened to a story. I liked it because if I ever saw him again, that's the version of his face I thought I would see.

"Gangster," Leon said. "He's all"—he imitated my dad, folding his own elbows behind his head, puffing out his chest. Then he scrunched his face and nodded, tough-like.

"He wasn't really a car person either." My father almost exclusively drove old cars, including the green minivan that he drove through three presidencies. "One of his cars was stolen and used in a robbery, actually." I rolled my window down, too, and rested my elbow near the old-fashioned lock. I could feel the night prick through my sweater. I tried to enter into the ministry of presence.

"For real?" Leon asked.

"For real," I said. My father's used gray Chevy had been stolen from where it was parked near the House and then used in a bank robbery. When it was found, abandoned, driven into a wall blocks from the bank, my father was brought in for questioning. My mother thought it was funny that he was a robbery suspect because he wouldn't even accept things he accidentally got for free. Like the time they went to pick up a used coffee table and the woman asked him for less than the stated price in the want ad and he gave her the full price because they had already agreed upon it. Or the time he was dispensed an extra twenty-dollar bill from an ATM during off-hours and he went back the next day to return it. Still, he stammered when he gave his alibi for the time of the robbery, that he'd been at a Department of Youth Services meeting and there were plenty of people who could corroborate his story.

"And when he got the Chevy back," I told Leon, "there was damage to the front of the car and the inside was spattered with maroon paint from the dye bombs that the teller had put in the money bags. And he had the hood fixed, but he left the spray paint across the dashboard, the inside of the passenger door, and the ceiling."

"For real?" Leon asked again.

"Yeah," I said. "He said it added character." He liked to tell the story to friends we carpooled with. "You can ask Arlette. I bet she remembers. I think she was one of his witnesses."

"See?" Leon said, looking at the picture of my father again. "Gangster." He studied it, then asked, "You think he robbed the bank?"

"No." I laughed.

"I think he could've," Leon said, staring at my father's face. "Maybe that's what he's trying to tell you now, through that psychic guy. So you could know the truth."

I said "Maybe" unconvincingly.

"You kind of do need to change your attitude," Leon said. "If this dude had something to tell me, I would listen to him."

A FEW WEEKS after Leon turned twenty, I turned thirty. I had grossly underestimated how much I would know and be by twenty-nine and was starting to seriously doubt if there was such a thing as being grown-up. How do you know exactly who you are supposed to be in the world, and when? Who gets to choose when they feel ready to live on their own? For all I didn't know, I knew that if I could invite any five people, living or dead, to my birthday dinner, I would only choose one.

Of Mice and Men and Fire

O ne night during that second spring of cooking together, Frank met me on the landing and pulled the door closed behind him. He must have heard the rustle of bags or the sound of my shoes on the stairs.

"I did something you're going to say is real bad," he said.

In the time I had known him, Frank had been in trouble a number of times: an altercation with a police officer who tried to break up a fight between Frank and another student at school; the incident with the homeless man about the two dollars; various marijuana infractions, both in the House and in public; truancy and other miscellaneous school stuff. When we talked about any of these things, he never expressed concern that I'd say they were bad.

"What happened?" I searched his face. I braced myself.

"I seen my moms the other day," he told me, looking at my shoes.

Prior to that moment, the only mention of Frank's mother was in references other boys made about Frank's having been born substance dependent; the prescription medications he took and the partial funding he received from the Department of Developmental Services were fodder for their jokes about him being slow, or his mom being on drugs. What must have been years into this banter, Frank never denied it or got angry or embarrassed by the insinuations. He would say things like, "Yeah, my moms shared that shit with me when I was a baby," or "I know it, I started being badass way back then." His retorts made the others quiet.

Until he mentioned seeing her, I didn't know Frank's mother was still alive.

"You saw your mom?" I tried to read his eyes as he studied the concrete-colored carpet covering the stairs. "For real?"

"Yeah," he said. It was a different *yeah* than when he said "Yeah" when I asked whether he had gone to school when I knew that he probably hadn't, or "Yeah" when I asked if he wanted me to get shrimp, too, when I knew he definitely did.

"Did you go to see her?" I asked. Some of the boys talked about having home visits; Frank never had.

"Nah, I went to see someone who lives near where she lives and she was just there outside," he said, using more words than he usually did at one time.

"Did you talk to her?"

"Yeah," he said. Then he shrugged. "I mean, nah, not really."

"What did you say?"

"Nothing," he said. "I knew it was her, though." His tone changed.

"Frank, did she say something to you?" I asked.

He paused.

"What did she say, Frank?"

Frank kept looking at the stairs. "She looked at me all hard and told me 'I had a son who looked like you once.'" He looked up, then back down.

"What did you say?" I knew he wasn't finished talking because he didn't walk away.

He shifted his weight. The stairs creaked under us.

"When she said that, Frank," I asked cautiously, "what did you say?" I thought his response must be the terrible thing he warned me about.

He looked at the floor. I looked at his face.

"Nothing," he said. "I just looked at her and walked away."

I didn't say anything.

He shifted. "I did say something actually. I said, 'I don't know what you're talking about.' Then I walked away."

I took a breath. I kept looking at his face.

Frank looked up. "It's wrong, right?" he asked. "You think what I did is real wrong, right?"

He looked at me, then back at the floor.

"No, Frank. I don't," I told him. "I really don't." I looked at him, then up at the ceiling. It was all plaster and water stains, lit by one bald bulb screwed into a socket. "You know what?" I said. "I think sometimes you have to say what makes sense at the time. And sometimes it doesn't feel like it was the right thing later, when you keep thinking about it. But it was the right thing when it happened. So it's the right thing. It was the right thing, Frank."

"Yeah?" he asked.

"Yeah," I said. "I don't think it was wrong. I can't think of a better thing that you could have said to her right then." I tried to imagine the face of the woman who was Frank's mother. I tried to imagine her that day, and in all her years without Frank.

He stared at the wall behind me.

"You know, I think I probably would've done the same thing," I said. I thought of my own mother's face, her eyes. Tears closed my throat and I swallowed them down. I made tighter fists around the bags.

"Yeah?" he asked, looking at my shoes.

"Yeah," I told him, looking at his eyelashes.

"Yeah, right?" he said. He nodded to himself and I nodded along. "I'm about to go wash my hands. What're we having for dinner already? You brought me Code Red?"

"You know it," I said. I held the bag up so he could see the bright red bottle gleam through the plastic.

He let go of the doorknob and reached for the bag. I followed him through the door and shut it behind us.

IT WAS JUST the two of us in the kitchen for a while. Leon was working and living in his new place; Wesley and Joseph were in their rooms. While Frank was either peeling or cutting, and I was either spicing or stirring, I saw a flash of motion out of the corner of my peripheral vision. I gasped, despite myself.

"What happened?" Frank asked.

"I think I saw a mouse."

"Probably did," he said, returning to his cutting and peeling.

"Have you seen mice in the kitchen before?"

"Yup. We got mad of 'em here."

I looked from the baseboard to the bottom cabinets to the trash can.

"It's true. Matter of fact," Frank continued, "they don't just have babies here. They have like, triplets."

I laughed.

"What?" he asked. "It's true."

"No, I believe you. It's just funny, how you said they were having triplets. You're funny, Frank." I scrunched my nose. "I hate mice. I mean, I don't hate them. I just— Every time I see them, I get . . . I just don't like them." I shrugged. I felt like I had to apologize for the gasp.

Frank narrowed his eyes and looked at me. I wondered how many times he must have seen mice run across the floors of places he had lived; I wondered if he thought about how I hadn't. As self-conscious as I was about the way I had winced, I was struck by the way that he didn't flinch.

Joseph lumbered into the kitchen wearing a fresh tie-dye T-shirt, with eyelids heavy from sleep or medication or some combination of the two, ready to mix something or set the table.

Wesley came around the corner next, holding a plastic cup. He reached for the milk, but when he saw the soda piled sideways in the fridge, he grabbed the Pepsi. He clinched the cup in his teeth as he held the bottle with one hand and unscrewed the cap with the other. As he poured himself a drink, he joined the conversation. He'd been listening to the mouse exchange from across the hall. "Sometimes we exterminate them," he said, inhaling a first sip. "In a homemade way," he added.

"What do you mean?" I had to ask. "The mice?"

"Yeah," he said between sips. "We trap them in the corner, and then punish them."

"No," I said. "Please tell me that's not true."

"It is," Wesley said, smiling behind his cup. "It's true."

"Please tell me it's not," I continued. "Because do you know what they look for in serial killers?" I waited for some sort of reaction, some sort of connection. "Torturing small animals, setting fires, and bed-wetting."

There was a pause.

"I got two," Frank said, pouring himself some soda.

"Me too," Wes said. He smiled wider and finished his Pepsi in one gulp.

"I set a fire when I was five," Joseph said in his slow, deliberate way from where he was standing across the kitchen. He paused. His head was tipped to the side; he was thinking. "I was five, I found matches. I wanted to see what you could do with them."

The other boys looked at him. Frank stood holding the knife he had used to cut the chicken; he held the blade away from his body. Wesley crumpled the empty plastic cup into a ball.

"So, I think," Joseph continued, "I got three." He looked up out of the corner of one eye, over the rim of his glasses, as if he was counting scenes as they flickered across the HDTV screen of his memory.

Frank and Wes looked at each other, then they looked at me. We all looked at Joseph.

Joseph blinked and nodded. "Yup, I got all three."

He laughed. The other two boys laughed. We all laughed together.

Done with the confessional component of the evening, Wesley slam-dunked his cup into the trash can, shaking his head, and left to do laundry or smoke before we sat down to eat. I gave Joseph the cookie mix in a bowl and an egg, some oil, and a spoon to assemble our dessert. Frank turned back to the sink to wash the knife, slicing the blade through the water. When he finished rinsing the soap off it, he handed me the knife, and I put it in my purse.

Until It Rolls Down Like Waters

In May, Frank debuted a black T-shirt with a giant screen-printed stop sign outlined in white. The familiar red octagon stretched across his chest. STOP was printed in white Highway Gothic across the middle and SNITCHING was spray-painted in bubble letters below it, also white. At the table at the House, we tended not to talk about tangential things like family, politics, and God and stuck instead to issues bound by immediate relevance like food, fighting, school, and sometimes girls. But Frank's T-shirts sometimes took us in new directions. While I generally supported his engagement in grassroots movements, I had reservations about the stop snitching campaign that was gaining momentum around the city as summer beckoned and the streets heated up. The shirts were controversial in Boston that year; at one point, the mayor tried to prevent stores from selling them as a matter of public safety and the ACLU got involved because it was a question of free speech.

"Aren't you guys tired of the stop snitching stuff?" I asked, pointing at Frank's shirt. How could a campaign deterring witnesses from reporting criminal activity to the police serve the best interests of the community, or protect the people who were most vulnerable and most in need of protection? Pressure to stop snitching seemed more like intimidation and less like honor to me. But how I understood the meaning of loyalty and the ways fear factored into codes of silence, as well as how I felt the dimensions of the ongoing problem of police violence, were all shaped by my white female body. I lived in a world where I asked police officers for directions when I was lost in a new city; I called 911 when I heard gunshots or witnessed a person drag another into an alley. The first time I remember meeting a police officer was in kindergarten; he introduced himself to me. He was part of the new landscape I was learning, like the strawberry milk in the cafeteria, the collection of small mats we rotated for circle time, and my teacher's wedding dress, which was rumpled in the box of costumes in the make-believe play corner. I didn't know what a divorce was, but I knew that was why she had cut off the bottom of her sparkly dress and brought it to school for us to play with, because I had overheard her tell my mom. And I didn't understand the contexts of school desegregation in Boston or appreciate the debate about whether police belonged inside schools, but I remember feeling like the tall, uniformed men were there to protect me. It seemed like they must be there to protect all of us; we were so little, walking from our buses in the schoolyard through long hallways into our brightly lit classroom, comparing the colors of our hands as we traded puffy Michael Jackson stickers and fruity scratch-and-sniffs and buddied up in line and practiced taking turns to answer questions. I know now that I wasn't wrong, that the officers were there to protect me, but I also know now that my sense that their presence was benevolent to all of us wasn't entirely correct.

"Seriously, though," I said to the boys. "What's the point of that?"

"Oh, that?" Wesley gestured with his chin at Frank's shirt.

"Yeah. I mean, don't you think it's kind of harmful?" I asked.

They kept eating. Wesley nodded at the Pepsi and Frank passed it to him. Somebody changed the subject and said something that somebody else said was fucked up.

"Did anybody hear what happened to Ronald?" I circled back. Arlette told me that Michael Peters's roommate, Ronald, who was paralyzed from the waist down, had recently been arrested on weapons charges. He'd been hanging out with some people who, when they saw the police coming, had lifted him out of his wheelchair to place their guns underneath him and then fled the scene on foot.

"The dude in the wheelchair? Who lives where LeBron lives?"

Wesley asked. Most of the boys at the House had a sense of who was at the other residences and what was happening there, at least in terms of placements, removals, and anything involving police.

"Yeah," I said.

"Yup," Wesley said. "Heard that. Bad break."

"Yup," Frank agreed.

"Nobody thinks what happened to Ronald is fucked up?" I asked.

"You don't usually talk like that," Leon said. He was back for dinner; he'd taken his uniform shirt off before he made his biscuits and was in a white undershirt and his khakis.

"You know what," I said, "I don't know how else to talk about it."

"It's how it goes," Frank said, shaking his head.

"How it goes?" I asked. "A kid gets messed up in gang stuff and gets shot and paralyzed, and then he doesn't want to stay away from people he thinks are his friends, so he goes back to them. And then one night they're stopped by cops and one of them *lifts* him up *out of his wheelchair*—because he doesn't have control of his own body—to put their guns underneath him. And when the cops lift him up and find the guns, nobody admits anything and they just let him get locked up for possession. And that's just *a bad break*?"

"They probably didn't think that the cops would lift him up like that," Leon explained. It was always Leon who tried to explain so that I would understand.

"Arlette told me it was the first place the cops looked." I couldn't stop. "Are you really defending people who lifted up a paralyzed boy—people who that boy thinks are his *friends*—who lifted him out of a wheelchair to put their guns underneath him, then let him take the blame for it?" I looked at Wesley.

Frank was quiet.

"Like I said, it was a bad break," Wesley said. He poured himself more soda and screwed the cap on the bottle.

"A bad break?" I repeated. I opened my mouth to say something else, then I closed it.

"You're heated, dawg," Frank said, to me but in the direction of his plate.

"How are you guys not heated?" I asked.

"It's. How. It. Goes," Wesley said again, more slowly, sipping.

"Snitches get stitches." Frank articulated the subtext of his T-shirt.

People mumbled in agreement.

I wanted to understand. "But how's that right? How's that honor? You're supposed to not turn someone in, but the person who's actually guilty isn't supposed to take responsibility for his own actions? How's it not more offensive to not take responsibility for your own actions than to tell the truth?" It wasn't that I didn't know that was how it went, but that I wondered if that was how it had to go.

"Not snitching to the cops *is* responsibility," Wesley said.

"But how?" I asked. "What about responsibility to each other?" I wanted to understand how they understood the epidemic of gun violence that was leaving legions of young men in wheelchairs, paralyzed. There was so much injury. And that night, injury had a face: it was Ronald's. Ronald, whose family left him in the system when he got paralyzed and who was unable to care for himself, whose friends left him with their weapons underneath him and who was unable to get away fast enough on his own. I had met Ronald once at an event for the House and introduced myself to him. I told him that my father had been concerned about him after his accident and was so relieved when he was okay; he told me he thought my dad was real nice but he never knew he worried about him like that. "Wes, how is that how it has to go?"

"She's definitely heated," Wesley said to the other boys, looking away from me.

I had slid back into a third-person stranger at the table. It didn't make sense to them why I would care about a boy who we didn't know together, and charges that might not even stick. I thought about Ronald, who had survived violence only to endure more violence. What would become of him, of all of the paralyzed men who survived shootings, who navigated worlds that were inadequately accessible to them even before accidents that left them less equipped? How do we make sense of these systems of violence? I thought of the projected lifespans of the boys at the table. I imagined their home lives and school lives and work lives, past, present, future. I studied their faces as they kept eating. This was about Ronald, but it was also about each of them. Who would protect them? (And who would guard the guards?)

It was easy for me to believe that wasn't how it had to go; it's easy to believe in systems that are built to protect you. My anger didn't make sense to the boys because the stakes weren't the same for us; we didn't have the same skin in the game. I could imagine myself into their *we*, but it was only at the table they could feel a part of mine, for a few minutes; outside the House, *we* barely existed. They were them and I was me. We lived in the same neighborhood, but different worlds. And the police were on my side. "I don't know." I retreated. "I just feel bad for Ronald."

Plastic forks scraped paper plates.

"Don't feel that bad for him," Leon said, reaching for the bottle of Sprite. He twisted the cap and it let out a carbonated fart. "He's got a girlfriend."

"What do you mean?" I asked.

"I mean," Leon continued, "Ronald's got a girlfriend, so don't feel *that* bad for him."

FRANK INTRODUCED ANOTHER statement piece later that spring: a hand-painted design with a giant likeness of Barack Obama's face airbrushed onto the front of an XXXL white shirt. Obama's nostrils were the size of quarters, his ears were the height of a grown man's hands. "BELIEVE" was written in block letters underneath the then-senator's larger-than-life chin. Barack Obama was not yet the presumptive presidential nominee, but Frank was already on board.

When we were in the kitchen doing prep work as usual, I asked Frank whether he believed. He looked puzzled. I pointed to his shirt. He looked down at the letters on his chest and said it just came like that.

"But seriously," I asked, "what do you think of Barack Obama?"

"Never going to happen," Wesley said, entering the kitchen mid-conversation, like he did. "That shit's never going to happen."

"He's very dynamic," I said. "He's an amazing speaker. He's brilliant, so charismatic. People love him. I mean, look! He's got Frank—"

"Yeah, I've got to be with Wes," Leon said. "I mean, I want it to, but it's not. Something's probably going to happen."

"No way a Black dude's going to be president," Wesley said definitively. "That white lady's going to get it."

"She might not." I shrugged. "Some people are more afraid of women than Black people, believe it or not," I joked, a joke that wasn't a joke. *Afraid* still wasn't the right word, but it's the word I said.

Frank narrowed his eyes. Obama peered dreamily through the space between his arms.

"I don't know about that," Wesley said, pouring himself a second cup of soda.

"Hey, you know what you know and I know what I know, right?" I smiled.

"True." Wesley shrugged then sipped his Pepsi.

"At the same time," Leon said, evenly, "I could kind of see how people could be afraid of you." He sat, nodding to himself.

"Afraid of me?" I opened my mouth and feigned shock.

"I'm just saying," Leon said seriously, his head tilted to the side. "People don't really like teachers, no offense. Don't give me the Liz eyes." He shielded his face.

"Yup." Frank nodded along, still eating.

"I mean, could we stop calling me a teacher, at this point?" I asked. "Seriously. This isn't school."

"What are you, then?" Leon asked me over his cup.

It was a good question. Who did I think I was to them? What was I trying to be? Who were we to each other? Cooking, talking, choosing to sit down with each other, able to walk away from the table at any time. I suggested that we were neighbors, fellow city people. I lived streets away. This was my neighborhood, too. "We're neighbors having dinner. We're all neighbors on this planet."

"That's such a teacher thing to say, yo," Wesley said.

Frank agreed and Leon said that he did too, no offense.

—

WHEN OBAMA GOT the Democratic nomination in June, I couldn't wait to hear what Wesley had to say.

"Wes, he did it!" I said. We both knew whom I meant without having to say more.

"Yeah, I saw that," he said.

"It could change things, Wes."

"We'll see," he said, on the way to do laundry or smoke before dinner. "I just hope that dude don't get shot."

NEW BOYS MOVED into and out of the House over the summer, sometimes two FNGs at a time. Frank and Wesley and Joseph all had new roommates; none seemed to stay very long. I remembered what Gerry had told me, that he had less and less control over the placements and the particular kids who were assigned to the agency's care over the course of the year. This meant that, as the months went on, most of the new boys moved in and out quickly, some under particularly difficult or violent circumstances. By the fall, some had come and gone before we could cook together.

The other big news of the summer was that Leon's caseworker located his biological mother and put the two in touch. The effort on the part of the caseworker was part of a larger plan for Leon's transition out of youth protective services and into the adult sector of the system, but he didn't understand it like that. He told me casually about seeing her, as if she had been in the picture all along. He told me about meeting her and her other kids, and about his plans to buy her things with money he'd earned from his job. I told him I was happy for him, and I worried something terrible was going to happen.

Wesley continued to be more interested in eating than in cooking, but he encouraged others to cook for their own well-being. I overheard him tell one FNG why he should cook. "You better listen to what she tells you, dawg. 'Cause you're mad ugly and you're probably never going to get a girl. If you don't listen to her and be

able to cook for yourself, you're going to starve." His endorsement
seemed like the kind of thing I should put on a brochure; it captured my mission and weaponized it.

I recounted the Wesley exchange to a friend over drinks, when he
asked what I'd been up to.

"You're still doing that cooking thing?" he asked. "Do you keep
doing that because of your father, or because you actually want to
do it?"

It was a question I had asked myself many times since I had
started, when I was running late, as I was swiping my debit card at
the supermarket, each time I arrived in an empty kitchen. I supposed the answer was located between the two; what began as one
became the other. My father never wanted me to follow his path; he
wanted each of my siblings and me to make our own choices. I
wasn't trying to be more like him, but to know more than I had gotten to ask him before he died. The project was less about retracing
his steps than understanding the map of the world he lived in, to
figure out how it might also be mine. It was hard to explain why I
kept doing the cooking thing. I said that somehow, it felt like a right
thing to do even when it felt like a thing I didn't feel like doing.

My friend said I was making a riddle out of a simple question.

I said that sounded about right.

A BOY NAMED Jesús moved into the House in September. I don't
know who had told him what, but his first words to me were "No
forget Jesús's birthday." It was in December, he said. I told him I
wouldn't. He reminded me every time I saw him, twice per night on
nights he was there.

ONE NIGHT WHILE Leon was mixing brownies and Frank was buttering tortillas for quesadillas, Jesús came into the dining room where
I was preparing the chicken and sat down across from me at the
table. I was pulling the meat off two rotisserie chickens, separating

the skin and bones and wings into one bowl and the white meat we were going to use into the other.

Jesús nodded at the bowl with the bones in it and asked, "You going to throw that away?"

"Yeah." I looked at the pile of chicken skin and wings entangled with a sticker and string.

"I could have that?" he asked.

"Of course," I said, embarrassed I had designated it trash. As discreetly as I could, I pulled the paper and string away from the chicken remnants and passed him the bowl.

"This is the part I like," he said, taking it. He worked the dark meat off the bones swiftly and sucked at the wings and salty skin.

It was a hot, fall-but-still-feels-like-summer day. Jesús was wearing a white tank undershirt so thin I could read the giant arch of a woman's name in the Old English letters on his chest: MARÍA ELISA.

"Who is María Elisa?" I asked.

"My mother," he said. For some of the boys, tattoos they wore were the only mention they made of their families. If they were in conspicuous places—arms, shoulders, back, neck—we sometimes talked about them.

"Has she seen your tattoo?" I asked.

He kept eating.

"So, Jesús. You're from Mexico City and before this you lived in L.A., you like to draw, you like chicken, you have a tattoo for your mom. And your birthday's in December. What else should we know about you?"

"That's it," he said, in between bites.

"No puede ser todo," I tried in Spanish, thinking he might say more; it can't be everything. He had told me once he didn't speak English very well, which Wesley translated as "that dude just doesn't want to talk to you."

"It is," he said, sucking the last flavor from the bones. He thanked me and told me he wouldn't be around for dinner. Then he smiled and reminded me, "No forget Jesús's birthday."

Not long before he was gone, Jesús spent a night in jail. He came back to the House with a cane and a limp and stories about how cold it had been in the cell.

"Are you okay?" I asked him in English. I stopped trying in Spanish because he'd only ever answered me in English. I didn't ask why he'd been taken in.

"Yeah, I'm okay. It was mad cold there."

"You know why they do that?" Greg asked. He was on duty that night. It wasn't clear if he was clarifying for my benefit or for Jesús's. "For the addicts and drunks, so they sober up. Most of them're taken in drunk so that cold wakes you up. Real quick."

"They don't give you blankets or nothing," Jesús said. "It's mad cold."

Prison was never far from conversation at the table. It was a constant reminder that jails and prisons were more part of the boys' stories than colleges and jobs, the things I was used to talking about with my students at school. The boys often talked about people they knew who were locked up, and they talked about not wanting to get locked up, or not caring if they were locked up. There was nothing subjunctive about how they talked about it; juvenile detention was the simple past, incarceration, the simple future. Like day and night, the boys talked about inside and outside. Joseph's father was locked up for homicide and died in prison. Michael Peters's brother was locked up but he never talked about why. Frank's sister was locked up; it was the only thing he told us about her. And Frank's brother, P, whom I had met the time he came by the House, was on the run in Georgia, because he wasn't going to get locked up again. And when Wesley spent the night in jail in Connecticut and bumped into his cousin in the holding cell, and I asked him if he thought that bumping into people he knew in jail in a different state was an indication that he needed to start making some different choices, he had replied, "When you put it like that, yeah, maybe," and he laughed. Then we all laughed like we were all in on the joke.

Greg told me that Jesús had a court date and he shook his head no when I asked how he thought it would go. "It's one thing when it's assault and the other person doesn't show up. But when it's drugs . . ." He shook his head no for the rest of the answer.

"I had two court dates before," Joseph, who must have overheard my exchange with Greg, told me at dinner. "One of them was a misunderstanding."

At the shift change, Prof asked how dinner had gone, and I told him that drugs and court dates had been the talk of the day. Prof and I had started to overlap with some frequency. It was only ever for a few minutes but the talk was never small. I learned that Prof had worked for the agency full-time as a houseparent before going to school to become a high school history teacher. But, he said, he wanted to stay connected to the House, so he kept working one evening shift per week. Sometimes, we exchanged school stories, notably about testing and sexting, which were both making head-lines. One night, he asked me if I'd ever done hard drugs, as a point of reference for a story about a friend, whom he was helping with a situation. "Because it changes your perspective, and you can't un-derstand what that's like unless you've experienced it. And that feel-ing, once you've had it, you'll do anything to have it again." He said he knew, and maybe someday I would understand. This night, he asked if I'd read the book he was carrying, which compared the Roman Empire with the American Empire.

"No, I haven't heard of it. I don't think I've ever even thought of America as an empire," I said apologetically.

"Sure is," he said. "Look around. These kids here, this is the un-derclass."

I scribbled *Look around. These kids here, this is the underclass* on an index card in my schoolbag when I got into the car, for future refer-ence; I also wrote down Jesús's birthday, so I wouldn't forget. I stuck the card to my fridge when I got home.

A few weeks later, I asked Frank where Jesús was. He said, "That Spanish dude's dead."

"I think he's Mexican, and I don't think he's dead," I said, getting technical.

"What's the difference, dawg?" Frank asked me, cutting up some chicken.

When I asked Gerry, he didn't share details. He simply said, using the historical present, the way some people tell stories about the past in the present tense to drive the story home, "If Jesús is going to bring the street into the House, we will not have that. He cannot stay."

THAT OCTOBER WAS the third October of cooking at the House, and the last one, though I didn't know that yet. There were more boys for shorter periods of time, and fewer placements overall. The changes on the horizon that Gerry had speculated about were coming into focus. The table was starting to feel smaller. Though Leon had moved out in March and was holding a steady job, he came back to the House for dinner whenever he could make it. Frank was still going to math class and skipping other classes and smoking, and cooking every time. Wesley wouldn't make anything besides his own quesadillas or calzones, but he kept joining us in the kitchen to drink milk or soda while we were working, and then coming to eat. And Joseph was still Joseph, slow and quiet except when he was loud and violent, and always hungry. Other boys were moved in and barely introduced themselves before they were moved out; when I'd ask Frank or Wesley their names, they'd ask why they mattered.

I switched our Tuesday cooking nights to Wednesdays, because I was taking a class on the social contexts of literacy on Tuesday nights that semester. I felt bad about disrupting our routine, but the course was required for my degree. Frank said he didn't mind the change. Wesley said he never cared anyway. Leon asked, "But didn't you finish enough school already?"

Like most of Leon's questions, it was a good one. I was nearly finished with a graduate degree in education, and I needed the credential to keep my teaching job, I told him.

"Most people be trying to get out of school," Leon said when I told him, "and you just keep trying to get back in." I laughed, and he said, "But I'm serious, though."

Around Halloween, Leon told me that Wesley had gotten suspended for bringing a box cutter to school.

"Wes, is that true?" I called into his room from the kitchen. "Wes? Are you in there?"

He walked past me to the refrigerator and reached for the milk. "Yeah, it's true," he said.

"A box cutter?" I asked. "What were you thinking?"

He shrugged, unscrewed the cap, and poured.

"What happened, Wes?" I asked. "Why would you do this? I don't get it."

He shrugged, took a sip, and said, "People think I do that shit anyway, so I just did it."

I felt his words in my stomach. "What happens now?"

"Same old," he said between deep sips. "New school. Same shit."

I didn't know what the weapons charge meant in regard to transferring schools or continuing to live at the House. I didn't know what to ask or what I was allowed to know.

"It doesn't matter," he said. "I'm out when I'm eighteen anyway, like in a month."

I had heard Wesley was aging out, but this was the first time he mentioned it. "So, is it going to be different at the new school?" I asked.

He sipped and shrugged.

Leon shook his head no at the sink, where he was quietly bathing the vegetables.

I thought we should at least pause to appreciate the dramatic irony of the situation. "Wes, how is it that I haven't been able to get you to pick up a knife in *the kitchen*," I asked, "where, I'd like to note, it's appropriate to have knives. Yet, you felt compelled to bring a box cutter to *school*, where, I'd like to also note, it's widely considered unacceptable to carry sharp blades?"

Wesley laughed. "Well, when you put it like that," he said. He finished the milk in two gulps, then destroyed the cup and threw it away.

THE WEEK OF the presidential election, Frank was wearing his Obama T-shirt when I arrived. It soon became clear that he hadn't taken it off for a while. Change was the talk of the House: Barack Hussein Obama had been elected the first Black (second Irish American) president of the United States, and Frank Jones needed to change his clothes.

The houseparent on duty that Tuesday had let the boys stay up until all of the ballots were tallied and the new president was named on every channel.

Leon recounted the night's events and the bets that were placed on who would win in the end. He peppered his account with additional bits of commentary, like: "No offense, but that white lady on the other side is crazy."

"None taken," I assured him, amused but alarmed that he imagined an automatic allegiance between Sarah Palin and me just because we were both white women.

Frank stood with his fingers hooked into the wooden beam of the doorway. He leaned forward, bare feet planted, chin up, listening. As Leon got to the end of his story, Frank joined in. "You saw the different states and it was going back and forth. Bam, bam, bam!" He let go of the beam and waved his arms, pointing. "This side, this side, that side. Bam! Blue, bam! Red, bam! Blue, blue, blue! Bam! Bam! Bam!" He made fists and cheered. "Then Obama's side just blew up. Bam! Bam! Bam, bam, bam!" He shook his shirt for the final bams, shaking Obama's giant face in a final frenzy.

"I always knew he was going to win," Leon said solemnly.

"That dude's such a liar. Nobody knew," said Wesley, who appeared quietly in the other doorway. He rolled his eyes at Leon.

"He did it, Wes," I said. "It could change things." I said *things*, but I was thinking about democracy and representation, labor rights and mass incarceration, poverty and access to education. And I said *change* as if change were a mappable, transactional possibility, the annoying way that teachers state ideas as facts, as if real change could happen neatly, as if meaningful change didn't require a violent dismantling of existing systems, and careful examination of the ways of life and interrogation of the philosophies that produce and reproduce inequality, racism, and other crimes against humanity and democracy, like Dr. King had said that long-ago day in Memphis, when the reckoning he imagined was still so far off.

"We'll see," Wesley said. "We'll just see about that."

Wesley said "We'll see" the way my father used to say it when we would ask for things and he didn't want to say no right away. What kind of change would be meaningful change? What good is hope when people are hungry? How much can one person do? It all remained to be seen.

Wesley Not Applicable

Two truths guided Wesley's role in the project: he wasn't really interested in participating and he really liked dessert. He made both clear on the first night and at almost every subsequent dinner.

"Are we ever going to make cheesecake?" he asked one night. I knew that cheesecake was his favorite, and that by "we" he meant me. For someone who wasn't interested in helping, he wasn't shy about suggesting what *we* should or shouldn't make.

Given his sweet tooth, it made sense that Wesley was the one with the theory that there is always room in your stomach for something sweet. "Tell him about your dessert theory!" I'd say, as someone was switching out the used dinner plates for fresh ones for dessert, or I was cutting cake or scooping ice cream.

And Wesley would look at me and roll his eyes, and then sigh deeply and stand up to recite it, with his hands in an almost heart shape just below his actual heart: "Everyone's got room for dessert . . ." I liked it as a kind of icebreaker because it showed the FNGs that Wesley wasn't as tough and unapproachable as he seemed. How can you be afraid of someone with a sweet tooth?

I told him that yes, *we* could make cheesecake. It was around the time that Philadelphia, the brand famous for cream cheese, came out with their prepackaged tubs of cheesecake filling, so I cheated and bought that, in the interest of time. I also bought toppings and vanilla wafers and cupcake foils, with the idea that we could assemble the mini cheesecakes that one of my aunts made. Plus, the individual size would allow each boy to choose his own toppings.

"Can I have the extra?" Wesley asked of a second, unopened tub of cheesecake filling, after everyone else had finished eating.

"Sure," I told him. "That's what it's there for."

"The whole thing?" he asked, his voice cracking in excitement.

"If you want," I said. I started washing the pans, a head start for whoever was on Kitchen A. "But maybe don't eat it all at once. Please don't get sick."

Wesley dumped all the toppings into the tub of cheesecake filling: the rest of the canned cherries, a fistful of chocolate chips, a cup of strawberry slices. He mixed it all into a soft swirl of colorful mess and started eating standing up because he couldn't wait to taste it.

"Are you really going to eat all of that?" I asked over my shoulder from the sink. I sounded like my grandmother. I didn't say it was going to give him a bellyache, but I thought it.

"Could I?" he asked, a heaping spoonful of everything cheesecake en route to his lips.

I nodded and he took a massive bite.

"How is it?"

"I love it," he said, smiling. It was the only time I ever heard Wesley say *love*.

The next time, I wanted it to be better. I told my librarian friend at school who sometimes helped me find recipes that I needed a good recipe for real cheesecake and he gave me his old boyfriend's gourmet recipe. I followed it closely, and asked Wesley what he thought.

"It's okay," he said. "No offense, but the other one was better. It tastes more like real cheesecake, like from Old Country Buffet and stuff."

I told him I wasn't offended, and said we would make the real kind next time.

"I'll still finish it, though. Could I have the rest of the cherries?" He smiled. Wesley averaged one smile per night, and if you missed it, you missed it.

Whenever we spoke of him, Gerry consistently referred to him as Wesley Not Applicable, in reference to the survey the first night and Wesley's "N/A" answer next to most of my questions, including his last name. "Not applicable, because nothing matters to him, and he doesn't think he matters to anyone," Gerry would say. "That says it all, now, doesn't it?"

That November, as Wesley's eighteenth birthday approached, he proposed a dinner plan. "This is supposed to be a big one, because it's my last," he said, as if he were on death row, entitled to a final meal. "You know," he continued, "I'm not going to live here anymore." For most teens, adulthood doesn't happen overnight. On the outside, turning eighteen is almost arbitrary, except that legally you can vote, get married, buy cigarettes and lottery tickets, and join the army, if you want to do any of those things. You can't buy beer yet; you can already drive. But on the inside, in the eyes of the state, a youth becomes an adult one minute to the next. Between 11:59 and midnight, a body assumes responsibility for itself. After his birthday, Wesley would move out of the group home and out on his own. It didn't seem to matter whether he was ready, or strong enough, or knew how to pay bills and make dinner for himself.

"So I was thinking," he said, "we should have lobster for my birthday dinner."

"Okay," I said.

"I could have it?" he asked, shocked. "I could have lobster?"

"Yeah, I think it makes sense, Wes. You're right. It's a big birthday. I think I can figure out a way to do it," I told him. "I don't know if I'll be able to get lobster for everyone—I'll have to see about that. But I'll get them for you, for your eighteenth birthday. Definitely."

"I don't care about anybody else—" he started to say, then stopped himself.

"Well, I know that already," I said.

He laughed. "I didn't mean it like that—"

"Except kind of." I laughed, too.

"Well, yeah." He laughed again. We laughed together.

"Do you know what's going to happen after the House?" I asked him quietly.

"Not really," he said. "But you're serious, I could have lobster?"

I nodded. He sort of sang, "Thank you!" and shot his smashed cup toward the trash can, making the basket without hitting the rim.

Gerry was more averse to the idea of lobster for Wesley's birthday than I thought he would be. It wasn't exactly about the expense; he knew I wasn't expecting him to fund it. I had paid for the majority of groceries out of pocket since I started, and Gerry gave me occasional checks that covered a portion of the total cost. It was about appearances, he said. By then, there were fewer and fewer referrals; there weren't enough youth placements to fill all of the programs, so some of the homes run by the agency had started to close. Gerry told me that he thought it would be problematic if word got out that there were lobster dinners at the House while the fate of the agency was unknown.

"How is word going to get out?" I asked. "Do you think Leon will report us to the boards? Nobody seems concerned that a whole population of kids who are already pushed around are going to be further displaced, but you think someone will think a dozen lobsters bought by a volunteer is somehow inappropriate?" I probably shouldn't have laughed, but I laughed.

He said that it wouldn't look good if anybody got wind of it. He was serious.

I became serious, too. "Gerry, it's Wesley's last dinner at the House. I can't change anything that happened to him, or what his life will be after this. But I can give a stupid lobster dinner for his eighteenth birthday. If anybody says anything about it, blame me. Tell them an aggressive bleeding heart with a dead dad insisted on feeding these homeless kids lobster and did it without your consent. Blame me. I already told Wesley I'm getting lobster. I have to get it."

Gerry narrowed his eyes. I kept talking. I told him the lobster story from my family mythology, which took place while my parents were working at the orphanage run by the Daughters of Charity where they met. The sisters and staff took the kids on a trip to the beach, and at dinner they told the kids they could order anything they wanted. A boy named Matty O'Sullivan said that he wanted lobster. The sisters had to tell him no, because it was too expensive; they hadn't expected the kids to ask for lobster, and they didn't have the budget for it. Matty wailed when they told him no. He said that he didn't want it anyway, he just wanted to see if he could have it. He said he knew they would say no, he knew the adults were lying when they told the kids they could have whatever they wanted.

In our house, when I was growing up, Matty O'Sullivan was a cautionary tale about testing and expectations, and being satisfied with what you have. But my mother said she always wished she could've just gotten him that lobster, as if a dinner could change a course of history.

I told Gerry that I didn't want Wesley Not Applicable to be my Matty O'Sullivan.

Gerry didn't laugh. He just looked at me. Then he reluctantly agreed.

When I told my mother about Wesley and the lobster dinner, she insisted that she pay for the lobsters, for everyone.

I BORROWED METAL crackers for the claws, melted butter, and Frank and I made an array of sides, including corn on the cob, which Leon referred to as Normal Corn. I bought the lobsters steamed. As I pulled their bound bodies out of the bags one at a time, I reconsidered the high road I had taken during the torturing-small-animals conversation we'd had a few weeks before.

Wesley sat in his usual chair and tied a plastic bib around his neck ceremoniously after everyone else was seated. He hadn't believed he'd get the lobsters until they were stacked in front of him.

Joseph had said he wanted one, but when he unwrapped it, its face surprised him. "I just don't think I can do it. I can't do it. I can't eat this." He pushed his chair back from the table. "No, no, no, I can't," he squealed. "I'm sorry, I just can't." He folded his arms and shook his head no. "I'm sorry, I can't." He started rocking back and forth.

"It's okay, Joseph," I said. I picked up the lobster so he didn't have to look at it and asked if he wanted chicken. We had also made some chicken, because Frank said from the beginning that he wasn't interested in lobster.

"See, like I said, that shit's nasty," Frank said. "Smells nasty, looks nasty, probably tastes nasty, too." He waved around a plastic fork with a block of barbecue chicken on it. "That's why I ordered this." He took a bite for emphasis.

"I'm sorry, I just can't," Joseph repeated. "I can't. I'm sorry."

"Can I have his?" Wesley asked.

"Sure," I said, placing Joseph's lobster on Wesley's plate next to his birthday two.

"I'm sorry, I just couldn't," Joseph kept saying as I served him chicken. "I'm sorry."

"It's fine, dawg. Now stop apologizing," Wesley said to Joseph. "That shit's annoying."

When everyone was seated, served, and already eating, I suggested that we toast Wesley.

Javier, the FNG, kicked us off, lifting his cup. He was never particularly interested in helping prepare dinner, but when he moved in, he and Wesley got into the habit of going out to smoke and coming back just in time, enthusiastic about eating. The first time I met him, Wesley told me Javier was his cousin and I believed him, even though he was Black and Javier was Latino. I accepted that they were related because of how they looked out for each other and how bloodlines aren't always obvious. Wesley had laughed and said, "Liz, you believe anything."

"Wes, you've always been a fun guy," Javier started. "A good cousin." Everybody laughed. "Are we going out later, or what?"

"Javier, usually people don't ask questions in the middle of toasts," I said.

Wesley said, "Yeah, dawg, and you're supposed to stick your pinky finger in the air like this." And he lifted his littlest finger off his red cup, cocked his head to the side, swished the Pepsi around in his cup, and said, "Now toast me, fools."

The other boys raised their cups, laughing.

I lifted my pinky, too, and asked Leon if he'd like to offer a toast.

Leon began, "First, I'd just like to say that it was my birthday, a couple times, and I didn't have nothing like this. I mean really, there was no lobster or anything like that. I mean, no offense. It was okay, but it wasn't like this." He made a sweeping gesture in the direction of the cornucopia of crumpled tinfoil, cracked red carcasses, and heaping plates.

"Leon," I interrupted. "Usually people don't use toasts as a space to complain or talk about themselves."

"And I mean," Leon continued, "this dude's not even going to say thank you."

"Leon!" I interrupted him again. "And people definitely don't usually criticize people while they're toasting them."

Leon reeled himself in for a genuine finish. "Anyway, Wes, happy birthday. And I hope things go good for you now." He raised his cup, then added, "I hope you don't mess up too bad"—everyone clicked cups—". . . like you usually do."

"Leon," I said again, giving him Liz eyes.

"Well, it's true," he said into his cup but loud enough for all of us to hear.

Joseph giggled. "Happy birthday, Wesley," he said.

"Thanks, Joe," Wesley said.

"Same," said one voice.

"Same," said another.

"Same," a third voice said.

All of the cups were up, with pinkies lifted in the air.

"Happy birthday! We all wish you the best, Wes," I said. "Always."

And then everybody ate everything on his plate, and then a little bit more. And we sang to Wesley over a strawberry shortcake, as we had twice before, this one lit with a wax 1 and 8. It was one of those rare moments when even while it's happening, it feels right.

As we were clearing the dishes, before everyone left to take care of his chore for the night, Wesley walked over to me. "I was going to say thank you, Liz." His voice was soft when he said it. "I'm not just saying it 'cause Leon said to."

"I know, Wes," I told him.

"Thank you," he said quietly. "For everything."

"You're welcome, kiddo. Happy birthday," I said.

I looked at him. He looked at me. It felt like an ending.

"No seriously," Wesley said, again, deliberately. "I mean, like, for *everything*."

"Seriously, Wes. You're very welcome." I wrapped my arms around his shoulders. I thanked him back. I wished him luck. I told him to be careful. I asked him to not be a stranger, to keep in touch.

He hugged me hard and said he would. I wanted to believe him.

Milk, Eggs, Bread,
Pedro Martínez

I don't know if it is movies or religion that makes us think that the meaning of life can ever be clear. We want to know everything, say everything, be told everything. We believe there must be reasons for things, and we want to understand those reasons. Because if there's no good reason, then what's the point of anything? Despite our best logic, we crave that kind of understanding. We use religions as frameworks, metaphors as surrogates, and other people's tragedies as rehearsals. When our time comes, we want to be ready. I can't be the only one who used to think it was possible to be ready.

When my grandmother died in January of 2004, it wasn't a surprise. She had suffered the slow erosion of dementia for over a decade by then. One visit at a time, I saw how she was replaced by a different version of herself with deceivingly familiar hands but distant eyes.

When my father died in December of the same year, it felt more like being hit by a truck. He fell into a coma within hours of the natural disaster that devastated Indonesia that year. Over the beep and trill and snoozing alarm sounds of the machines in the intensive care unit, we watched continuous footage of homes being swept up like sandcastles, with animals and people flailing like matchsticks. We listened to the urgent voices of reporters, counted the tallies of victims that scrolled across the bottom of the screen, waited for it to stop and for there to be some kind of resolution. At some point, my mother looked at me over my father's chest as it rose and fell with the respirator and said, "We were hit by our own tsunami."

While I was a volunteer teacher after college in Chicago, the parent of one of my ninth graders suffered a fatal heart attack. I watched my student try to figure out why her mother died and whether life would ever be normal again. I helped organize a memorial service at school so we could come together as a community to support her. Friends and classmates contributed food and talents. Somebody sang "Amazing Grace" a cappella; many people brought family-sized bags of hot Cheetos and liters of soda. The girl's father attended with her younger sibling. The student said ahead of time that she wanted to speak.

Holding herself together, she stood in the middle of a crowd of teachers and friends. She thanked everyone for coming, then pulled out a piece of paper from her pocket and said she had to tell us a story. She said that she was doing laundry and found her mom's housecoat. She had pulled it in close to her face to smell her mom's smell another time, then emptied the pockets and found this note. She held it up and said, "I was so excited when I found this! I thought finally, I found her secret letter to me. I was sure that it would say that she loved me, or what I'm supposed to know. You know?" she asked. Everyone nodded.

"You know, I thought at least it would say *goodbye* or something. Because she didn't even say goodbye." People were crying; she was so matter-of-fact. "Anyway, I opened it up." She opened the folded sheet to its full size, the size of an index card, and flipped it around for everyone to see. "It says '*Leche, huevos, pan, algo para cenar.*'" Through tears, everyone laughed at the punch line: *Milk, eggs, bread, something for dinner*. The secret note was a grocery list. As the girl laughed, her eyes started to well up. Two friends rushed up to hug her. "I know she loved us," she continued. "And you know, this makes sense, because she was always cooking and taking care of us. I just thought it would be nice to have a letter or something."

I may have been thinking of that index card when I casually gave my father a new Moleskin journal a few weeks after he was diag-

nosed. Never a diary guy, he accepted the book with gracious skepticism and put it on the shelf by his bed. My wanting more words
from him was a recurring theme in our relationship. It started when
I went to Girl Scout sleepaway camp in fifth grade and I asked him
if he was going to send me care packages, and he asked me what he
would send. I suggested Swedish Fish, the penny candy I liked to
buy from a corner store when we stopped on the way home from
my children's theater group. So while I was away at camp, he sent a
tiny bag of the candy in a large manila envelope with a one-sentence
note: *Dear Liz, Here are the fish. Love, Dad.* When I got home, I
thanked him and asked if he could write more next time. He said he
didn't know if there would be a next time.

The March before life split into before and after, we had gone to
Fort Myers for what had become our annual family trip to spring
training: one long weekend with mornings planned around baseball
games and batting practice and evenings planned around dinner at
chain restaurants like Bennigan's. My dad would time dinner to
catch the sunset and would pull over on the ride back to the hotel if
we weren't going to make it back to the beach in time, and make us
get out of the car to watch it. My brother and sisters and I would
indulge him this, mocking how his sentimentality was increasing
with age. He turned the volume way up when Sheryl Crow sang
about soaking up the sun; my brother and sisters and I rolled our
eyes and sang along. That trip, he was tired even after the second
day of vacation and he had a persistent cough. It was a normal-
sounding cough, the way that something can seem normal right up
until the second you know it isn't. He made the appointment when
we got back.

He died nine months later.

Of course, we didn't realize he would only have nine months.
Even in retrospect it's hard to delineate between denial and hope. I
think we really believed that he could defy the odds, or at least be on
the more-time versus less-time end of the spectrum. He was young.
He always did what he was supposed to do. He was ours. These
seemed like good reasons to believe; that every third person in Bos-

ton was wearing shirts that said "Believe" that fall only reinforced the point.

As our family life came apart at the seams, the Red Sox won their way to their first World Series in decades. We rode waves of desperation and elation. Two months later, my father was lying in a coma. We kept a kind of vigil by his bedside for eight days. We planned. We talked. We worried. We played music, and sang along. We sat. We sat a lot. We cried. We waited. We also ate. The windowsill of his intensive care unit room was lined like a concession stand. My sisters and I communicated through shared raspberry and cream cheese croissants. Though there was a lot of uncertainty about what was happening, there was continuity in eating. We didn't have the right words, but we had plenty of snacks. Food, at least, was real.

People came in to see him, to say goodbye. And people said the kinds of things people say in the worst of times: comforting, cryptic, random, well intended but poorly executed, kind.

One of the last days, when it was just my mother and sisters and a family friend in the room, I mentioned the journal. I confessed that I had read it. Only three pages were inscribed with my father's large, crooked cursive writing. In the book I had given him to write what he could not say, he wrote one sentence about disliking acupuncture and several entries about Pedro Martínez and his pitching.

My mother softly asked whether he mentioned her.

"Did he call you Pedro Martínez?" I asked.

We all laughed.

"Sometimes," she said.

We laughed harder, tears streaming down our faces.

There was no script. We were on our own to make sense of things, through makeshift frameworks. We were hit by our own tsunami. My mother and brother and sisters and I had to figure out how to rebuild our interior and exterior worlds, together and separately, inundated by grief. My siblings built families of their own. And I found a kind of refuge, for a while, in an upstairs room of my father's unfinished work, cooking to remember him and honor him and to try to understand his life better, determined to keep moving through doing, trying to do the best I could.

In December 2008, Gerry wrote a letter stating that the agency would close on June 28, 2009. By then, they had closed the girls' residence and one of the other boys' residences and were in the process of closing the others. They had only twenty-two youths in their care, and they could not afford to continue. They expected to have twelve boys living in two residences at the end of June; the youths they would continue to serve in the final months were individuals with education plans and planned terminations; the June plan would enable them to finish the school year before being moved to new placements. I would learn later that Gerry called these seven months, between declaring that the House and all of the agency's residences would close and their actual closing, the death march. He would tell me when it was over that he was grateful that I had been there, in my father's stead, that he saw a symmetry in how my father had been there in the beginning and I was there in the end. He quoted Walt Whitman at dinner when he told me: "'Sail Forth—steer for the deep waters only, / Reckless O soul, exploring, I with thee and thou with me, / For we are bound where mariner has not yet dared to go, / And we will risk the ship, ourselves and all.'"

It was a while before any of the boys said out loud that the House was going to close, or talked about where they would be moved when it did.

There was snow that winter and it was cold as always, but Wesley never ate with us again after his lobster dinner. I saw him one more time, that December. He was on the couch waiting for Javier, who was still living at the House, though not for much longer. I told Wesley I heard he had switched schools again, and he said he didn't like people talking about his business. I told him I wouldn't have to ask around if he would tell me himself; I had given him my number when he left and told him to be in touch if he wanted. He shrugged and said he was fine, and school was school, and he asked what was for dinner. I said he was welcome to stay and he said yeah, he knew that already. But when I went back into the TV room to tell him the food was made, he was gone.

I thought Wesley would come back. I bought him a sweater that I knew he would like, along with the other Christmas presents for Frank and Leon and the FNGs who were living at the House. I kept that sweater for weeks afterward, wrapped in a box, in the back of my car with the knives. Eventually, I brought it back to the store. When the cashier asked me why I was returning it, I wanted to tell her everything. Instead, I just said that I had made a mistake.

Tell All the Truth
(But Tell It Slant)

For Frank's birthday in February, I thought it would be a treat to order out for Chinese food, because he said his next favorite thing, besides cheese and shrimp, was crab Rangoon. We tried to make them once. I thought they tasted like leaves slathered in cream cheese, but Frank ate all of them and said he liked them. It reminded me of the time we made breakfast for dinner and the omelets had to be pried off the cheap pan in stubborn yellow forkfuls and I apologized profusely, but he insisted, "They're good, dawg. Stop stressing." I asked if he wanted to order out or if he had a different idea for his birthday. He said he was thinking about the rainbow cupcakes.

WHEN I CALLED ahead to ask Frank what he wanted me to order, he asked me what they had. I told him they had all the usual things Chinese food restaurants have. He said all he knew was crab Rangoon. I asked if he wanted to check out the menu online, and he told me, "Just get what you think." So I ordered us what my siblings and I usually order: sweet-and-sour chicken, teriyaki beef, fried rice, lo mein, plus crab Rangoon. I also made Funfetti cupcakes. When I pulled candles out of my purse, Frank said there weren't enough people to light them, but he would keep them anyway. He took the waxen 1 and 7 and put them away in his room. Frank turned seventeen, and Wesley wasn't around to suggest that he was really only turning sixteen.

I thought about Wesley and Leon as we sat at the mostly empty table. There were only five boys living at the House by February, and I hadn't met two of them. Gerry and the staff were working to line up next placements for each of the boys who were still there, along with all of the young people living in the remaining eight residences the agency ran. It was hard to say how the kids' transitions would go. I thought about what Greg had told me about Javier's departure when I asked about when he had left.

Greg shrugged and said, "He asked me to give him the money in the petty cash envelope."

"What do you mean?" I asked.

"So he'd have some money in his pocket. He said to just tell Gerry that he robbed me."

I sighed. "He was so nervous about leaving." Javier had told me that they were moving him back to live with his mom, whom he hadn't lived with for three years; she lived with her boyfriend and their daughter, a half sister Javier had never met. "What did you say?"

"I said, 'You know I can't do that, man.' I said all I could give him was his haircut money, plus the tip." Greg shrugged again.

"Dude could've just robbed you but instead he asked." Frank said what I was thinking.

It was just Frank, Michael Peters, Joseph, and me at dinner, and Joseph left to watch a movie in his room after his cupcake.

As I smoothed the tiny printed message from my fortune cookie, I explained to Frank and Michael Peters how I always read my fortunes. I always think they might be right. I keep them in a drawer, as if all together they might add up to something: "To avoid criticism, do nothing, say nothing, be nothing." "Have the courage to live creatively." "You will attract cultured and artistic people to your home." "Seek the significance of your problem at this time. Try to understand."

"Do you guys ever read your fortunes?" I asked.

"Nope," Michael Peters said, not reaching for a little wrapped package.

I looked at Frank, who ate his cookie and left the paper on the table.

"I don't like reading," he told me for the hundredth time.

"It's just a sentence, Frank." I tried persuasion.

"It's still reading, dawg." Frank went with reason.

"He's right." Michael Peters laughed.

"Okay, but are you even going to finish this?" I gestured to the remaining crab Rangoon and rice. "Are you on a diet, Frank?" I asked jokingly. "You used to eat so much, but you don't anymore."

"I know, I used to be mad hungry every time," he told me. "But then when you kept coming, I don't know. I stopped being so hungry."

WHEN I TOLD Frank a couple weeks later that I had a favor to ask of him, he narrowed his eyes and asked me what it was. When I asked him if I could interview him for a class I was taking about reading, he said he would think about it. The assignment for my literacy class was to first interview a student about their experience with reading and school, and then reflect on the student's answers in the context of the course readings. In class, we tended to talk about literacy as a liberatory practice and reading disorders as obstacles that could be overcome with the right instructional practices; in class discussions there seemed to be a general consensus that if a student wanted to read—and was inspired by an enthusiastic educator and innovative pedagogy—they certainly could. I considered interviewing one of my students from school for the paper, but since I assessed their reading and comprehension skills in Spanish rather than English, and since the power dynamic was such that my students were reliant on me for grades and they might feel compelled to agree even if they didn't want to participate, I didn't think it was ideal. And, as I made my way through the course readings and listened to classmates discuss the pathways and social contexts of literacy throughout the semester, I kept thinking of Frank. I kept thinking about the conversations we'd had about his reading. And I knew Frank would say no if he didn't want to spend forty more minutes talking to me about it. I assured him that it wouldn't take too long, that he didn't have to write anything, and that I would just ask him some questions, which I would then type up with some other notes and turn in to my teacher. He said, yeah, he knew what an interview was, and like he said before, he would think about it.

Frank had told me on multiple occasions that I asked too many questions. But he usually answered them, with yeahs or yups or nopes; or sometimes he would just sigh a response: a slow, exasperated sound, like a balloon having the air let out of it. Frank rarely asked me questions, except about what time we were eating and whether I would buy him shrimp. And he had told me he didn't like reading, but he had never exactly said that he didn't want to talk about it. We hadn't discussed it much since our impromptu poetry reading in the TV room; I occasionally asked how school was going and he sometimes assured me that yeah, he'd been going. I thought my chances for being granted the interview were at least fifty-fifty.

The next week, while we were unpacking groceries, he told me, "I'll do the thing." I knew he knew he was helping me out. We set the time for the following Saturday at 3 P.M., at the coffee shop around the corner from the House.

At 3:18, as I sat at a colorful café table with an iced coffee next to my open notebook and a sweating can of Red Bull in front of an empty chair across from me, I debated whether or not to call the House to see if Frank was there. At twenty-two minutes after, I called. One of the other boys answered and said that Frank was in his room. After a moment, Frank picked up.

"Hello?" Frank said, like a question.

"Hey Frank, it's Liz—"

"I'm leaving already," he said before I could say anything else. "Be there in five minutes."

"It's the place around the corner," I said, wanting to be sure he knew where I was.

"I know, dawg," he said. "I'm gone already." He hung up.

At 3:27, Frank pushed the door of the café open while pulling a black sweatshirt over his white T-shirt and sleepy hair. He nodded at me from the doorway, then walked toward my table in wide strides, sat down, and opened the can with his teeth.

Looking at Frank Jones, I had wondered more than once what it must be like to be the Boo Radley of your own life. I witnessed how other boys were with him; they called him slow, they said he stunk, and they made crack-baby jokes when they were fighting or being familiar. I had seen people outside the House cross streets to avoid his tall body and oversized clothes. Frank never flinched. His gaze was usually fixed somewhere else.

At sixteen or seventeen, Frank had told me that he read at "one of them three levels," which I took to mean a third-grade reading level, which somebody must have told him, in some classroom along the way. His school history read like a disjointed overview of public schools and juvenile detention facilities in Massachusetts. Since kindergarten, he had attended at least five schools that he remembered. His home history was a list of group-living and direct-care facilities dating back to before he could walk, when he was removed from the custody of his mother.

When I asked him if he remembered learning how to read or who taught him, he said, "Nope."

When I asked how often he read, he said, "I don't." When I reminded him that I knew for a fact he owned a copy of *Harry Potter*, he reminded me that he read one page a year and he had read it already.

When I asked how he feels when someone asks him to read, he said, "Not good, like I don't want to do it."

When I asked what his favorite book was, he said it was the one about the girl.

When I asked him what the first part would be about if someone was going to write the story of his life, he said he didn't know what I meant. "All stories start someplace," I said. "Where does your story start?"

"I don't remember," Frank said as he took a sip from the sweaty can.

"You can't think of anything?" I asked. "A memory?"

"Nope." He sipped.

When I asked the most interesting thing he ever did, he said, "Math. I'm good at math."

When I asked what was different about math than reading, he said, "The difference is that I like it and I'm good at it. It's money." He put the can down. I noted in the margin of the page that *money* and *the truth* were synonyms he used for *good*. I wondered what was happening in his math class that wasn't happening in his other classes. I had to imagine that it wasn't just about the numbers.

When I asked Frank what his best school memory was, he scrunched his nose into his forehead; he looked confused. I amended the question. "Can you think of a time that you didn't hate being in school, or maybe even liked it?"

"Oh," he said. "Yeah, gym."

Twice during the interview, I told Frank that we could stop if he wanted; my questions about literacy and school seemed so useless as I heard myself ask them.

Twice, Frank shook his head no and said, "You always ask a mad lotta questions, dawg. I'm used to it already."

When I asked him how many years he had left in school, Frank said, "Probably like three."

When I asked what he would do next, after high school, he said, "Probably college."

When I asked what he wanted to study in college, he said, "Probably construction."

Then, when I asked Frank if he wanted to change how he read, to be able to read better, he said, "Yup," as if it were obvious. When I followed up with, "Is there something you think would help with that?" he paused and said, "I don't know," as if there must be a right answer, but he didn't know it, something that might have been in one of the books that he never opened up.

—

IN MY PAPER, I tried to capture Frank's views about school in words he used to talk about his experience during our interview. I also wrote about his attention span and the jokes the other boys made at his expense. I wrote about the punishment essays Frank said he was assigned for skipping classes—which he didn't write because he struggled with reading and writing, which is why he skipped the classes in the first place. I described how I had watched him stumble over reading instructions on the backs of bags of frozen vegetables and boxes of rice, and speculated about how he could be expected to navigate a novel or a biology textbook and what kind of support he would need to do it. I tried to imagine how he must feel in school, and how getting in trouble for not going must have felt less embarrassing than going. There was plenty more to Frank's school story than what he told me in our thirty-four-minute interview, in the short answers he provided to my prescriptive questions. But there was also so much in what he said.

It was hard to justify my belief that schools are supposed to distribute opportunity, not reproduce inequality, in the context of how I understood Frank's experiences in classrooms and with teachers; the possibility for social mobility in his school story wasn't easy to locate. What kind of intervention would it take to change Frank's trajectory—in school, in work, in life—in a meaningful way, for the better?

"Social promotion," Greg, the houseparent, had told me when I asked him if there was a plan in place for Frank in school. When Greg would tell me about Frank's truancy, I would ask about his access to support services. Frank was getting up and going to school; it wasn't that he didn't want to be in school or that he was refusing to go. He was showing up, and not getting the services he needed. This infuriated me. Who was advocating for Frank for the services he deserved? Greg shrugged. "You're a teacher. You know what social promotion is. That's the plan for Frank. They don't care if he can't read. They've got to know he can't."

The *they* were Frank's teachers and guidance counselors and administrators; as I wrote my paper, I kept thinking about them. I tried to reconcile how, as a teacher, I was part of the same system of schooling that was a ladder for some students and a maze for others. I thought about the night Frank read to me from the old book I found in the cabinet, and how I had thought the Emily Dickinson poem about telling the truth would be simple and relatable: familiar words, in short sentences, about a topic we both knew. I thought reading the poem would be a good thing, because that's how I think about poems, as little stories with beginnings, middles, and endings that you can ingest and talk about. But it was like the basil had been with Wesley. The poem was another test for Frank, and by the time I realized, it was too late. If I stopped him before the last line, I thought he would feel like he had failed the test, so I didn't stop him. He kept going. I kept listening, and saying words when he looked at me for help. The most striking line of the truth poem was the one Frank added at the end, eight syllables like the first: "See, that's why I don't like reading."

I had approached the interview as an opportunity to understand Frank's experience as a student in the context of my experience as a teacher. I had taken my teaching job the fall before my dad died because I wanted a change and I wanted to work at a job that I believed was good work, and I believed in schools and education; I believed that education is architecture, not alchemy—transformation by a different name. Systematic inequalities didn't fit neatly into my philosophy of teaching. I didn't know if teaching was the one thing I wanted to spend my life doing, but I knew that even on hard days, working with students felt like good work. I was almost finished with the coursework for this credential I needed to keep my job. In theory, I understood the ideas and practices of many dimensions of American schools and schooling and student life. But I struggled to conclude what it would take to actually, meaningfully change the shape of Frank's experience in schools, or whose responsibility it was to make that happen.

Frank approached our interview as further proof that he knew what he was talking about when it came to reading. He knew his story already; I was the one who didn't get it.

"Schooled the teacher," I could almost hear Wesley say, from wherever he was.

THE INSTRUCTOR WROTE a single-sentence assessment in red on the bottom of the last page of my paper: "You've failed to capture anything positive about the educational experience of your subject."

Life of the Party

When Gerry said the boys wanted to cook for me for my birthday that March, I couldn't imagine that it was their idea. When I called before I left school to confirm that I shouldn't bring food that week, he said that Arlette had made Jamaican curry chicken. Then I called upstairs like I usually did to see how many boys were around, and I offered to bring dessert. My favorite cake is chocolate with vanilla frosting, like James's was; I thought I might bring cupcakes.

"You could bring soda and quesadilla stuff," Frank said.

I said I had heard that they were making Jamaican curry chicken for me.

"Yeah but nobody likes that," Frank said. He'd heard the plan but had a different one in mind.

"Oh," I said, recalculating. "Gerry told me not to bring anything because you guys were going to cook for me . . ."

"I mean, Arlette made that. But nobody's going to eat it," Frank said.

"So," I clarified, "you want me to get quesadilla stuff, too? Were you thinking that we'd use the curried chicken? Like, curried chicken quesadillas?"

"You could have that if you want, but nobody really likes that," Frank said. "So you could bring regular stuff for us."

"So I should get a rotisserie chicken and tortillas and cheese?"

"And shrimp," he said. "Could you get shrimp, too?"

"Sure," I said. "Should I get some cupcakes?"

"For what?"

"In case it's anyone's birthday."

"It's not," Frank said. "LeBron already had his. Remember? We made sundaes. He's the only one with the birthday in March."

When I arrived with arms full of quesadilla stuff and soda, the kitchen was empty. I followed the pinging sound of videogames around the corner and found Frank on the couch. He sighed when he saw me, and then stood up, still attached to the TV, as if the controller cord were umbilically tying him to it. He played a little bit more as he started to walk away; moving faster for the last seconds. Then he sighed again, paused the controller, and tossed it onto the sofa. He didn't look at me.

"I really appreciate your help, Frank," I said to his back, as I followed him into the kitchen.

He didn't turn toward me as he grunted his "mmhmm" response.

When he got to the kitchen, he flicked on the faucet sighingly to wash his hands with water and dish soap, then dried them on his jeans. "You brought the quesadilla stuff? What you want I should do?" he asked the floor in front of me. "Butter the bread things, and do the shrimp?"

"That'd be great," I told his shoulder.

"K," he told my shoe, hooking a finger through the plastic bag, tearing the tortillas open.

"Thanks, Frank," I said to his hand.

"Yup," he told the plastic wrapper as he threw it away.

As I washed my hands and rolled up my sleeves to pull apart the chicken, Leon came in with Flaco, the FNG who had moved in a few weeks before.

Without prompting, Flaco searched the cabinets for frying pans, found two in two different places, washed and dried them, and handed one to Frank, who accepted it with a nod. "I'm about to cut up some onions and peppers and fry them up so if people want to put them in, they could," Flaco told me.

"Perfect," I said. "They should be in one of those bags. And Leon, want to put the soda in the freezer? And then maybe help Frank butter the tortillas?"

"I was already doing that," Leon said, reaching into the bag for the bottles. On his way back from the refrigerator, Frank tossed him the other package of tortillas and he caught it.

Flaco sliced the peppers into narrow, uniform strips and slid them into the pan with a quick flick of his knife. And when he finished, he handled the onion quickly and neatly, without blinking or tears.

Frank watched him, over his shoulder. "You did that real fast, dawg," he said.

"It's real easy once you do it a couple times," Flaco said. Greg, the houseparent, who'd started talking to me more, told me he'd heard that Flaco's placement in the House was related to a child labor law violation; he said he was pretty sure Flaco had worked in a restaurant, so he'd probably be helpful in the cooking program. Greg thought I'd be happy about that.

"Not for me," Leon said, spreading a glob of margarine across a tortilla.

"You could probably do it if you tried," Flaco told him. Then Flaco told me he knew a guy who knew a guy who was having a tattoo party at his house, and the boys were going to get tattoos there on Saturday.

My instinct was to report it to someone. Tattoos were only recently legal in Massachusetts. Until 2001, they'd been considered a "crime against a person." Minors still needed permission and accompaniment to get them. And I was skeptical about the safety and sanitization protocols in the friend of a friend's kitchen. I asked, "What're you going to get?"

"My girl's name over my heart," Flaco said, as if it was obvious. He hit his heart with the flat palm of his left hand.

"That's a big decision," I said in my best grown-up voice. I couldn't help myself. "How do you know you'll always want her name on your chest?"

"I will," Flaco said, as if you don't need a reason if you just know.

"I'm getting a rose," Leon said. "I'm getting it for my mother."

"Don't know what I'm getting yet," Frank said, as he thawed and shook the shrimp.

"You want to come to the party?" Flaco asked me, sincerely. "You could if you want."

In the Wes Anderson–film version of my life, I go to that party. I drive there in my light-blue Matrix girl car with my Clinique cosmetic case of knives in the trunk. I wear what I always wore, black pants, a tank top, and a cardigan, plus a pair of my grandmother's rhinestone earrings; I bring a batch of black bean empanadas. Leon meets me at the door and takes the plate and Flaco shows me where the other boys are; we all hang out together. There is music. Maybe there is dancing. Someone brings a decorated cake. Nobody matches, but it all makes sense.

When it's my turn for the tattoo, I get a Swedish Fish on one wrist and the word *love* followed by a comma (*Love,*) in the thick, felt-tipped font of my dad's handwriting on the other. I close my eyes and flash back to me at Girl Scout camp. I am eleven. It's mail time at the picnic tables outside the cabins. I hold a manila envelope with my name and cabin number typewritten on the front and spill its contents into my lap. There are fifty Swedish Fish in a small paper bag and a note on a piece of lined paper from a yellow legal pad, folded into thirds. I open it and it says: "Dear Liz, Here are the fish. Love, Dad." I fold up the note, look off toward the lake in the distance, and blink. Tom Hanks plays my father at the typewriter at the House, colorful tie thrown over his shoulder, addressing the envelope at work, a flashback inside of a flashback. Then I'm back at the party. Both tattoos are done. The guy from 7-Eleven offers me some Mountain Dew Code Red; we all toast each other, laughing. This is the version of the story where we can hang out and be familiar and exist together without complicated power structures or pretenses. The scene goes black.

I told Flaco that I really appreciated the invite, but I wouldn't be able to go to the party.

"What? You don't like tattoos?" he asked. "You're afraid?"

I said it wasn't that. Tattoos are scars we choose. Signs, symbols, names, dates—when it's not enough just to remember some piece of our story, we have it sewn into our skin. There's a terrible kind of beauty in that kind of writing. But I didn't say that. And I didn't say that both going to a party with the boys and getting tattooed on a stranger's kitchen table made me uncomfortable; I was trying to shake my teacher reputation. Instead, I said, "I already have a tattoo, and one's enough for now." I was ready to tell him my own crazy illegal tattoo story, but he wasn't interested, and Frank and Leon weren't either.

"If you change your mind, you could still come," Flaco told me.

I told him I would let him know.

"You're afraid it'll hurt too bad, right?" he asked.

I cringed and then smiled as if maybe that was it. But everybody knows the body forgets pain; it's the mind that won't let go.

Flaco shrugged and flicked a glob of butter onto a hot frying pan. It sizzled.

There was an enormous pot of curried chicken on the back burner. It smelled delicious and simmered like a best-laid plan. We cooked around it.

Give a Man a Fish

It was strange to think that spring, as life resumed, expanding, and trees looked like trees again with branches full of leaves, that the House was closing. For nearly four decades, that brick building with the green door had housed Community Caring, an agency whose name had changed over the years but whose work had remained the same, even as its daily tasks adapted to meet the needs of its young clients. The agency formed part of the parallel world of human services, part of a world that people on the outside refer to as "The System," as if it were one cohesive organism. I knew it was easier to critique the worst-case scenarios that made the news than to recognize the problem of care as a systemic problem of resources: in most cases, it isn't that the care is bad, it's that there is simply not enough—not enough staff, not enough training, not enough supervision, not enough support. There has never been enough, and there will never be enough. It's not that there are no good people who do this work—it's that there are simply not enough. As someone who had worked in schools and hospitals, I had an impressionistic sense of the shape-shifting nature of budgets and policy relating to social services; still, as an outsider, I didn't understand the logic of specific initiatives like family reunification, one of the driving forces behind the House's closing. One problem with the statewide shift in youth services from a residential model to a family model, Arlette would say later, was that "a family model assumes that the boys know what that even means. And they don't. It's not their fault. They never had successful families. If they did, they wouldn't be here in the first place." For the most part, the boys didn't seem to know where they would go next, whom they would live with, or how it would be.

"You know, Community Caring's closing soon, so you're going to have to find something else to do," Leon told me sympathetically. He was in the hospital again. When I called to touch base about dinner logistics, Gerry told me that Leon had gone in for another procedure. Gerry had kept in close touch with Leon through his move out of his placement at the agency into a public housing unit, from one sector of state care into another. Leon was struggling with life on his own, and his body was a contributing factor to the instability of his young adulthood. I went to visit him one afternoon after school. I parked on the street, bought ice cream from the convenience store on the corner, stopped in the cafeteria for a plastic spoon and two sodas, and took the elevator up to his unit. The nurse at the station asked our relationship; I said we were neighbors.

I appreciated Leon's concern that I wouldn't be able to fill my evenings once the House closed. I worried about what it meant for the boys who were still there and bound for displacement, especially Frank. It was late April, so there was a little over two months left. Until what, was still unclear.

Leon's head was shaved and he wore a navy hoodie zipped over a flimsy hospital gown. He sat propped up in bed, under one of the blankets Arlette had made for him.

"Cherries are the best part, right?" I said as I watched him dig through the ice cream.

"You should've got yourself some, too," he said through a mouthful of Ben & Jerry's. Then he told me how he had met a girl in one of his group therapy sessions and had been writing her songs and sending messages through his music therapist. When I asked if she had sent any messages back, he said, "Not yet."

When I asked him how he was feeling, he said same old. When I asked about his job, he explained between bites that he was taking a break from work because with his health stuff it was too hard for them to make a schedule; he said he was going to tell them when he was ready to go back. I didn't ask about his mother, but he brought her up. She was busy, he said, or she'd come to visit. When I asked him what he thought would happen to Frank and Joseph and Gerry when the House closed, which was also a way of asking him how he was handling all the changes, he shrugged.

"Things change," he said as if it was obvious. He kept eating.

He told me when I was leaving that he might come to cook the next week, *if* he was discharged, and *if* he didn't have anything else to do.

I told him he was welcome, but that we probably wouldn't be cooking. Frank had asked if we could go to Gina's Pizza Heaven, and I had said yes.

Leon's contingencies melted at the promise of a steak bomb with everything. "If we're definitely going to Heaven, I'm going," he said.

LEON WAS AT the door like old times when I arrived the next week. His hair was starting to grow out and a bandage was visible above his neck.

"You come on time now?" Leon asked, in lieu of hello.

"I wasn't always late," I said. It was good to see him standing.

"You say that now," he said. He shook his head. "But I was there. I know how it was." He held the door open to let me step into the gray stairwell. "And I don't know if you know this, but there're mad people upstairs."

I stepped in and then aside to let him lead up the stairs. "What do you mean?" I asked.

"Dunno," Leon said. He stopped and lowered his voice to tell me, "There's like a hundred people up there. I hope you brought a lotta money."

"Always," I said. "You know I always have a lot of money, 'cause I'm a teacher."

He shook his head no. "You still don't even have one of them clickers. I saw you, all reaching over to lock your doors."

The hundred were four boys in the kitchen: Frank, Hayden, the FNG I'd met once before, plus Michael Peters and another boy I didn't recognize. I introduced myself.

"I'm Nigel," he said, reluctantly shaking my hand. "I don't have to come."

"You're welcome to come," I said. "I think we're going to Gina's Pizza Heaven to get food instead of cooking." I turned to Frank for verification. "Is that still the plan?"

"Yup," he said.

"Where we going?" someone asked for clarification.

"Heaven," Frank said.

"How come she calls it by the whole thing?" someone asked.

I had a hard time calling the little place with stained tables and plastic silverware Heaven.

"She just does, dawg," Frank answered.

"Yeah, she does that with everything," Leon explained. "She likes whole names. She's a teacher. She kind of has to."

I was an alien again in the end, as I had been in the beginning. Or I was an alien all along.

"Is Joseph here?" I asked. "Or is he on a visit?" I looked at Frank.

The other boys looked at Frank.

"Don't know." Frank looked at me then looked away. "Don't look at me, dawg. Why's everyone looking at me?"

I walked down the hall to Joseph's room and knocked.

Joseph opened the door, in a thin nylon jacket over a brightly colored T-shirt, ready to go.

THE WALK TO Heaven was short and pleasant. Leon led the way. The stoplights turned in our favor as the April sun warmed our faces. When we arrived, the place was nearly empty. Michael Peters and Frank pushed two tables together. Leon grabbed an inch of napkins, a handful of utensils, and one shaker of hot pepper flakes in three trips to the counter and put all of it in the middle. When the table was set, the boys placed their orders and picked their spots for dinner.

Michael Peters pulled a chair out for me. "Here you go, miss," he said.

I thanked him and Leon rolled his eyes and said nobody ever noticed when he did nice things, and looked at me so I knew that I was the nobody he meant.

The boys talked to each other across each other.

I asked about people's weeks and school.

Nigel, the boy who had just introduced himself to me, was the first to answer. "They're giving me an iPod and a hundred-dollar mall gift card when I graduate," he told us. It turned out Nigel wasn't an FNG; he lived at one of the other residences. "I'm getting my own place, too." He explained that he was going to finish high school at the end of the month and be moved into his own apartment two weeks later, a few weeks before the House and the other residences were set to close. The subtext was that Nigel was transitioning out of direct-care services, but we focused on the consolation prizes.

"What kind of iPod is it?" Frank asked. "The big one or the little one?"

"I know what I would do with a hundred dollars," Leon said.

"Where's your apartment going to be?" I asked. "Will you have a roommate? Are you excited?"

Nigel shrugged and said he didn't know any of it—the size of the iPod, where he would live, what he would buy with one hundred dollars because he needed everything.

"Would it be helpful if I got you some stuff for your kitchen?" I asked. I wondered if he knew how to cook.

He shrugged again.

The boys claimed their orders when they were called at the counter. Soon, everyone was eating.

"When I was here," Leon told the table, "we didn't just *get* all this."

The boys paused to look at him.

"I think we did," I said.

"But not like *this*," he said. Leon gestured at the stuff on the table, his eyes closed as he made his point. "With subs with everything and a whole pizza for ourselves."

Joseph's gaze never strayed from his pizza. Piece by piece, he engulfed his small cheese.

Leon continued, "When I was here, we had to *work* for it."

The other boys returned to their subs. Frank ate slowly.

I squinted, trying to remember the hard labor regime that Leon was recalling.

"*We* had to work for it," Leon continued. "She would've stopped coming if I hadn't kept doing everything. Everybody peaced out and I was all, 'Fine, I'll help.' Y'all are lucky I kept doing it." He unscrewed the cap of his Pepsi.

It was hard to hear which was louder, the *fsh*-ing of the Pepsi cap or Frank's *pff*-ing sigh.

"Y'all have all this 'cause of me," Leon said. He bit into his steak and cheese, chewed, and swallowed a satisfied bite.

Frank squinted at Leon and pursed his lips. Leon raised his eyebrows.

"I definitely remember Frank being there, too, Leon," I said.

"I mean, yeah, Frank was there a few times," Leon said, sipping. "But I—" he started.

Frank widened his eyes and looked at me; I nodded. Frank knew that I knew that he had been there every time, that there wouldn't have been cooking if it hadn't been for Frank. Each time I had started to tell him, so that he could hear me say the words, he told me to not be so loud about it. He turned back to his steak and cheese with extra cheese and mushrooms, shook his head, and sighed. "You forced it, LeBron."

Leon sipped a purposeful sip of soda.

"What should we make next week?" I asked the table.

"Actually, I'm busy next week," Leon said.

"You don't even live here no more, dawg," Frank said. "She's not even talking to you."

"We should make something *real*," said Hayden, the FNG, when someone suggested quesadillas and someone else seconded it. "Like salmon!" he said, smiling. Hayden was sixteen, had moved to Boston from the Bahamas when he was little, and had moved to the House from his neighborhood in Boston a few weeks before. "'Cause there're no jobs there" was what he said about his parents' first move; "'Cause, you know" was all he said about his own.

"Nah, dawg." One of the other boys vetoed the fish initiative immediately.

Frank said he didn't know what it was, so no.

"It's a kind of fish," I told Frank. I described its pinky color and mild flavor and told him I thought he might like it, since he liked shrimp.

"I won't," Frank said. "I'm not eating nasty shit, so I'll have chicken and Sierra Mist." Amidst the tides of change, Frank had switched from Mountain Dew Code Red to Sierra Mist.

I asked Joseph, who was finishing his last slice of pizza, if he might try salmon.

"Nooooo," he said pleasantly.

Hayden tried to convince them. "You people don't know what's good."

I told Hayden we could make salmon, despite the majority rule, and told the others that we would make something else, too. And by "we," I meant Frank, who suggested barbecue chicken.

"Were you thinking we'd bake the salmon?" I asked Hayden. "Or pan sear it?" Broken since I started there, the broiler had become a storage drawer.

"I don't really know how to make it, to tell you the truth," Hayden said apologetically. "But I know I like it, 'cause I had it before."

"What flavors do you like?" I asked. "Teriyaki? Dijon mustard? Lemon and dill?"

"Probably lemon," he said. "Tell you the truth, that's the only one I know of what you said." He laughed. "They said you come like every week?"

"I do," I said.

"And you don't even remember her pops?" Hayden asked Frank, and all the boys looked at Frank.

"Nah, dawg, I told you," Frank said to Hayden. Then he looked at me, then down at the table. "I don't remember him. I'm sorry."

"Oh," I said, not expecting this now. In explaining me was the story of my father, and apparently the FNG had pieced together a time line; since Frank had arrived at the House in my father's last months, he thought Frank should know my dad. Apparently, they'd had this conversation before. I didn't know it was something the boys talked about, or that it made Frank feel bad that he didn't remember. "I wouldn't expect you to remember," I told Frank. "He wasn't in his office much those months, when you first got here. He was really sick."

"I wish I did but I just don't, dawg," Frank said.

On the walk back to the House, I kept thinking about that unexpected burst of sympathy, of empathy, the clumsy grace of it, and how it had been there all along. And I made a mental note to find a recipe for salmon; if it was going to taste real, I had to do some research.

THE NEXT WEEK, I again enlisted my librarian friend, Steve, for help after school. After our short investigation, he printed the recipe for baked salmon with the fewest steps and asked, "Hey, how's the cheesecake kid?" I told him I was pretty sure he was the only person in the world who thought of Wesley as "The Cheesecake Kid," and that I didn't know how he was. I explained that Wesley had been gone for months. Then Steve asked me how much longer I thought I'd keep doing the program. I told him that it wouldn't be much longer because the place was closing.

"Closing-closing?" he asked, surprised.

"Closing-closing," I said definitively.

"What's gonna happen to those boys?" He asked what any reasonable person would ask.

I shrugged and told him I didn't really know.

HAYDEN AND FRANK were in the kitchen by the time I climbed the creaky stairs.

"You brought it?" Hayden said, smiling.

I nodded and held up one of the bags.

"You brought the chicken, too?" Frank asked. "'Cause I'm not eating pink fish."

"You know you want to, Frank," I said.

"I don't," he said seriously. He reached for the second bag and I handed it to him.

Frank took the bag, checked inside, and put it by the side of the sink. He washed his hands.

I reached toward the stove and saw that it was already preheated.

"Did you already turn on the stove, Frank?" I asked. I tried not to sound too excited.

"Yup," he said. He dried the fronts and then backs then fronts of his hands on his jeans. With a steak knife, he sliced the package open, then started with the chicken. As he finished, he stacked the pieces on a wad of paper plates.

I reminded him to be careful. He reminded me that he wasn't the one who ever cut himself.

Meanwhile, Hayden unwrapped the salmon and scrunched his nose at its saltwater smell.

"Is it supposed to smell like this?" he asked. "Nasty?"

I leaned over to make sure it didn't smell like ammonia. "Yeah, it's supposed to smell like that," I told Hayden. "Like the ocean." I closed my eyes and breathed it in.

"Told you that shit's nasty," Frank said over his shoulder, still cutting chicken into strips.

"The beach smell goes away when you cook it," I said. I covered one of the two cookie sheets in aluminum foil and asked Hayden to cut one lemon into fourths and the other into slices.

"We're going to put the slices on the cookie sheet and then rest the salmon on top of it," I told him. "Do you want to do that or want me to?"

"How about I do the lemons and you do the fish?" he said. "I'm going to eat it and everything, but I don't really want to touch it raw." He looked at the fleshy pink slab as if it had offended him.

"Sounds good," I said.

"Sounds like I was right," Frank said from the stove, twisting the barbecue sauce open.

I covered the brownie pan in foil and handed it to Frank for the chicken.

He took the pan, emptied the bottle of sauce into the bottom, and nestled in the chicken.

Hayden arranged the lemon slices on the covered cookie sheet and I placed the salmon on top of the yellow pinwheels. I spread butter on top. Hayden held two lemon quarters between his thumbs and index fingers and squeezed one and then the other. The smell of citrus filled the kitchen. I opened the plastic box of dill and held it out to him.

He reached for it. "We're putting grass on it, too?" he asked reluctantly.

"No!" I said. "Well, kind of. It's an herb. This is dill. It'll add a little flavor."

He took all of the dill in his fist. "Just drop it all on?"

"I think we'll take the stems off and just use the fluffy parts," I said, pulling a stem apart.

Hayden broke off small puffs of green hyphens and dropped them strategically on the salmon, careful not to touch his fingers to the fish. "Smells kind of like pickles," he said.

"Yeah, exactly," I nodded. "This is where some pickles get their flavor."

"This is mad soft," he said, brushing his cheek with stems of dill.

"It is," I agreed.

Hayden reached toward Frank's face with the dill. Frank swatted him away and sighed heavily as he slid the pan of chicken into the oven. He closed the door with a thud.

I noticed a second oven rack when he opened the door.

"Somebody found the second oven rack?" I exclaimed. It had disappeared sometime before we started cooking; everything took longer without it.

"Yup," Frank said, unmoved by the reappearance. He filled a pot with water for rice.

"Where was it?" I asked. "We've been looking for that for years." There were only four boys living in the House now; soon there would be none. We had only a few dinners left. Where was that rack when we had needed it? The stupid oven rack! Where had it been all this time? What good was it now? I projected my disappointment about everything onto the oven rack.

"Don't know," Frank said. "Want me to make the corn, too?"

"Yes, please," I said. "Is the salmon ready to be put in the oven?" I asked Hayden.

"Almost is," he said. With a fork and knife, he rearranged the salmon on its lemon bed so it sat in the exact center of the pan. Then he gave it to me to place on the prodigal rack.

Then Joseph emerged in the doorway and asked what he could do.

I asked Frank if he minded if Joseph added the rice to the boiling water on the stove.

Frank said no, and watched quietly as Joseph tore the box of rice pilaf open and dumped its contents into the water, packet of seasonings and all.

"Knew that was going to happen," Frank said to the corn as he stirred it.

Hayden looked at me. I looked at Frank. Joseph looked at the paper envelope as it bobbed in the bubbling water.

"Is that dude serious?" Hayden asked Frank.

"Yup," Frank said, stirring.

"I'm just going to grab this," I said, plucking the packet out of the boiling water. "The flavor actually absorbs a little better when you open the packet first."

"Ooooookay," Joseph said, unfazed.

"Did he really just do that?" Hayden asked Frank.

"Really did," Frank replied, shaking his head.

I asked them to please set the table and they headed toward the pantry, leaning in to each other, laughing. Frank set four plates and forks for us as Hayden hunted for napkins.

Gerry came upstairs that night to check in. When he saw the salmon on the table, he said he was going downstairs for his camera. "Because this . . ." And he looked at me, his voice trailing off. "This is camera worthy."

"It was Hayden's idea," I told him.

"Is that right?" he asked.

Hayden beamed. "Yeah."

When Gerry came back, he took a close-up of the salmon, buttery and specked with dill, stretched out on a cookie sheet covered in tinfoil, with lemon slices on top. In the picture, you can't see the old table or the broken chair or the disposable dinnerware. Up close, it looks elegant. Hayden was satisfied with the finished product; he said it looked *real*.

Gerry had never eaten with us, though he, like Arlette, came upstairs from time to time to see how things were going. That night, he cut himself one small piece of salmon, and then another.

Frank watched Gerry's face as he savored the fish and said aloud, "Chicken's better."

"I always like chicken," Joseph said into his plate.

"Yup," Frank agreed. "Joe knows what's up."

"You don't know what's good," Hayden told the chicken eaters.

Gerry told me he would be in touch and left.

"You ever think that dude looks like a wizard or some shit like that?" Hayden asked.

"Yup," Frank said. "Everybody said that already. All the time. That and Santa."

I loved the idea of Gerry as a wizard, of a wizard eating salmon, of a book of spells among the many that populated the bookshelves downstairs.

"You know, the day after my birthday, June thirtieth, is when it's closing," Hayden said.

I knew by *it* he meant the House. Gerry had told me that July 1 was the official end date, but this was the first time I heard any of the boys other than Leon mention it. I didn't know Hayden's birthday was during that last month; this was the first he told me.

"Do you know what you're going to do?" I asked.

"I want caviar," Hayden said.

I meant after the House closed, but I said okay and asked, "Do you like caviar?"

"Never had it. But they said you said that we could get what we want for our birthday. And I want that." Hayden sat back in his chair and gestured to an imaginary spread on the table. "I want to eat like rich folk."

"I'll get it, but I don't know if people will like it," I said. "It's like really salty tapioca. Or salty little bubble tea. Have you ever had bubble tea? Or like goopy little sour grapes. Really salty, really tiny peeled grapes," I said. I had tried it on a trip to Russia; I didn't appreciate its taste. "I don't really like it, but you might."

"You're always telling us to try new things and now you're telling him not to," Frank said to me. "But it sounds kind of nasty, dawg," he said to Hayden.

"I still want it," Hayden said.

"I'll get it," I said. "But we definitely need something else, too."

"Let's just have chicken," Frank said.

"So we'll have caviar and chicken in three weeks for Hayden's birthday," I said. "What should we have next week?" I knew that the following week was likely Joseph's last week at the House. I didn't know about the other boys yet, but Gerry had told me that Joseph would be moved early enough in the month that there was time to move him in somewhere and then out again if it didn't go well. I suggested his favorite. "Should we make pizza?"

"Yeah," Joseph said, giggling. "I like pizza so much it's funny."

"I know," I said. "Me too." It was still light out even though it was night when we said goodbye, one of the last goodbyes.

Life Is Obvious!

The end of June came hot and fast. The air conditioner hummed in the window as we cooked our last dinners, which didn't feel like last dinners, except that they were. Junes always felt like final chapters to me, in school, but the bitterness of ending is tempered by the sweet excitement of summer vacation and graduation. Teaching had made me comfortable with the strange intimacy of caring for other people's children within a particular context. I had learned how to establish a professional distance, how to engage the emotional and intellectual investment and then step away; I knew how to say that kind of goodbye and good luck. But this was different. This was termination, not graduation. I had no official role here. This context felt uncertain. The boys were headed toward futures they never applied for.

Joseph was the first to be moved.

We made pizza, as we planned, the week before he left. We were Frank and Hayden and Joseph and me.

"I don't know if I could eat a whole pizza." Hayden laughed as we placed the fourth one on the table.

"If you don't, that dude'll have yours," Frank said, nodding at Joseph.

"It's true." Joseph laughed, getting in on the joke.

"Sumo," Frank said, nodding at Joseph.

"Should we switch nights next week?" I asked Frank once we had all sat down. "Gerry said some people might be going to a Red Sox game on Wednesday."

"Not me," Frank said. "Nobody even likes that shit."

"Baseball!" I exclaimed. "What do you mean nobody likes base-ball? It's our national pastime!" I grew up in a house where most nights of the week between April and September we were at a game or there was one on the radio in the car or playing on the kitchen television, on mute if it was dinnertime. I had a short and under-whelming career in the sport, but my sisters were great softball players and my older brother played baseball through college. I was more of a dandelion picker, but my brother was a left-handed pitcher who walked up to the plate like he was born to do it. And he has the same kind of discipline off the field; when I need help gaug-ing what's foul and what's fair, I know I can call him. Baseball is still the fifth season in our family life. If there is a heaven and it has a sound, I believe it's the hum of a crowd in a stadium. "Who doesn't like baseball?"

"Me," Frank said.

"Me either, dawg." Hayden laughed.

"But wouldn't you want to go to a game? The tickets are free. You could get snacks and be outside . . ." I imagined the fresh smell of cut grass that hits you as you climb the metal stairs up to your seats, the tang of mustard on the first bite of a ballpark frank. "Are you sure you don't want to go?"

"Yup." Hayden laughed.

"Yuuup," Frank echoed. "That shit's boring as hell. Nobody likes it."

"But, like, what are you going to tell the guy that got the tickets, who wants to take you to the game? Just 'No, thank you?'" Gerry had told me it was the same guy who had donated Celtics tickets, who made annual donations to supplement the Christmas gift al-lowances; he had either been in the system, or one of his parents had, and this was how he paid it forward. "I bet he's going to be so disappointed."

"You could go with him." Frank redirected.

"What?" I laughed, imagining the guy's face if I showed up in-stead of the boys. "I don't think I'm invited. You think I should just go and be like, *Hey, I'm Liz. Frank told me to come?*"

"You could," Frank said. "I'm not going, so."

"Me neither, dawg." Hayden laughed, making his way through his whole pizza.

"It's weird," Joseph said, on his penultimate slice. "I'm not going to be here anymore. I'm going to be somewhere else."

"It is weird," I agreed. "How do you feel about moving?"

"It doesn't really matter." Joseph shrugged. "I have to do it anyway." He giggled.

I thought about the last two lines of the poem of his that he had copied for me because I said I liked it one of the nights during our Joe-and-Liz time at the table. "Nothing really matters / The whole world is scattered."

Joseph finished his last slice in three bites, then said, "I think I'm too tired for poetry tonight."

When Frank and Hayden left to start chores, Joseph and I said goodbye in the kitchen, one word and two waves, the scattered world between us. I thought about his poem again, how he'd written out the long stanza in wide, deliberate letters, handed it to me, then took it back to underline the title: *"Life Is Obvious!"*

LEON WAS BACK again the next week. He shielded his eyes from the sun in what looked like a salute as he stood keeping the green door open; his other hand was tucked behind him.

"Hey, stranger!" I called through my open window as I parked.

"You trying to say you forgot me already just 'cause this's almost over?" he said.

"I could never forget you, Leon. I was just trying to be funny." I slammed my door.

"What're we having anyway?" He watched me pull the bags from my backseat.

"Chicken and caviar," I said. It sounded ridiculous. "It's Hayden's birthday; that's what he wanted." I held out a bag for him to carry upstairs.

"You know I don't live here anymore, so I don't have to help." He stiffened his arms by his sides.

"I know, but don't you want to?" I asked. I reached around to lock my back door.

"*Chict-chict.*" Leon aimed a fist at my car and made his clicking sound, then sighed and reached for a bag. "I can't even stay the whole time, I've got to go meet someone. *Chict-chict*," he said again. "Here, I got you a clicker." He held out his fist and waited for me to shift my bags and open a hand under his so that he could deliver my invisible gift.

"I'm glad you're here for however long you can stay," I told him on our way upstairs.

"Yeah, I figured I should come even if I could only come for a little," he said, kicking the kitchen door open.

I followed the sound of zooming and gunshots into the TV room and found Frank and Hayden on the couch with Michael Peters, who had also come for dinner. Frank stood before I said anything and said, "All my lives are over anyway, so I'll just come help already."

It was Frank and me and Leon in the kitchen for a few minutes before the other boys finished their game and joined us. It was like old times, washing and cutting and cooking, except that Frank was taller and Leon was sicker, though I didn't know how sick. Frank put the soda in the freezer to chill, then cut the chicken without bones in it, which was familiar to him now. Leon made his from-the-heart biscuits and said he'd set the table, too. At the counter, I cut the vegetables, normal ones, nothing too small or too weird. Then I made Hayden's cake.

As Frank flicked the chicken over in the pan to cook it from all sides, I asked if he needed anything for his move, if there was anything I could bring him. As soon as I said it, I wished I could pull the words back into my mouth. What could I bring to make his move smoother?

He asked if I had a bag. "But not like the one you got Mikey, like a bigger one," he specified.

I remembered the *preface* night, and adjusting the straps of my backpack to fit Mikey's shoulders on the sidewalk, sure the bag wasn't mine anymore. "You want a duffel bag instead of a backpack?" I asked. "Yeah, I can get you one. Do you just need one? How big do you want it?"

"I got one," he said. "But all my stuff won't fit in it. It all fit when I moved here, but I got more stuff now than when I moved in, so I thought if you had one you could bring it. But if you don't, it's okay."

"I can definitely bring one." I held out my hands the length of a hockey bag. "Like this big?"

He set the spatula down across the lip of the pan. With his index fingers, he tapped my hands once and then again, so that the space between them was closer to the size of a carry-on. "Like that," he said.

I told him I would find a bag like that. I asked what color, and he said it didn't really matter.

When everything was ready, we sat down at the table that Leon had set. He was already sitting, to be sure that there was no question about which seat was his. Frank sat down in his usual spot, too, and Hayden and Michael Peters sat across from each other. I pulled my chair out too quickly from under the table and its arms lifted out of it.

"You want a chair that isn't broken, miss?" Michael Peters started to stand up, to switch my chair for his.

I thanked but no thanked him.

"I would've given her mine. But," Leon said, pointing to the broken chair, "that's her chair."

"No offense, but these containers are kind of small," Hayden said, as he opened the cups of caviar and placed them in front of himself.

"I know," I said. I had brought two small portions of red and black varieties, along with some sour cream and crackers. "I wanted you to try two kinds. If people really like it and want more, I'll get more and bring it next week, of whichever kind you like. But I'm not sure people will like it. So I thought we'd start with a little."

Hayden took a cracker from the package and ceremoniously dipped it into the black caviar and put the whole thing in his mouth. He closed his eyes as he chewed and swallowed. He repeated this with the red caviar. He took another cracker, plunged it into the other mound of fish eggs, and closed his eyes as he ate a second heaping pile. Then he patted his lips clean with a napkin. "Rich folk be eating nasty shit," he declared. "Where's that chicken at?"

"Told you," Frank said, passing him the dish of chicken.

"Does anyone else want to try caviar?" I held up the containers in Frank's direction.

"You're trying to feed us nasty shit?" Frank said.

"It's good caviar! You might like it, Frank," I said. "Some people love it. It's a delicacy. This is expensive shit right here." I pointed to the price tags.

"You're going to eat it, then?" Frank asked me.

"Well, no," I said. "I don't really like it."

"So you're trying to feed us *nasty* stuff *you* wouldn't even eat," Leon said. He gave me Leon eyes. "That's just wrong, fam."

Michael Peters laughed at us and ate his chicken.

"Leon," I said, "I'm not trying to feed anybody anything nasty. Hayden wanted this for his birthday. I went all the way to a different town to go to a Russian market to get good stuff."

"He's kind of right," Hayden agreed.

"Hayden! *You* asked for this. I told you that you might not like it. I told you that *I* don't like it." I wanted us to have real food and now here we were, fighting over caviar.

"You could've told me harder," Hayden said.

"But aren't you glad you tried it?" I asked. "So you know?"

"Not really," Hayden said, chugging a second cup of soda, sticking his tongue out between sips. "I can't get that taste out of my mouth."

"Are we really going to waste the rest of this caviar?" I asked.

"Unless *you're* going to eat it," Leon said.

Nobody ate the rest of the caviar. Someone cleared the plates. I lit the candles in the kitchen and carried the ice cream cake to the table ablaze. Leon shut the lights off and we all sang to Hayden. If he made a wish, he didn't say.

Leon left when it was time to start chores. I stayed to help with the dishes.

"Was anybody around when Joseph left?" I asked Frank and Hayden and Michael Peters, who'd been spending a lot of time at the House. "Do you know if he was okay?" I scanned the walls and windows for signs of distress.

The boys looked at each other.

"I'm worried about him," I said. I thought Joseph would be the most resistant to change of all the boys; he was the least stable and the most dependent, in my estimation. He'd been moved into a community-based care facility for people with mental illness.

"Yeah, we were here when they took him," Frank said. "Dude kicked in a window when they took him out. I told you he was sumo." Frank kicked the air and made a crashing sound.

"Oh no," I said. "Was he okay? Did he calm down?"

"I mean no, but yeah," Frank said.

"What do you mean, 'No, but yeah'?"

Michael Peters lowered his voice. "He cried a little bit." He must have read my face, because he added, "But he was okay, miss."

"Why you worried about him for?" Hayden asked me.

I looked at him.

"That dude's got it made for the rest of his life," Hayden said.

"I know, right?" Frank said.

"What're you talking about?" Hayden looked at Frank. "You do too, dawg." I understood it as a reference to Frank's partial funding from the Department of Developmental Services.

"Nuh-uh. My check could cut at any time," Frank said, "if they decide I'm not crazy enough. That shit's not guaranteed." I had never heard Frank talk about it so directly.

"Yeah, you just got to stay crazy, dawg," Hayden told Frank. "But not me, yo. I turn eighteen and that's it, I'm on my own. I'm screwed." I remembered how one of the nights at the table with Joseph, Hayden had come back to the table with his own poems. He let me read one of them from a marbled composition notebook filled with rhyming lyrics about love and money. The poem he opened to ended with the line "and return me to my spot in poverty," as if there were assigned seating in the world, as in classrooms, theaters, and baseball stadiums, as if people got preprinted tickets and Hayden already had his stub. His notion that every person has a future that will reveal itself to us, already imagined and intact, was not so different from my own. Except that it was so different from my own.

I kept washing the dishes, soaping, scrubbing, rinsing. Frank grabbed the broom and swept his way back into the dining room. Hayden started drying. I asked Michael Peters if he knew where he was moving when the agency closed.

"You don't have to worry about me, miss," he said. His hat was off; he held it in his hands.

I remembered a couplet from Hayden's poem: "No father, no money, no house / That's just how that shit goes."

My MEMORY OF our last dinner together at the House is a dream. It's not just Frank and Hayden and Michael Peters and me; the other boys are there, too—even the ones who stayed for only a few dinners, and the ones who never sat down to eat with us. Leon sits at the head of the table, where he always sits, and tells it like it is. Joseph waits to take seconds and then thirds. Wesley pours soda for everyone, and then two cups for himself, full to the brim. Carlos sits with his legs outstretched under the table; he smiles, his real smile. James comes late, but he comes; his hand and neck are healed. It is a miracle of chicken and soda and supernatural bread. There is more than enough; there's plenty, for once and for all. The table is a raft, and we are all holding onto it. I will my father into the scene, but he doesn't sit down with us. His face is a blur in a doorway or outside a window; his voice calls up from downstairs.

It's strange how we remember life out of order, how our minds rearrange days we've lived in order to make them more coherent. What we know for sure rushes in like sand to fill the gaps and change the shape of the past into something that makes sense. This is a trick that memory plays over and over when people die, or we suffer other endings or try to write history. I don't remember what we actually made the last night, what we ate and talked about, or how much was left over. There must have been bread, because there was always bread. We knew it was the end, and we cooked around it.

I GAVE FRANK the bag he asked for after dinner, after we washed the dishes, when it was time for me to go. He inspected its zippers and pockets and nodded that it was as he imagined it.

I stood across from him, twisting my keys in my hand. I don't remember when I realized he was the tall, quiet kid who had been standing next to Leon the night I met them for the first time at Gerry's party months before we started cooking; Frank had been part of the story the whole time. "Hey, Frank, can I give you a hug?"

"Oh yeah," he said. "This's it. I forgot already." He leaned down toward me and put his hands lightly on my arms. He turned his cheek so it almost touched my cheek.

"You keep getting taller," I said. I looked up into his eyes. I wondered if I would see him again, whether we would recognize each other. It was a question I couldn't bring myself to ask out loud. "You're taller than me now!"

"I know, dawg," he said, as if he, too, was surprised by the fact. "And you're tall."

"I wonder if you'll be as tall as your brother," I said. I wondered who Frank would be when he grew up. I wondered where he would live, what he would do for work, whom he would love. I hoped he would never be hungry.

"Don't know, dawg," he said.

There were so many things I wanted to tell him: to be kind, to be strong, to be safe.

I thought of what my grandmother used to tell us at the end of every visit during the decade she dissolved into dementia. "Thank you, God bless you, I love you." She told the doctors, orderlies, nurses, and patient care assistants, too—as if she remembered any of us, or meant it for all of us, as if in her altered state when past was present and present was an unfamiliar institution, familial distinctions were abstractions and care was care.

"Thank you, Frank," I said. "You've always been the best helper."
I told him again like I had told him before. "You know we couldn't
have done any of this without you."

"Yup," he said. He stepped away from the embrace, his gaze fixed
on the kitchen counter.

I couldn't say goodbye. I kept turning my keys in my hand. Traffic purred and honked through the open June window. It was still
light outside; it didn't feel like night, but it was. Sirens whirred. All
the small things outside were annoyingly unstoppable. It didn't feel
like the end, but it was.

"K," Frank said to me and the sink. He nodded, a tilt of his chin
toward my face. "Bye already."

Something Happened Here

"How did everything go?" I asked Gerry as I sat down for dinner. He was already seated and I was late. Even in the end, I didn't know what I was allowed to know but I felt vested and thought if I asked he might tell me. "How did the boys do?"

"Well," he started, "how much time do you have to discuss it? A year? A lifetime?"

"A dinner will have to be enough for now," I said. Our usual place was a new restaurant in the same space. The walls and menus had been renovated; the continuity was in the chicken. I said that I already missed the old place, and remembered the restaurant that had operated in this location before that one, and the bar before that. People say the restaurant business is tough, as if nearly every human endeavor weren't a sweaty game of dollars and chance. "Can you even imagine a business with such high turnover?"

"In fact, Elizabeth, I can," Gerry said.

A server appeared at the table. "Do you know what you want?" she asked.

"Do we know what we want?" Gerry repeated. "Even if we know what we want, is there any guarantee that we can have it?"

"I think so," the server stammered. "I mean, we aren't out of anything. It's early."

"He'll have the merlot blend," I said. "And I'll have a gin and tonic, please."

She nodded, marked her pad, and left us to our drama.

Gerry folded his hands on the table and looked at me, his blue eyes focused. "As of end of business on June thirtieth, we are closed," he said. The last kid moved out on the twenty-eighth and it took two more days to finalize the paperwork. "After forty years of providing direct-care services, we have officially stopped accepting referrals. There are no youth in our care." Each time he said *care,* the word hung in the air. The House was dismantled a room at a time. The boys left one by one, with their stuff in boxes and backpacks, in one or two trips down the stairs. Each of the residences was emptied accordingly. Caseworkers came to pick up, sign out, and transport kids to their next placements.

"So that's it?" I asked. "That's all?"

"That is all," he said. He sighed. "Indeed, that has been everything."

"Gerry, how many kids would that be?"

"Thirty-seven this year," he said. "Twenty-two young men and fifteen young women."

"What about ever?" I asked. "In all the years."

"Ever?" He leaned in to me, his bushy white eyebrows furrowed.

"How many kids would that be—total, since you opened your doors?" I asked.

My father had instilled in me an appreciation for inventories, and the comfort of counting to know exactly what you had. During our last walks, he talked through some of the tallies he had been taking, of the obvious, the obscure, and the in-between. Among them: how old he was; how much he weighed; how many days he had worked; how many times he had gone to church; how many children he had; how many wives (he chuckled with this one); how many people he counted as friends; how many degrees. He was careful in this accounting. Some lists were a little more mundane: how many books he estimated he had read in his life; how many hours of television he had watched; how many sandwiches (mostly peanut butter and jelly) he had made for us to take to school for lunch (four kids times one hundred eighty days of school times twelve years of school); how many piles of dog shit he had picked up—his words, not mine (two dogs times one walk per night times ten years for one and eleven for the other). Life was unfair, but lists were straightforward.

"Are you asking for a total number of young people, in forty years of programs?"

"Yeah," I said. It seemed like a reasonable question.

"I could not say," Gerry said. He lifted his wine. "Your father almost certainly could."

"That's kind of what I was thinking," I said. I could smell the lime in my glass as I took a sip. "To all of the kids," I said. "Wherever they are."

"To all of them," he said. His eyes welled. I looked away.

I asked about the boys' moves, and Gerry told me what he knew.

Gerry was preoccupied with one of the kids I had never met, from one of the other residences, whose transition had been particularly difficult. He had panicked about living alone in the apartment he was moved to because he had never lived on his own; he was only eighteen. The second night in his new place, he knocked on the door of a female neighbor in the building and told her he wanted to have sex with her. He just stood there. Gerry believed he knew she would call the police, that he wanted to be taken back into custody. Now Gerry was working on a new plan for him. Because of the kid's age, it was complicated.

"It doesn't seem logical that crime is his only way back into care," I said. A similar thing had happened with Nigel, the boy who had come to dinner at Gina's Pizza Heaven and talked about moving into his own place after graduation. The day before his scheduled move, he pulled a knife on Flaco and was arrested. Flaco had asked me to translate his subpoena and asked whether I thought he would be deported if he appeared in court about the assault. As Flaco explained his immigration status, as he understood it, I kept thinking about how scared Nigel must have been to do that. And I really hoped it wasn't a knife I had given him in a box of things for his new kitchen that Nigel had pulled on Flaco. It felt like an O. Henry story I'd read in high school. But without irony; it wasn't poignant, it was just pathetic. I sighed from the weight of it. "It doesn't seem humane."

"It is not humane," Gerry said simply. The candlelight illuminated the lines in his face.

Joseph was doing "as well as can be expected," Gerry said. Every day, once per day, Joseph left messages on the answering machine at the House. They were always the same. A beat. Then, "Hello, Gerry. This is Joseph." Another beat. Then, "I am okay." And then he disconnected.

When Hayden left, he left without incident. So much so that nobody could remember where he was placed next. He had turned seventeen on his caviar birthday. He had at least one year left in the system, so he was somewhere.

Leon was still going to school, which was good. He was having some trouble with people who said they were family taking his assistance money, which also meant trouble with the police. Gerry hoped Leon wouldn't have to move as a result of it. "There's simply no way to know what will happen with Leon Williams," Gerry said. "I told him when he graduates, I will host a party for him. I would assume that you will come if it happens."

I promised I would.

FRANK WAS THE last kid to leave the House. His social worker came to pick him up. It made sense that he was the last to go because he'd been there the longest of everyone in the last bunch, over four years. It was a long time for an interim placement and one of the longest stays Frank had stayed anywhere. He'd lived in all the rooms of the House, and he'd had the most roommates: because he snored, because he didn't haze FNGs, because he didn't steal, because he didn't have anything to steal.

He didn't swear or kick in any windows when he left. He didn't punch a hole in a wall or ask for money or cry, as other boys had. Frank left quietly.

He packed most of his clothes into two duffel bags and one garbage bag, leaving the white suit he'd worn to prom on its wire hanger. He took the TV he'd gotten for Christmas, his radio from the Christmas before, and a plastic grocery bag of toiletries.

He also untacked the two photographs stuck to the bulletin board over his desk. In one, he was sitting with a group; it had been taken for some sort of article. The other was of him, sitting on a bench outside his school, the night of his prom. He went with Arlette to pick out his suit and shirt and shoes and a striped tie. He was wearing the red rose boutonniere I had brought over for him while he was getting ready; he's smiling at the camera, or at Arlette who must have been the one who took the picture. Those photos, I imagined, were the last things Frank packed when he emptied his room. Both taken since he'd moved into the House, they were the only pictures of himself that he owned. I imagine that he slid them into one of the pockets of a duffel bag. I can't say whether he took *Harry Potter* with him or left it behind, spine unbent, one page read.

I imagine that he carried his stuff out of his bedroom, both hands full, through the kitchen, down the back stairs to the sidewalk, and then, one bag at a time, loaded his social worker's car: the trunk, the floor or the backseat, maybe the front seat.

He had told her beforehand that he wanted to ride his bike to his next place, to his new placement across the city.

"There was liability involved," Gerry told me when he told me all of this. "If anything happened to him in those interim minutes, with him on his bike, in the street, between placements, I do not know what would have happened, who would have been at fault." He shrugged. "But his social worker let him go."

I asked if Frank knew the way to where he was going.

"I suppose he must have," Gerry said. "He got on his bike and rode, and she started her car and drove along behind him." As Gerry told me, the scene replayed in his memory.

Frank, who had been born substance dependent, whose exact date of birth was unknown; Frank, who liked cheese with everything except Chinese food and liked shrimp best of all; Frank, who covered his mouth when he smiled, because he was self-conscious about the space between his front teeth; Frank, who always believed his family would come for him, but always said he didn't care anyway because he could take care of himself. Frank, who had helped more than anyone, was the last man standing. He packed his things without anyone's assistance and convinced his social worker to let him get himself to his next place. And then, as if it were all on his own terms, he rode himself across the city, squinting into the sun.

"Frank," I said, as if I knew him. I swallowed. "It's unbelievable. All of this."

"Unbelievable! That's a good word for it," Gerry said. "There is nothing left to believe."

I took another sip. "I just can't believe that it's over."

WHEN I TOLD my mother that the agency was closing, she sighed and said it was a long time coming. She said she had worried for years that my dad would never be able to retire because the finances of the agency were so inconsistent. I knew this. I remembered the conversations that became fights, how my dad would raise his voice and talk about the kids, how she would say he had to think about his own kids, too, and he would ask how she could say that. "But—" she started, unable to finish the sentence. Her eyes filled. She bit her lip. I knew the rest: but then my dad died when he was fifty-seven, eighteen years before he planned to retire and enjoy leisurely breakfasts on weekdays and *Murder, She Wrote* reruns at any hour of any day.

"You know, when I went to see Leon in the hospital, he told me that I was going to have to find something else to do with my time when the House closed," I told Gerry.

"Is that right?" Gerry asked, amused.

"Yes," I said. "I think Leon is worried about us. He says that things change and that's life. But he doesn't think we get it. And, Gerry, he's probably right about that, too. But I can only speak for myself." I hate the helplessness of endings. I hate knowing that change is not necessarily inflected with improvement. I hate how it feels to be sad. I remembered a car ride with my dad the month after one of my students was killed in Chicago; I couldn't stop crying. I don't remember where we were going. My dad looked over and saw my face leaking and asked what was wrong. And I said I couldn't believe the Red Sox had lost the night before. And he knew what I was saying and what I wasn't saying, and he said, "Sweetheart"—and he never called me sweetheart—"the more appropriate response is rage."

"Leon Williams is an exquisite human being, isn't he," Gerry said.

"He is," I agreed. I'm always torn between believing there are reasons for why we meet the people we meet and knowing that life is mostly luck, the way our world and bodies are mostly water. "Will he graduate, do you think?"

"I certainly hope so," Gerry said. "You will come to the party, won't you?"

"You know I'll be there," I said again. I pretended that this was not the end.

He sighed and sipped more wine. The chicken had come and gone. This was it.

"I guess this means you'll have to find another vanity project," I said. "For the next forty years."

He laughed. "That's right. A vanity project." Then Gerry got serious. "You have to tell the story. That something happened here. Or there will be no trace of any of it. There is nothing left." His eyes welled again.

I looked out the window. What is left of a job when it's done? How do we count what we have made and known, and let go of what escapes us? How do you accurately inventory a life, and track its various intersections with other people's lives? How does the work of our life become the work of our life? Who cares? I squinted across the street at the brick building with the door and shutters the color of the third row of a memorized rainbow. The light in my father's office was off.

LEON GRADUATED TWO months later. It was momentous. His team from the hospital attended the ceremony; his surgeons, two nurses, and a resident went to cheer him on. He was happy they were there but was distracted by his elation that his mother had also shown up. When the state had located his biological mother months before he was moved out of the agency's care and into independent living, there was a general assumption that the fact of locating her would save him. Gerry called this one of the great fallacies of idealism: believing that if you find the mother, the child will be accepted and all will be made right.

When Leon told Gerry he was hoping really hard that his mother would be at his graduation, Gerry vowed to do whatever it took to get her there.

She arrived late, but she arrived.

Gerry brought his camera to the ceremony to properly document the occasion. He snapped pictures of Leon listening to the principal's speech to the graduates, several of him walking up to receive his diploma, one of him with a giant smile, clutching the paper in his fist. He took shots of Leon talking to classmates afterward, and a series with Leon posed next to the podium with the school logo, and with the medical team, some of them still in scrubs, having rushed over from the hospital to make it on time. And when Leon said he wanted one with his mother, Gerry snapped that picture, too. Leon's smile is widest in that one. He's beaming, leaning in to her. She is standing straight.

Leon preemptively told Gerry that he didn't need a ride afterward because he was leaving with his mother.

Gerry nodded that he understood. Then he waited. He put his camera away and shook the hand of the principal, thanked him for his good work. By the time he was putting his jacket on, Leon was standing by his side.

"Actually," Leon told him, "I'll take the ride. My mother has to be somewhere."

Gerry nodded and gently said, "All right." Then he put his arm around Leon's shoulder, and led him home.

As PROMISED, GERRY threw a party at the House to celebrate Leon's graduation. Arlette reached out to the other boys to tell them about the celebration, but none of them made it back to the House that night. Leon's mother said she would come, but she didn't show up in the end. Gerry also invited everyone in the reach of the agency and the various community programs that continued to run under its not-for-profit umbrella so the first floor was crowded and people were sitting and laughing on the beige couch like I'd never seen before. I met the accountant whose name I'd heard for years.

"You can't be Charlie's daughter," he greeted me.

"I am," I said, and introduced myself.

"Oh," he said, confused. "The picture Charlie had in his office is of little kids, so I thought you guys were much younger." He hesitated. "Did he have a second family?"

I knew the picture he was talking about; a larger copy hung in my parents' hallway. It was the only family portrait we'd ever had taken. We didn't really have money for those things, except that it was part of a Girl Scout fundraiser in a church hall. My brother is wearing one of my dad's ties; I was in my First Communion dress; my sister Juli, who hated girls' clothes, had been forced into a purple dress with a bow; my sister Laura, then a toddler, sat in my mom's lap. If you look closely, I think you can see that we were all getting over the chicken pox.

"No second family, he just hadn't updated his family picture since 1986," I said. I think he had a copy of the same picture in his wallet until the last day he carried it. "Unless you know something we don't know," I added, laughing.

"Oh, no! No!" the accountant said, laughing. He became serious. "Your dad was a real good guy," he said. "You know, he wouldn't let us get an air conditioner in the offices downstairs because the kids didn't have one upstairs, or in any of the other residences. I tried to tell him, 'Charlie, you gotta get an AC in here! You're baking in this office! The heat's brutal!' But he refused and said he wouldn't until there was money to put them in all the group homes. He had a sweat rag, you know, to sop up the sweat. He sweat a lot, God love him. And the next week when I got there, he'd put a sweat rag on my chair for me, so I knew that was it. No more discussion about that. There aren't a lot of people like that in the world." He nodded, remembering. "People tell you ya look like him? I see it now."

I nodded, suddenly unable to say more in this familiar unfamiliar place.

"What a party, huh?" The accountant gestured to the decorations.

There were balloons and streamers, and Gerry blew up pictures from the graduation and made two posters. In one, Leon was nearly life-size in his tan suit and blue shirt and striped interview tie. The other was a collage of smaller pictures taken on graduation day. During the party, Leon stood next to the poster of himself, greeting guests like the celebrity he was, towering plate of pad Thai in one hand, plastic fork in the other, smiling proudly. He was very popular.

I SAW LEON again a few months after that, again with pad Thai. Gerry invited me to lunch at a Thai restaurant on Centre Street where he and Leon and Arlette occasionally met to eat and talk.

Arlette usually ordered pad Thai without sprouts. Leon had copied her the first time they went to lunch and liked it, so he made it his usual, too. This time, she ordered something different. So when it was his turn, Leon paused and told the server he wanted pad Thai. He closed his menu and added, "Without the Brussels sprouts."

Arlette turned to the server to explain what Leon meant, but before she could say anything, the server nodded that he understood.

We talked about life since the agency's closing. Arlette gave updates on the staff: who'd gotten jobs, where, and what they were doing now; who was still looking. I asked about each of the boys I had known.

Leon loved being at the grown-ups' table. He sipped his Pepsi, nodded in agreement, and added bits of commentary when he felt moved to do so.

Arlette said that Joseph was still at the place he was moved to when the House closed. He was doing "as well as can be expected."

"What about Frank?" I asked.

"John sees Frank," she said. John was a houseparent at another of the residences. A former foster kid himself who came up in the system, he tried to keep track of departed boys. "Frank's still living in the place near Heath Street." That wasn't far from where I lived. "John says he's doing okay, and he has a job at a Stop and Shop." She paused. "So that's good."

"Which Stop and Shop?" I asked. I thought I might see Frank again.

"The one near Fenway, I think," she said. It wasn't far from the school where I worked. I imagined orchestrating some kind of bump-in. But what then?

"What about Wes?" I asked.

"Wes," she said, shaking her head, "I think he's locked up again."

I looked at her. She knew my question.

"Drugs, I think. Or weapons charges."

I tried to calibrate the thought of Wesley charged with drugs or weapons with my memory of the sound of Wesley's giggle, the time he asked me whether I had ever laughed so hard that milk came out of my nose.

I ticked down the list of the rest of the boys I had known. She shook her head no to most of them, that she didn't know, and nobody she knew was in touch with them.

"Oh, what about Michael Peters?" Even though he hadn't lived at the House, he came over from his residence for dinner pretty regularly during the last few months.

"He's locked up." There was no question in Arlette's voice.

"No, I mean Michael Peters. The short kid who was friendly with Frank," I clarified.

"Yup," she said. "Theft or drug charges, something like that."

"The Michael who said thank you—Frank's friend, who told me my plantains tasted like his auntie's. The one who—" I touched my cheek, about to say something about his acne.

"With the skin. Yeah, Liz, I know who you mean." She smiled gently and lowered her voice a little. "He's locked up," she repeated.

"I always said thank you," Leon interjected.

"I know you did," I said. I was still thinking about Michael Peters. I turned to Leon. "I know, Leon, you always did. You're the best." I smiled. "You know that."

"And I laughed at your jokes. Even when they weren't funny," he added, loud enough for the table to hear. "People don't treat me like I'm the best."

Arlette looked at him and then me and smiled again.

By this time, our food had come.

"Want to give us your update, Leon?" I asked. "Now that you're a graduated man."

He puffed his chest out. "I *am* a graduated man."

Leon was hesitant to offer his own update of his post-graduation life. He knew that we knew versions of what had been happening. He was on probation at the public housing unit where he was living. Some people who identified themselves as his cousins kept bringing trouble to the elderly people and people with disabilities who lived in his apartment complex when they came to visit him the time of the month when Leon got his social security checks. He couldn't put his money in the bank because his identity had been stolen and his social security number was compromised, so he had to cash the checks and keep the cash in a strongbox in his closet. When the cousins came around, they asked for money to party, and at first he gave it to them. But then when he started refusing them, explaining that he was trying to save some money, they jumped him and took the cash. Neighbors who weren't angry were afraid. Leon had to move.

"And the cops keep picking me up for public intoxication, but they don't get that this is just how I walk," he explained. He sipped his Pepsi.

We nodded. I looked at him. Was he drinking and smoking again? Did it matter? Where would he live next? Gerry and Arlette and I avoided each other's eyes.

We talked and ate and laughed and listened until our plates were empty.

Leon turned to Gerry, more like a business partner than a former resident. "Man, Gerry, Community Caring, that was a journey and a jungle."

Gerry closed his eyes to take in that truth. Community Caring, the agency he started the year Buzz Aldrin landed on the moon and my dad was drafted to go to war in Vietnam, was closed. Closed-closed.

Arlette laughed her big, deep laugh. I looked at Leon and smiled.

"I'm being serious," Leon said evenly. "You're all laughing but I'm serious."

"I am not laughing," Gerry told him. Gerry wasn't laughing.

"Because, I mean," Leon continued, "some of it was crazy." He widened his eyes and shook his head disapprovingly.

"Yes, it was," Arlette agreed, nodding and smiling widely.

"To the journey and the jungle!" I toasted, lifting my glass. "They say it's bad luck to toast with water. But why start listening to them now?"

"Now, I will lift my glass to that," Gerry said. "Let's not listen to them now."

We laughed and raised our glasses to toast each other. The clink of melting ice against glass made the softest background music.

"But it *was* a journey and a jungle," Leon told us over the tip of his glass. "I'm serious."

Nobody disagreed with him. And we stayed until there was nothing left on the table.

A Journey and a Jungle

Leon Williams died on a Sunday. His last stay, he was in the hospital for 104 days. He was in a medically induced coma for many of them. The appointment started like all of them started, wading through the invasive smell of disinfectant, waiting for lethargic elevators, walking in his leaning way around the labyrinthine hallways. He wasn't afraid. He couldn't have known how the infections would avalanche this time, or that he would never make his way out. His heart stopped on September 4, 2011. He was twenty-three.

Gerry visited him every day, some days twice a day. He asked the nurses questions, talked to the doctors, and told a semi-sleeping Leon that he was there. He may have also prayed.

Leon's body lay for nearly two weeks in the hospital morgue after he died, unclaimed because the woman listed as his next of kin would not return the hospital's calls. She was not his biological mother, but his adoptive mother, who had given him back, whose house he called until the week before he fell into the coma, who had stolen his identity because she had access to his social security number because she had been his guardian when he was younger.

The lawyer who handled the details of his death was the same lawyer who was assigned to his case when he was born. Leon had been the lawyer's first case her first week of work at the hospital, she explained to Gerry as they worked together to track down the woman listed in the file. The lawyer cried as she told Gerry that she couldn't believe the coincidence. Gerry listened as she recalled being present the afternoon that Leon's biological mother signed him over to the state. Gerry had heard versions of Leon's immediate entry into the system but didn't meet Leon until he was a teen-ager being placed at the agency. The lawyer lowered her voice as she recalled what Leon's mother said when the doctors introduced her baby to her. Leon was sick and small, with tubes across his face and in his head. His mother asked the doctors if they could just kill him. The doctors said they wouldn't, but informed her that she could refuse her responsibilities for him. The lawyer remembered draw-ing up the papers for his mother to sign before she left. She de-scribed Leon's fragile baby body; she didn't remember who had given him his name. She told Gerry how the case had shaken her, how she wondered what this baby's life would be, how many times she had thought of him since. She cried for him twenty-three years later, assigned to close his case for the public record, lamenting the partial answer of his partial life.

The woman they were looking for, listed as his next of kin, had adopted him as a toddler. If he knew, Leon never said why she relin-quished custody of him as an adolescent. His last communication with her was after she was identified as the culprit of his identity theft, a year before he died. She had opened multiple credit cards in his name and charged numerous purchases that he could not pay for; it was because of her that he couldn't open a bank account, or have a credit card of his own. But somehow, his paperwork had never been updated and she was still listed as his "in case of emer-gency" contact. When Gerry and the lawyer and the nurses kept calling to ask for her permission to release his body, she thought they were calling about the identity fraud; she didn't pick up. They left a flurry of messages. The woman wouldn't respond.

I asked how it was possible that a person who had stolen Leon's identity could be listed as his next of kin. Gerry answered my ques-tion with a question: "How is any of this possible?"

Every day that Leon's body lay in the hospital morgue, Gerry made phone calls and wrote letters. He petitioned the state, politi-cians he knew, anyone he could think of for the release of Leon's body for burial.

After ten days, he left this message on the woman's voicemail: "Leon is dead. Please allow me to cremate and bury his body."

She called back and asked how much it would cost. Gerry promised that he just needed her signature; he would take care of the rest. She finally agreed.

There was no wake and no funeral. Leon was laid to rest in a numbered grave in the public section of a cemetery with a name like *New Hope*.

It sounds like an allegory of abandonment, except that it's the story of Leon's life.

Gerry organized a memorial service for Leon the following month. It took place in the funeral home across the street from the House, the one that the boys joked about when they joked about people dying after they left the group home.

I told Gerry I would do whatever he asked me to do. Call people, bring flowers, find pictures, print programs, cook food; I knew the list.

He asked me to speak at the service. I said that I would, because I couldn't say no. But what could I say? What do you say when a man who is barely past boyhood dies? How do you honor an unfinished life?

I started writing about how for some of us there is a gap between what our life is and what we want it to be. I wrote that how we fill that gap and manage the desire for something else is what defines us as individuals. I tore that draft in half and walked to 7-Eleven for a pint of Cherry Garcia for inspiration. I hoped against hope that I would bump into Frank on my way through the neighborhood. I hadn't seen him in two years. I wondered if he knew that Leon died, who had told him, and how he took the news.

ON THE DAY of the service, the first thing I saw in the funeral home was Leon's smile. Gerry positioned the posters from the graduation party on easels so that the giant one of Leon was visible from the doorway. Seeing Leon's face there but not there was too much. I scanned the crowd for the other boys. I didn't see them. Hardly anyone seemed to know each other.

Someone ushered the small crowd of us into a room with chairs.

Gerry welcomed everyone and thanked us all for being there. He said he was moved that so many people had come. We were a roomful of people who had nothing but Leon in common: doctors and nurses, classmates, friends, houseparents and staff from the agency, community members. Astonishingly, Leon's kindergarten teacher was there, and she asked to speak; she said that she'd read the obituary and remembered him as a toddler, climbing into her lap. "He knew he wanted love and would take it where he could get it," she said, "even as such a little boy." Arlette talked about Leon's goodheartedness; she told the room that Leon did have a family. "We are his family," she said. "So that makes us family to each other, too." The principal of the school he had graduated from, which served students with substance dependency, said it was important to remember that Leon wasn't broken, or ever looking to be fixed. "He just wanted some company along the way." He wiped tears from his eyes. "We were his company."

When it was my turn to speak, Gerry introduced me. In the program, next to my name he had written "friend and volunteer," but when he called me up to the podium, he said I was the daughter of his longtime business partner and dear friend, Charlie Hauck. I realized then that part of why Gerry had asked me to speak at the service was as my father's proxy. It was a memorial for Leon, but it was also a kind of wake for the agency. The House and all of the group homes were closed. I was there for Leon, and for all of the youth they had served. Gerry told the room that I had taught Leon to cook and that he was sure that Leon had taught me some things, too.

Everyone looked at me.

I took a deep breath and I read so that I wouldn't stumble; I wanted to sound official. I couldn't look at his picture, but I imagined Leon was listening.

> Leon Williams was the kind of person who stuck out in a crowd, partly because he meant to and partly because he couldn't help it. His way of walking, talking, and looking at you were distinctive. He stood with one shoulder a little higher than the

other and his head was fixed at an angle so when he looked at you, it was more out of one eye than the other. His walk was an unsteady saunter. But he never pretended that his body was not unusual. Because of how he was, there was no forgetting Leon; you either knew him or you didn't. And if you knew him, you had to like him. And if you liked him, you probably loved him.

Leon was a believer. He had a unique way of seeing, and he named the real. Somehow, he mostly saw good in this dilapidated world from the vantage point of his imperfect body. And though he doubted his own infinite goodness, Leon recognized the good in other people. He gave us what some might call the benefit of the doubt. Leon would probably say, "No, it's the benefit of belief."

The first time I met Leon was at Gerry's birthday party. He was with Frank, who was standing behind him. When I asked them questions, Leon answered for both of them. This would be the case for as long as I knew Leon, that he would translate for other people, including me. The next time I met him was at the House. When I asked him whether he thought that the guys upstairs would like to do a cooking program, in which we'd cook for an hour and then eat for an hour, Leon said, "To tell you the truth, I think everyone would like it better if you just cook and then we eat." It was not the answer I was hoping for, but it was the truth.

That we did the cooking program for nearly three years, longer than anyone expected, was in no small part because of Leon. He was the leader, the taste-tester, the brownie maker. He showed up first and set the tone; the other kids followed. They joked and fought and as far as I could see, Leon tried to be the kind of older brother to the other boys that he never had.

I don't know how he learned to be kind in the midst of the life he was dealt, but he did. More than his shoulders or his walk, Leon's kindness was his most defining feature. During one of his hospitalizations, I told him I was sorry he was sick. And he told me, "You can't be sorry, this is how it is with me."

In his time of need, he had the compassion to help me feel better about his suffering.

Dilapidated world or not, Leon was hopeful about possibility when it presented itself to him. Before I went to visit him after another of his procedures, Gerry told me about their plans to watch the Superbowl together, and how he had put a ten-dollar deposit on the one visitor seat in Leon's hospital room. So as I was leaving, I told Leon that I'd heard he had already sold the seat to watch the Patriots play that Sunday and he replied, "Yeah, but at the same time, how much were you thinking of offering?"

During our last meal together, Leon told Gerry something about the agency that could also be said about his life, that it was "a journey and a jungle."

I think Leon would have loved to be here. He would have told Gerry, "Look, these people are here for me." And he would have smiled his megawatt smile, his head tilted, eyes closed like when he was making a point. And he'd be right; here we are, for him.

The first time we cooked and sat down together at the House—because Leon insisted that we sit down and eat together "like a family, not like a buffet"—he said that sitting together like that was the truth. And then he explained that when something was good, it was the truth. I think if he were here he might say that we are the truth. We were the love he found. We were his family. We were his company. Let's give each other the benefit of belief, to honor him. We are bound together. Let's try to be each other's truth.

AFTERWORD

The Problem of the Millions
and the Work of the Dozen

Two days after my first meeting with the boys in 2006, Gerry sent me a letter confirming that we would try the dinners one night at a time, and he enclosed a copy of one of the pictures that the photographer who had been there that first night had taken. There are hints in the photo of so much of what would come. The bottom half of the frame is mostly table. You can see how sturdy it is, and how the chairs have an institutional sensibility to them, all built for function, not form. Four of the boys who would be at the House the longest are there.

Carlos is in a crisp white T-shirt, looking in my direction, smiling. Wesley is to his right, standing not quite against the wall, not quite at the table, the expression on his face serious and turned away from the camera. Gerry is next to him, also standing. Nearly the same size, they are a study in contrasts: young and old, Black and white, T-shirt and collared shirt, closed fists versus open hands.

In the photo, I'm seated at the table. You can see my profile, which I mostly hate, except that the crooked line of my forehead is a copy of my father's and it's hard to hate what was his, even in myself. I made a paparazzi joke when the photographer positioned us for the shot, and Wesley isn't budging but Carlos and Leon are laughing and Frank is almost smiling. Frank stands behind me in a baggy black sweatshirt, leaning in. Leon is seated to the left of us, smiling. A brownie sits in a napkin in front of him because he was the first to say he would have one, and he's waiting until the others get served to take a first bite. You can't see from this angle how different his posture is from everyone else's. You can't see any of his scars; besides dark circles under his eyes that could indicate any civilian level of tiredness, you can't see that he is sick. His smile is the widest.

That photo is the only proof that we were ever all around the same table, for a while. It was stuck to my refrigerator for years. I couldn't open my freezer for ice without seeing Leon's face and wondering what happened to Carlos, where Wesley was living, who Frank would be when he grew up—and whether any of us would recognize the other if we passed each other on a street in our city in the middle of a day.

Here is what I wish I could tell you now: that everything turned out okay. And by everything, I mean the boys. And by boys, I mean the men who they have become. I want to tell you that they are all right in the world, that they have enough—of food, of clothing, of shelter, of healthcare, of education, of heat, of love. I want to tell you that they are alive, with jobs and homes of their own. I want to report that they have overcome the obstacles and systematic injustices that landed them in the House, for a while. I want to say they are all in better places. Because kids deserve chances. Because this is America.

I want to say that they are all safe and they are all well, but it's simply not true.

ALL OF THE young men in this story are real, and all of the stories here are true. I have changed individual names and some identifying characteristics to protect their privacy, but there are no composite characters. Over the course of the three years and about one hundred dinners that I cooked with the boys at the House, twenty-seven kids were moved in and out, a number that does not reflect the kids who visited from other group homes, which had similarly high turnover. Most of the boys were between fourteen and seventeen, old enough to be placed in a semi-independent living situation, too young to live on their own. Several had lived with foster families previously; two had been adopted and returned to state care. Nearly all of them had siblings in other state-appointed placements. Most but not all of them were Black or Brown. Two of them were undocumented, without proof of citizenship anywhere. One had lived much of his previous life in a mental health institution, and was readmitted to another when the House closed. Most had served time in juvenile detention facilities, at least once. One had never been in any kind of placement before the House; within months he was returned to his biological family. One was kicked out of his family home when he came out to his mother as gay. One had no memory of ever living with his biological family. If the details of the lives of the boys blur together, it is because there is a systemic story here: of the lottery of birth, the cycle of poverty, life in a carceral state, structural racism, and the unequal distribution of economic and educational opportunity—and the fallacy that hard work is enough to dissolve these nearly impermeable inequalities.

All of the boys I met at the House made references to other homes they'd lived in, and to biological and sometimes foster families, but none talked about how or when he entered the child welfare system. The vast majority of children's entries into the child welfare system begin with reports of neglect; sometimes cases open in response to reports of physical or sexual abuse, or abandonment, whether intentional or unwillingly after a parent's incarceration or deportation. Not all children who experience mistreatment are referred to social services, and not all children who are referred to social services are placed in foster care, but all children who are placed in the foster care system have been screened and found to have experienced neglect or some significant emotional, physical, or sexual abuse or abandonment. It is also important to note here that the trauma children experience when they are removed from their families and homes through this process is itself harmful, and some studies have found removal to be more detrimental to children's well-being than marginal neglect and abuse experienced at home. Furthermore, some children experience maltreatment while in state care. Data show that these children, who spend part of their childhoods involved in the child welfare system, and the adults they become are a most vulnerable population, one that is disproportionately Hispanic and Latino and Black, disproportionately poor, and disproportionately criminalized; meaningful interrogation of this finding requires that we seek to understand the causal links herein. There is much to be unpacked, but as Anthony Barrows, a policy expert and former classmate of mine who spent part of his adolescence in foster care, posited, "How do we disentangle race from class, and how do we disentangle the harms those cause from the harms of abuse or neglect and then again from the trauma of removal itself?" Like other systems—such as public education, healthcare, and public housing—the child welfare system operates within and across multiple, simultaneous, tangled contexts. Furthermore, these very systems at times contribute to the marginalization of the vulnerable populations they intend to protect.

In Massachusetts, there are about 11,000 children living in foster care; for these kids, the state is their parent. On a given day, there are nearly 450,000 kids in foster care in the United States, a number that spiked in 2014 with the opioid epidemic and is further complicated by how undocumented immigrant children factor in and out of federal policy. Twenty-six percent of children enter foster care at age one or younger; 25 percent are between the ages of twelve and seventeen when they enter. Almost 50 percent spend less than a year in foster care; about 24 percent spend between one and a half and three years; 14 percent spend between three and five years, with 5 percent of children spending more than five years in foster care while growing up. About 16 percent of these kids are transitional age, between sixteen and eighteen; about 7 percent age out every year. This means that each year in the United States, about 18,000 young adults are released into their cities and towns, a figure that reflects only those who are counted; the total number of young people who survive beyond youth welfare system census is unknown.

Youth who age out of the foster care system are significantly less likely than youth in the general population to graduate from high school and college. Research has shown that they are more likely than their peers with forever families to experience homelessness, unemployment, sex trafficking, and incarceration, by overwhelming margins. Experts are constantly working to improve those odds and provide consistent, longer-term care services for these young people. As a result of federal legislation like Fostering Connections, which has both advocated for policy changes and lobbied for funding to support them, twenty-five states have extended foster care past age eighteen. And, as initiatives like Re-Envisioning Foster Care in America highlight, many innovators who are reimagining foster care are alumni of the foster care system committed to changing the narrative and serving children and youth living in foster care.

The foster care system forms part of a constellation of interconnected federal and local systems designed to address patterns of inequality and violence, which often simultaneously, though not intentionally, reproduce inequality and violence. The public education system, the public housing system, the healthcare system, and the juvenile justice system are other, inextricably intertwined, excruciatingly unequal systems. Each of the boys who lived in the House navigated all of these systems and experienced overlapping inequalities and compounded violence—already, before he was old enough to make big decisions on his own. Abuse and abandonment experienced in childhood, including the trauma of being removed from one's home and the maltreatment foster kids sometimes experience while in the care of the state, have been proven to have devastating and lasting effects on a person, on the state, and so on society. This book is my story about dinners and conversations with six boys, or twenty-seven boys, living in foster care who were assigned to a group home run by the human services agency my father had cofounded, during the three years I ran a weekly cooking program there as a volunteer. It's a story about the interconnectedness of food and memory, and community service and community care. This is also a story of modern America.

There exists no single intervention that could compensate for the gaps in opportunity that the boys experienced and other kids in foster care experience over the course of their childhoods. No singular policy change could guarantee improved, never mind equal, outcomes for these marginalized young people. One place to start would be at the nexus of the foster care system and the juvenile justice system by focusing on the ways that kids move and are moved between these systems and identifying points of contact where small interventions could have a significant impact on the lives of young people and their families. Our existing juvenile justice system fails to meet the rehabilitative goals that guided its founding, particularly in relation to youth of color. Nearly all of the kids who lived at the House were already designated court-involved youth, which means that, as teenagers, they had already been, in their words, "locked up," and they were already, in my words, "on track" to experience incarceration as adults. All have shorter life expectancies than their peers outside the foster care system. Furthermore, as Black and Brown youth, most were even more likely to be stopped by police, suffer at the hands and badges of police, and be arrested, often without cause, which compounded the problem. And they knew it. Police—and so police brutality, crime and criminalization, and juvenile detention facilities and the prospect of prison—were never too far from their minds. Everybody at the table had at least one story about drugs, theft, vandalism, assault, or possession of dangerous weapons; some of the boys also held on to the uniforms and distaste for institutional food that they acquired in lockup. To a certain extent, the boys' relationship to the criminal justice system was the one they could be sure of, a through line between their pasts and imagined futures. This played out particularly heartbreakingly in the stories of the boys who aged out at eighteen and committed or threatened to commit crimes as a path back into state care; this was the story with Nigel, a kid from one of the other residences, who pulled a knife on Flaco at the House the day before he was supposed to move out so that his tenure was extended a few weeks to deal with the resulting court case, and another who, a few nights after being moved out and into an apartment of his own, knocked on his female neighbor's door and told her he wanted to have sex with her, aware that she would call the police to have him arrested.

Punishment is not care, and poverty is not a crime. We need to create safe, supportive pathways for reentry into the community for all people and especially young people who are left out and act out. Interventions like decriminalizing youthful indiscretions for juvenile offenders and providing foster children and their families with targeted services and support would require significant investment and deliberate collaboration at the community, state, and federal levels, as well as a concerted commitment to dismantling our carceral state. These interventions happen automatically and privately for young offenders who are not poor, whose families can access treatment and hire help, and who have the privilege of living and making mistakes in neighborhoods that are not over-policed. We need to provide, not punish, and to foster belonging and self-sufficiency for our neighbors' kids. More, funded YMCAs and community centers and summer jobs, for example, would help do this. These kinds of interventions would benefit all the Carloses, Wesleys, Haydens, Franks, and Leons, and would benefit our collective well-being. Only if we consider ourselves bound together can we reimagine our obligation to each other as community.

When we consider ourselves bound together in community, the radically civil act of redistributing resources from tables with more to tables with less is not charity, it is responsibility; it is the beginning of reparation. Here is where I tell you that we can change this story, now. If we seek to repair systemic inequalities, we cannot do it with hope and prayers; we have to build beyond the systems and begin not with rehabilitation but prevention. We must reimagine our communities, redistribute our wealth, and give our neighbors access to what they need to live healthy, sustainable lives, too. This means more generous social benefits. This means access to affordable housing, well-resourced public schools, affordable healthcare, jobs, and a higher minimum wage, and, of course, plenty of good food. People ask me what educational policy reform I would suggest investing time and money in, if I had to pick only one. I am tempted to talk about curriculum and literacy, or teacher preparation and salary, to challenge whether police belong in schools, to push back on standardized testing, or maybe debate vocational education and reiterate that educational policy *is* housing policy and that we cannot consider one without the other. Instead, as a place to start, I say free breakfast and lunch. A singular reform that would benefit all students is the provision of good, free food at school.

(Data show that this practice yields positive results; but do we need data to know this?) Imagine what would happen if, across our communities, people had enough to feel fed.

INDEED, THERE ARE people in the trenches, already reimagining, constantly building and rebuilding, who have been doing this work and fighting this fight for a long time. Community Caring began as a community residence called DARE. Gerry's goal was to provide troubled young men a community setting, rather than an institutional one, in which to grow up and live. At the time, institutions were closing and there was no place for kids who had histories with crime and who had been removed from their parents' custody; the Department of Child and Family Services didn't yet exist. Gerry had opened the first home in 1964, the first year of the War on Poverty. Its purpose was to provide an alternative, rehabilitative placement for kids who had been placed in larger correctional facilities; Gerry believed that a direct-care rather than correctional approach would provide an environment in which they could gain the skills to graduate from high school and get jobs. After four years of running the residence with a married couple, social workers also committed to the mission, Gerry says he was convinced that nonprofessional people with supervision and training would also be able to work with difficult kids, like a boy who broke the ribs of his psychologist at a different facility, and another who was referred because his mother had taken to locking him in closets to contain him. In 1968, Gerry expanded the agency's reach, opening another residence; he says the places were not halfway houses, but community residences. Still, it took time for the common language to catch up with the mission.

In 1969, *The Boston Globe* published an article about DARE, its founder, and his innovative mission. Gerry is quoted in the piece saying, "Halfway House is a very descriptive term. We're not at the top trying to pull the kids up. We're all together. All halfway there, struggling together." Later in the article, he explained the scale of his approach: "There are too many committees trying to solve the problems of the millions. We're rolling up our sleeves and going to work with a dozen." To Gerry Wright, then thirty-four years old and described as "a stocky man with the neck of a wrestler and mismatched blue eyes," acceptance meant "the rejection of rejection." Expectations for the youth in his care were not long-term dream goals, but measurable daily things: getting up, going to work, cleaning up after oneself, maybe going home, maybe not.

Gerry gave me a copy of the article sometime after the House closed, after he told me that I needed to write about my experience cooking with the boys at the House so people would know that something had happened there. He said he'd come across it and thought I might like a copy. I didn't recognize his face in the photograph; I never knew him without his beard and white flyaway hair.

I told him I barely recognized him in the picture and he laughed his rumbly laugh. "I was young once, Elizabeth! You don't have to sound so surprised." In the picture, he was just a bit older than I was at the time.

And then I noticed the other, smaller picture beneath it of Gerry with boys at a table, and I recognized the conscientious objector assigned to this program for his alternative national service just months before: my father as a twenty-two-year-old kid in profile, his candy-bar sideburns, Clark Kent glasses, my forehead; he barely looked older than the other kids at the table. How could he have known he would spend the rest of his life immersed in that same work? How do you ever know for sure what you should do with your one life? What does it mean to try to solve the problem of the millions by settling in to work at the scale of the dozen? How much can one person do? How much is enough?

I NEVER EXPECTED my cooking project to lead me to another cemetery. The first time I went to see where Leon was buried, I got lost in the looping driveway and crowded emptiness. I circled back to ask a woman who worked in the main office for directions.

"Are you sure that's the part you're looking for?" she asked me. She adjusted her glasses and clarified, "The section for *indigents*?" The word, like her hairstyle, was from a different time.

She stared into my face. I could feel her question about how I knew the young man whose grave I had come to visit; it was the question in convenience stores, at the hospital and the pizza place, on the street, above the table as we sat together at the House: who were we to each other?

"Yes." I nodded. I read her the row and space number I had written on the back of a receipt in my wallet. I watched as she circled the farthest section on the cemetery map with a blue highlighter and put an *X* where she said she thought Leon's plot was. I listened as she told me that the only marker would be a metal plate about the size of two postage stamps, imprinted with a letter and a number, screwed into a concrete runner in the ground. I thanked her and said that he had been my neighbor.

I've settled on *neighbors* to describe our relationship, in part because I can see Frank and Wesley and Leon roll their eyes like they did when I suggested it. We were neighbors who ate some dinners together. The really radical act of hospitality was not that I showed up with groceries, but that the boys let me into their kitchen and extended their table, and that we all sat down together. The hardest part was not the actual cooking—because Frank did most of the cutting, and the cooking was mostly assembly. The hardest part was the passing. Not because of the manners, but because of the care. It took weeks before the boys wouldn't just serve themselves, weeks before they'd wait with a dish, hold it out for the kid sitting beside him, nod, and pass it on to the next. That was the eventual grace, and that was all that was actually homemade. The food, the flavors, the sharing: it was all the truth. Sometimes improvisation in kitchens is disastrous. But sometimes, a combination of elements produces something spectacularly unexpected. I think that's why, when we don't know what else to do, we feed our neighbors: because the chance of grace outweighs the probability of mess.

When we claim our neighbors we commit to our communities, and when we feed our neighbors, we serve them. When we consider ourselves bound together in community, the radically civil act of redistributing resources from tables with more to tables with less is our responsibility; it is the social, practical work of justice.

WHEN COMMUNITY CARING closed, and Gerry told me that I had to tell the story of the dinners, to capture some part of the work of the agency so people would know that, after nearly forty years and thousands of kids who had been assigned into and out of the House, something had happened there, I couldn't refuse him. To watch my father's work disappear was to lose him a second time. But what I saw and did at the House was such a small slice of what happened there; I was just a volunteer who ran a community service project one night a week for three years—I was around for only a few minutes of the life of the agency. Who am I to tell this story? I wasn't staff or a social worker; I didn't balance any budgets, win any grants, or defend anyone in court; I wasn't a journalist or researcher; and I certainly didn't save anyone. My range of motion was small, and our cooking operation was far from perfect. If I knew then what I know now, I would have done some things differently. I would have gotten Teflon pans before suggesting breakfast for dinner; I might have made a more concerted effort to implement some kind of re-cycling program; I probably should have been more careful in how I talked to Frank about his reading and asked him to practice it; I wish I could have prevented James from running away, the first time. But that's not how real life works. You can't go back and do it again, even though you can revise the way you tell the story. So, I have told my version of this story as I knew it as best I can, as Charlie Hauck's daughter. My dad had worked downstairs at this place as a direct-care provider and the chief financial officer of this human services agency, one of so many like it. I was just a volunteer who showed up to the House for about a hundred dinners. We're better-safe-than-sorry people who know that life is not fair and believe that the world is good, two truths that compete with but complement each other, like vinegar and oil. We know that systems fail, but food is revolu-tionary. When in doubt, we focus on the food.

Here is where I want to say that I found what I was looking for and that, in time, the fog of losing my dad has lifted. But that's not true either. I have taken to driving the longer but less trafficked routes through Boston that he would drive. When I remember a thing he used to say, I write it down so that I don't forget, as if, like fortune cookie fortunes, these sentences on index cards and the backs of envelopes might all add up to something. I maintain irrational attachments to Tom Hanks and Pedro Martínez. Sometimes while making dinner, I pour half a glass of beer and put on "Hey Julie" and remember how he would dance around the corner from the living room, eyes closed, hands pulsing back and forth, not so unlike Leon's rhapsodic empanada moves. It has been fifteen years since my father died; I keep looking for him.

Sometimes I find him in unexpected places. While searching for Christmas decorations in the attic, I found part of his personal statement for divinity school, which became his application for conscientious objector status. "I will attempt to develop the structures of a worldview with guidelines for change," the kid who became my father had written. "I want to construct models for a society and teach the tools for developing them, intuitively sensing that to nurture the consciousness of an ability to construct a society might prompt some to construct or reform theirs, I think this approach is necessary to solve the problems facing a society, for to act best one has values and an image of what one will create." I took a picture of the page.

This is the closest I have come to an answer for why he did the work he did, and what compelled him to stay so long after his service was up. Every time I read it, I imagine him writing it at twenty-two, with no sense of the shape of what his life would be, but a clear conviction of how he planned to live it. And then I remember him, on one of our walks when he was dying but we didn't want to say it out loud. "Your life is happening all around you," he told me. "You have a job. You are surrounded by people who love you. If you think something needs to be changed, change it. That's up to you, not anyone else. Nobody is going to fix your life. It's your life. Do something. Or don't. But don't talk nonsense." He was telling me in plain

English that I needed a worldview with guidelines for change that were built on epistemological frameworks, not epiphanies. And he was telling me to appreciate that what I already had was enough, and that the idea that my life hadn't started yet was bullshit.

I've studied that page of my father's application as if it were a map to an ancient city whose borders have been redrawn. I've read and reread what he wrote about his concern with the question of God, his notion of community as having its own creative potential, and how he sought wisdom "in the Confucian way the individual orders his mind, his heart, and his will, and in so doing, realizes the ordering of his family, his state, and his kingdom." When faced with a duty that lay closer, he pivoted toward it. He had planned to be a scholar; he didn't plan to be a social worker, but it was more practical; one choice led to another, of mind, of heart, of will. He didn't plan to be a father either.

My father never wanted children. I asked him once, one of the last months of all of us living in the same house, possibly while my mom and sisters and I were fighting, if he ever thought he would live surrounded by so many women. "Not in my wildest dreams," he said. "I never wanted children," he added. I knew this. My mother had been told she couldn't have children; when they married, they planned to run a group home in which they would foster other people's children. (My baby sister had been a little scandalized when she asked him how many children he'd wanted when he was little, and he happily answered, "None!") "But," he added, after pausing the way he used to pause when he was considering an idea, "children were the greatest surprise of my life." Having us was his greatest surprise. And, in what my mother would call a twist of fate, losing him too soon was the greatest surprise of ours.

Life continues without him, but he's not gone. I finished my degree the spring the House closed and my mom took the day off from work to accompany me to the commencement. In a real small-world moment, I was seated at the ceremony next to the daughter of a woman who had not only worked with my dad at the House, but had met him when he was an undergraduate at Boston College and put him in touch with Gerry, the young sociologist-preacher who was starting a community residence and had a job opening that qualified as an alternative service placement. And now, more than forty springs after my dad's college graduation, I was graduating from his alma mater with an advanced degree in education along with his former colleague's daughter, who was also pursuing a version of her parents' work. The colleague, whose picture was on the mantel in the waiting room at the House next to my father's funeral program, had died some years before he did. My mother recognized the woman's husband and checked the program to verify his name. After the ceremony, my mother and my classmate's father embraced and they marveled at how much time had passed and how funny life is. There we were, in a familiar place, without our people and also, in a way, each other's people.

I have stopped trying to reassemble my father from the objects he left behind; I try instead to recognize him in dimensions of thought, feeling, action, expression, and relation. Despite myself, I still sometimes hope to see epiphanies in stained glass windows. I sometimes catch myself waiting for my real life to start. I still have so many questions I wish to know his answers to; I'll never know if he robbed that bank. And I still dream about our walks, though the dreams are so much less frequent now. Life's not fair. I can see the pores on my father's nose when I imagine him reminding me, one long hair escaping a nostril. He's not old, because he never got to be old. And it's not his voice anymore, because I've forgotten the pitch of his voice. His voice is my voice now. Life is not fair. But that's not an answer; it's the starting point. It's where the answers begin.

SOME PLANS ARE made of hunger. The cooking project was one of those. It became a kind of project of the dozen, but it started as an idea, driven by the same instinct that compels a person to try to catch a thing that's falling, or to mark the place of someone important who has died. The dinners we actually made were not as exciting as the ones I envisioned. But what we made was good, or good enough. Another difference between food and love is that in addition to sustenance, a meal can provide a kind of closure, even in the midst of fog. Meals have beginnings, middles, and ends; even modest meals are real. This story was never supposed to be a book, because books are supposed to have calibrated worlds and endings that make sense, where heroes you root for don't die, and boys whom you meet in the beginning—the ones who make jokes while cutting chicken and help to feed other people and keep showing up to do it again—get to be heroes by the end of the story. This book doesn't make that kind of sense.

I have done my best to depict the boys the ways they showed themselves to me, in as close to their own words as I could, in order to present them as three-dimensional people with hope and anger and love and appetites, and to describe who we were to one another through our conversations. This is my story. The scope of what I can convey about the lives of the boys is limited to the stories they shared in the kitchen and at the table of the House, in almost every instance tied to food or flavors, or being fed. All of the dialogue has been written from my recollections and is not intended to serve as a transcript; what we said to each other was recorded only on the flawed machine of my memory. Any error in reporting is mine. Indeed, my biggest preoccupation with writing this all down has been doing the boys justice, not betraying their confidence but honoring it; I was just a volunteer. I believe that the boy whom I call Leon would especially like this story, and that he would love the chance to be loved, over and over again, in these pages. Here is the thing that even true stories with real endings can have in books: life after life.

ACKNOWLEDGMENTS

A book is a fraction of one life, and refracts the light of so many intersecting lives and stories. During one of our walks, one night while my father was dying, he told me his hope for each of his kids was that we would have a constellation of people who would be around for us, in the moments he couldn't be. He gestured to the sky when he said this, his hands open to the stars above us. Years later, in his stead, I remembered his wish to my sisters as I toasted them at their weddings, looking out into the glittering candlelit tables full of people there to support them and their new husbands, my new brothers. As I think about the people I have to thank here, and how I can't possibly thank everyone who deserves it, I recall the constellation my dad imagined in place for me. Indeed, I am deeply indebted to a small crowd of people who have fed me and eaten with me, traveled beside me and accompanied me from a distance, listened to me and argued with me, and sat in silences alongside me. My teachers, my family, my friends, my students, my companions, my city, my stars: you know who you are. Thank you for showing up. Like everything, the list that follows is incomplete.

I am especially grateful to each of the kids who cooked with me and ate with me at the House for the nearly three years I ran this back burner project. You number in the dozens. In a perfect world, or even a slightly better one, we would never have shared a table; I don't think any of you would have chosen to spend your teenage Tuesdays with me and my cheesy teacher questions and basic recipes, and so much extracurricular chicken. But there we were, in the world we have, buttering bread and laughing. Those dinners were a kind of reprieve in my grieving weeks, too. You suggested what we make and helped make it, lit the gas stove because I hate matches, set a place for me at the table, taught me how long it takes to heat oil and how it's both a privilege and a waste of time to worry too much about getting burned, and that good enough is good. Without you, there would be no story here. Thank you for showing up, for extending your table, for being good neighbors. I hope we share a meal again, someday.

I also thank the staff and care workers at the House for unlocking drawers and making sure the sink was clear to start with, most nights, and for letting me in; I especially appreciate all of the conversations. And to each of the staff and affiliates of Community Caring with whom I crossed paths on regular nights, at celebrations, or the memorial service: thank you for sharing your memories of my dad with me. I'm particularly grateful to the incomparable Arlette Grant-Brown, whose name is one of two I didn't change in this story. Your faith inspires me and your smile is a light. Thank you for the visits upstairs and for your example of serving the people most in need, for so long. And to Gerry Wright, for looking toward the horizon and steering for the deep waters only. You do contain multitudes. Thank you for getting down and always keeping it real, like someone we knew used to say.

The idea for this little community service project was mine, but the ways I imagined the cooking program and how I understood my role as the adult in the kitchen and a volunteer in the community were informed by my previous training as a volunteer and a teacher, and also by my experiences as a student and kid in the city of Boston. Many adults helped shape my own adolescence and young adulthood and my worldviews in messy, interesting ways. I would say that you know who you are, but the likelihood is that some of you don't know the magnitude of your impact. It is by the shimmer of your example, not coincidence, that I gravitated toward being that presence and facilitating those spaces for other kids. You led clubs and choirs, directed plays, and chaperoned trips and clubs, and only when I became a teacher myself did I appreciate how undercompensated or uncompensated you were for your time and this "extra" work in extracurricular spaces that hosted some of the most important educational experiences of my younger self, especially during high school. At Boston Latin School: to Roseanna Fernandes, whose music room in the basement was a haven for me and so many friends during Gospel Choir many after-school Mondays, for teaching us to memorize lyrics and think about what they meant, and to know when to whisper and when to get loud; to Jack Regan, for Classical Club and opening a space for the performing arts and casting me in it; to Mary Colvario for The Register, and demanding close reads and caution with clichés; to Mary Alice Hantout, for the Costa Rican Exchange Club and the trip that inaugurated my wanderlust and thirst for translation, and later for recommending me and mentoring me as a Spanish teacher at Latin; and also to Meg Shannon, who shed a lot of light on my path; to Malcolm Flynn, for advising many utility periods of student council chaperoning, and later for mentorship when I returned as a teacher and floor master at Latin; and to headmasters Michael Contompasis and Cornelia Kelley, who instilled in me a deep respect and gratitude for public education and a sense of responsibility to serve the city that provided it. I am grateful to all of my teachers, including my students, who taught me so much.

As a city kid, I benefited from several after-school and summer programs designed to provide opportunities to city kids who might not have them otherwise. These free programs made the world of the arts accessible to me, and I am grateful to both the people who imagined them, the people who funded them, and the people who staffed them. These kinds of programs make city life more robust and kids' lives healthier. I can't remember all of them, but I will never forget Days in the Arts camp at Tanglewood the summer of seventh grade, which changed how I listen to music, and my briefest stint as a sailor through Community Boating that taught me, among other things, how to come about quickly and the logic of "when in doubt chicken out," that even if you have the right-of-way, the better path is to steer away from doing harm. Michelle Barri-McCourt's Neighborhood Children's Theatre helped so many kids find our voices. To Wendie and Kaleel Sakakeeny for creating and directing Vox Juvenum, and setting a stage for voices of youth. To Nancy O'Malley and Joe Check of the Writers' Workshop at UMass Boston: thank you for summers of classes and guest speakers and readings by real writers for me and for so many other kids. And to all the teachers and supporters of the after-school studio art classes for public school kids at the Museum of Fine Arts—these classes three days a week for four years gave me entry into a world filled with art and inadvertently prompted the many rides home with my dad; to Kathleen Marsh, especially, for the balance of careful instruction and freedom, and for teaching me that good critique begins with honest praise and art doesn't require outside validation. Thank you.

I'm also grateful to many people who trained me and accompanied me at multiple volunteer placements; each of you shaped how I understand community and the reciprocity of humanity—at Holy Name Parish Church, the Soldiers' Home in Chelsea, and the Emerging Leader Program, Shaw, 4Boston, Appalachia Volunteers, and Ignacio Volunteers programs at Boston College, as well as at the Pine Street Inn, the Suffolk County House of Corrections, and last but not least, Cristo Rey Jesuit High School. I am grateful to so many friends and neighbors, especially my Pilsen housemates, who shared the struggle, the lightbulbs, and so many frozen pizzas (with a little extra cheese and garlic salt because that really did elevate our five-dollar dinners). I borrowed heavily from 4Boston to develop a small group-reflection element for the Rudy Lozano tutoring program that I ran in Chicago, and then those pizza reflection sessions inspired my vision and confidence for this cooking program in Boston. As it turns out, everything is connected. (Thank you, especially, Sergio García, for assuring me that if you bring soda, people will come. You were right, wherever you are.)

When Gerry greenlighted this project, I sent a mass email to all of my contacts announcing this cooking program and asking for good, easy meal ideas; some friends responded with recipes and good wishes, and some contributed even more. Lisa, thank you for the knives from your dad's collection. (They might still be zipped in a cosmetic case in my trunk.) Steve, thank you for all the printouts and for asking about my boys; Leigh, thank you for funding Frank's one take-out birthday dinner; Nancy, thank you for giving to the Christmas fund one year in memory of your own dad. Juli, thank you for all the emergency meatballs and directions; Lou, thank you, too, for always listening to my stories; and, of course, Mom, thank you for buying the bundle of controversial lobsters. Several people read early versions of these essays (thank you, Thalia, Fel, Kathleen, Stephan, and Katie—who also dug that outhouse beside me). Others gave me keys to quiet, beautiful places to write and edit (thank you Dorelia and Aunti Cath, for two perfect writing Julys), provided excellent notes on recent chapters and accountability to the writing (thank you, Jennifer, Eleni, Mercy, and Michelle) and brainstormed the title of this thing over Moscow mules and campfire light (Catherine and Brie). And also texted articles, fact checks, and check-ins (thank you, Isaac, Erin, Dan, Kyle, Molly, Caitlin, Huimin, Abby, and Chris), staffed tech-savvy happy hours (Bri), zoomed encouragement in pandemic (Sheila, Rebecca, Jen, Esther, and Jackie) and hosted a real salon when the world was open (Allana, Caitlin, and Malka).

And thank you to Mark and Kelly for the dinners and tax advice, to Sue and Uncle Bill for the lunches, to Leo for the backup plans, and to Betty Ann and Peggie for the white light. And to Cioci Chris (and Uncle Joe), thank you for the snowball cookies and other sweetness. Thank you, also, to Jess, Meredith, Wendy, Thuy, Kay, John, and Lynn—for being my best teaching crew; and to Christina, Deb, Meg, Kristin, Colleen, Elena, Saya, Anya, and Kathryn—for every little thing, for so many years. And thank you to my one Twitter follower, who knows who he is. I'm also grateful to Anthony Barrows for careful notes on my afterword, and then on the whole manuscript. And to Carolyn Alessio for writer and good-teacher-with-weird-earrings things, to Tony Ortiz for S'mores and more, Joseph Appleyard, S.J., for generations of guidance, and to Barbara Abercrombie for the space and company in the woods to write. And to Roseanne Aversa and Mike McCormick, who served with my Dad in the early days and shared stories over an epic pre-pandemic lunch about what it was like to be a CO, how they made sense of the work in real time, and how my Dad ate a whole pan of moussaka in one sitting. In Madison, most recently, I'm also grateful to the historians Adam Nelson, Bill Reese, Walter Stern, and Jennifer Ratner-Rosenhagen—for expanding my questions and sharpening my answers. Thank you all, and more.

Many thanks are due to my extended family, my aunts and uncles and cousins, for a lifetime of good food and care. And to my brothers and sisters: John and Heather, Juli and Jesse, Laura and Nick—

you are my village. And to my nephews and nieces: Charlie, Claire, Teddy, Maddie, Abby, Kathryn, James, Matthew, Carly, and Johnny— may you know the grandfather you never got to meet a little better through this story. He would have given anything to know you; his shyness and his kindness, and his appetite and willingness to help, along with his fang tooth and crazy hair, are all yours already. And to Mom, you are our anchor and we are your millions.

And here, I thank my kitchen gods: my grandma Ruth Hauck, who woke early to feed the birds and let me sprinkle as much powdered sugar onto my French toast as I wanted; my dziadzi, John Ziemba, a baker who taught me to make bread and let me sneak the raisins; my babci, Sally Ziemba, who let me help even though she knew I'd make a mess and shared her ginger ales even as she lost herself; Sister Mary Patricia Finneran, who taught me to crack an egg with one hand and that it's natural and necessary to care for other people's children; Natalie Corrigan Ungari, who should still be here for boozy brunches, whose voice I still hear asking, *What is taking you so long?;* and my dad, Charlie Hauck, whom I miss every day, especially during a nail-biter game or a good meal.

A lot of people say this, and I'm not sure if that makes it more true or less true, but this really wasn't meant to be a book. This is an accidental memoir, with many beginnings and an unfinished ending. Some friends have emails with the seeds of these stories; others listened as I recounted the funniest parts and the saddest parts, and encouraged me to write them down for a wider audience. To Carrie Friedman Lloyd, my writing partner, and to Jennifer Hollis, my Perfect Reader, you read all of these pages over and over again, through years of editing; I have no words for the depth of my gratitude for your careful edits, your generosity, and your friendship. And to Christina Thompson, my teacher and friend, thank you for your keen eye, sharp wit, and for everything. This book is an actual book because of you. I am particularly grateful to Colin Dickerman for investing in an earlier version of this book. To my editor at The Dial Press, Whitney Frick, and to Brettne Bloom, my agent at the Book Group: thank you for believing in this story and in my ability to tell it. Finally, Dear Reader, thank you. That you have read this far means the world.

NOTES

EPIGRAPHS

1 "We've got to be as clear-headed about human beings as possible, because we are still each other's only hope.": James Baldwin, in *A Rap on Race* (1971).

1 "Hunger is the best sauce in the world.": Miguel de Cervantes Saavedra, in *Don Quixote,* part II, chapter V, first published in 1615.

129 "The ache for home lives in all of us, the safe place where we can go as we are and not be questioned.": Maya Angelou, in *All God's Children Need Traveling Shoes* (1986).

247 "Sometimes at that moment a wave of light breaks into our darkness, and it is as though a voice were saying: 'You are accepted. You are accepted, accepted by that which is greater than you, and the name of which you do not know. Do not ask for the name now; perhaps you will find it later.' ": Paul Tillich, in *The Shaking of the Foundations* (1948).

247 "We are each other's harvest; we are each other's business; we are each other's magnitude and bond.": Gwendolyn Brooks, in "Paul Robeson," originally published in *Family Pictures* (1971), also collected in the Freedomways anthology, *Paul Robeson, the Great Forerunner* (1978).

AFTERWORD

351 All of the boys I met at the House: The House was a group home, one of several the agency ran; I volunteered there between 2006 and 2009. The data I quote in my afterword is recent, to give a sense of current context rather than historical context, including data from a 2018 report from the Children's

Bureau, an office of the Administration for Children & Families. It seems worth noting here that the 2018 report shows that a group home was the most recent placement for only 4 percent of the population of children in child welfare services, or 19,253 children. The same report shows that 52 percent of the total population in foster care was male, so of 226 children, 156 boys. See: www.acf.hhs.gov/cb/resource/afcars-report-26.

351 The vast majority of children's entries into the child welfare system begin with reports of neglect: The process through which children enter foster care, and the data that capture their demographics and specificities, has been documented in many reports, articles, and websites, including the 2018 report by the Children's Bureau AFCARS, which cites neglect as the leading circumstance of removal with 62 percent of cases, or 162,543 children, who entered into foster care in the United States for the reported year. The next-leading circumstance for removal is drug abuse (by parent) with 36 percent of cases, or 94,386 children, who entered into foster care that year. See: www.acf.hhs.gov/cb/resource/afcars-report-26.

351 Not all children who experience mistreatment are referred to social services: This is to say that there are different contributing factors in which cases are reported, and how. Recent scholarship addresses the new "Jane Crow" in the foster care system, which refers to how policy shapes the practice of separating children from their poor mothers deliberately and with disproportionate frequency. One place to start to understand this practice is the 2017 *New York Times* article, "Foster Care as Punishment: The New Reality of 'Jane Crow'," by Stephanie Clifford and Jessica Silver-Greenberg.

351 [S]ome studies have found removal to be more detrimental to children's well-being than marginal neglect: In a well-known paper on child protection and child outcomes, Doyle tried to estimate the harms of removal itself and found that marginal abuse and neglect is less harmful than removal. See: J. Doyle, "Child Protection and Child Outcomes: Measuring the Effects of Foster Care," *American Economic Review,* December 2007,

1583-1610. A February 2020 article by Eli Hager on the Marshall Project reported on "The Hidden Trauma of 'Short Stays' in Foster Care." See: www.themarshallproject.org/2020/02/11/the-hidden-trauma-of-short-stays-in-foster-care.

351 [S]ome children experience maltreatment while in state care: There is much reporting on this topic, plenty on Massachusetts alone. A national campaign called CHAMPS (Children Need Amazing Parents) was just launched in June 2020 to improve the quality of foster care and training and retention for foster parents. For more information, see: www. fosteringchamps.org.

351 [A] most vulnerable population, one that is disproportionately Hispanic and Latino and Black: The demographics of race and ethnicity of children in foster care is not proportionate to the demographics of race and ethnicity of the general population. For example, according to the 2018 AFCARS Report, 44 percent of children in foster care, or 193,117 individuals, identified as white/non-Hispanic, compared with the U.S. Census Bureau's estimate, as of 2017, of 60.7 percent of the country's population. For information on how other races and ethnicities are represented in the child welfare system, see: www.acf.hhs .gov/cb/resource/afcars-report-26.

352 "How do we disentangle race from class, and how do we disentangle the harms those cause from the harms of abuse or neglect and then again from the trauma of removal itself?" Anthony Barrows asked this question in notes on my afterword. For data on kids in foster care to be meaningful, we must better try to understand multiple, simultaneous contexts and factors.

352 In Massachusetts, there are about 11,000 children living in foster care: The FY 2019 Massachusetts Department of Children and Families (DCFS) Annual Progress and Services Report indicates that 10,328 children are living in foster care, and more than 50,000 total are served by the department; not all children who are served by DCFS in a given year are entered into foster care. See: www. mass.gov/doc/fy19-oca-annual-report.

352 [T]here are nearly 450,000 kids in foster care in the United States:

In 2018, this number was reported at 437,283. See: www.acf
.hhs.gov/cb/research-data-technology/statistics-research/afcars.

352 [A]bout 7 percent age out . . . about 18,000 young adults are
released into their cities and towns: According to the Congressional Coalition on Adoption Institute (CCAI), "17,844 (7%)
aged out of the U.S. foster care system, and a majority left without the emotional and financial support necessary to succeed
in life that other children can receive within a family." See:
www.ccainstitute.org/resources.

352 Research has shown that they are more likely than their peers
with forever families to experience homelessness: Many organizations related to foster youth and dedicated to serving foster
youth who age out cite similar findings. Once again, see: www
.ccainstitute.org/resources/fact-sheets; see also: Foster On:
www. fosteron.org/facts/.

353 [T]wenty-five states have extended foster care past age eighteen: Fostering Connections made it possible to use IV-E funds
to extend care past eighteen, and most states do this now. See:
www.congress.gov/bill/110th-congress/house-bill/6893. Though
how the policies are applied varies state to state, twenty-five
states have extended foster care past eighteen because of
Fostering Connections. See: www.ncsl.org/research/human-
services/extending-foster-care-to-18.aspx. The law was shep-
herded by a variety of lawmakers and advocates, including
foster youth and alumni.

353 [M]any innovators who are reimagining foster care are alumni
of the foster care system: Much effective work is being driven
by centering the voices of the people who are most affected by
these agencies. For example, there is a long history of foster
youth and alumni doing policy-relevant work. From the Massachusetts Network of Foster Care Alumni, or MassNFCA, and
the New England Youth Coalition, or NEYC (both of which
Anthony Barrows helped launch), to Foster Youth in Action,
the Foster Care Youth and Alumni Policy Council, and the previously cited Congressional Coalition on Adoption Institute, or
CCAI, there are many organizations trying to live the "Nothing

about us without us" ethic when it comes to reimagining these systems.

354 [A]s Black and Brown youth, most were even more likely to be stopped by police, suffer at the hands and badges of police, and be arrested, often without cause: Much has been written on the criminalization of Black bodies, police shootings, and activism to protest and raise awareness about the long history of violence against Black people in the United States. See, for example, Devon Carbado and Patrick Rock's October 2016 article in *Harvard Civil Rights-Civil Liberties Law Review* 156, "What Exposes African Americans to Police Violence?"

354 Interventions like decriminalizing youthful indiscretions for juvenile offenders and providing foster children and their families with targeted services and support: In a recent study in *Future of Children,* sociologists Youngmin Yi and Christopher Wildeman wrote that "given that children placed in foster care come from communities and families that are also disproportionately likely to be involved with the criminal justice system, successful interventions in the child welfare system could reduce criminal justice inequality and minimize harm to children in foster care—or perhaps even vastly improve their lives." For full article, see: Yi and Wildeman, "Can Foster Care Interventions Diminish Justice System Inequality?" Vol. 28, No. 1: Spring 2018, 41.

355 [S]ummer jobs, for example, would help do this: For more on this topic, see: www.brookings.edu/research/how-can-summer -jobs-reduce-crime-among-youth/.

356 Data show that this practice yields positive results: Much has been written on universal free meals at school. Boston Public Schools, for example, joined this program. From the BPS website: "The Boston Public Schools will serve free meals—both lunch and breakfast—to all students, regardless of their income status this year. Boston becomes one of the largest cities in the nation to join a program aimed at serving healthy meals to more children and save families money." For more, see: www .bostonpublicschools.org.

356 [T]he Department of Child and Family Services didn't yet exist:
      DCFS was founded in 1978.
356 "Halfway House is a very descriptive term.": All the quotes in
      this paragraph are from Ellen Goodman's article about Gerry
      Wright and his agency: "They're daring to succeed," in *The Bos-
      ton Globe,* November 23, 1969.

A PORTION OF the author's royalties will be donated to projects with
missions dedicated to food justice and community service.

HOME MADE
LIZ HAUCK

Random
House
Book Club

Because
Stories Are
Better Shared

TM

A BOOK CLUB GUIDE

Q&A WITH LIZ HAUCK

1. How did this story become a book?

I'm sure a lot of people say this, but this was never supposed to be a book. Cooking with the kids at the House started as a suggestion I made to my dad, almost as a joke; then, after he died it was going to be one dinner for checking a box to say I'd done it. When the kids kept showing up, we kept cooking and it took on a life of its own. Then, when the agency closed and my dad's business partner urged me to tell this story, I couldn't refuse him. Sharing the story became a way to put something in the place of absence. This book is a kind of monument to my dad and his work— as well as a tribute to a child's love and longing for a lost parent, and a love letter to all the people involved in care work at the margins.

Writing the book was much harder (and so much lonelier) than cooking with the kids. I didn't keep good notes in real time, but I captured the funniest dialogue in emails and catch-ups with friends; I still occasionally find index cards that I used as bookmarks, with phrases scribbled on them, like, "Can't cook tonight, dawg. Gotta drop and roll." I also have a little archive that contains things like the knives with wooden handles that I started bringing for cooking when the knives at the House kept getting locked up, a few photos that Gerry sent me, some recipes (like the one for the infamous fried chicken, and the one I printed out for salmon), as well as the paper with all of the boys' birthdays and favorite cakes written on it from that first night. I also keep a letter my dad wrote to me with that archive. It seems worth noting here that the letter is mostly about getting my taxes done and an update about old car repairs rather than the Deep Life Content I was always hoping for, but I've grown to really love the sight of his messy handwriting, even more so as time passes. When I would get frustrated with the writing and editing process, I would open that folder and study these things like artifacts to ground myself in the real. The shape of the book changed a little over during the process of writing it, but the conversations with the kids have always been the heartbeat of this story.

2. *Home Made* is a book about food and it's also not really about food. What do you make of that?

So much about who we are is present in what we eat, who feeds us, and who we eat beside—all our lives, but especially in childhood and adolescence. Beyond binaries like gourmet or not, there's so much to say here about taste, nourishment, access, and memory. *Home Made* touches on these themes while focusing on descriptions of ordinary food and the basic choreography of cooking. Sometimes making dinner is a way of connecting with others and sometimes it's a form of defense; both things are true.

3. Of all the meals you cooked at the House, did you have a favorite?

If I had to pick, I would say the birthday dinners were my favorites. They were by no means extravagant, but each one was special—much like the birthdays in my house growing up. My mom would make our cakes and decorate them with an assortment of plastic figures from past cakes that she kept in the drawer under the stove in one of those blue tins from Danish sugar cookies. My cakes, for example, usually had vanilla frosting (my favorite) and a couple of ballerinas (because that's what I wanted to be), a shamrock (because my birthday is on St. Patrick's Day), and candles—though never the number kind, which was always a point of contention. And my three siblings and I each got one gift on the other's birthdays, which meant less jealousy-fighting among us, but also meant that we really looked forward to each other's birthdays. The presents were never expensive, but that didn't detract from the celebration.

This is the spirit I tried to replicate with the birthday dinners and with all of the dinners at the House, really. I tried to produce what the kids asked for whenever I could; there's a deep vulnerability in asking for a thing you want, and I tried to create a safe space where that asking was possible and honor it. When new kids started going out of their way to tell me their birthdays and their favorite flavors because the longer-term residents encouraged them to, I knew that we had reached a different level of community, however fleeting.

4. A thread through the various chapters is grief. Can you talk about the role that grief plays in the story?

Grief is a big part of the landscape of this story, like Boston and state care. The obvious grief is over losing my dad. I don't think it's an exaggeration to say that I didn't really confront and process the emotions of losing him until I began to write about the time I spent in the place where he'd worked, and what I thought I would find there after he died. The hardest parts to write were the paragraphs about him. But the kids' grief is also part of the story. Part of why the boys sat down at the table with me was about being hungry. But I think part of it was the grief; I think they recognized my grief even though their own grief was often misidentified as anger or treated as violence, withdrawal, and neglect. Nobody had the luxury of checking their baggage at the door at the House; everyone just kind of sat down at the table with their stuff, together. That was the mess and grace of it. I don't think we talk enough about grief in American culture. But we have gotten really good at tweaking recipes for casseroles.

5. What did this experience teach you about community and the various ways people make family?

Chosen family is often the primary support for kids in care and this was certainly the case for many of the kids at the House; I didn't appreciate that dynamic before spending time cooking and listening to how the kids talked about their allegiances, relationships, and support networks. I gained a new appreciation for how YMCAs and summer jobs are essential services, for example, along with a new skepticism for how much public schools can do. At some point, (the kid who I call) Frank stopped addressing me as "miss" and started addressing me as "fam," and I felt like something shifted, but I can't say whether he or any of the kids came to think of me as family. I do believe they trusted me enough to know that I would keep coming back and that if they asked for something I would at least try to deliver— even if it was a little hard for some of them to understand why, since I wasn't getting paid to be there. Certainly, that trust and accompaniment bound us together. The question *Who are we to each other?* becomes a kind of refrain in the book as a way of energizing the space between me and the boys and me and the world more broadly. For me, the short answer is *community,* and it's a continuous loop that begins and ends with showing up.

6. What is a thing that surprised you about the process of writing and publishing *Home Made*?

One thing that continues to surprise me is receiving notes about the book from readers I don't know. The messages come to my school email address, through my website, and some through Instagram or Twitter. Some are mentions and recommendations, tagging friends who might be interested in the story. Some say thank you or offer a blessing. But some are really more like deeply personal letters about grief or care work. Those tend to begin with an aspect of the book and then go on to share a story about the letter writer's own life and work or grief, sometimes about the loss of a parent or child, but often about how the kids in my story remind them of kids or vulnerable adults in their own stories, and how their lives were also shaped by this care work. I've read books that I would consider what one of my mentors calls "companion books"— books that resonate in a particular way, that stay with you and that you return to; but I've never written to an author, so I just I didn't expect that people would write to me. And I couldn't have anticipated how moving it would be, to receive these notes— unexpectedly, on random Tuesdays or during insomniac email checks. Each one is a kind of testament to how most of us read for two reasons: to learn about other worlds and to know that we are not alone.

7. What is the best advice about writing you have ever received?

I had the opportunity to hear Mary Oliver speak at a high school event several years ago, around the time I did the cooking program. During the Q&A, a rising senior asked the poet how to know what course of study to pursue in college, because it seemed like a decision that would shape her life. And the audience laughed because it was such a big question and the poet laughed because we were over time but she had to offer an answer. She paused and then said something along the lines of "Find something real and particular, and just sort of do that thing. If it has meaning to you, it will likely have meaning to others." This wasn't directed at me, nor was it specifically about writing, but it's advice I often come back to—because things said by people you admire have a different weight, but also because it's very good advice. I don't think you have to look hard for the stories you have to tell; I think you are already part of them.

8. If there's one message you hope readers will take away from *Home Made,* what is it?

Show up. Especially as we emerge from the COVID-19 pandemic. There are so many ways for us to show up for each other. Seek out those opportunities to donate time or money (or both) to people and organizations that need you, or recognize the opportunities when they present themselves. Step through the initial awkwardness. And like my dad would say, just do the best you can.

DISCUSSION QUESTIONS

1. Consider the title of Liz Hauck's memoir. How does the title capture the various themes you encountered in *Home Made*? What is her ultimate message, and how does the title support that message?

2. Before she begins the story, Hauck tells her readers that she "wasn't trying to save anyone" with her volunteer work. Why does she insist that in this memoir, "salvation was never on the table?"

3. The author highlights her four principles of volunteering: Show up when you say you'll show up; know your one small task and do it the best you can; prepare to improvise; and leave when you're supposed to and then come back again. In which scenes do you see these principles play out, and to what effect? How is Hauck's approach like or unlike your own approach to volunteering or care work?

4. What do you think it means to *show up*? And how is—and isn't—showing up for family different than showing up for strangers? When do the kids start and stop showing up, and how does that shape the story?

5. An optional weekly cooking ritual is a small, low-intensity intervention of sorts in the complicated lives of the residents at the House. What do their various ways of responding to the cooking nights tell you about the personalities and previous experiences of each of the residents of the House? Do you think it made a difference? If so, how would you describe the possible difference it made in the lives of these kids?

6. Over the course of nearly three years of weekly dinners, we meet many different kids in the kitchen and at the table at the House; only Frank and Leon remain at the center of the story throughout. Which kid or kids stood out to you? Which details of the residents' lives seemed to blend together? Do you think there is a star of the book? Why, or why not?

7. Some of the faces kept changing in the story, but lot of the food kept repeating. Which dishes did you notice the most? What do you make of the repetition in the meals? Does this ring true to your experience? What's a food that you associate with a specific time and place in your life? Or, what's your standby dinner, and why? What, if anything, do you think a person's tastes tell you about a person?

8. How do we encounter race at different moments in the story? What does Hauck mean in "Show Me How You Make Your Chicken and I'll Tell You Who You Are" when she says about race: "Until the fried chicken, we cooked around it"? What happened in that chapter that felt different?

9. The author never sugarcoats the difficulties of the boys' lives and the bare-bones institutional shabbiness of the House. Which descriptions of the House and aspects of life there stuck out to you? Which descriptions of the trenches of human services surprised you—or didn't?

10. What does *Home Made* suggest about the accessibility of the American Dream? How do the personal circumstances of the boys that Hauck portrays impact their ability to achieve it?

11. What does the American Dream mean to you? Do you think your definition of this dream is different from that of

your parents, guardians, or grandparents or older relatives? How has the meaning of the American Dream changed over generations in your family? Is the American Dream still alive in the United States? Do you think it's accessible to everyone in this country?

12. Part of the landscape of *Home Made* is grief. The decision to cook with the residents at the House was a way for Hauck to manage her grief following the loss of her father, Charlie. What are some components of grief you recognize in the author's story? What do you think Hauck means when she writes that "grief is the ultimate marinade"? Do you think this is a suitable metaphor for grief? In what moments of the story is it especially clear that the boys are also experiencing grief? Do you think it's possible to resolve grief?

13. Hauck's father, Charlie, is a significant character in the book, though he has already died before the story begins. What do we learn about him, and how? What do you think of Hauck's occasional observations about the light in her father's office? Why do you think she includes her father's aphorisms alongside the weighty sayings of famous writers before each of her memoir's major sections? How are Charlie Hauck's quotations similar to or different from those of thinkers like Baldwin, Angelou, Tillich, and Cervantes? What is the impact on the reader of including quotations by Hauck's dad?

14. How and through which characters does Hauck address the theme of family? How do you define *family*? Can people have more than one family? What binds people to their care units beyond biological connection? What other kinds of kinship shape who we consider family? How does *Home Made* enhance or challenge your ideas about biological families and chosen families?

15. The memoir concludes with two celebrations, one for Leon's graduation from high school, and the other for Leon's short life. How do these two powerful scenes answer the essential question of this memoir: What are we to one another?

ENHANCE YOUR BOOK CLUB

1. **Cooking:** What is a flavor or dish that reminds you of people you love or a particular moment in your life? Maybe it's a ritual food you make to mark a certain occasion; maybe it's something you used to make that reminds you of a specific memory. Make this dish for your book club and share its special meaning with the group.

2. **Poetry:** Read "Perhaps the World Ends Here" by Joy Harjo, former U.S. poet laureate. Discuss the role the kitchen table plays in the world—first, according to Harjo, and then draw connections to Hauck's memoir and to your own life.

3. **Acknowledgments:** In the acknowledgments of *Home Made*, Hauck thanks a variety of people who showed up for her, including teachers and after-school program chaperones. Bring a stack of postcards to your book group—one for every member. Designate 5 to 10 minutes at the beginning or end of your meeting for each member to write thank-you notes to someone in their life who had some impact on their formation as a person, to ground the discussion in reflection and gratitude.

4. **Local Context:** The story of *Home Made* takes place in one group home in one city in one state; in the afterword, Hauck uses data from local and national organizations to provide a much larger context for the situation of kids in state care. Prior to your book club meeting, do some online research about the numbers of kids in care in your area, and share information about some of the organizations doing work to support them. Are there ways you and your neighbors or workplace can engage with kids who are

aging out of the system, or one of the organizations that support them?

5. **Showing Up:** Whether your book group is meeting in person or in a virtual space, your community is likely still feeling the effects of the COVID-19 pandemic, which has illuminated so many fractures in the systems in place to support us. Spend some time during your book club meeting to share about things you've done to help those in need, to listen about your friends' experiences doing care work, and to brainstorm ways that you can show up for one another and show up for your community.

LIZ HAUCK is an educator and writer from Boston, Massachusetts. Liz has worked in three schools and one hospital, and her volunteer placements have included teaching literacy in a shelter for people surviving homelessness, digging an outhouse on a mountain in Virginia, and cooking with teenagers in state care. She's currently completing her Ph.D. in educational policy studies and history at the University of Wisconsin–Madison, and she holds a B.A. and M.Ed. from Boston College. *Home Made* is her first book.